MIGRANT LABOUR AND THE RESHAPING OF EMPLOYMENT LAW

The presence of migrant workers has become a central feature of labour markets in highly developed countries. The International Labour Organisation estimates that in 2013 there were 112 million resident migrant workers in the 58 highest-income countries, who made up 16% of the workforce. Non-resident workers have also increasingly become part of the labour available for employment in other states, often on a temporary basis.

This work takes a thematic and comparative approach to examine the profound implications of contemporary labour migration for employment law regimes in highly developed countries. In so doing, it aims to promote greater recognition of labour migration-related questions, and of the interests of migrant workers, within employment law scholarship.

The work comprises original analyses by leading scholars of migration and employment law at the European Union level, and in Australia, Canada, Germany, Italy, the Netherlands, Spain, the United Kingdom and the United States. The specific position of migrant workers is addressed, for example as regards equality of treatment, or the position in employment law of migrant workers without a right to work. The work also explores the effects of migration levels and patterns upon general employment law – including the law relating to collective bargaining, and remedies against exploitation.

Migrant Labour and the Reshaping of Employment Law

Edited by
Bernard Ryan
and
Rebecca Zahn

•HART•
OXFORD • LONDON • NEW YORK • NEW DELHI • SYDNEY

HART PUBLISHING
Bloomsbury Publishing Plc
Kemp House, Chawley Park, Cumnor Hill, Oxford, OX2 9PH, UK
1385 Broadway, New York, NY 10018, USA
29 Earlsfort Terrace, Dublin 2, Ireland

First published in Great Britain 2023

A catalogue record for this book is available from the British Library.

Library of Congress Cataloging-in-Publication Data

Names: Migration and Employment Law in Comparative Perspective (Conference) (2017 : University of Leicester) | Ryan, Bernard, 1966- editor. | Zahn, Rebecca, editor.

Title: Migrant labour and the reshaping of employment law / edited by Bernard Ryan and Rebecca Zahn.

Description: Oxford ; New York : Hart, 2023. | "based on papers first presented at a workshop entitled Migration and Employment Law in Comparative Perspective held at the University of Leicester in September 2017"—ECIP preface. | Includes bibliographical references and index. | Summary: "This book examines the implications of labour migration for employment law regimes in highly-developed countries. It adopts a comparative approach, with some chapters providing thematic overviews of the challenges posed by migration for employment law, and others addressing the main effects of migration upon employment law in particular countries. The context of the book is the increased importance of actual and potential migration to the labour markets of highly-developed countries. Resident migrants' share of the labour force has increased markedly since the early 1990s, with the International Labour Organisation estimating that in 2013, there were 112 million migrant workers in the 58 highest-income countries, who made up 16% of the workforce. In addition, non-resident workers have increasingly become part of the labour available for employment in other states, often on a temporary basis as posted or agency workers. This evolving labour market context has led to a series of challenges for, and effects upon, employment law"— Provided by publisher.

Identifiers: LCCN 2022057456 | ISBN 9781509919147 (hardback) | ISBN 9781509968329 (paperback) | ISBN 9781509919161 (pdf) | ISBN 9781509919154 (Epub)

Subjects: LCSH: Foreign workers—Legal status, laws, etc.—Congresses. | LCGFT: Conference papers and proceedings.

Classification: LCC K1841.A46 M544 2017 | DDC 344.01/544—dc23/eng/20230403

LC record available at https://lccn.loc.gov/2022057456

ISBN: HB: 978-1-50991-914-7
ePDF: 978-1-50991-916-1
ePub: 978-1-50991-915-4

Typeset by Compuscript Ltd, Shannon

Preface

The chapters in this book are based on papers first presented at a workshop entitled *Migration and Employment Law in Comparative Perspective*, organised by Bernard Ryan with funding from the British Academy, held at the University of Leicester in September 2017. The subsequent publication plans were unavoidably disrupted and delayed by external events, including the playing-out of Brexit, the COVID-19 pandemic and lockdowns, and intermittent industrial action in UK universities. Despite that, the central premise of the book remains valid and timely: the value of bringing together insights from leading international scholars on the relationship between migration phenomena and employment law. These two aspects of contemporary labour markets are inherently inter-connected in practice, yet often treated separately in academic literature. This collection attempts to bridge that gap. The questions which contributors were asked to explore included the effects of migration levels and patterns upon general employment law; the extent to which migrant workers are treated as equals in law with resident workers; avenues for the redress of exploitation; and the position in employment law of migrant workers without a right to work under immigration law.

In his first chapter, Bernard Ryan sets the scene for the work by showing the ways in which increases and changes in labour migration in developed states lead to pressures for re-regulation in employment law. Drawing on a range of statistics, his chapter provides a broad comparative account, which identifies the similar trends, but distinct outcomes, across destination states in Europe and North America, and in Australia.

The book then considers the interplay between immigration and employment law under three broad headings. A key assumption underpinning this structure is that migrant workers are frequently in a distinct socio-economic position to resident workers. Employment and immigration law regimes can therefore be considered in relation to how they provide for equal status for migrant workers (Part I); how they counter exploitation (Part II); and, how they reconcile migration phenomena and employment law (Part III).

The four chapters contained in Part I provide a diverse picture of the extent to which labour migrants have an equal status with resident workers in different countries. Petra Herzfeld Olsson focuses on the measures taken by the Swedish legislator to provide decent working conditions, and examines whether these include labour migrants. Maria Ontiveros analyses the contemporary situation of noncitizen immigrant workers in the United States, grounding that examination in an understanding of its historical antecedents. Olaf Deinert focuses on *Willkommenskultur* ('welcoming culture'), a famous phrase in public debate in

Germany, which came to prominence during the refugee crisis of 2015–2016. He examines the extent to which German labour law (broadly defined) constructs such a welcoming culture for migrant labour. Ferran Camas Roda compares non-EU migrant workers' access to employment and decent working conditions with that of Spanish nationals.

The chapters in Part II focus on measures taken in employment law (or not) to counter exploitation, broadly understood to include both protection against vulnerability and systems to ensure compliance with labour standards. Sarah Marsden provides an overview of the legal avenues available to migrant workers in Canada, and casts doubt on their capacity to provide redress for workers and to deter labour abuses by employers. Laurie Berg and Bassina Farbenblum's chapter explores the unsettled legal framework in Australia concerning the entitlement of unauthorised workers to basic employment protections. Tesseltje de Lange discusses sanctions against employers for the informal employment of migrants staying irregularly in the EU under the Employer Sanctions Directive 2009/52/EC. Alan Bogg's chapter considers the operation of the illegality doctrine in English law as it relates to irregular migrant workers, as they are particularly exposed to it by the criminalisation of work in breach of immigration permission. He develops an argument based on the constitutional principle of legality to support restricting the impact of criminalisation in extinguishing migrants' fundamental social rights. William Chiaromonte's chapter provides an overview of the law and context of undeclared work and the exploitation of migrant workers in Italy, and explores the ways in which Italian legislation concerning labour migration contributes to the irregular situation of many migrant workers.

Part III of the work contains chapters which explore how employment laws and legal scholarship have attempted to reconcile the challenges of migration with employment law regimes. Rebecca Zahn focuses on the central and eastern European Union enlargements (2004–2013) to question to what extent migration controls affect actual migration flows and, by extension, labour law systems. Mimi Zou's chapter seeks to develop a normative basis for redesigning temporary labour migration programmes, many of which have been criticised for severely curtailing migrants' legal rights in the host country, in order to enable migrants to exit from any employment relationship at any stage of their migration projects. In her chapter, Tonia Novitz considers the policy options open to the UK post-Brexit, given that the EU system for 'posting of workers' is no longer applicable. She considers different justifications for regulatory action in light of the decisions now being made by the UK, as reflected in the newly adopted UK-Australia and UK-New Zealand Free Trade Agreements, while recognising scope for future policy development. Finally, Bernard Ryan concludes the book by focusing on scholarship in the United Kingdom, providing a survey of the treatment of migration-related questions by employment law scholars based in the UK. He shows that migration-related questions are now widely understood to fall within the employment law field of inquiry, but argues that there remains a division between scholarship which favours resident workers (which he terms 'methodologically nationalist') and that which gives recognition to migrant workers as well (which he terms 'cosmopolitan realist').

We would like to thank the chapter authors for their contributions to the collection, and for their patience with the delays in its emergence. It is our hope that the final product will contribute to the understanding of the significance of migration for contemporary employment law regimes, and that it will encourage further exploration of comparative research on that subject.

The chapters in the collection were finalised in 2022.

Bernard Ryan,
University of Leicester
Rebecca Zahn,
University of Strathclyde

Table of Contents

PART III
RECONCILIATIONS

List of Contributors

Laurie Berg is Associate Professor in the Faculty of Law, University of Technology Sydney, Australia.

Alan Bogg is Professor of Labour at the University of Bristol, and Emeritus Fellow of Hertford College, Oxford, UK.

Ferran Camas Roda is Professor of Labour and Social Security Law and Director of the Chair of Immigration, Rights and Citizenship at the University of Girona, Spain.

William Chiaromonte is Professor of Labour Law at the University of Florence Law School, Italy.

Olaf Deinert is Professor of Civil Law, Labour Law and Social Law at the Institute of Labour Law of Göttingen University, Germany.

Bassina Farbenblum is Associate Professor in the Faculty of Law & Justice, UNSW Sydney, Australia.

Petra Herzfeld Olsson is Professor of Labour law at Stockholm University, Sweden.

Tesseltje de Lange is Professor of European Migration Law and Director of the Centre for Migration Law, Radboud University Nijmegen, the Netherlands.

Sarah Marsden is Associate Professor of Law at Thompson Rivers University, Canada.

Maria Ontiveros is Professor of Law at the University of San Francisco, USA.

Tonia Novitz is Professor of Labour Law at the University of Bristol, UK.

Bernard Ryan is Professor of Migration Law at the University of Leicester, UK.

Rebecca Zahn is Reader in Law at the University of Strathclyde, Glasgow, UK.

Mimi Zou is Professor of Commercial Law at the University of Exeter, UK.

1

From Labour Migration to Employment Law Reform: A Comparative Interpretation

BERNARD RYAN

I. INTRODUCTION

THIS CHAPTER IS concerned with the ways in which contemporary labour migration in developed states leads to re-regulation in employment law.[1] Increased labour migration in these states has been a central element of the transformations of neoliberal globalisation, which accelerated after 1989.[2] The theme explored here is that of connections between increased labour migration and pressures upon employment law regimes in those states. This phenomenon has been considered in the existing literature on employment law primarily in respect of migrant and posted workers in the European Economic Area, subsequent to the enlargements of the EU which began in 2004.[3] The aim here is a more general comparative account, which identifies similar trends, but distinct outcomes, across destination states in Europe and North America, and in Australia.

A key assumption in this chapter is that migrant workers are frequently in a distinct socio-economic position to resident workers. Their personal economic priorities often differ from resident workers, due to ongoing attachments and commitments in places of origin.[4] They may lack social capital in the place of

[1] Throughout this chapter, the terms 'labour migration' and 'migrant workers' will be understood to cover all foreign-born workers who are part of the labour force available to employers in a given state, including those who work and reside there, and more mobile workers, who work in a state without having their primary residence there.

[2] See S Castles, H de Haas and M Miller, *The Age of Migration: International Population Movements in the Modern World*, 6th edn (London, Bloomsbury Academic, 2019) 51 and 127–34.

[3] T Krings, 'East-West Mobility and the (Re-)egulation of Employment in Transnational Labour Markets' in J Dølvik and L Eldring (eds) *Labour Mobility in the Enlarged Single European Market* (Bingley, Emerald Publishing, 2016); R Zahn, *New Labour Laws in Old Member States: Trade Union Responses to European Enlargement* (Cambridge, Cambridge University Press, 2017).

[4] For the classic exposition of this argument, see M Piore, *Birds of Passage: Migrant Labor and Industrial Societies* (Cambridge, Cambridge University Press, 1979) ch 3.

employment, in the sense that they are constrained by unfamiliarity with the working language, local workplace and social norms, and resources for workers (including trade unions).[5] They may face discriminatory treatment, due to embedded social prejudice on racial and ethnic grounds, or for religious or cultural reasons, which in turn enables unequal treatment and segmentation in the labour market.[6] Limitations to the immigration status of many migrant workers, through ties to employers or irregular status, also leave them in a comparatively weak position in the labour market.[7]

In addressing the interaction between labour migration and employment law, the chapter will draw upon the well-known 'varieties of capitalism' typology in comparative political economy. That literature distinguishes between liberal market economies in English-speaking countries, co-ordinated market economies in Northern Europe, and 'mixed' regimes in southern Europe (France, Italy, Greece, Portugal and Spain).[8] Liberal market economies have labour market regimes characterised by general skills acquisition, weak state regulation and trade unions, decentralised wage-setting, extensive low-wage employment, and a subsistence-oriented welfare state.[9] Co-ordinated market economies are taken to have labour market regimes characterised by high-skill and high-wage employment, comparatively high levels of regulation, and extensive collective bargaining.[10] The mixed regimes in southern European states are characterised by strong state institutions and weaker voluntary co-ordination structures, which in the labour market is associated with weaker trade unions and collective bargaining, and often with extensive informal employment.[11] It may be added that France is anomalous in this scheme: though not truly a co-ordinated market

[5] Lack of social capital leads to the development of migration-supporting networks and institutions: see D Massey et al, *Worlds in Motion: Understanding International Migration at the End of the Millennium* (Oxford, Oxford University Press, 1998) 42–45.

[6] For the post-war decades in Europe, see S Castles and G Kosack, *Immigrant Workers and Class Structure in Western Europe* (London, Institute of Race Relations/ Oxford University Press, 1973) 107–112 and R Miles, *Racism and Migrant Labour* (London, Routledge and Kegan Paul, 1982).

[7] B Anderson, 'Migration, Immigration Controls and the Fashioning of Precarious Workers' (2010) 24 *Work, Employment and Society* 300.

[8] P Hall and D Soskice, 'An Introduction to Varieties of Capitalism' in P Hall and D Soskice (eds), *Varieties of Capitalism: The Institutional Foundations of Comparative Advantage* (Cambridge, Cambridge University Press, 2001).

[9] K Thelen, Varieties of Liberalization and the New Politics of Social Solidarity (Cambridge, Cambridge University Press, 2014) ch 1.

[10] ibid. The list in Hall and Soskice (n 8) comprises four Nordic countries (Demark, Finland, Norway and Sweden), five other European states (Austria, Belgium, Germany, the Netherlands and Switzerland), and Japan. Some authors have proposed to separate the Nordic countries from the others: see C Devitt, 'Varieties of Capitalism, Variation in Labour Immigration' (2011) 37 *Journal of Ethnic and Migration Studies* 579, 586. This approach is not followed here, as it appears unnecessary to a discussion of labour migration trends or of employment law regimes.

[11] In general, see P Hall and D Gingerich 'Varieties of Capitalism and Institutional Complementarities in the Political Economy: An Empirical Analysis' (2009) 39 *British Journal of Political Science* 449; for the labour market, see Devitt (n 10) 586.

economy, its effective systems of state governance leave far less space for informality in the labour market than in other states classed as 'mixed'.[12]

This three-part categorisation will be deployed as a framework for discussion both of labour migration trends in developed states, and of related reforms in employment law regimes. In broad terms, it will be shown that, for most states in all three groupings, there have been sustained increases in labour migration over recent decades (section II).[13] Instead, a 'varieties of capitalism' approach is more relevant to understanding how employment law regimes have responded to contemporary labour migration (section III). In both liberal and 'mixed' economies, the focus is more commonly upon the exploitation and abusive treatment of migrant workers, with reforms to the enforcement of employment law and/or in the criminal law. In co-ordinated market economies, the primary purpose of reform is the prevention of undercutting, by ensuring that migrant workers who are present on the labour market are covered by collectively agreed standards. The chapter will conclude by arguing that, in a world where labour migration is commonplace, we expect to observe widespread pressures for re-regulation in employment law. In that regard, the most effective reform strategies will be those that aim at a reconciliation and balancing of the interests of resident and migrant workers.

II. CONTEMPORARY LABOUR MIGRATION

The decades since the second world war have seen two distinct transformative periods of labour migration to the developed liberal democracies covered in this volume. The first covered the post-war decades, roughly from the 1950s to the 1970s. In Northern Europe, that period saw a steady rise in labour migration, linked to the post-war boom.[14] By 1973, France and West Germany had approximately 2.5 million foreign workers each (10–12 per cent of the labour force), Switzerland had 600,000 (30 per cent), and Belgium and Sweden had 200-220,000 (6–7 per cent).[15] In Great Britain, census data showed an increase in the number of non- UK-born persons in employment from 0.7 million

[12] On the distinctiveness of France's state-led variety of capitalism, see B Hancké, M Rhodes and M Thatcher, 'Beyond Varieties of Capitalism' in B Hancké (ed), *Debating Varieties of Capitalism* (Oxford, Oxford University Press, 2009) 291.

[13] Data is considered systematically only up to 2019, because of the varied and uncertain effects of the COVID-19 pandemic upon labour migration in subsequent years.

[14] Castles and Kosack (n 6) ch 2; R King, 'European International Migration 1945–90: A Statistical and Geographical Overview' in R King (ed), *Mass Migration in Europe: The Legacy and the Future* (London, Belhaven, 1993).

[15] J Salt, 'International Labour Migration in Western Europe: A Geographical Review' in M Kritz, C Keely and S Tomasi (eds), *Global Trends in Migration* (New York, Center for Migration Studies, 1981) 139.

(3.0 per cent) in 1951 to 1.7 million (7.2 per cent) in 1971.[16] In these states, that phase of labour migration came to an end in the period from the mid-1970s onwards, when new labour migration was officially curtailed.[17] The foreign-born share of the working population did not reverse, however, due to the arrival of family members, refugees/asylum seekers, and irregular migrants.[18] In the post-war decades, Australia, Canada and the US took a somewhat different route. In the 1950s and 1960s, they did not have the same pressures to import labour for post-war reconstruction, and maintained racially selective immigration policies, which in turn limited immigration rates. Instead, the pivotal moment was the end to preferential treatment for immigrants from Europe and the Americas, which started in Canada in 1962, the US in 1965, and Australia in 1973.[19] Thereafter, both permanent and temporary labour migration would start to rise in all these states.[20]

The second period of sustained growth in labour migration started with the end of the Cold War in 1989. That had long-term effects on international migration, including labour migration, by liberalising travel and mobility rights in many regions, and by triggering new refugee flows.[21] A recent picture of the extensive current scale of labour migration in all highly developed economies is provided by the ILO's *Global Estimates on International Migrant Workers*, for 2017.[22] That found 164 million migrant workers across the world, making up 4.7 per cent of the global workforce.[23] Of those, 111 million were in the 57 countries designated as high income, where they made up 18.5 per cent of the workforce.

[16] C O'Muircheartaigh and T Rees, 'Migrant/ Immigrant Labour in Great Britain, France and Germany' (1976) 4 *New Community* 493, 495.

[17] S Castles, 'The Guest-worker in Western Europe – An Obituary' (1986) 20 *International Migration Review* 761.

[18] R Penninx, 'International Migration in Western Europe since 1973: Developments, Mechanisms and Controls' (1986) 20 *International Migration Review* 951, 962–63; S Castles, 'Guestworkers in Europe – A Resurrection?' (2006) 40 *International Migration Review* 741, 744.

[19] N Kelley and M Trebilcock, *The Making of the Mosaic: A History of Canadian Immigration Policy* (Toronto, University of Toronto Press, 1998) 332–33 and 351; C Keely 'The Development of US Immigration Policy since 1965' (1979) 33 *Journal of International Affairs* 249; G Tavan, 'The Dismantling of the White Australia Policy: Elite Conspiracy of Will of the Australian People?' (2004) 39 *Australian Journal of Political Science* 109.

[20] For the 1970s, see C Keely and P Elwell, 'International Migration: Canada and the United States' and J Zubrzycki, 'International Migration in Australia and the South Pacific', both in Kritz, Keely and Tomasi eds (n 15).

[21] These effects were especially pronounced in Europe (though not confined to it): see C Bonifazi, 'Evolution of Regional Patterns of International Migration in Europe' in C Bonifazi, M Okólski, J Schoorl and P Simon (eds), *International Migration in Europe: New Trends and New Methods of Analysis* (Amsterdam, Amsterdam University Press, 2008) 118–21 and R King and M Okólski, 'Diverse, Fragile and Fragmented: The New Map of European Migration. (2019) 8 *Central and Eastern European Migration Review* 9.

[22] International Labour Organization, *ILO Global Estimates on International Migrant Workers: Results and Methodology*, 2nd edn (2018). These estimates refer to persons who are foreign-born, with information on persons who hold a foreign citizenship used as a substitute where necessary. The ILO report does not provide country-level information.

[23] ibid, 9. An earlier edition of the report, published in 2015, estimated a global share of 4.4% in 2013.

In contrast, in the 131 other countries surveyed, there were an estimated 53 million workers, who made up 1.8 per cent of the workforce.[24] The share in the 30 states and territories of northern, southern and western Europe was 18 per cent (39 million), while in Canada and the US, taken together it was 21 per cent (38 million).[25]

In the rest of this section, the typology of liberal market economies, co-ordinated market economies, and 'mixed' regimes is used to analyse recent labour migration trends in developed states. In the literature, varieties of capitalism approaches have been taken to imply significant differences between different categories of state/economy.[26] First, it has been anticipated that the less regulated labour market regimes of liberal market economies are especially likely to see significant inward labour migration.[27] The primary reason is thought to be the lack of impediments in such economies to low-wage employment, which attracts mobile migrant workers seeking labour market opportunities, but not resident workers with family ties and social rights.[28] There are also often greater reasons for migration in skilled work categories, as liberal market economies are frequently characterised by under-investment in training.[29] Second, constraints upon lower-waged labour migration have been expected among the co-ordinated market economies of northern Europe. One account has focused on labour standards, arguing that collective and statutory labour market norms are generally more onerous, and compliance with them more effectively monitored, through the activities of trade unions and/or state bodies.[30] Others have focused on the political sphere, where the expectation is that governments will face penalties if they pursue an overt strategy of promoting low-skilled labour migration.[31] Third, labour migration in 'mixed' regimes in southern Europe has been expected to provide a combination of these two elements. In regions and sectors where there are effective labour standards, it is expected that there will be less demand for foreign-born workers, while in regions and sectors which are less well-regulated, the regime will in practice be more akin to the flexible ones of liberalised market economies, with an expectation of greater recourse to migrant labour.[32]

[24] The region with the highest estimated share (40.8%, equating to 23 million persons) of migrant workers covered twelve Arab states in Asia: ibid, 15.

[25] ibid, 15. It is not possible to identify a share for Australia from the ILO study.

[26] See Devitt (n 10) and G Menz, *The Political Economy of Managed Migration* (Oxford, Oxford University Press, 2009) ch 1. M Ruhs, 'Labor Immigration Policies in High-Income Countries: Variations across Political Regimes and Varieties of Capitalism' (2018) 47 *Journal of Legal Studies* S89, includes a contrast between liberal and co-ordinated market economies (at S97-S100), while recognising 'mixed' market economies (at S120).

[27] See A Afonso and C Devitt, 'Comparative Political Economy and International Migration' (2016) 14 *Socio-Economic Review* 591, 601–2.

[28] Devitt (n 10) 587.

[29] Devitt (n 10) 590 and C Wright, Immigration Policy and Market Institutions in Liberal Market Economies' (2012) 43 *Industrial Relations Journal* 110.

[30] Devitt (n 10) 588–9 and Ruhs (n 26) S98.

[31] Menz (n 26) 10.

[32] See Menz (n 26) 11 and Devitt (n 10) 588–9.

The remainder of this section will consider the empirical support for this account, drawing upon census and labour force survey data on foreign-born populations and workers, with a focus on the period from the mid-1990s to 2019. It will show that it is not possible to simply read off trends in labour migration from varieties of capitalism categories. Rather, it appears that significant labour migration is a pervasive feature of contemporary developed economies, across different regime types.

A. Liberal Market Economies

It will be shown here that there have been substantial increases in the share of foreign-born labour since the 1990s across five liberal market economies: Australia, Canada, Ireland, the UK and the US. In **Australia**, the number and share of foreign-born workers rose from 7.6 million and 25 per cent in 1991 to a high of 12.5 million and 32 per cent in 2021.[33] These trends were linked to policy developments, as can be seen from Table 1, which provides annual averages for five-year periods from 1984 to 2019 in the number of visas issued in work and study categories.[34] The number of persons granted visas in the skilled migration stream increased markedly from 1999 onwards, and averaged above 120,000 per annum for the most recent decade (2009–2019).[35] The number of persons admitted in temporary skilled migration rose, especially from 1997 to 2018, when the 457 visa class permitted employers to hire skilled workers for up to four years, often without a requirement to demonstrate a labour market need.[36] The working holidaymaker category expanded significantly, with an increase in the annual average from nearly 90,000 in 2001–2004 to an average

[33] Australian Bureau of Statistics, Labour force status by Age, Major country group of birth, and Sex, January 1991 onwards (September 2021 release).

[34] Data from the following sources. *Skilled stream* – J Phillips and J Simon-Davies *Migration to Australia: a quick guide to the statistics* (Parliament of Australia Library, January 2017), Table 1, and Department of Home Affairs, *Permanent Migration Program (Skilled & Family) Outcomes Snapshot: Annual Statistics: Program years 2011–12 to 2020–21*, Table 2; *457/ temporary skilled visa* – Phillips and Simon-Davies, Table 2 and Department of Home Affairs, *Australian Migration Statistics 2019–20*, Table 2.0; *Working holidaymakers* (data starts in 2001–2002) in Department of Home Affairs, *Australian Migration Statistics 2019–20*, Table 2.0; *Students* – Phillips and Simon-Davies, Table 2 and Department of Home Affairs, *Australian Migration Statistics 2019–20*, Table 2.0; *Post-study work* – Department of Home Affairs, *Temporary Graduate visa program* data.gov.au/data/dataset/temporary-graduate-visas (updated 28 November 2021) [last accessed 04 September 2022]. Annual data is for June–July, so that the periods cover five rather than six years. All data refer to visas granted, rather than actual admission.

[35] On policy changes, see L Hawthorne, '"Picking Winners"? The Recent Transformation of Australia's Skilled Migration Policy' (2005) 39 *International Migration Review* 663, 681–8 and A Boucher and A Davidson, *The Evolution of the Australian System for Selecting Economic Immigrants* (Migration Policy Institute, May 2019) 4–9.

[36] On the evolution of the 457 visa, see I Campbell and J-C Tham, 'Labour Market Deregulation and Temporary Labour Migration Schemes: An Analysis of the 457 Visa Program' (2013) 26 *Australian Journal of Labour Law* 239. On its replacement with the when Temporary Skilled Shortage visa in 2018, see Boucher and Davidson (n 35) 10–11.

above 210,000 in 2009–2019.[37] The number of international students – who are permitted to engage in paid employment – increased markedly, with an annual average of nearly 350,000 visas in the most recent five-year period.[38] Finally, graduates have been permitted to remain for post-study work since 2008, with the numbers obtaining visas under this route rising to 63,994 in 2018–2019.[39] While concerns over employer abuse and worker exploitation have more recently led to changes to the scope of work and study visas in Australia, and to reductions in the number being issued, nevertheless the longer-term picture has been one of marked expansion in the number of those permitted to work in Australia.[40]

Table 1 Annual visas granted in work and related categories, Australia, five-year averages, 1984–2019

Period	Permanent skilled stream	Temporary skilled	Working holidays	Students	Post-study work
1984–1989	29,600	–	–	–	–
1989–1994	36,700	–	–	–	–
1994–1999	30,344	–	–	–	–
1999–2004	54,174	37,978	89,294	150,862	–
2004–2009	99,291	84,225	141,889	239,145	–
2009–2014	120,974	101,635	219,384	265,063	24,372
2014–2019	120,141	83,144	214,380	347,491	42,474

In **Canada**, the foreign-born share of the employed workforce reached 21.5 per cent in 2006 (3.5 million) and 27.9 per cent in 2019 (5.3 million).[41] The background was a series of changes to liberalise labour migration policy from the 1990s onwards. That can be seen from Table 2, which shows the number of admissions in the permanent economic, temporary foreign worker and international mobility categories from the early 1980s.[42] Canada's policy on permanent economic

[37] Boucher and Davidson (n 35) 13–14.

[38] The policy change was announced on 25 April 2008: H Spink, *Overseas students: immigration policy changes 1997–2015* (Parliament of Australia Library, 25 February 2016) 28. On the employment of international students, see J Howe, 'A Legally Constructed Underclass of Workers? The Deportability and Limited Work Rights of International Students in Australia and the United Kingdom' (2019) 48 *Industrial Law Journal* 416, 425–29.

[39] On the establishment of the scheme, see L Doyle, *The Other Temporary Skilled visa* (Parliament of Australia Library, 23 March 2013). Data in Department of Home Affairs, *Temporary Graduate visa program (updated 28 November 2021)* data.gov.au/data/dataset/temporary-graduate-visas [last accessed 04 September 2022].

[40] On both points, see Boucher and Davidson (n 35).

[41] Based on Statistics Canada, *Labour force characteristics of immigrants*. 2006 is the first year for which this data appears to be available. Information for 2020 has been disregarded: it showed a fall of 986,000 in total employment, and roughly the same percentage of foreign-born (27.8%).

[42] The figures for permanent economic admissions are based on the following, published by Citizenship and Immigration Canada: 1980–2015 – 'Permanent Residents – Ad Hoc IRCC (Specialized Datasets) – Canada – Admissions of Permanent Residents by Immigration Category,

migration categories came to provide a range of new avenues for skilled workers who were nominated by provinces or territories, who had a job offer, with high skills or skills in shortage, or who had 'Canadian experience' through study or work.[43] The number of admissions within the temporary foreign worker program, for which a labour market assessment is required, also rose from the mid-1990s until policy changes in 2014.[44] The international mobility program, which does not require a labour market assessment also continued to expand markedly.[45]

Table 2 New admissions in economic categories, Canada, five-year averages, 1980–2019

Years	Permanent economic stream	Temporary foreign workers	International mobility
1980–1984	42,420	–	–
1985–1989	61,282	–	–
1990–1994	97,635	–	–
1995–1999	113,499	43,959	62,596
2000–2004	137,511	63,813	67,214
2005–2009	145,728	105,170	96,514
2010–2014	163,464	111,308	171,840
2015–2019	173,748	82,386	233,083

1980 – Q2 2016', www.cic.gc.ca/opendata-donneesouvertes/data/IRCC_PRadmiss_0002_E.xls [last accessed 04 September 2022]; 2016–2019: 'Permanent Residents – Monthly IRCC Updates – Canada – Admissions of Permanent Residents by Country of Citizenship and Immigration Category' at www.cic.gc.ca/opendata-donneesouvertes/data/IRCC_M_PRadmiss_0013_E.xls [last accessed 04 September 2022]. The figures given include both principal applicants and spouses and dependants. The figures for the Temporary Foreign Worker Program and the International Mobility Program are based on the following, published by Citizenship and Immigration Canada: 1994–2006 – *Facts And Figures: Immigrant Overview – Temporary Residents 2013*, Tables 2.1 and 2.2, publications.gc.ca/collections/collection_2015/cic/Ci1-8-10-2013-eng.pdf [last accessed 04 September 2022]; 2007–2014 – *Facts and Figures 2017 – Immigration Overview – Temporary Residents*, Tables 3.1 and 3.2, www.cic.gc.ca/opendata-donneesouvertes/data/Facts_and_Figures_2017_TR_EN.pdf [last accessed 04 September 2022]; 2015–2019 – *Temporary Residents: Temporary Foreign Worker Program (TFWP) and International Mobility Program (IMP) Work Permit Holders – Monthly IRCC Updates*, data on the year when permits became effective, open.canada.ca/data/en/dataset/360024f2-17e9-4558-bfc1-3616485d65b9 [last accessed 04 September 2022]. Due to small discrepancies in the data in different publications, the last published source was used for any given year.

[43] On the development of Canada's permanent economic migration policy, see A Green and D Green, 'The Goals of Canada's Immigration Policy: A Historical Perspective' (2004) 13 *Canadian Journal of Urban Research* 102, 127–34; A Ferrer, G Picot and W Riddell, 'New Directions in Immigration Policy: Canada's Evolving Approach to the Selection of Economic Immigrants' (2014) 48 *International Migration Review* 846; D Hiebert, *The Canadian Express Entry System for Selecting Economic Immigrants: Progress and Persistent Challenges* (Migration Policy Institute, 2019).

[44] For an earlier analysis, see J Fudge and F MacPhail, 'The Temporary Foreign Worker Program in Canada: Low-Skilled Workers as an Extreme Form of Flexible Labour' (2009) 31 *Comparative Labor Law and Policy Journal* 5.

[45] See L Vosko, 'Temporary Labour Migration by Any Other Name: Differential Inclusion Under Canada's "New" International Mobility Regime' (2020) *Journal of Ethnic and Migration Studies* (online version).

In **Ireland**, the share of foreign-born workers increased sharply as a consequence of a period of significant economic growth and development from the mid-1990s onwards. The available census data on the foreign-born employed is summarised in Table 3.[46] As recently as 1991, the proportion of the employed labour force born outside Ireland and the UK was only 1.8 per cent.[47] The decades thereafter saw a rapid change, with a much larger employed workforce, an increased share of workers born outside Ireland (23.5 per cent in 2016) and outside Ireland and the UK (16.2 per cent in 2016).[48] Policy changes played a significant part, including a relaxation of the work permits regime in the early 2000s.[49] Also significant was the opening of the labour market to central and Eastern European states in 2004: in 2016, 10.7 per cent of employees had been born in an EU Member State other than Ireland and the UK.[50]

Table 3 Foreign-Born Employed in Ireland, 1971–2016

		Born outside Ireland		**Born outside Ireland and UK**	
Year	**Total**		%		%
1971	1,119,531	42,403	3.8	9,134	0.8
1991	1,382,870	113,125	8.2	25,321	1.8
2006	1,930,042	376,754	19.5	228,049	11.8
2016	2,001,953	469,932	23.5	323,726	16.2

For the **UK**, the period between 1971 and 1991 saw a levelling-off in labour migration, as a policy environment unfavourable to new migration saw the number of non-UK-born increase from 7.2 per cent (1.7 million) to 7.6 per cent (1.9 million).[51] In contrast, the period from the mid-1990s saw a sustained increase, with Labour Force Survey data (summarised in Table 4) showing that the number of foreign-born workers in employment rose from 1.9 million in 1997

[46] Table 3 is based on varied census data published by the Central Statistics Office available at www.cso.ie [last accessed 04 September 2022]. For 1971, the data is from *Census of Population*, vol 11, table 9, and concerns persons aged 14+ gainfully employed. For 1991, the data is from *Census of Population*, vol 8, table 36, and concerns persons aged 15+ in the labour force. For 2006, the data is from *Census of Population*, volume 7, Table C0734, and concerns persons aged 15+ at work. For 2016, the data is from *Census of Population*, Profile 11, Table EB006, and concerns employees, employers and self-employed.

[47] Until the 1990s, most UK-born persons resident in Ireland were either from Northern Ireland or were the children of Irish-born parents who had returned with them to Ireland. Neither group can be considered typical migrant workers.

[48] The foreign-born share of *employees* was slightly higher in 2016: 24.5% were born outside Ireland, and 17.4% outside Ireland and the United Kingdom.

[49] M Ruhs, Managing the Immigration and Employment of Non-EU Nationals in Ireland (Dublin, Policy Institute, 2005).

[50] Census data for 2016 (n 46).

[51] Information from Office of Population Censuses and Surveys, *1991 Census: Ethnic Group and Country of Birth: Great Britain*, vol 2 (1993), Table D. On the policy context, see Z Layton-Henry 'Britain: The Would-Be Zero Immigration Country', in W Cornelius, P Martin and J Hollifield (eds) *Controlling Immigration: A Global Perspective* (Stanford, Stanford University Press, 1994).

(a 7.3 per cent share) to 5.8 million in 2019 (a 17.8 per cent share).[52] The increase was greater for non-EU countries (up by 2.1 million) than for EU Member States (up by 1.7 million). These changes were linked to policy developments. Labour governments between 1997 and 2010 favoured economic migration, including opening the labour market to nationals of new EU Member States in 2004.[53] New migration would continue to be substantial even after 2010, as Coalition and Conservative governments enabled higher-skilled employment from outside the EU, while demand for lower-waged immigration was met by EU workers.[54] As the free movement of persons regime ceased to apply to the UK at the end of 2020, a new labour migration policy substantially liberalised the previous skilled worker regime, including by removing the resident labour market test and caps, and by lowering the minimum skill level and salary.[55]

Table 4 Employed persons by birthplace, United Kingdom, 1997 and 2019 (in thousands)

	Total	UK	non-UK	non-UK %	EU	EU %	non-EU	non-EU %
1997 Q1	26,245	24,323	1,921	7.3	638	2.4	1,283	4.9
2019 Q1	32,641	26,838	5,796	17.8	2,420	7.4	3,376	10.3
Increase	+6,558	+2,706	+3,849	+10.3	+1,730	+5.0	+2,119	+5.5
% increase	+25%	+11%	+200%	–	+271%	–	+165%	–

For the **US**, the share of foreign-born labour increased consistently from 5 per cent in 1970 to 17 per cent (28.4 million) in 2019.[56] This sustained increase in the foreign-born labour force was the product of several long-term policy developments. The Immigration Act 1965 ended national origins quotas, thereby enabling permanent immigration from Asia in particular.[57] The Immigration Act 1990 increased the quota for employment-based acquisitions of permanent residence status, from 54,000 to 140,000 annually.[58] Employment in temporary (so-called 'non-immigrant') work categories in the US grew substantially, as can

[52] Based on Office for National Statistics dataset, *EMP06: Employment by country of birth and nationality* (release of 16 November 2021).

[53] W Somerville, *Immigration under New Labour* (Bristol, Policy Press, 2007).

[54] See Migration Advisory Committee, Migrants in low-skilled work: The growth of EU and non-EU labour in low-skilled jobs and its impact on the UK (June 2014); M Sumption, *Labour Immigration after Brexit: Trade-offs and Questions about Policy Design* (Oxford, Migration Observatory, January 2017).

[55] J Portes, 'Immigration and the UK Economy after Brexit' (2022) 38 *Oxford Review of Economic Policy* 82.

[56] The figures for the intervening decades were as follows: 1980 – 7.1 million (6.7%); 1990 – 11.6 million (9.3%); 2000 –17.3 million (12.5%); 2010 –14.4 million (15.8%). Information for 1970–2000: taken from E Newburger and T Gryn, 'The Foreign-Born Labor Force in the United States: 2007' (US Census Bureau, December 2009), which draws upon census data. Information for 2010 and 2019: author's calculations, from Bureau of Labour Statistics/ Current Population Survey data, www.bls.gov/webapps/legacy/cpsatab7.htm [last accessed 04 September 2022].

[57] See B Ong Hing, *Making and Remaking Asian America, 1850–1970* (Stanford University Press, 1983) especially ch 3.

[58] The actual number has typically been close to the quota: for example, in the years 2017–2019, the average number of employment-based acquisitions of permanent resident status was 138,495: Department of Homeland Security, *Yearbook of Immigration Statistics 2019*, Table 6.

be seen from Table 5, which gives the annual average in the main categories for five-year periods from 1985 to 2019.[59] The largest numerical increases were among H-1 skilled workers and H-2 visa holders in agriculture, food processing and construction.[60] Finally, the US has a significant presence of workers lacking a right to work under immigration law, whose number is estimated to have increased from 3.6 million in 1995 (2.7 per cent of the workforce) to a peak of 8.2 million in 2007 (5.4 per cent of the workforce) in 2007, before falling to 7.8 million in 2016 (4.8 per cent of the workforce).[61]

Table 5 Non-immigrant work visas, US, 1984–2019

5-year average	H1 Skilled	H2 Agriculture, food processing and construction	L1 Intra-company	O1 High ability	Total
1985–1989	37,159	9,430	13,514	0	60,102
1990–1994	51,231	18,527	18,166	983	88,907
1995–1999	81,534	35,423	35,564	3,651	156,172
2000–2004	132,013	95,177	58,403	6,344	291,937
2005–2009	131,299	144,944	74,275	7,942	358,461
2010–2014	162,239	157,376	71,513	12,706	403,834
2015–2019	189,847	302,424	76,988	17,751	587,010

B. Co-Ordinated Market Economies

Whereas the rises in foreign-born labour in liberal market economies are consistent with the varieties of capitalism approach – for the reasons explained – it is striking that the recent period has also seen marked increases in foreign-born employment in co-ordinated market economies in Northern Europe. An overall picture of the change may be obtained from Table 6, which summarises European Labour Force Survey data on the foreign-born employed in 2006 and 2019 for 11 Northern European states.[62] Taken as a group, these had an increase

[59] Calculations based upon US Department of State, *Nonimmigrant Visa Statistics*, various years. See further the discussion by Ontiveros in ch 3 of this volume.

[60] See S Pierce and J Gellat, Evolution of the H-1B: Latest Trends in a Program on the Brink of Reform (Migration Policy Institute, March 2018) and Congressional Research Service, H-2A and H-2B Temporary Worker Visas: Policy and Related Issues (June 2020).

[61] J Passel and D Cohn, *US Unauthorized Immigrant Total Dips to Lowest Level in a Decade* (Pew Research Center, 27 November 2018), 13. These figures include employed and unemployed. A separate estimate found 7.3 million unauthorised workers in 2019, and 6.8 million in employment: Migration Policy Institute, *Profile of the Unauthorized Population: United States*, www.migrationpolicy.org/data/unauthorized-immigrant-population/state/US [last accessed 04 September 2022].

[62] Based on Eurostat data on 'Employment by sex, age and country of birth' (lfsq_egacob) available from ec.europa.eu/eurostat/web/lfs/data/database [last accessed 04 September 2022]. The figures are for Q2 in each year.

in the number of foreign-born employed from 9.1 million to 14.0 million, with an increase from 13 per cent to 18 per cent in the share. The largest absolute number of foreign-born workers in 2019 was in Germany (7.7 million, 19 per cent), with the highest shares in Luxembourg (57 per cent), Switzerland (32 per cent), Austria and Sweden (both 21 per cent). Over the period from 2006 to 2019, there were sizeable increases in the share in Luxembourg (+14 per cent), Norway (+11 per cent), Switzerland and Sweden (both +8 per cent). For the 10 states other than Germany, there was an increase of 1.3 per cent in the share from pre-2004 Member States (the 'EU15') over the period, 1.7 per cent in the share from post-2004 Member States (the 'EU13') workers, and 2.9 per cent in non-EU, for a total increase of 5.9 per cent.[63] As of 2019, the foreign-born employed comprised 4 per cent from EU15 states, 4 per cent from the EU13, and 11 per cent from outside the EU.[64]

Table 6 Foreign-born employed, Northern European states, 2006 and 2019

	All (thousands)		% of all employed		% increase 2006–2019			
	2006	2019	2006	2019	EU15	EU13	Non-EU	All
Luxembourg	85	166	43.8%	57.4%	3.8%	4.1%	5.7%	13.6%
Norway	171	488	7.4%	18.7%	2.0%	4.0%	5.2%	11.2%
Switzerland	960	1,460	24.3%	32.2%	4.6%	1.4%	2.0%	7.9%
Sweden	540	1,023	12.4%	20.7%	–0.4%	1.2%	7.4%	8.2%
Belgium	461	840	11.0%	17.5%	0.5%	2.4%	3.6%	6.5%
Austria	572	909	15.2%	21.3%	1.6%	2.6%	1.9%	6.1%
Iceland	10	20	5.8%	10.5%	1.0%	2.2%	1.4%	4.7%
Denmark	156	285	5.7%	10.2%	1.0%	1.0%	2.5%	4.6%
Germany	5,248	7,671	14.4%	18.9%	–	–	–	4.5%
Finland	68	154	2.8%	6.1%	0.1%	0.9%	2.2%	3.3%
Netherlands	789	1,025	10.1%	11.8%	0.3%	1.0%	0.4%	1.7%
11 states	9,061	14,041	13.2%	18.4%	–	–	–	5.2%
10 excluding Germany	3,812	6,370	11.9%	17.9%	1.3%	1.7%	2.9%	5.9%

The case of **Germany** illustrates how migrant labour supply and policy change have led to increased migration. The period from the 1980s saw labour market

[63] The 2006 data for Germany does not include a breakdown by place of origin which precludes a comparison with 2019.

[64] Not shown in Table A. The EU15 figures exclude the state in question if it is an EU15 state. The breakdown figures do not add up to 18% due to rounding. More precise figures are 3.7% for EU15, 4.1% EU 13, 10.5% non-EU, and a total of 18.4%. For the ten other states the changes from 2006 were as follows: +1.3% EU15, +1.7% EU13, +2.9% non-EU.

reforms aimed at enabling fixed-term contracts and part-time work; an erosion of the coverage of trade unions and collective bargaining; and, an increased concentration of migrant workers in low-wage employment, especially in services.[65] In respect of labour migration, public policy overtly shifted towards encouragement of highly-skilled immigration.[66] The EU enlargements from 2004 also increased the supply of migrant workers to Germany, initially in atypical categories such as posted workers and self-employed, and then as employees.[67] Overall, the pace of recent changes in the labour market may be seen from Table 7, which shows the number of immigrant workers, for 2005, 2011 and 2019.[68] It shows a 67 per cent increase in all such workers over the period (+3.1 million), with nearly half of the increase among non-EU workers (+1.5 million, up 49 per cent), and a similar increase among new EU Member States (+1.4 million, up 154 per cent).

Table 7 Immigrant workers, Germany, 2005–2019 (thousands)

	2005	2011	2019	Increase 2005–2019	
EU15	747	761	996	249	33%
EU13	882	1,246	2,241	1,359	154%
Non-EU	3,069	3,502	4,586	1,517	49%
Total	4,698	5,509	7,823	3,125	67%

Sweden is a second country in which new labour supply and neoliberal policy developments has prompted significant increases in labour migration.[69] In 2004, it was the only Northern EU Member State to open its labour market from the

[65] For a detailed review, see T Krings, '"Good" Bad Jobs? The Evolution of Migrant Low-Wage Employment in Germany (1985–2015)' (2021) 35 *Work Employment and Society* 527.

[66] H Kolb, 'From Brakeman to Booster: Policy Change in Germany's EU Labour Migration Policy' (2017) 55 *International Migration* 11, and J Chaloff, 'The Impact of EU Directives on the labour migration framework in EU countries' (OECD Social, Employment and Migration Working Papers No 180, 2016) 39. Germany issued an annual average of 14,991 such permits between 2012 and 2019, which was 83% of the total for the EU as a whole: Based on Eurostat, 'EU Blue Cards by type of decision, occupation and citizenship' (migr_resbc1) available at ec.europa.eu/eurostat/web/products-datasets/-/migr_resbc1 [last accessed 05 September 2022]. Germany has deployed the 'blue card' as a new labour migration category which can lead to permanent settlement, whereas other northern European states have treated it merely as an alternative to parallel national schemes: Kolb 16.

[67] B Wagner and A Hassel, 'Move to Work, Move to Stay? Mapping Atypical Labour Migration into Germany' in Dølvik and Eldring (n 3).

[68] Author's calculations, based on Statistisches Bundesamt, *Fachserie 1 – Bevölkerung und Erwerbstätigkeit*, Rehihe 2.2, Table 16I, column on employed persons ('Erwerbstätige'), for each year. The data does not refer to all foreign-born persons, but instead those with their own 'migration experience ('eigener Migrationserfahrung') among those with a 'migration background' ('Migrationshintergrund'). It therefore excludes persons born as German citizens abroad who subsequently moved to Germany.

[69] On neo-liberalism in respect of non-EU migration: see D Frank 'Changes in Migration Control During the Neoliberal Era: Surveillance and Border Control in Swedish Labour Immigration Policy' (2014) 7 *Journal of Political Power* 413, and C Hedberg and I Olofsson, 'Negotiating the Wild West: Variegated Neoliberalisation of the Swedish Labour Migration Regime and the Wild Berry Migration Industry' (2022) 54 *Environment and Planning A: Economy and Space* 33.

outset to workers from the eight Central and Eastern European states which joined then (the 'EU8').[70] That was followed by a policy shift in 2008 concerning non-EU workers, at all skill levels: where previously work permits had been subject to a labour market test, and there was a practice of allowing trade unions a veto, employers became free to nominate migrant workers without those constraints, subject to respect for employment laws and the terms of collective agreements.[71] The result was a marked expansion of non-EU migration into lower-waged occupations where there was not a shortage of labour.[72] The EU Labour Force Survey data in Table 6 confirms that the greatest part of the rise in foreign-born workers between 2006 and 2019 was among non-EU born workers (an increase of 7.4 per cent in their share of the workforce).

In other Northern European states, recent increases in labour migration were largely influenced by labour supply factors. In **Austria**, the share of workers with foreign *nationality* increased gradually, from around 5 per cent in the late 1980s to 12.3 per cent in 2007, largely due to arrivals from the former Yugoslavia (often refugees), East Germany (post-reunification) and the post-2004 EU Member States.[73] After 2010, there were further increases, due to the lifting of labour market restrictions upon EU13 workers (2011 onwards), new arrivals from Germany and southern European states, and new refugee flows.[74] That is reflected in the EU Labour Force Survey data summarised above, which shows an increase of 5.1 per cent in foreign-born workers in Austria between 2006 and 2019, with increases in all of EU15, EU13 and non-EU categories. In **Norway**, labour migration from EU8 states was permitted from 2004, subject to the person having a full-time contract, and being employed on the terms set out in collective agreements or at the going rate.[75] The result was substantial labour migration in occupations and locations which were unattractive to Norwegian workers.[76] In line with that, the EU Labour Force Survey data summarised above shows that the share of all EU13 workers in the employed workforce increased from 0.4 per cent in 2006 to 4.4 per cent in 2019.

[70] For an account emphasising inter-party dynamics, see L Berg and A Spehar, 'Swimming against the tide: why Sweden supports increased labour mobility within and from outside the EU' (2013) 34 *Policy Studies* 142.

[71] For a discussion, see Frank (n 69) 421–25.

[72] See H Emilsson, 'Recruitment to Occupations with a Surplus of Workers: The Unexpected Outcomes of Swedish Demand-Driven Labour Migration Policy' (2016) 54 *International Migration* 5 and O Frödin and A Kjellberg, 'Labor Migration from Third Countries to Swedish Low-wage Jobs' (2018) 8 *Nordic Journal of Working Life Studies* 65.

[73] E Walterskirchen, 'The Dimensions and Effects of EU Labour Migration in Austria' in B Galgóczi and J Leschke (eds), *EU Labour Migration since Enlargement: Trends, Impacts and Policies* (2009) 151 and 155–56.

[74] Krings (n 3) 192–193.

[75] JE Dølvik and L Eldring, Mobility of labour from new EU states to the Nordic Region – Development trends and consequences (Nordic Council of Ministers, 2008) 17.

[76] JH Friberg, 'New Patterns of Labour Migration from Central and Eastern Europe and its Impact on Labour Markets and Institutions in Norway: Reviewing the Evidence' in Dølvik and Eldring (n 3) and M Slettebak, 'Labour Migration and Increasing Inequality in Norway' (2021) 64 *Acta Sociologica* 314.

The European Labour Force Survey data, together with these selected examples, cast doubt on the position that Northern European economies are inherently less likely than liberal market economies to see significant shares of foreign-born workers. Instead, the pattern has been of increases in the share of foreign-born workers, especially among EU13 and non-EU workers. There have of course been national differences in the nature and extent of labour migration trends in Northern Europe in recent times. Not all states have participated equally in increases: there is for example an interesting contrast between Belgium (+ 6.5 per cent share over the period) and the Netherlands (+1.7 per cent). Overall, however, a combination of employer openness to labour migration, the availability of migrant labour supply, and policy reforms, have led to sustained increases in levels in many of these states.

C. Mixed Regimes

European Labour Force Survey data for 'mixed' regime states for 2006 and 2019 is summarised in Table 8. As of 2019, the overall share of employment for foreign-born workers across these states was 14.0 per cent, with the highest shares in Spain (17.6 per cent) and Italy (14.5 per cent). Between 2006 and 2019 the overall share of foreign-born workers rose from 10.2 per cent to 14.0 per cent across these states. The greatest part of this increase came from non-EU workers (+2.7 per cent), with only modest increases among EU13 (+0.9 per cent) and EU15 (+0.1 per cent). Both the foreign-born shares, and the increases, were therefore lower than in northern Europe, while the increased labour supply from the EU13 did not have as dramatic an effect in southern Europe.

Table 8 Foreign-born employed, mixed regime states, 2006 and 2019

	All (thousands)		% of all employed		increase 2006–2019			
	2006	2019	2006	2019	EU15	EU13	Non-EU	All
Italy	1,879	3,311	8.3%	14.5%	–0.1%	2.3%	4.0%	6.2%
Portugal	366	510	7.7%	11.0%	0.8%	0.0%	2.5%	3.3%
Spain	2,832	3,444	14.3%	17.6%	0.4%	0.8%	2.0%	3.2%
France	2,391	3,271	9.6%	12.2%	–0.1%	0.3%	2.4%	2.6%
Greece	364	316	8.2%	8.2%	0.1%	–0.5%	0.3%	0.0%
Total	7,832	10,852	10.2%	14.0%	0.1%	0.9%	2.7%	3.7%

The southern European states in this group have had similar migration trajectories in recent decades. Having previously been countries characterised by emigration, including in the post-war period, they each experienced a rapid rise in immigration in the 1990s and 2000s, before seeing reduced immigration in the aftermath of the post-2008 financial and Eurozone crises, followed by a resumption in recent years.[77] This recent pattern of 'boom and bust' shows how migration can respond flexibly to changing demand, and as such is consistent with a varieties of capitalism interpretation of mixed regimes, and with the broader view of labour migration as a widespread phenomenon.

These points may be illustrated by reference to the cases of Italy and Spain. In **Italy**, the number of foreign nationals who were resident rose rapidly from around 1990 onwards.[78] Census data show an increase from 356,000 in 1991 to 4.335 million in 2011 (from roughly 0.6 to 7.2 per cent).[79] The 'immigration boom' of these decades came to an end with the economic downturn and public expenditure cuts in Italy in the post-2008 crisis.[80] Nevertheless, the foreign population continued to grow in the 2010s: more recent estimates, based on population registers, show 4.96 million foreign nationals, comprising 8.35 per cent of the population, in 2018.[81] The share of foreign workers also grew steadily throughout the period from 2006 to 2018, with only a slight fall recorded in 2019.[82] These continued rises presumably reflect the concentration of foreign workers in low-skilled work: foreign nationals made up an estimated 33 per cent of all unskilled workers in the period 2011–2016, with high concentrations in domestic care work, in smaller industrial firms, and in construction, hospitality and agriculture.[83] Across the economy, the significance of low-wage employment, often with casual and/or irregular employment, and weak compliance regimes, tend to enable migrant work.[84] The particular significance of migrant domestic work in Italy is closely linked to the 'Southern European' character of its labour market and welfare state arrangements, which assume that families will take responsibility for their members.[85]

[77] D Maddaloni and G Moffa, 'Migration Flows and Migration Crisis in Southern Europe' in C Menjivar, M Ruiz and I Ness (eds), *The Oxford Handbook of Migration Crises* (Oxford, Oxford University Press, 2019).

[78] A Colombo and G Sciortino, 'Italian Immigration: The Origins, Nature and Evolution of Italy's Migratory Systems' (2004) 9 *Journal of Modern Italian Studies* 49, 55–57; T Perlmutter, 'Italy: Political Parties and Italian Policy, 1990–2009' in Hollifield, Martin and Orrenius (n 51) 342–44.

[79] Census figures for foreign national residents for 1991–2011 are in A Colombo and G Dalla-Zuanna, 'Immigration Italian Style, 1977–2018' (2019) 45 *Population and Development Review* 585, 589. The total resident population is estimated to have been 56.8 million on 1 January 1992: Istat, *Popolazione Residente Ricostruita: Anni 1991–2001* (available at www.dati.istat.it [last accessed 04 September 2022]).

[80] Colombo and Dalla-Zuanna (n 79) 605–8, and Chiaromonte, ch 10 in this volume.

[81] The quoted figure is for 31 December, from Istat, *Anni 2002–2018: Ricostruzione della popolazione residente* (17 March 2021). That document also shows a total resident population of 59.8 million on that date.

[82] The figures for 2006 and 2019 are given in Table I in the text. The peak number of foreign-born workers (3.3149 million) and share (14.53%) were recorded in 2018, with modest falls of 4,000 workers and 0.04% in the 2019 figures.

[83] Colombo and Dalla-Zuanna (n 79) 597–601, and C Devitt, 'Shaping Labour Migration to Italy: The Role of Labour Market Institutions (2018) 23 *Journal of Modern Italian Studies* 274, 275–77.

[84] Devitt (n 83) 280–84.

[85] G Sciortino, 'Immigration in a Mediterranean Welfare State: The Italian Experience in Comparative Perspective' (2014) 6 *Journal of Comparative Policy Analysis* 111.

Spain experienced a more pronounced 'boom and bust' in immigration levels in recent times.[86] Significant inward labour migration to Spain began in the mid-1980s, linked to its accession to the EU in 1985. Census data show that the number of foreign-born in the population rose rapidly from 0.84 million (2.2 per cent) in 1991 to 6.3 million (13.5 per cent) in 2011.[87] The number of foreign-born residents peaked in 2012 at 6.8 million (14.3 per cent), then fell for four years, before again reaching 6.8 million (14.4 per cent) in 2019.[88] A similar pattern can be seen in the employment sphere: EU Labour Force Survey estimates show that foreign-born workers in employment rose from 439,000 (3.2 per cent) in 1998 to a peak of 3.4 million (16.6 per cent) in 2008, then fell for six years, before increasing to again reach 3.4 million (17.6 per cent) in 2019.[89] Here too, the principal sectors in which there was demand for migrants were domestic service, agriculture, construction and hospitality.[90] In this case, labour supply from the EU13 was less significant, with increases in the population from Latin America and Morocco providing larger contributions to the foreign-born population by the late 2010s.[91] State policy also played a part: in the 2000s, a new labour migration policy was put in place, which permitted recruitment in shortage occupations, and circular migration under bilateral arrangements with states of origin.[92] Also significant is Spain's preparedness to regularise undocumented migrant workers: some 1.2 million people were covered by collective regularisations between 1986 and 2005, while provision for individual regularisation has been included in its immigration law since 2004.[93]

The case of **France** remains atypical among so-called mixed regimes. After France experienced significant labour migration in the post-war decades, for 25 years the foreign-born share of the population remained relatively stable, standing at 7.4 per cent in 1975 and 7.3 per cent in 1999.[94] It then increased

[86] M Hazán, 'Spain: The Uneasy Transition from Labor Exporter to Labor Importer and the New Emigration Challenge' in Hollifield, Martin and Orrenius (n 51); R Ferrero-Turrión, 'Migration and Migrants in Spain after the Bust' in D Papademetriou, M Sumption and A Terrazas (eds), *Migration and the Great Recession: The Transatlantic Experience* (Washington DC, Migration Policy Institute, 2011). In relation to Spain, see too Camas Roda, ch 5 in this volume.

[87] 1991 information taken from D López de Lera, 'Panorama de la Inmigración' in A Izquierdo Escribano and D López de Lera (eds), *Demografía de los Extranjeros* (Bilbao, Fundación BBVA, 2006) 36. 2011 figures calculated from Instituto Nacional de Estadística, *Censos de Población y Viviendas 2011: Población por sexo, nacionalidad y país de nacimiento*, available at www.ine.es [last accessed 04 September 2022].

[88] Calculations based on Instituto Nacional de Estadística, *Principales series de población desde 1998: Total nacional: Población por País de Nacimiento, sexo y año*, available at www.ine.es [last accessed 04 September 2022]. The equivalent figures for 2021 were 7.3 million and 15.5%.

[89] Calculations based on Eurostat data (n 62).

[90] Hazán (n 86) 378–79 and K Hooper, *Spain's Labour Migration Policies in the Aftermath of Economic Crisis* (Brussels, Migration Policy Institute Europe, 2019).

[91] Hooper (n 90) 5–6.

[92] ibid 16–19.

[93] ibid 11–15.

[94] INSEE, 'L'essentiel sur … les immigrés et les étrangers' available at www.insee.fr/fr/statistiques/3633212#tableau-Tableau1_radio1 [last accessed 04 September 2022].

gradually, reaching 8.1 per cent in 2006 and 10.0 per cent in 2019.[95] The European Labour Force Survey data for the foreign-born employed (above) also show a gradual increase, from 9.6 to 12.2 per cent over the same 2006–2019 period. A feature of French employment patterns is a relatively low level of EU migration, with EU13-born making up only 0.5 per cent of the employed in 2019, compared to 9.0 per cent among non-EU born.[96] This suggests less demand for lower-skilled migrant labour in France than in almost all of the liberal, co-ordinated or mixed regimes states considered above. It is also in line with an ambivalence in state policy concerning labour migration, with calls for '*immigration choisie*' (ie, selective immigration) since the mid-2000s not matched by significant changes in practice.[97] France therefore appears as an atypical case where a strong state does not actively favour labour market flexibility, and so has not seen the more substantial changes in labour migration which flexibility enables.

III. THE INFLUENCE OF MIGRATION UPON EMPLOYMENT LAW

The sustained rise in labour migration in developed states can be understood as a key aspect of the globalisation of labour markets since the 1990s. Generally, globalisation of economic activity is thought to have encouraged states to adopt neo-liberal strategies of 'making labour law more business-friendly'.[98] On this view, competition for work and investment exerts downward pressure upon existing standards, while deterring innovation to improve labour standards.

It is however sometimes possible to see effects in the opposite direction, as changes associated with international economic integration generate pressure – from unions, or the electorate – for *greater* regulation. For example, the development of EU labour standards after 1989 was inextricably linked to the completion and expansion of the EU single market over the same period.[99] Similarly, the increased prominence of the ILO in the current era of globalisation, reflected in new conventions and declarations, has been linked to calls for limits to liberalisation in the international labour market.[100] Other more specific cases

[95] ibid.

[96] Calculations based on Eurostat data (n 62).

[97] M Samers, 'The Regulation of Migration, Integration, and of Multiculturalism in Twenty-First-Century France' in R Mielusel and S E Pruteanu (eds), *Citizenship and Belonging in France and North America* (London, Palgrave Macmillan, 2020) 61–63.

[98] H Arthurs, 'Who's Afraid of Globalization? Reflections on the Future of Labour Law' in J Craig and S Lynk (eds) *Globalization and the Future of Labour Law* (Cambridge, Cambridge University Press, 2006) 56–57; K Rittich and G Mundlak, 'The Challenge to Comparative Labor Law in a Globalized Era' in M Finkin and G Mundlak (eds), *Comparative Labor Law* (Cheltenham, Edward Elgar, 2015) 85–86.

[99] See F Hendrickx and S Giubboni, 'European Union Labour Law and the European Social Model: A Critical Appraisal' in Finkin and Mundlak (n 98).

[100] See B Hepple, Labour Laws and Global Trade (Oxford, Hart, 2005) ch 2 and International Labour Organization, *Declaration on Social Justice for a Fair Globalization* (Geneva, 2008).

may also occur where the effects of internationalisation are immediately visible: an example at the EU level was the adoption of a directive concerning information and consultation rights as a belated response to the closure of the Renault plant in Vilvoorde (Belgium) in 1997.[101] A more recent example concerned the dismissal in 2022 of the crews of P&O ferries, who had been covered by UK collective agreements, and their replacement by agency workers hired outside the UK, who were not. That prompted the Conservative Government to take steps to extend the UK national minimum wage to ferries using British ports.[102]

This section will consider ways in which increases in labour migration can lead to forms of re-regulation in employment law. Two types of such change are distinguished here: those which respond to *exploitation*, and those which respond to *undercutting*. It will be seen that reforms to employment law to address exploitation are more common in liberal market and mixed regimes, as a counterpoint to the extremes produced by labour market flexibility.[103] In contrast, employment law reforms to address undercutting are more typical of co-ordinated market regimes, where the goal is to protect collective labour standards against pressures linked to labour mobility.

A. Exploitation

Within the literature on labour migration and employment law, there is a consensus that situations of exploitation are to be distinguished from 'decent work' on the one hand, and 'forced labour' – which implies a lack of consent – on the other.[104] Between the poles of decent work and forced labour, two approaches to conceptualising exploitation may be distinguished. The broadest treats exploitation as involving persistent violations of the rights guaranteed by employment law.[105] The alternative treats exploitation as relational, in the sense

[101] Directive 2002/14/EC establishing a general framework for informing and consulting employees in the European Community [2002] OJ L80/29: for the background, see M Fuchs, 'The Bottom Line of European Labour Law (Part I)' (2004) 20 *International Journal of Comparative Labour Law and Industrial Relations* 155, 167.

[102] 'P&O Ferries: new powers to protect maritime workers', statement by Secretary of State for Transport, Grant Shapps, *House of Commons Debates*, 30 March 2022.

[103] In this vein, see J Fudge and J-C Tham, 'Dishing up Migrant Workers for the Canadian Food Services Sector: Labor Law and the Demand for Migrant Workers' (2017) 39 *Comparative Labor Law and Policy Journal* 1 and J-C Tham and J Fudge, 'Unsavoury Employer Practices: Understanding Temporary Migrant Work in the Australian Food Services Sector' (2019) 35 *International Journal of Comparative Labour Law and Industrial Relations* 31. For a discussion of exploitation in relation to temporary labour migration programmes see Zou, ch 12 in this volume.

[104] K Skrivankova, *Between decent work and forced labour: examining the continuum of exploitation* (York, Joseph Rowntree Foundation, November 2010); J Fudge and K Strauss, 'Migrants, Unfree Labour, and the Legal Construction of Domestic Servitude: Migrant Domestic Workers in the UK' in C Costello and M Freedland (eds) *Migrants at Work* (Oxford, Oxford University Press, 2014).

[105] For an example of use of that approach to analyse patterns of violations, see A Boucher, '"What is exploitation and workplace abuse?" A classification schema to understand exploitative workplace behaviour towards migrant workers' (2021) *New Political Economy* (published online 28 October 2021).

that it involves an employer taking advantage of a worker, essentially because the worker is vulnerable in some way.[106] We will see in the discussion here that both approaches are of relevance in interpreting actual reform developments.

Among the liberal market economies, **Canada** has seen the most extensive series of reforms linked to exploitation in the first sense – ie, breaches of employment law standards – primarily in respect of migrant workers on temporary work schemes. This has been described as a '"protectivist" vector shaping migrant worker policy', which covers 'rights shortfalls, exploitation and abuse of migrant workers'.[107] These reforms have included provincial legislation concerning employment standards, for migrant workers specifically, and for workers in general, and changes to federal immigration policy to uphold provincial employment law.

Several examples may be given of legislation concerning foreign workers adopted at province level.[108] In *Manitoba*, the Worker Recruitment and Protection Act 2008, requires employers to register if they wish to hire migrant workers through Canada's immigration programme, while recruiters of such workers must be licensed.[109] Both employers and recruiters are prohibited from charging fees to workers, and the terms and conditions agreed with a worker cannot be reduced.[110] In *Ontario*, legislation adopted in 2009 placed legal obligations upon employers or recruiters of live-in caregivers, which were extended in 2014 to all workers covered by federal immigration schemes.[111] This legislation requires employers and recruiters to provide specified information to foreign workers; prohibits the charging of fees to foreign workers; prohibits employers from recouping costs from foreign workers; and, protects foreign workers both from reprisals and from the withholding of their property.[112] In *Nova Scotia*, amendments to the labour code in 2011 required employers of foreign workers to register, and recruiters to possess a licence; protected foreign workers' agreed

[106] C Rijken, 'When Bad Labour Conditions Become Exploitation: Lessons Learnt from the *Chowdury* Case' in C Rijken and T de Lange (eds), *Towards a Decent Labour Market for Low-Waged Migrant Workers* (Amsterdam, Amsterdam University Press, 2016); V Mantouvalou, 'Legal Construction of Structures of Exploitation' in H Collins, G Lester and V Mantouvalou (eds), *Philosophical Foundations of Labour Law* (Oxford, Oxford University Press, 2018). See too the discussion by Zou in ch 12 in this volume.

[107] S Marsden, E Tucker and L Vosko, 'The Trilemma of Canadian Migrant Worker Policy: Facilitating Employer Access while Protecting the Canadian Labour Market and Addressing Migrant Worker Exploitation' in C Dauvergne (ed), *Research Handbook on the Law and Politics of Migration* (Cheltenham, Edward Elgar, 2021).

[108] See Marsden, ch 6 in this volume, and Marsden, Tucker and Vosko (n 107) 70–71.

[109] Information from 'Employer Registration Information' and 'Foreign Worker Recruitment Licence Information' Government of Manitoba factsheets, at www.gov.mb.ca/labour/standards/wrpa.html [last accessed 04 September 2022].

[110] Worker Recruitment and Protection Act 2008 (Manitoba) ss 15, 16 and 17.

[111] Employment Protection for Foreign Nationals Act (Live-in Caregivers and Others) Act 2009, amended by the Stronger Workplaces for a Stronger Economy Act 2014. For a critique of its complaints-based model, rather than registration, see F Faraday, *Canada's Choice: Decent work or Entrenched Exploitation for Canada's Migrant Workers?* (Toronto, Metcalf Foundation, 2016) 45.

[112] Employment Protection for Foreign Nationals Act 2009 (as amended), ss 7–11, and discussion by Marsden in ch 6 in this volume.

terms and conditions; and, prohibited employers and recruiters from taking possession of a foreign worker's property (including their passport and work permit).[113] In *Saskatchewan*, the Foreign Worker Recruitment and Immigration Services Act 2013 required the registration of employers, and the licensing of foreign worker recruiters and immigration consultants; prohibited fees to workers; prohibited the retention of a worker's passport, other official documents or property, and threats of reprisals; and protected migrant workers' agreed terms and conditions.[114] A notable aspect of both the Nova Scotia and Saskatchewan legislation is that they apply to the recruitment of *all* foreign workers other than permanent residents, and not only those within designated federal immigration schemes.[115]

There has also been innovation at the provincial level concerning general employment standards and their enforcement, linked to poor treatment of migrant workers. *Ontario* saw a series of enhancements of its employment law regime between 2003 and 2017 including increases in the minimum wage; limits to excessive working time; requirements on all agencies to provide specified information to workers, and not to charge them fees; and, equal treatment for agency, casual, part-time and temporary workers with full-time permanent workers with the same employer.[116] There have also been policy changes aimed at promoting employer compliance, including the introduction of new administrative penalties in 2000 ('notices of contravention') and 2004 ('certificates of offence', or 'tickets').[117] The legislation in Ontario is a significant example of how poor treatment of migrant workers can lead to labour law reforms of wider application.[118] The reforms of 2011 in *Nova Scotia* already mentioned included prohibitions on the charging of fees to workers in connection with finding them employment, and on the recovery of recruitment costs from workers by employers.[119]

[113] Labour Standards Code (Nova Scotia), sections 89H, 89T, 89F and 89G. This development is discussed in D Gesualdi-Fecteau and D Nakache, *Employment Standards for Mobile Workers* (St John's, On the Move Partnership, 2017).

[114] Foreign Worker Recruitment and Immigration Services Act (Saskatchewan) 2013, ss 4, 14, 22 and 23.

[115] Labour Standards Code (Nova Scotia), s 2(fa) and Foreign Worker Recruitment and Immigration Services Act (Saskatchewan), s 2(g) (discussed by Marsden in ch 6 in this volume).

[116] For a detailed account of these developments, see L Vosko, *Closing the Enforcement Gap: Improving Employment Standards Protections for People in Precarious Jobs* (Toronto, University of Toronto Press, 2020) 30–37.

[117] For a discussion of these innovations, and their role in practice, see R Casey, E Tucker, L Vosko and A Noack, 'Using Tickets in Employment Standards Inspections: Deterrence as Effective Enforcement in Ontario, Canada?' (2018) 29 *Economic and Labour Relations Review* 228.

[118] For a government publication showing this link, see Ontario Ministry of Labour, *The Changing Workplaces Review an Agenda for Workplace Rights* (May 2017) 36–37. See also M Gellatley, *Still Working on the Edge: Building Decent Jobs from the Ground Up* (Toronto, Workers' Action Centre, 2015). Some of these reforms – including the equal treatment provisions – were subsequently reversed by a pro-business government: Vosko (n 116) 37.

[119] Labour Standards Code (Nova Scotia), ss 89B and 89E.

Furthermore, at the federal level, concerns over employer practices led the Canadian Government in 2015 to make respect for federal and provincial employment standards a condition of authorisation to recruit workers within such schemes.[120] The new policy meant that breaches of provincial employment standards could trigger compliance measures by the immigration authorities and by Economic and Social Development Canada.[121] The manner of incorporation of employment standards into the immigration regime has been criticised for its dependence upon employee complaints, and because it may affect the right of an employer to continue employing its current migrant workforce.[122] Nevertheless, the ambition to actively promote employment standards enforcement through immigration law is a significant development.

Australia too has seen labour law reforms to address the exploitation of migrant workers, understood as a persistent violation of employment law rights. These reforms have mainly concerned the enforcement of labour standards by the federal agency concerned with labour inspection, which was renamed the Fair Work Ombudsman (FWO) in 2009.[123] From 2012, the FWO identified migrant workers as a specific group of concern, and a priority group for both compliance activity and education.[124] From 2015, research by academics and others called attention to systematic underpayment of migrant workers in two temporary visa categories (international students and working holidaymakers), particularly in the horticulture and retail sectors.[125] The subsequent political debate would label the treatment of temporary migrant workers 'a national disgrace'.[126] The Fair Work Amendment (Protecting Vulnerable Workers) Act 2017 strengthened the Fair Work Act in several key respects: employers were prohibited from unreasonably requiring employees to make payments to them; liability for Fair Work Act violations could be extended to a franchisor or parent company; penalties for serious contraventions of the Act were increased; and,

[120] Marsden, Tucker and Vosko (n 107) 71–74.

[121] See Marsden, ch 6 in this volume.

[122] S Marsden, E Tucker and L Vosko, 'Flawed by Design? A Case Study of Federal Enforcement of Migrant Workers' Labour Rights in Canada' (2021) 23 *Canadian Labour and Employment Law Journal* 71.

[123] T Hardy and J Howe, 'Partners in Enforcement? The New Balance Between Government and Trade Union Enforcement of Employment Standards in Australia' (2009) 23 *Australian Journal of Labor Law* 306.

[124] See Berg and Farbenblum, ch 7 in this volume, and B Farbenblum and L Berg 'Migrant Workers' Access to Remedy for Exploitation in Australia: The Role of the National Fair Work Ombudsman (2017) 23 *Australian Journal of Human Rights* 310, 311 and 315.

[125] For evidence of systematic underpayment, see L Berg and B Farbenblum *Wage Theft in Australia: Findings of the National Temporary Migrant Work Survey* (Sydney, UNSW/ UTS, 2017); S Clibborn, 'Multiple Frames of Reference: Why International Student Workers in Australia Tolerate Underpayment' (2021) 42(2) *Economic and Industrial Democracy* 336; and E Underhill and M Rimmer, 'Layered Vulnerability: Temporary Migrants in Australian Horticulture' (2016) 58 *Journal of Industrial Relations* 608. See too the discussion by Berg and Farbenblum in ch 7 in this volume.

[126] Parliament of Australia, Senate Education and Employment References Committee, *A National Disgrace: The Exploitation of Temporary Work Visa Holders* (March 2016).

the FWO acquired new investigative powers.[127] In practice, the FWO has been focused upon compliance and enforcement action relating to migrant workers.[128] The policy debate linked to the exploitation of migrant workers has moreover continued, with a government taskforce recommending in 2019 that a criminal offence be introduced for 'the most serious forms of exploitative conduct, such as where that conduct is clear, deliberate and systemic'.[129]

In **Ireland** too, labour migration has contributed directly to recent changes to the enforcement of employment law. Two political and industrial relations controversies in 2005 over migration triggered a transformation in the institutions supervising compliance with employment standards.[130] The first concerned Gama, a prominent contractor in public construction projects, which was alleged to have paid its Turkish workforce below the legally-binding collective agreement for the construction sector.[131] The second concerned Irish Ferries, which announced that 543 Ireland-based crew were to be replaced with agency workers from eastern European states on far lower rates. In that case, it was eventually agreed that they would receive at least the Irish minimum wage, rather than the collectively agreed rates.[132] These controversies led the Irish trade unions to obtain a government commitment within social partnership negotiations for the overhaul of the inspection and enforcement regime relating to labour standards.[133] Initially, the relevant unit within a government department was expanded and re-branded as the National Employment Rights Agency.[134] The Workplace Relations Act 2015 then introduced a new system of inspection, compliance and adjudication under the Workplace Relations Commission.[135]

In contrast, labour law developments in the **UK** have followed a relational approach, prioritising migrants and other workers vulnerable to exploitation, and can be grouped into three phases. The first steps were in response to the

[127] Summary based on M Rawling and E Schofield-Georgeson, 'Industrial legislation in Australia in 2017' (2018) 60 *Journal of Industrial Relations* 378, 380–84.

[128] See for example the information concerning migrant workers in Australian Government, *Fair Work Ombudsman: Annual Report 2020–21* (2021) 20–21.

[129] Australian Government, *Report of the Migrant Workers' Taskforce* (March 2019) 86–87.

[130] See G Flynn, 'Mobile Worker Disputes Jolt Ireland's "Social Partnership" Model' [2006] *Transfer* 267; T Krings, '"Equal Rights for all Workers": Irish Trade Unions and the Challenge of Labour Migration' (2007) 16 *Irish Journal of Sociology* 43. See too the discussion by Zahn in ch 11 in this volume.

[131] During 2005, the company succeeded in blocking publication of a labour inspectorate report into these allegations of underpayment. For a summary of the information in the public domain, see M Doherty, 'Posting of Workers before Irish Courts' in Z Rasnača and M Bernacia (eds), *Posting of Workers before National Courts* (Brussels, ETUI, 2020).

[132] T Dobbin, 'Irish Ferries dispute finally resolved after bitter stand-off' (European Foundation for the Improvement of Living and Working Conditions, 20 December 2005).

[133] See speech by David Begg, then Irish Congress of Trade Unions General Secretary, 'Managing the Labour Market: Implications of EU Expansion and Ireland's Experience' at the University of Notre Dame, October 2007 available at www.ictu.ie/sites/default/files/publications/2021/managing_the_labour_market_notre_dame_oct_07.pdf [last accessed 04 September 2022].

[134] P Teague, 'Reforming the Anglo-Saxon Model of Labour Inspection: The Case of the Republic of Ireland' (2009) 15 *European Journal of Industrial Relations* 207.

[135] A Kerr, 'The Workplace Relations Reform Project' (2016) 7 *European Labour Law Journal* 126.

Morecambe Bay tragedy of February 2004, when 21 Chinese nationals in an irregular immigration situation drowned while collecting cockles.[136] That led to the Gangmasters (Licensing) Act 2004, which established a licensing and compliance system, overseen by the Gangmasters Licensing Authority, for intermediaries in agriculture, horticulture, shellfish collection and related processing and packaging, which mainly concerned employment law.[137] A second phase – between 2011 and 2016 – saw increased prominence given to criminal sanctions and policing in the work of the GLA. The government re-directed it to focus on serious and organised crime (2011); transferred responsibility for it from the Department for Environment Food and Rural Affairs to the Home Office (2014); and the Immigration Act 2016 then renamed it the Gangmasters and Labour Abuse Authority, with new investigation and enforcement powers in respect of the minimum wage, employment agency regulations, the GLA 2004 and the Modern Slavery Act 2015.[138] A third set of developments has seen the government attempt to unify enforcement of core employment laws to cover the minimum wage, employment agencies regulations and holiday pay.[139] This initiative is said to reflect the state's 'important role … in protecting the most vulnerable workers from exploitative practices'.[140] Throughout these developments the position of migrant workers has been key. For example, in 2004, it was understood that migrants worked extensively in the sectors initially covered by the GLA, while the stated aim of the policy which led to the changes made by the Immigration Act 2016 was to prevent employers taking advantage of migrants or others.[141]

The similar experiences in Canada, Australia, Ireland and the UK, of developments in labour enforcement regimes, linked to the exploitation of migrant workers, have not been replicated in the US. It has a well-established labour enforcement architecture, with federal agencies responsible for federal laws on wages and hours, employment equality and health and safety, while many individual states have stronger wages and hours laws, with enforcement agencies to

[136] For details, see 'Chinese cockler tragedy', *Guardian*, 26 March 2006.

[137] B Ryan, 'The evolving legal regime on unauthorised work by migrants in Britain' (2005) 27 *Comparative Labour Law and Policy Journal* 27, 49–57.

[138] Department for Environment Food and Rural Affairs, *Consultation on changes to the scope and governance of the Gangmasters Licensing Authority* (April 2013); Gangmasters Licensing Authority, *GLA moves to Home Office* (9 April 2014); Immigration Act 2016, ss 10–30. For a summary of the 2016 Act provisions concerning the GLAA, including LAPOs, ACL Davies, 'The Immigration Act 2016' (2016) 45 *ILJ* 431, 432–33.

[139] Department for Business, Energy and Industrial Strategy and Home Office, *Good Work Plan: Establishing a New Single Enforcement Body for Employment Rights: Consultation* (July 2019) and Department for Business, Energy and Industrial Strategy, *Establishing a New Single Enforcement Body for Employment Rights: Government Response* (June 2021).

[140] Department for Business, Energy and Industrial Strategy and Home Office (n 139) 3.

[141] Speech by Jim Sheridan MP, *House of Commons Debates*, 27 February 2004, cols 515–523; Department for Business Innovation and Skills and Home Office, *Tackling Exploitation in the Labour Market: Consultation* (October 2015) and *Tackling Exploitation in the Labour Market: Government Response* (January 2016). See too the discussion by Zahn in ch 11 in this volume.

support them.[142] While there have been many criticisms of the inadequacy of these enforcement regimes, both generally and in respect of migrant workers, these have not led to significant reforms.[143] Instead, there has been incremental policy change, such as a more strategic policy of fair labour standards enforcement by the Department of Labour, including the hiring of officials able to communicate in key foreign languages.[144]

Among the continental EU Member States considered here, the starting-point of highly-regulated labour markets has implied less scope for fundamental reforms concerning enforcement. Instead, the main examples of reform have concerned not the classic sphere of employment law but new criminal offences concerning labour exploitation. In **Austria**, the aliens law was amended in 2000 to provide a penal sanction for exploitation of a foreign national, defined as obtaining a continuous income from a person who lacks immigration permission or a work permit, or who is otherwise in a situation of special dependency.[145] **Italy** criminalised the actions of both intermediaries (2011) and direct employers (2016) which lead to exploitative conditions for workers, by taking advantage of their situation of need (*stato di bisogno*), in order to address labour abuses involving foreign workers lacking immigration permission.[146] In 2016, **Germany** criminalised the act of exploitation as such, in addition to forcing a person into exploitative employment.[147] In either case, the offence depends upon the person's 'taking advantage of another person's personal or financial predicament or helplessness on account of being in a foreign country'.[148] In 2017, **Sweden** passed legislation concerning the trafficking of human beings which included a new criminal offence of human exploitation.[149] That offence is

[142] D Kerwin and K McCabe, *Labor Standards Enforcement and Low-wage Immigrants: Creating an Effective Enforcement System* (Washington, Migration Policy Institute, 2011) 5–17. On state wage and hours laws, see I Lurie, 'Enforcement of State Minimum Wage and Overtime Laws: Resources, Procedures, and Outcomes' (2011) 15 *Employee Rights and Employment Policy Journal* 411.

[143] See D Weil, *The Fissured Workplace: Why Work Became So Bad for So Many and What Can Be Done to Improve It* (Cambridge, MA, Harvard University Press, 2014) ch 9; Kerwin and McCabe (n 142); D Kerwin, 'The US Labor Standards Enforcement System and Low-Wage Immigrants: Recommendations for Legislative and Administrative Reform' (2013) 1 *Journal on Migration and Human Security* 32.

[144] D Weil, 'Creating a Strategic Enforcement Approach to Address Wage Theft: One Academic's Journey in Organizational Change' (2018) 60 *Journal of Industrial Relations* 437, generally and at 454.

[145] Fremdenpolizeigesetz [Aliens Police Law], s 116. Information concerning its adoption is in EU Fundamental Rights Agency, Severe Labour Exploitation: Workers Moving with into the European Union: States' Obligations and Victims' Rights (Vienna, 2015) 38.

[146] *Codice Penale*, s 603 bis. Information taken from Chiaromonte, ch 10 in this volume.

[147] Fundamental Rights Agency, Protecting Migrants in an Irregular Situation from Labour Exploitation: Role of the Employers Sanctions Directive (2021) 35; Strafgesetzbuch §232b (forced labour) and §233 (exploitation of labour).

[148] See translations of §232b and §233 at www.gesetze-im-internet.de/englisch_stgb/ [last accessed 04 September 2022].

[149] The offence is that of *människoexploatering* in Swedish Criminal Code, ch 4, §1b. For a discussion, see E Sjödin, 'Criminalisation as a Response to Low Wages and Labour Market Exploitation in Sweden' (2021) 12 *European Labour Law Journal* 529, 539–45.

committed when a person 'by unlawful coercion, deception or exploitation of another person's position of dependence, defencelessness or difficult situation, exploits another person in forced labour, labour under clearly unreasonable conditions or begging'.[150] In addition, in almost all EU Member States, the 2009 Employer Sanctions Directive requires that criminal penalties be in place for the employer of an irregularly present worker, inter alia where there are 'particularly exploitative working conditions'.[151] As a result, in many Member States, severe exploitation is a constituent element in a criminal offence of employing a worker lacking immigration permission.[152]

B. Undercutting

These examples in co-ordinated market economies of reforms linked to notions of exploitation focused on the criminal law, rather than employment law and its enforcement, fit with the emphasis in those states upon the labour market as a relatively well-ordered sphere. For the same reason, the major focus of employment law reform linked to migration in those states has been upon the undercutting of collectively agreed labour standards. In practice, this question has primarily concerned workers posted within the EU, especially from EU13 states. There have been reforms of posted workers legislation at the EU level, and contributed to significant innovations in employment law in Austria, Germany, Norway and Sweden, which are summarised here.

At the EU level, political concerns over posting of workers go back to the 1990s, and led to the adoption of the Posted Workers Directive in 1996.[153] In respect of employment law, the 1996 Posted Worked Directive had apparently defined a set of standards which Member States were either obliged to extend, or permitted to extend, to incoming posted workers. As regards legal standards, in all sectors, Member States were obliged to extend terms of employment which were 'laid down … by law, regulation, or administrative provision', including minimum rates of pay and limits on working time.[154] Member States were also – apparently – permitted to extend labour standards on unlisted matters.[155]

[150] Translation from www.government.se/government-policy/judicial-system/the-swedish-criminal-code/ [last accessed 04 September 2022].

[151] Directive 2009/52/EC providing for minimum standards on sanctions and measures against employers of illegally staying third-country nationals, [2009] OJ L168/24, Art 9(1)(c). 'Particularly exploitative working conditions' are said to exist when there is a 'striking disproportion' in working conditions by comparison with workers who are legally employed: Art 2(i). The 2009 Directive does not apply to Denmark or Ireland.

[152] See information in European Commission, Communication on the application of Directive 2009/52/EC of 18 June 2009 providing for minimum standards on sanctions and measures against employers of illegally staying third-country nationals (COM (2021) 592), Table 2.

[153] Directive 96/71 concerning the posting of workers in the framework of the provision of services, [1997] OJ L18/1.

[154] The list of topics is in Directive 96/71, Art 3(1).

[155] Directive 96/71, Art 3(7) and Art 3(10), first indent.

As regards collective standards, in the construction sector, Member States were required to extend the provisions of collective agreements or arbitration awards which had been declared universally applicable, concerning the same list of subjects.[156] They had two further options as regards collective standards: to extend such agreements/awards to posted workers in other sectors; and, in any sector, in the absence of such agreements, to extend the terms and conditions which were 'generally applicable', or agreements concluded by the most representative employer and labour organisations at national level.[157]

Concerns about posted work gained particular resonance from 2004 onwards, with the enlargement of the EU. It was possible for service provides to post workers from EU8 states in central and eastern Europe to older Member States, at a time when they typically faced transitional restrictions upon direct employment for up to seven years.[158] The increase in posted work would moreover continue after those transitional periods, having become embedded as a practice in labour markets.[159] Critics argued that the EU legal regime concerning posted work – covering labour law and social security rules, and the enforcement of both – was too weak, as it did not prevent cross-border competition by service-providers on the basis of lower home state labour costs.[160]

The Commission's proposal for a Services Directive, which had been made in January 2004, was the first battleground concerning the posted work regime.[161] The 'country of origin' principle was the central element of that proposal: as far as possible, service providers would be subject to the standards and controls of their home Member State alone. In relation to posted workers, the proposal set out exemptions from the country of origin principle *only* for 'matters covered by' the Posted Workers Directive, and implicitly not for others.[162] The proposal also precluded host states from placing obligations upon employers to make a declaration of posting, and to hold and keep employment documents on the host state territory.[163] These constraints upon the enforcement powers of the host state of posting were only in theory off-set by duties of co-operation upon the authorities of the *home* state.[164] These aspects of the package were criticised

[156] Directive 96/71, Art 3(1) and Annex.

[157] See Directive 96/71, Art 3(10), second indent and Art 3(8), respectively.

[158] See J Arnholtz and N Lillie, 'European Integration and the Reconfiguration of National Industrial Relations: Posted Work as a Driver of Institutional Change' in J Arnholtz and N Lillie (eds), *Posted Work in the European Union: The Pollical Economy of Free Movement* (Routledge, New York, 2020).

[159] F De Wispelaere and J Pacolet, 'The Benefits of Posting: Facts and Figures on the Use and Impact of Intra-EU Posting' in Arnholtz and Lillie (eds) (n 158).

[160] J Cremers 'Free Provision of Services and Cross-Border Labour Recruitment' (2013) 34 *Policy Studies* 201; M Houwerzijl, '"Regime Shopping" Across (Blurring) Boundaries' in S Evju (ed), *Regulating Transnational Labour in Europe: The Quandaries of Multilevel Governance* (Oslo, University of Oslo, 2014).

[161] European Commission, Proposal for a Directive on services in the internal market COM (2004) 2.

[162] COM (2004) 2, Arts 17(5) and 24(1).

[163] COM (2004) 2, Art 24(1). The proposed bar on requirements to hold employment documents (item (d)) was at odds with the Court's decision on that subject in C-369/96 *Arblade* [1999] ECR I-08453.

[164] COM (2004) 2, Art 24(2).

for favouring deregulation, not least because home states might have neither the means nor the incentive to supervise work activity taking place in another country.[165] The proposed Directive proved highly controversial, with the provisions concerning posted workers among the elements to which the greatest objections were raised.[166] A trade union-led march in Brussels on 19 March 2005 attracted a reported 80,000 participants.[167] That was followed by a European Council meeting on 22–23 March 2005, at which the French Government called for changes to the proposal, with support from Belgium, Germany, Luxembourg and Sweden, while being opposed by the UK and the EU8.[168] The European Parliament, as co-legislator, removed the 'country of origin' principle and deleted the posted workers clauses in amendments adopted in February 2006.[169] Its approach to the posted workers provisions was then followed by the Commission, when it proposed its own amendments in April 2006, and that text became the basis for the Directive 2006/123 on services in the internal market.[170]

A second battleground then emerged, when the Court of Justice's judgments in *Laval*, *Rüffert* and *Commission v Luxembourg*, effectively treated the 1996 Directive as a ceiling on the extension of terms and conditions to posted workers.[171] In particular, that meant that it was not generally possible to go beyond the matters listed in the Directive, for example by extending rates of pay other than minimum standards.[172] Moreover, the ruling in *Laval* limited the possibility to rely upon collective bargaining and industrial action, rather than legislation, as the means to extend a sectoral collective agreement to posted employees.[173] The Court's position was that such action would violate an employer's EU law right to provide cross-border services because its scope went beyond the matters listed in the Directive, *and* because of a lack of transparency as to the employer's eventual obligations.[174] These judgments on posted workers were extensively

[165] F Hendrickx, 'Monitoring of Labour Standards in Case of Posting: Some Troublesome Issues under the Proposed Services Directive' in R Blanpain (ed), *Freedom of Services in the European Union: Labour and Social Security Law: The Bolkestein Initiative* (58 Bulleting of Comparative Labour Relations Series Set, Kluwer, 2006) 113.

[166] J Flower, 'Negotiating European Legislation: The Services Directive' (2007) 9 *Cambridge Yearbook of European Legal Studies* 217, 221–224.

[167] ibid 224.

[168] ibid 225 and 'Blair Attacks Chirac over EU Reforms', *Independent*, 25 March 2005.

[169] European Parliament resolution T6-0061/2006, 16 February 2006.

[170] Amended Proposal for a Directive on Services in the Internal Market, COM (2006) 160 and Directive 2006/123 on services in the internal market, [2006] OJ L376/36.

[171] Case C-341/05, *Laval un Partneri* [2007] ECR I-11845; Case C-346/06 *Rüffert* [2008] ECR I-1989; Case C-319/06 *Commission v Luxembourg* [2008] ECR I-4323.

[172] See *Laval*, paras 80 and 81; *Rüffert*, para 33; and *Commission v Luxembourg*, paras 26 and 31. For a discussion of the combined effects of the rulings, see C Barnard, 'The UK and Posted Workers: The Effect of Commission v Luxembourg on the Territorial Application of British Labour Law' (2009) 38 *Industrial Law Journal* 122.

[173] A Davies, 'One Step Forward, Two Steps Back? The *Viking* and *Laval* Cases in the ECJ' (2008) 37 *Industrial Law Journal* 126, 127–33.

[174] *Laval*, paras 96–111. The approach in this part of the judgment in *Laval* built upon the Court's ruling in *Viking*, delivered a week earlier: there, industrial action against reflagging a vessel to permit a reduction in workers' terms and conditions was rejected by the Court, on the grounds that it

criticised for restricting the options under the Posted Workers Directive and the Treaty for host states and collective bargaining to extend terms and conditions to incoming posted workers.[175] A further issue concerned the disruption caused by the *Laval* ruling to Nordic industrial relations systems which relied upon collective bargaining, without legislative extension, to ensure that collectively agreed standards applied to posted workers.[176]

These controversies over the EU posted work regime would lead to two legislative developments. The first was the adoption of the Posted Workers Enforcement Directive in 2014 to reinforce compliance with the obligations in Directive 96/71.[177] It included provision inter alia for the designation of competent authorities in each Member State, and mutual assistance among them; for criteria for identifying a genuine posting; for the power of Member States to require a declaration of posting and the provision or retention of employment documents; for effective checks and monitoring by both states concerned; for legal proceedings in the host state; and for chain liability for sub-contractors (which was made obligatory in the construction sector).[178] The 2014 Directive prompted significant changes in the legislation of many Member States, for example in respect of declarations and sub-contractor liability.[179]

Second, and more significantly, amendments to the Posted Workers Directive in 2018 strengthened the obligations of host Member States to extend labour standards to incoming posted workers.[180] In particular, the provision for the obligatory extension of labour standards relating to 'minimum rates of pay' was changed to cover all 'remuneration'; labour standards which are not specifically listed are ordinarily to be extended to posted workers after 12 months' employment in the host state; and, universally applicable collective agreements and arbitral awards are to be applied to posted workers in all sectors, and not only in construction.[181] The amendment Directive did not resolve every issue with the posted worker regime, especially in Member States where collective agreements or arbitral

violated the business's EU law freedom of establishment: Case C-438/05 *Viking Line* [2007] ECR I-10779.

[175] In practice, this critique frequently covered the *Viking Line* ruling as well, because of its close factual and legal links to the *Laval* judgment. For an overview, see C Barnard, 'The Calm after the Storm: Time to Reflect on EU (Labour) Law Scholarship Following the Decisions in *Viking* and *Laval*' in A Bogg, C Costello and A Davies (eds), *Research Handbook in EU Labour Law* (Cheltenham, Edward Elgar, 2016).

[176] R Eklund, 'A Swedish Perspective on *Laval*' (2008) 29 *Comparative Labor Law and Policy Journal* 551 and M Rönnmar, 'Free Movement of Services versus National Labour law and Industrial Relations Systems: Understanding the *Laval* case from a Swedish and Nordic Perspective' (2008) 10 *Cambridge Yearbook of European Legal Studies* 493.

[177] Directive 2014/67 on the enforcement of Directive 96/71/EC concerning the posting of workers in the framework of the provision of services [2014] OJ L159/11.

[178] Directive 2014/67, Arts 3–4, 6 and 9–12.

[179] See European Commission, Report on the application and implementation of Directive 2014/67/ EU, COM (2019) 426.

[180] Directive 2018/ 957 amending Directive 96/71 concerning the posting of workers in the framework of the provisions of services [2018] OJ L173/16.

[181] The key amendments were made to Directive 96/71, Art 3, by Directive 2018/ 957, Art 1(2).

awards are not made universally applicable in a given sector, as there is neither an obligation to extend nor specific protection for trade union intervention.[182] Nevertheless, it is significant as a deliberate effort at re-regulation, in order to ensure the equal treatment of posted and host state workers.[183]

The arrival of posted and other migrant workers also had significant effects upon several *national* employment law systems within the European Economic Area, especially after the EU enlargements of 2004 and 2007. The most significant of these were in states which had previously not had an extensive practice of extending collective agreements to non-parties. In **Germany**, the starting point was that the extension of sectoral agreements was comparatively unusual – even tending to decline – up to the mid-1990s, largely due to employer opposition.[184] A first change had come in 1998, when Germany's Posting of Workers Act was amended to enable the extension of collective agreements in the construction sector – to both resident and posted workers – by government order, without social partner agreement, and that step was then taken.[185] After the 2004 and 2007 enlargements, Germany restricted access to migrant workers from the new Member States for seven years, and exercised a special option to restrict the posting of workers in a more limited range of service sectors.[186] These delays in fully opening the labour market did not prevent labour mobility in that period, however, because of the possibility of self-employment, and of posted working in other sectors, such as meat processing.[187] Towards the end of the transitional period, and immediately after it, the possibility of direct employment of migrant workers from the new Member States, and unrestricted posting of workers, led to significant further reforms. From 2009, legislation permitted government regulations to extend collective agreements in sectors other than construction, and that was then done inter alia for cleaning, security and meat processing.[188] In 2014, a more general reform saw the introduction for the first time of a statutory minimum wage.[189] These developments show the impact of

[182] R Zahn, 'Revision of the Posted Workers Directive: A Europeanisation Perspective' (2017)19 *Cambridge Yearbook of European Legal Studies*187, 205–7.

[183] On the EU political process leading to the Directive, see Zahn in ch 11 in this volume. Novitz, ch 13 in this volume, explores options for the regulation of posted work by the United Kingdom, post-Brexit.

[184] T Blanke and E Rose, 'Erosion or Renewal? The Crisis of Collective Wage Formation in Germany' in T Blanke and E Rose (eds) *Collective Bargaining and Wages in Comparative Perspective* (The Hague, Kluwer, 2005).

[185] See Deinert, ch 4 in this volume.

[186] The sectors which Germany was free to exclude were construction, industrial cleaning and interior decoration: see list of sectors in Annex II to the 2003 Act of Accession ([2003] OJ L236/33) and Annex VI to the 2005 Act of Accession ([2005] OJ L157/203).

[187] Wagner and Hassel (n 67); B Wagner and A Hassel, 'Posting, Subcontracting and Low Wage Employment in the German Meat Industry' (2016) 22 *Transfer* 145.

[188] Wagner and Hassel (n 67) 131. For the current list, see the webpage 'Conditions of employment as laid down in collective bargaining agreements and legal provisions' at www.zoll.de [last accessed 04 September 2022].

[189] See D Mabbett, 'The Minimum Wage in Germany: What Brought the State in?' (2016) 23 *Journal of European Public Policy* 1240; G Bosch, 'The Making of the German Minimum Wage: A Case Study of Institutional Change' (2018) 49 *Industrial Relations Journal* 19.

EU enlargement, by enabling lower-wage labour migration, as a central factor driving reform.[190]

In **Norway**, the historic policy of non-extension was abandoned when the 'Act on the generalization of collective agreements' was adopted in 1993, as part of the preparations for its joining the European Economic Area on 1 January 1994.[191] The Act's main purpose was to ensure that the wages and other labour standards of 'foreign workers' from within the EEA – both migrants and posted workers – were equal to those for resident workers.[192] Linked to that purpose, the extension mechanism permitted either unions or employers to apply, and gave neither side a veto over the government decision.[193] The Act would become relevant in practice from 2004, as migrant and posted workers arrived from the EU8 states (discussed above), which prompted a series of requests for extensions by the Norwegian Confederation of Trade Unions (the *Landsorganisasjonen i Norge*) between 2004 and 2007.[194] The extension of collective agreements would come to cover construction, the onshore petroleum sector, shipyards, fish processing, agriculture, transport and cleaning.[195]

The case of **Sweden** is quite different, as it did not give up its tradition of reliance upon collective action, rather than state intervention, to extend collective agreements to non-parties. That tradition of non-intervention has meant that the social partners did not support a statutory extension mechanism when the Posted Workers Directive was implemented in the mid-1990s.[196] The period after the 2004 EU enlargement saw increased numbers of migrant workers and the pursuit of a more neo-liberal socio-economic policy (see above). Both the tradition of non-intervention and the neo-liberal approach would shape the response to the *Laval* ruling. Rather than create an extension mechanism, in 2010 a centre-right government legislated to confirm restrictions on the right to take industrial action against posting employers.[197] In particular, it was provided that industrial action could not go beyond minimum rates of pay, and that there was no right at all if an employer could prove they were already contractually obliged to pay equivalent rates to the workers in question. In 2014, the second of these limits was removed by a centre-left government, while legislation adopted in 2020 after the amendment of the Posted Workers Directive (above) implies that all aspects of remuneration can be the subject of industrial action.[198] It appears therefore that posted work, and the EU regime relating to it, provided a

[190] See Krings (n 3) 189–192; Mabbett (n 189).

[191] *Lov om allmenngjøring av tariffavtaler* (1993). See K Alsos and L Eldring, 'Labour Mobility and Wage Dumping: The Case of Norway" (2008) 14 *European Journal of Industrial Relations* 441.

[192] Alsos and Eldring (n 191) 446–47.

[193] ibid 448.

[194] ibid 450.

[195] Friberg (n 76) 37.

[196] K Ahlberg and N Bruun, 'Sweden: Transition through Collective Bargaining' in Blanke and Rose (eds) (n 184) 122.

[197] M Rönnmar, '*Laval* Returns to Sweden: The Final Judgment of the Swedish Labour Court and Swedish Legislative Reforms' (2010) 39 *Industrial Law Journal* 280, 284–86.

[198] See Herzfeld Olsson, ch 2 in this volume.

challenge to the Swedish labour law system, but without generating a transformation within it.

A final example among co-ordinated market economies is **Austria**, which has near-complete coverage of collective agreements through statutory extension.[199] Its first policy response to the enlargement of 2004 was shaped by the fact that it bordered four of the new Member States.[200] Initially, its policy focus was on controlling access to the labour market by nationals of the new Member States.[201] In addition to taking advantage of the seven-year transitional period, Austria negotiated and implemented a specific option to restrict posted work in a broad range of service sectors, covering construction, cleaning, horticulture, home nursing and security. As transitional measures came to an end in 2011, the focus shifted to ensuring *compliance* with collectively-agreed labour standards. As Zahn explains in this volume, in 2011 the Anti-Wage and Social Dumping Act[202] was adopted, which made it an administrative offence to fail to pay posted workers the minimum collectively agreed wage. That was amended in 2014 to provide for administrative penalties where a posted worker was paid less than a comparable worker. These penalties are supported by an active enforcement system in respect of posted workers, including the *Kompetenzzentrum LSDB*, a new body established by the 2011 legislation.[203]

Among liberal market economics, examples of legislative reforms to prevent undercutting by migrant or posted workers are far rarer, which can be traced back to the lack of extension mechanisms. A partial exception in **Ireland**, where there is a system for the extension of sectoral collective agreements to non-parties, which does not appear to have been affected by recent labour migration.[204] In the **UK**, where a neo-liberal policy of promoting labour market flexibility, with limited or no support for collective bargaining, has held sway since the 1980s, labour law reforms have not generally aimed at prevention of undercutting. That was seen in particular when protests over the hiring of posted workers in the energy construction sector in 2009.[205] At that time, the Labour Government

[199] See Zahn, ch 11 in this volume.

[200] Krings (n 3) 193.

[201] Zahn (n 3) 157–59.

[202] Lohn- und Sozialdumpingbekämpfungsgesetz (2011).

[203] See the discussion in ch 11 in this volume.

[204] The extension of collective agreements has been subject to constitutional challenge in Ireland in the past decade. The current system, put in place by the Industrial Relations (Amendment) Act 2015, enables the Minister of Labour to convert certain collective agreements into 'sectoral employment orders', after a process which includes approval by both houses of the Irish Parliament. That was found to be compatible with constitutional requirements in *Náisiúnta Leictreach Contraitheoir Eireann v The Labour Court* [2021] IESC 36: see A Eustace, 'The Electrical Contractors Case: Irish Supreme Court Illuminates Collective Bargaining and Delegated Legislation' (2022) 85 *Modern Law Review* (published online).

[205] This episode is examined by Ryan in ch 14 in this volume.

broadly took the view that the protests concerned legitimate labour market competition, and that it would not look to re-instate statutory provision for the extension of collective agreements to non-parties.[206]

IV. CONCLUSION

This chapter has shown how labour migration can be a source of pressure to new regulation within the employment law systems of highly developed states. Contrary to the predictions of varieties of capitalism approaches, significant increases in labour migration have been observable not only in liberal market economies and in most mixed regimes, but also in many coordinated market economies. While national trajectories inevitably differ, in many highly-developed countries, we see a combination of employer demand for migrant workers, the availability of migrant labour supply from foreign workers, and policies which encourage labour migration, leading to an increased presence of such workers. That suggests that labour migration is likely to remain a key part of the context of these employment law regimes, going forward.

In the employment law sphere, we see something of a bifurcation, however. In liberal market economies and mixed regimes, with labour markets which are flexible de jure or de facto, and a high degree of employer freedom, the core issue is protection against 'exploitation'. As we have seen, that can be understood either as involving persistent non-compliance with labour standards, or taking advantage of a worker's position of vulnerability. That concern has led in particular to pressure for the regulation of labour market intermediaries, to a new orientation to the enforcement of labour standards, and to a growing role for the criminal law in respect of the most serious forms of exploitation. In contrast, in co-ordinated market economies, while there are examples of recent criminal law measures addressing exploitation, the primary emphasis has been on preventing undercutting of collectively agreed norms by migrant workers. That has led to reforms to the law on the posting of workers from other states (both at EU and national levels), with a particular focus on extension of sectoral collective agreements to non-parties. It has also led at times to the introduction of statutory minima, especially in relation to wages.

The comparative approach followed here could be used to analyse other questions at the intersection of immigration and employment law. One such is the question of upholding labour standards within immigration control systems (as has been done in both Canada and Sweden).[207] A second is the manner and extent

[206] Statement by Secretary of State for Business, Enterprise and Regulatory Reform, Lord Mandelson, *House of Lords Debates*, 2 February 2009, cols 472–74.

[207] See Marsden, ch 6 of this volume and Herzfeld Olsson, ch 2 of this volume, respectively.

of protection against discrimination, whether on grounds related to migration, such as race and ethnicity, or nationality and immigration status.[208] A third topic could be differences of approach concerning the possibility for workers without immigration status to rely upon employment law rights.[209] Finally one could envisage comparative work on the question of how right to work checks upon employers are structured and delivered.[210] In all these cases, one might anticipate a greater tendency to promote flexibility and individual rights in liberal market economies, with a preference for labour market order in co-ordinated market economies and – by extension – mixed regimes.

These comparative questions link to a deeper normative issue. In a context of extensive labour migration, which exerts pressure within labour markets, how should employment law regimes evolve in response? How are the interests of resident workers and of those who have migrated or moved for work, or who are available to do so, to be reconciled? What should be the policy on labour market admission and the right to work? What do non-discrimination and equality of treatment require? Any legal regime is likely to favour some workers over others, and as yet there is no consensus as to what the legitimate choices are, and how such choices should be made. An exploration of answers to those questions appears unavoidable as long as migration for work remains as extensive as it has become in developed states.

[208] For a review of the applicability of US discrimination laws to workforces which include migrant workers, see R Bloomekatz, 'Rethinking Immigration Status Discrimination and Exploitation in the Low-Wage Workplace' (2007) 54 *UCLA Law Review* 1963. See the discussion in the chapters in this volume by Deinert, Marsden and Ontiveros.

[209] See the discussion in the chapters in this volume by Berg and Farbenblum, Bogg, Camas Roda, Deinert, de Lange, Herzfeld Olsson, Marsden and Ontiveros. See also E Dewhurst, 'Models of Protection of the Right of Irregular Immigrants to Back Pay: The Impact of the Interconnection between Immigration Law and Labor Law' (2014) 35 *Comparative Labor Law and Policy Journal* 217.

[210] See B Ryan, *Innovations in Employer Sanctions* (Institute for the Study of International Migration, 2008), and the discussion in the chapters in this volume by Berg and Farbenblum and by de Lange.

Part I

Equality

2

The Same, Only Different: How to Make Swedish Labour Law Work for Labour Migrants

PETRA HERZFELD OLSSON*

I. INTRODUCTION

THE CHALLENGES TO ensuring decent working conditions for labour migrants have been widely explained and discussed.[1] This chapter builds on some of those insights, but takes a slightly different perspective. The focus here is on measures taken by the Swedish legislator to overcome such challenges. The question raised is: Are the measures taken likely to include labour migrants in the Swedish labour law model and to provide them with decent working conditions?

The Swedish labour law system provides strong protection for trade union members covered by collective agreements. For workers outside these structures – in many cases, labour migrants – the system is weaker.[2] There is no statutory minimum wage. The wage is the outcome of negotiations either in collective agreements or in the employment contract. Monitoring and enforcement, to a large extent, are built on collective agreements and trade union membership. Hence, the legislator has adopted measures to promote the application of Swedish labour standards to labour migrants and/or avoid exploitation. Many of the measures taken are driven by EU law. Our focus will be on prescribed

* This chapter is part of the project *An inclusive and sustainable Swedish labour law – the way ahead*, dnr. 2017-03134 financed by the Swedish Research Council. The author would like to thank the editors and other participants in this anthology for their helpful comments on earlier drafts of this chapter.

[1] See, eg, J Howe and R Owens, 'Temporary Labour Migration in the Global Era: The Regulatory Challenges' in J Howe and R Owens (eds), *Temporary Labour Migration in the Global Era: The Regulatory Challenges* (Oxford, Hart Publishing, 2016); M Freedland and C Costello, 'Migrants at Work and the Division of Labour Law' in C Costello and M Freedland (eds), *Migrants at Work: Immigration & Vulnerability* (Oxford, Oxford University Press, 2014).

[2] J Malmberg, 'The Collective Agreement as an Instrument for Regulation of Wages and Employment Conditions' in P Wahlgren (ed), *Stability and Change in Nordic Labour Law*, Scandinavian Studies in Law Vol 43 (Stockholm, Stockholm Institute for Scandinavian Law, 2002) 190.

wage levels for different categories of labour migrants and on monitoring and enforcement mechanisms adopted to ensure that these wage levels are upheld and/or prevent exploitation. These measures will be described and analysed in order to discuss whether it is at all possible to guarantee labour migrants decent working conditions within the so-called Swedish model.

The chapter is organised as follows. In section II, the characteristics of the Swedish labour law model are discussed. In sections III–V the three labour migrant groups in focus will be introduced: third-country national labour migrants (section III), intra-EU posted workers (section IV) and irregular migrants (section V). The law establishing their status, the rights conferred on them in relation to wages and the measures adopted in relation to a specific group of labour migrants with regard to enforcement and monitoring will be touched upon. The chapter ends with some concluding remarks (section VI).

The three groups of labour migrants chosen for this analysis differ in many ways. Nevertheless, they often work side by side at the same workplace and experience similar exploitation.[3] The challenges they face are explained by similar factors, such as the Swedish labour law system's difficulty in providing protection for those operating outside collective agreements and trade union membership, and the additional challenges related to labour migrants' strong dependence on the employer, established by migration law and EU law. The fear of expulsion often undermines the willingness to enforce labour rights. This makes it reasonable to discuss their situation in the same place.

II. THE SWEDISH LABOUR LAW MODEL

Collective agreements are the most important sources of norms regulating both wages and other employment conditions in Swedish law. There is no statutory minimum wage in Sweden. Wage levels are laid down in collective agreements or in individual employment contracts. These collective agreements are concluded at national sectoral level. The parties are normally national employers' organisations and national trade unions, representing a certain sector or industry.[4] In 2019, 85 per cent of the private sector labour force was covered by collective agreements, and 100 per cent in the public sector.[5] This is explained by the

[3] C Thörnqvist and S Bernhardsson, 'Their own stories – how Polish construction workers posted to Sweden experience their job situation, or resistance versus life projects' (2015) 21 *Transfer* 29 et seq; C-M Jonsson and G Larson, *Gäst i verkligheten – om utstationerad arbetskraft i praktiken* (Stockholm, Landsorganisationen i Sverige, 2013) 22–24 and by the same authors *Vinnare och förlorare: Om konkurrens om arbetskraftskostnader inom EU* (Stockholm, Landsorganisationen i Sverige, 2013) 56 et seq; S Lund 'Är papperslösa rättslösa?' *Arbetet*, 29 April 2016 available at arbetet.se/2016/04/29/ar-papperslosa-rattlosa/ [last acessed 1 April 2022]; J Söderqvist, 'De är räddare än någonsin' (2019) 10 *Arbetarskydd* 23.

[4] Malmberg (n 2) 192.

[5] Medlingsinstitutet, *Avtalsrörelsen och lönebildningen* 2020 (Stockholm, Medlingsinstitutet, 2021) 232.

high proportion of employers organised in employers' organisations. Organised employers employed 88 per cent of the labour force in 2019, whereas only 68 per cent of workers were organised.[6] In some sectors in which the number of labour migrants is particularly high, however, union density is substantially lower, including hospitality (30 per cent), berry picking (< 10 per cent) and cleaning (46 per cent).[7] Large segments of labour migrants also work in sectors in which collective agreement coverage in general is low, such as hospitality and IT.[8] Research has also confirmed that labour migrants often work in companies not covered by collective agreements.[9]

Collective agreements are binding on the signatory parties and their members. If the parties to the collective agreement or their members enter into an employment contract on terms that are in conflict with the collective agreement, the terms are void.[10] Employers bound by a collective agreement are also prohibited, in accordance with the general principles of labour law, from applying inferior conditions to employees who are not trade union members. If they do, they will be liable for damages towards the trade union. Non-member workers cannot themselves make claims based on the collective agreement, however, but only on individual agreements. In such cases, the individual agreement often refers to the collective agreement or it is an implied term in the employment contract.[11] Collective agreements cannot be extended to apply to a whole sector. Employers, not members of an employer organisation can instead conclude a type of collective agreement called an accession agreement with a trade union, which has the same legal effect as other collective agreements.

If the employer is not bound by a collective agreement, freedom of contract applies, so that the parties are almost free to set the wage they wish.[12] The only limitation is that the wage level must not be unjust under section 36 of the Contracts Act (1915:218) or discriminatory according to the Discrimination Act (2008:567).[13] According to section 36 of the Law of Contracts Act (1915:218) a contractual term may be modified or set aside if the term is unreasonable, having regard to the contents of the contract, the circumstances prevailing at the time the contract was entered into, and subsequently arising circumstances. When determining the applicability of this provision particular attention should be paid to the need to protect parties who are in an inferior bargaining position in the

[6] ibid 233.

[7] ibid 236; M Larsson, *Facklig anslutning år 2019* (Stockholm, Landsorganisationen i Sverige, 2019) 9.

[8] A Kjellberg, *Den svenska modellen i en oviss tid. Fack arbetsgivare och kollektivavtal* (Stockholm, Arena Idé, 2021) 62.

[9] O Frödin and A Kjellberg, 'Labour Migration from Third Countries to Swedish Low-wage jobs' (2018) 8 *Nordic Journal of Working Life Studies* 65, 77–78; P Herzfeld Olsson, *Equal Treatment for Highly Qualified Labour Migrants,* Working paper 2019:14 (Uppsala, IFAU, 2019) 25.

[10] Co-determination Act (1976:580) ss 26–27.

[11] Malmberg (n 2) 205.

[12] K Kjellström and J Malmberg, *Anställningsförhållandet*, 5th edn (Uppsala, Iustus, 2019) 191.

[13] Labour Court Cases; AD (1986) No 78 and AD (1982) No 142. The figure within parenthesis is the year when the cases were decided.

contractual relationship.[14] In the rare cases in which this provision is invoked in disputes that end up before the Labour Court, the Court looks for guidance on the reasonable level and what is customary in the sector. The Labour Court has clarified that the collective agreement applicable to organised companies in a sector plays a particularly important role in such cases.[15]

The legislator has, for a long time, systematically promoted strong collective agreements, largely through non-intervention; in other words, regulation of the labour market was left mainly to the parties to industrial relations. In the 1970s, after a period of industrial unrest, the legislator decided to take a more active role, and a number of important labour laws – such as the Employment Protection Act (1982:80) and the Co-determination Act (1976:580) – were adopted. All workers are now entitled in law to employment protection, paid holidays, regulated working time and employee involvement. But a large part of these provisions in law are semi-mandatory, meaning that it is possible for the trade unions and employers to deviate from them through collective agreements, and thereby to adapt the applicable provisions to the needs of the company or sector.[16] A collective agreement also carries with it a number of rights for the trade union party: for example, extended rights to information and consultation, protection of their representatives in the workplace and board representation in companies with at least 25 employees.[17] A collective agreement also gives the trade union a priority right of interpretation of the limits of the duty to work according to the employment contract. The employer is obliged to comply with the trade union's interpretation and to pay the workers accordingly, or else to bring the case to the Labour Court.[18] Another very important factor is the trade unions' extensive right to collective action when no collective agreement applies.[19]

All labour law disputes between parties to a collective agreement can be brought before the Labour Court. Labour law disputes cover, inter alia, disputes regarding collective agreements, labour law and employment contracts. Judgments from the Labour Court are binding. The trade union can always represent its members in such disputes without the need for formal approval.[20] Unorganised workers must start the process in the district court and can then, if specific circumstances are met, appeal to the Labour Court.[21]

[14] This follows from the first and second part of s 36 of the Contracts Act (1915:218).

[15] Labour Court Cases AD (1986) No 78 and AD (1982) No 142.

[16] K Källström, J Malmberg and S Öman, *Den kollektiva arbetsrätten*, 2nd edn (Uppsala, Iustus, 2019) 18 et seq.

[17] Co-determination Act (1976:580) ss 11, 12, 19, 34, 38–40; Board Representation Act (1987:1245) s 6; Trade Union Representative Act (1974:358) s 1.

[18] K Ahlberg and N Bruun, 'Sweden: Transition Through Collective Bargaining' in T Blanke and E Rose (eds), *Collective Bargaining and Wages in Comparative Perspective* (The Hague, Kluwer Law International, 2005) 123.

[19] Instrument of Government, ch 2, s 14, (1974) and Co-determination Act (1976:580) ss 41–44. Källström et al (n 16) 48 et seq.

[20] Act on Litigation in Labour Law Disputes (1974:371) ch 4, s 5.

[21] ibid, ch 2, ss 1 and 2.

The principles of collective autonomy and state non-intervention are also evident with regard to responsibility for monitoring whether employment conditions set out in law or collective agreements are being applied. This task is largely entrusted to the trade unions.[22] If the trade union suspects that a provision is not being applied correctly, the right to negotiation can be used to start discussions with the employer.[23] Such negotiations must take place before the parties can turn to the Labour Court.

Supervision is the responsibility of the public authorities only with regard to occupational health and safety provisions, the working time provisions (Work Environment Authority) and to some extent with regard to anti-discrimination (Equality Ombudsman).[24]

In practice, regardless of whether a collective agreement is in force, trade union members are normally supported by their trade unions in disputes, and the union also bears the costs of claims brought to court. Non-members normally do not get comparable support, though in some cases part of their costs can be covered by legal aid.[25] If the action is lost the claimant as a rule has to pay the winning party's costs, typically 4,000–6,000 euros, and this is not covered by legal aid.[26]

III. LABOUR MIGRANTS FROM THIRD COUNTRIES

A. The Employer Disposes of Entry and Stay

The Swedish rules on labour migration from countries outside the EEA changed radically in 2008. The system went from being strictly regulated, based on labour market tests conducted by the Employment Agency, to being open and employer driven. Today it is, independent of sector, individual employers who decide whether they need to recruit a worker from abroad. No labour market tests are carried out. The aim of the change was to facilitate recruitment of workers from third countries, to satisfy employers' labour needs both more fully and more quickly. According to the government, the change was to put recruitment of third-country nationals on a more equal footing with recruitment from within the EU.[27]

[22] J Malmberg, 'Enforcement of Labour Law' in B Hepple and B Veneziani (eds), *The Transformation of Labour Law in Europe* (Oxford, Hart, 2009) 262, 270 et seq.

[23] Co-determination Act (1976:580) s 10.

[24] Occupational Health and Safety Act (1977:1160) c 7. If working time issues are dealt with in a collective agreement, then the monitoring responsibility is transferred to the trade union. See Discrimination Act (2008:567) ch 6, s 2.

[25] Act on Legal Aid (1996:1619).

[26] Labour Court Cases AD (2017) No 67 and (2017) No 46; A Norrby and E Örnerborg, 'Special – Skenande kostnader i AD' (2013) 11 *Lag & Avtal* 21.

[27] Legislative Bill 2007/08:147, 1 and 25–26. A legislative Bill is sent by the government to the Parliament (Riksdag) with motivated legislative proposals. Such Bills including its motivations have an important value as a legal source when courts apply the law for example.

In Swedish law a non-EEA foreigner normally needs a work permit to work, and, for stays longer than 90 days, also a residence permit.[28] All Swedish work permits are issued on a temporary basis. They can last as long as the employment, but for a maximum of two years, and can then be extended. For the first two years the work permit is connected to a specific employer and a specific occupation. After two years it is connected only to a specific occupation.[29]

B. The Migration Law Perspective on Labour Law

There are no distinctions based on migration status or nationality in Swedish labour law. Employers and employees operating outside the collective agreement system, however, are normally free to set the wage level they see fit. This freedom is considered a risk within the labour migration system. The Swedish Aliens Act therefore requires that the employer must offer labour migrants employment and working conditions that correspond to the relevant collective agreement, or custom, in the relevant sector. This working condition requirement is intended as a safeguard, to ensure that the system does not enable irresponsible employers to obtain labour by offering working conditions worse than those applicable to workers already resident in Sweden.[30]

Nevertheless, the wage level prescribed in the Aliens Act for work in Sweden differs from that applicable to local workers. As already explained, Swedish resident workers do not have to abide by the collective agreement level or the custom in a sector if they are not organised, or organised but not covered by a collective agreement. The prescribed level in migration law is intended to ensure that labour migrants at least are not permitted to work on the basis of a wage below the level in the collective agreement or the norm in the sector. In order to enforce this requirement, the Migration Agency has been given the task of monitoring that the conditions are upheld during the application of the work permit.[31] Giving a monitoring task to a public body also differs from what otherwise applies: monitoring is normally the responsibility of trade unions.[32]

At first sight, therefore, it may seem that the Swedish admission conditions – part of migration law – will help to enforce a decent wage level and also other terms of employment for that matter. However, migration control and labour law remain two separate legal systems. Labour migrants cannot make any claims on the basis of the conditions in the Aliens Act. That is because the offer of employment for the purposes of the Aliens Act is not the same as an employment contract, which must be entered into separately. If the labour migrant is not a member of a

[28] Aliens Act (2005:716) ch 2, s 5. There are exceptions for Nordic citizens and for other EEA citizens.

[29] ibid, ch 6, s 2a.

[30] Legislative Bill 2007/08:147, 27.

[31] Aliens Ordinance (2006:97) ch 6, s 6a. (An ordinance is a provision adopted by the government. The authority is delegated in law by the Parliament to the government).

[32] B Nyström, 'Svensk arbetsrätt – på väg mot vad?' in K Ahlberg, P Herzfeld Olsson and J Malmberg (eds), *Niklas Bruun i Sverige: en vänbok* (Uppsala, Iustus, 2017) 330.

trade union that is party to a collective agreement applicable at the work site, the parties can agree on wages or other terms of employment below the requirements in the Aliens Act, and that would be lawful from a labour law perspective.[33] The labour migrant is in this case trapped in a difficult dilemma. If the labour migrant refuses to accept these conditions and no employment is entered into, the migrant can be removed; but that may also be the outcome if the Migration Agency finds out that the employment terms do not meet the admission conditions.[34] The employer, on the other hand, is not sanctioned in either situation.

This state of affairs has been intensively debated, and the government has sought a better balance between the relevant interests. The strictness of the provision – denying extension for even minor failures to apply labour law conditions – has been softened, so that the decision to extend a permit is now based on an overall assessment of the circumstances.[35] If the wage level provided has gone below the required level in the collective agreement for a certain period of time, but above for another period and it is clear that the low pay was a mistake and there was no intention to circumvent the requirement, the situation can still be accepted and an extension approved.[36] Separately, a government-appointed inquiry proposed in 2016 to criminalise employers who intentionally violate the admission conditions laid down in the Aliens Act.[37] However, a second government inquiry rejected the idea of criminalisation, because of the principle of legality, as the basis for criminalisation would be too vague and complex.[38] It suggested instead that the employer should be liable for non-punitive damages in such cases.[39] The government has not yet pursued this proposal.

A new inquiry was appointed in 2020 with a broader mandate. It should not only propose how to prevent exploitation of labour migrants, but also consider ways to promote the entry of highly qualified labour migrants.[40] The Parliament has so far adopted some of the proposals which entered into force in June 2022.[41] Of relevance in this context is, for example, the requirement for an employment contract instead of an employment offer when applying for a work permit. Another example is that employers are obliged to report a deteriorating change of the employment conditions to the Swedish Migration Agency. The employer may also be ordered to provide the Migration Agency with the conditions for

[33] See examples in Government Inquiry Report, SOU 2016:91, 61; P Herzfeld Olsson, 'Empowering Temporary Migrant Workers in Sweden – A Call for Unequal Treatment' in Howe and Owens (n 1) 211.

[34] Aliens Act (2005: 716) ch 7, s 7e.

[35] The Supreme Court for Migration Issues: MIGR (2017) Nos 24 and 25. The two judgments were issued on 13 December 2017; Legislative Bill 2016/2017:212, 4; Aliens Act (2005: 716) ch 7, s 7e third para.

[36] The Supreme Court for Migration Issues: MIGR (2017) No 25.

[37] Ministry Inquiry Report, Ds 2016:91 69.

[38] Ministry Inquiry Report, Ds 2018:7 42 et seq.

[39] ibid, 51.

[40] Kommittédirektiv 2020:8: *Åtgärder för att attrahera internationell kompetens och motverka utnyttjande av arbetskraftsinvandrare.*

[41] Legislative Bill 2021/22:134 *Skärpta och förbättrade regler om arbetskraftsinvandring*. The proposals are adopted by the Riksdag (Rskr 2021/22:238) and entered into force 1 June 2022.

the employment of a labour migrant.[42] Other proposals are still under consideration.[43] The government has not yet decided whether it will proceed with proposals such as the possibility to deny work permits connected to employers that previously have been sanctioned for employing labour migrants without the necessary permits or who have committed the crimes of human trafficking or human exploitation or who have failed to provide the Migration Agency with information about labour migrants' working conditions mentioned above. It is also still unclear whether the government will proceed to propose a new crime of *exploitation of foreign labour* which if violated would lead to imprisonment for a maximum of two years and if the crime was gross to imprisonment for at least six months and a maximum of four years.[44] An overall assessment of the above measures can be made when we know which of the proposals that will be pursued by the new government that took office in October 2022. It however seems that the focus on the measures suggested and considered is to put pressure on the employers to fulfil the requirements in the Aliens Act with the support of criminal and administrative sanctions. The government seems reluctant to give labour migrants any compensation for such failures. An important exception is the requirement for an employment contract as it will give the labour migrant something concrete to base claims on. This may be particularly effective if the government also criminalises disproportionate payments related to work permits, as one of the major problems reported is that labour migrants in many cases have to pay wages back to the employer, and such payments are often related to debts established in the work permit application process.[45] After this chapter had been written, in November 2022, Parliament decided to introduce a new wage threshold for labour migrants, to focus the system on the highly qualified. The level and scope of this threshold remain uncertain.

IV. INTRA-EU POSTED WORKERS

A. The Legal Starting Point: Being an Adjunct of a Service Provider[46]

An intra-EU posted worker 'for a limited period … carries out his work in the territory of a [EU] Member State other than the State in which he normally works'.[47]

[42] The new and revised provisions: Aliens Act (2005:716) are ch 6, s 2 and Aliens Ordinance ch 6, ss 6b, 6c, 6d and 6e.

[43] The result of the inquiry's work is published in two reports: *Ett förbättrat system för arbetskraftsinvandring*, SOU 2021:5 and *Ett förbättrat system mot arbetskraftsexploatering m.m.*, SOU 2021:88.

[44] The proposals were included in *Ett förbättrat system mot arbetskraftsexploatering m.m.*, SOU 2021:88.

[45] ibid, 27 and 179, 257 et seq.

[46] The phrase is borrowed from C Costello and M Freedland, 'Seasonal Workers and Intra-corporate Transferees in EU law: Capitals Handmaidens?' in Howe and Owens (n 1) 49.

[47] Directive 96/71/EC of the European Parliament and of the Council of 16 December 1999 concerning the posting of workers in the framework of the provision of services, Art 2(1) [1997] OJ L18/1 (hereafter Posted Workers Directive).

Posted workers differ from the third-country national workers discussed in the previous part of this chapter. It is not the posted workers themselves but their employer who has a right – namely, to provide services – that enables the worker to cross the border. The right to post workers is 'an inherent part of the freedom to provide services under Article 56 TFEU'.[48] This section will deal only with those posted workers who are not posted temporary agency workers, whose situation is dealt with somewhat differently.[49]

The regulation of posted workers has been described as 'a commodification of labour in the EU–made possible by the fact that labour mobility is part and parcel of market freedoms'.[50] As Costello and Freedland have pointed out, 'the posted workers route places workers at the disposal of their employer'.[51]

B. Equal Treatment or a 'Hard Nucleus'?

The question of what employment conditions posted workers should be entitled to has been discussed intensely over the past 15 years. The Posted Workers Directive (96/71) Article 3.1 originally stipulated that the *minimum* rates of pay, including overtime, set by law or regulation or for activities covered by an annex (all building work) to collective agreements or by arbitration awards that have been declared universal should apply to posted workers.[52] A description of such collective agreements or arbitration awards is included in Article 3.8 of the Directive. In Sweden, such universally applicable systems do not apply and a second possibility envisaged in the Directive suits the Swedish system better. In the absence of universally applicable systems Member States may, as Sweden has done, according to the second paragraph of Article 3.8, 'base themselves on: collective agreements or arbitration awards which are generally applicable to all similar undertakings in the geographical area and in the profession or industry concerned'.[53] Article 3.10 prescribed that a Member State can extend the application of such collective agreements also to other sectors than those mentioned in the Annex. The Annex enumerates sectors included in the concept 'building work'. Moreover, Article 3.7 states that Article 3.1 'shall not prevent application of terms and conditions of employment which are more favourable to workers'. However, the *Laval* case concluded that it was not possible to require a higher level of pay for posted workers, or to require other rights than those that are

[48] ACL Davies, *EU Labour Law* (Cheltenham, Edward Elgar, 2012) 93.

[49] For an overview of the differences see, P Van Nuffel and S Afanasjeva 'The Revised Posting of Workers Directive: Curbing or Ensuring Free Movement?' in N Cambien, D Kochenov and E Muir (eds), *European Citizenship under Stress: Social Justice, Brexit and other Challenges* (Leiden, Brill, 2021) 295–97.

[50] AH Van Hoek, 'Re-embedding the Transnational Employment Relationship – a Tale about the Limitations of (EU) Law?' (2018) 55 *Common Market Law Review* 449, 452.

[51] Costello and Freedland (n 46) 61.

[52] The concept of minimum rates of pay was one of the main subjects in Case C-396/13, *Sähköalojen ammattiliitto ry v Elektrobudowa Spolka Akcyjna*, judgment of 12 February 2015.

[53] Legislative Bill 2016/17:107, 28–29, 37.

part of the hard nucleus. In other words, the Directive provides both a floor and a ceiling.[54] In Sweden, this posed particular problems in the construction sector, where wage setting is rather complicated and the lowest wage level provided for in the collective agreement is never applied. It took the labour market parties in the construction sector a long time to reach a new collective agreement which included a level of pay fulfilling the requirements of EU law. In the spring of 2017, an agreement was eventually reached, although the wage level the parties agreed on was lower than the one guaranteed to resident workers.[55]

In 2018, however, the Posted Workers Directive was revised.[56] It now says that the Member States shall ensure that posted workers, on the basis of equality of treatment, must be guaranteed 'remuneration, including overtime rates' set by law, regulation or administrative provisions or collective agreement or arbitration awards which have been declared universally applicable or otherwise apply in accordance with Article 8 (without restriction to the building sector).[57] The revisions were transposed in Sweden in July 2020.[58]

With regard to the question of pay, the term 'minimum rates of pay' (minimilön) is replaced by the word 'remuneration' (lön). This means that:

> The remuneration demanded with the aid of industrial action is not to exceed the remuneration that an employer who is bound by the central collective agreement from which the remuneration demand derives is required to pay in an equivalent situation.[59]

It will continue to be incumbent on the labour market parties to decide the relevant level.[60] In line with the revised Directive, a number of allowances are explicitly included in the Swedish version of the hard nucleus, which could therefore be demanded through industrial action.[61] These terms and conditions include accommodation provided by the employer and allowances for or the reimbursement of expenditure to cover travel, board and lodging. This, however, applies only to allowances or reimbursement when posted workers travel to and from their regular place of work in Sweden, 'and when he or she is sent to by the employer to work at a different workplace than his or her regular place or work during the posting period'.[62]

[54] Case C-341/05, *Laval un Partneri* [2007] ECR I-11767.

[55] K Ahlberg, 'Byggbranchens parter enade om minimilön vid utstationering och offentlig upphandling', (2017) 3 *EU & arbetsrätt* 2.

[56] Directive (EU) 2018/957 of the European Parliament and of the Council of 28 June 2018 amending Directive 97/71/EC concerning the posting of workers in the framework of the provision of services, [2018] OJ L173/16.

[57] ibid, Art 3(a)1, the first indent and (c).

[58] Legislative Bill 2019/20:150.

[59] ibid, 50 et seq.

[60] ibid, 51.

[61] ibid, 52 et seq.

[62] ibid.

The outcome in the *Laval* case led to extensive changes to Swedish labour law, as a result of which it is no longer possible to use collective action to force a service provider to extend to posted workers the same collective agreement as applies to resident workers.[63] The trade union could, after *Laval*, only use collective action to demand a collective agreement that provides for the minimum level prescribed in the Posted Workers Directive, the so-called 'hard nucleus'. A heavily criticised caveat applied, however, namely that the right to take collective action presupposed that the service provider did not claim that that the 'hard nucleus' was already in general fulfilled through the applicable employment contract.[64] In such cases it was not possible for a Swedish trade union, with the support of collective action, to demand a collective agreement.

Other solutions, such as the extension of a collective agreement by legislative means, were discussed, but rejected by the Swedish legislator because it was considered alien to the Swedish labour law model, in which state interference should be avoided as far as possible. Such a system would give collective agreements statutory status and application would no longer be based on contractual rules and principles.[65] The measures adopted before 2014 were criticised by the monitoring bodies of the ILO and the European Social Charter, which concluded that Sweden no longer lived up to its obligations to respect freedom of association and the rights to collective bargaining provided for in ILO Conventions Nos 87 and 98 and in Articles 6.2, 6.4 and 19.4 of the European Social Charter.[66] The European Committee of Social Rights found that the provisions adopted, among other things, did not guarantee 'for foreign posted workers lawfully within the territory of Sweden treatment not less favourable than that of Swedish workers with regard to enjoyment of the benefits of collective bargaining'.[67] They have not yet evaluated the changes made in 2020.

C. Monitoring, Enforcement and Related Issues

The Posted Workers Directive of 1996 requires that the Member States shall guarantee posted workers certain working conditions. The Posted Workers

[63] Case C-342/05, *Laval un Partneri* [2007] ECR I-11767. For a discussion of the implications of the *Laval* case in Swedish law, see M Rönnmar 'Sweden' in M Freedland and J Prassl (eds), *Viking, Laval and Beyond* (Oxford, Hart Publishing, 2014) 251 et seq; J Malmberg 'Posting Post-Laval: Nordic responses' in M-A Moreau (ed), *Before and after the Economic Crisis – What implications for the 'European Social Model?* (Cheltenham, Edward Elgar, 2011).

[64] Act (1999:678) on Posting of Workers, amendment No SFS 2010:228) s 5a, (now repealed).

[65] Government Inquiry Report, SOU 2008:123, 250.

[66] Report of the Committee of Experts on the Application of Conventions and Recommendations, International Labour Conference, 102nd session, 2013, 178–180; Complaint No 85/2012, *Swedish Trade Union Confederation (LO) and Swedish Confederation of Professional Employees (TCO) v Sweden* (European Committee of Social Rights report, 3 July 2013).

[67] *Swedish Trade Union Confederation (LO) and Swedish Confederation of Professional Employees (TCO) v Sweden* (European Committee of Social Rights report, 3 July 2013) para 138.

Enforcement Directive adopted in 2014 was intended to sharpen this requirement.[68] In order to comply with it, in July 2017 new provisions on postings entered into force in Sweden.[69] The Swedish legislator adopted a number of important measures which deviated from the general labour law provisions applicable to other workers on the labour market. These measures also sought to meet the criticisms of the ILO and the Council of Europe, to which we referred above. It remains to be seen if the changes made altogether will satisfy the international bodies.

It can be argued that the 2017 changes sought to compensate for the fact that the Swedish model can only guarantee a certain level of protection if a collective agreement concluded with a Swedish trade union applies on the work site and the worker is a trade union member.

The most remarkable change was the introduction of a new form of collective agreement. A Swedish trade union can now, with the support of collective action, seek a collective agreement providing for the working conditions protected in the Posted Workers Directive, irrespective of whether the service provider claims that they already apply this level.[70] As with a regular collective agreement, if the posting collective agreement is violated, the trade union can claim damages.[71] However, this posting collective agreement has both more limited and more far-reaching legal effects than regular collective agreements. A regular collective agreement carries with it a number of additional rights for the trade union, which do not apply to a posted worker collective agreement, such as extended rights to information and consultation, protection of their representatives in the workplace and board representation in companies with at least 25 employees.[72] In contrast to other cases, however, the trade union is given explicit statutory rights to monitor whether the conditions in the posted worker collective agreement are being fulfilled. For example, it is entitled to documentation, such as employment contracts, wage slips and time reports.[73] To ensure that individual posted workers are provided with the rights they are entitled to, they, unlike other workers, are given a right to make claims based on the collective agreement, irrespective of whether they are trade union members or not.[74] These claims are, however, limited to the 'hard nucleus' in the Posted Workers Directive.

In addition, reprisals by employers against posted workers claiming their rights, provided for by the Posted Workers Directive, are prohibited, even though

[68] Directive 2014/67 on the enforcement of Directive 96/71/EC concerning the posting of workers in the framework of the provision of services [2014] OJ l 159/11, chs II–V, recital 7.

[69] Legislative Bill 2016/17:107.

[70] Posted Workers Act (1999:678) s 5a.

[71] ibid, s 24.

[72] Co-determination Act (1976:580) ss 11, 12, 19, 34, 38–40; Board Representation Act (1987:1245), Trade Union Representative Act (1974:358).

[73] Posted Workers Act (1999:678) s 5d.

[74] ibid, s 5c.

a similar provision for other workers only applies in relation to claims related to discrimination.[75] For violations of the new provisions in the Posting of Workers Act the sanction is damages both for economic loss and for the pain suffered.[76]

The Posted Workers Enforcement Directive also includes provisions on subcontracting liability.[77] Article 12.1 in the Directive prescribes that Member States may ensure that in subcontracting chains the contractor of which the posting employer is a direct subcontractor can, in addition to or in place of the employer, be held liable for outstanding remuneration corresponding to the minimum rates of pay in the Posted Workers Directive. For the activities mentioned in the Annex to the Posted Workers Directive (construction) the Member States, shall according to Article 12.2, provide for such liability as is described in Article 12.1. Hence, the only mandatory part is related to the activities mentioned in the Annex to the Posted Workers Directive, which covers construction.[78] It is an advantage for workers in subcontracting chains to be able, when the employer denies their rights, to make claims against other actors in the chain.[79] The question of subcontracting liability has been highly debated in Sweden, as no such statutory obligation previously existed, other than for irregular workers (section V, below). It is clear that a number of actors use subcontracting to circumvent their legal obligations and taxes.[80] Many stakeholders, including trade unions, had promoted the adoption of a general subcontracting liability provision. The legislator decided to meet these demands and a new law on subcontracting liability in both posting and purely domestic situations entered into force on 1 August 2018.[81] If the workers do not get paid by the employer they may turn to the contractor that hired the employer. If that attempt fails, the workers can turn to the main contractor.[82] The liability for the outstanding wages lies with the employer, and the employer is obliged to compensate the contractor or main contractor for the payment of the outstanding wages.[83] It is possible for the labour market parties to deviate from these provisions through a collective agreement. The collective agreement must fulfil the obligations in the Posted Workers Enforcement Directive.[84] In this case the government chose to raise the general level of protection, instead of adopting compensatory provisions only for posted workers.

[75] ibid, s 22 and Discrimination Act (2008:567) ch 2 s 18.
[76] ibid, s. 24.
[77] Directive 2014/67, Art 12.
[78] ibid, Art 12(1) and (2).
[79] M Houwerzijl and S Peters, *Liability in Subcontracting Processes in the European Construction Sector* (Dublin, Eurofound, 2008) 3.
[80] Legislative Bill 2017/18:214, 13.
[81] ibid and the Act (2018:1474) on subcontractor liability for outstanding wages.
[82] Legislative Act (2018:1474) on subcontractor liability for outstanding wages, ss 7–9.
[83] ibid, s 16.
[84] ibid, s 5.

The combination of a higher level of protection with the specific posting collective agreement and other enforcement promoting measures may help to improve the situation of posted workers in Sweden. The outcome will depend on whether the trade unions have a chance to reach the many small construction companies within the sector.[85]

V. IRREGULAR LABOUR MIGRANTS

A. Preventing Employment of Irregular Migrants

The EU has the competence to facilitate and encourage the adoption of measures to prevent and combat illegal immigration.[86] The EU adopted the Employers Sanctions Directive to 'counter the pull factor for finding work' for irregular migrants.[87]

In Swedish law, as mentioned, a foreigner needs a work permit to work, and, for stays longer than 90 days, also a residence permit.[88] It is a criminal offence for third-country nationals to stay or to work in Sweden without the necessary permits, and a criminal offence to employ a foreigner without the necessary permits.[89] The penalty for intentionally or negligently employing an irregular worker can be a fine or, if there are aggravating circumstances, imprisonment for a maximum of one year.[90] Negligent behaviour could be at stake when the employer does not check whether the foreign worker has the necessary permits for work.[91] Aggravating circumstances apply when there is a profit-making purpose behind the employment of the irregular worker, or when the employer operates on a large scale, meaning that they employ a large number of irregular workers.[92]

Irrespective of responsibility under the criminal provisions, a physical or a legal person who employs a third-country national without the necessary permits is liable to pay an administrative fine. This fine (or charge) may be reduced or

[85] The employers and trade unions in the construction industry have together put forward a number of proposals to combat work life criminality within the sector. One is directed to themselves, that they must be better in concluding collective agreements with smaller companies and ensure that they are applied, Byggmarknadskommissionens slutrapport, *Från svart till vitt – Vänd den osunda utvecklingen i byggbranschen* (Byggmarknadskommissionen & Premiss förlag, 2022) 12.

[86] Article 79 TFEU; C Costello, 'EU Migration and Asylum Law' in A Bogg, C Costello and ACL Davies (eds), *Research Handbook on EU Labour Law* (Cheltenham, Edward Elgar, 2016) 328.

[87] European Parliament and Council Directive (EC) 2009/52 providing for minimum standards on sanctions and measures against employers of illegally staying third-country nationals [2009] OJ L168/24.

[88] Aliens Act (2005:716) ch 2, s 5. There are exceptions for Nordic citizens and for other EEA citizens.

[89] Aliens Act (2005:716) ch 20, ss 1, 3 and 5.

[90] ibid, ch 20, s 5.

[91] Legislative Bill 2003/04:34, 84.

[92] Legislative Bill 1975/76:18, 145 and the Appeal Court Judgment *Svea HovR RH* (2013) No 7.

waived in full if there are special grounds for doing so.[93] The criminal provision requires intent or negligence, which is not the case for the administrative fine.

Against that background, the Sanctions Directive led to very few amendments to the criminal law provisions in Swedish law.[94] First, the provisions targeting employers were extended to include foreign workers who were not entitled to be in Sweden – previously they had applied only if the foreign worker lacked the necessary work permit. (In practice, this amendment had limited implications, as it is very rare that a person not entitled to be in Sweden would have a valid work permit.[95])

Second, the Directive led to employers being given new obligations aimed at preventing irregular migration.[96] Before a foreign worker takes up employment the employer is now explicitly obliged to check whether they have the prescribed permit to stay and work in Sweden.[97] A copy of the documents proving that the required permits were issued, or that permits were not needed, must be kept for the duration of the period of employment, and for 12 months after it has ended.[98] Employers also became obliged to report on new employment to the tax authorities, at the latest one month after it commences.[99] If the obligation to report the employment to the tax authorities is not complied with, the employer can be fined and, in aggravated circumstances, a prison sentence of up to six months can be imposed on the employer.[100]

Third, the liability to pay an administrative fine was expanded to cover illegal stays and not only when a necessary work permit was missing, as when the Sanctions Directive was transposed.[101] However some explicit exceptions to these provisions were also introduced through the Sanctions Directive. If the stay and/or work are irregular the employer can escape liability if they have checked the foreign worker's right to work and stay in Sweden, have kept a copy of the documents proving that, and have informed the tax authorities about the employment.[102] Exceptionally, if the documents are false, and the employer should have realised that, or did do so, the relevant checks are deemed not to have been made.[103] Before these amendments of the law, checks could have an impact on

[93] Aliens Act (2005:716) ch 20, s 12.

[94] Government Inquiry Report, SOU 2010:63, 107; Legislative Bill 2012/13:125, 41–42.

[95] Legislative Bill 2012/13:125, 45.

[96] ibid, 26–36.

[97] Aliens Ordinance (2006:97) ch 6, s 13a.

[98] ibid, ch 6, s 13a.

[99] ibid, ch 7, s 1b. If the obligation to report the employment to the tax authorities is not complied with, the employer can be fined and, in aggravated circumstances, a prison sentence of up to six months can be imposed. See Aliens Act (2005:716) ch 20, s 6. This obligation does not apply if the workers are EU long-term residents or EU citizens.

[100] Aliens Act (2005:716) ch 20, s 6. This obligation does not apply if the workers are EU long-term residents or EU citizens.

[101] Legislative Bill 2012/13:125, 55 et seq and 126.

[102] Aliens Act (2005:716) ch 20, s 12.

[103] Legislative Bill 2012/13:125, 50.

whether the administrative fine should be reduced or waived. In 2017 the fine was half of the base amount, of 22,400 SEK for each irregular worker employed, and the full base amount if the violation had been going on for more than three months. In order to further discourage the employment of foreign workers without the necessary permits, the level of the fine was doubled from 1 July 2018.[104] In 2021 the base amount was 47,300 SEK.[105]

Fourth, Article 7 of the Sanctions Directive led to the adoption of new sanctions for employers. An employer convicted of employing illegally resident workers according to the Aliens Act, chapter 20, section 5 can, in aggravating circumstances, meaning that the employer has been sentenced to prison, and if requested by the public prosecutor, be excluded, for a period of a maximum five years, from entitlements to some or all public benefits, aid or subsidies to which they are otherwise entitled.[106] The employer can also be obliged to pay back public benefits, aid or subsidies already received for a period up to 12 months preceding the time when the crime became known to the police.[107] The provisions in the Directive regarding possible exclusion from public contracts, the closure of establishments and the withdrawal of licences were already considered part of Swedish law.[108] The same was true of the liability of legal persons in Articles 11 and 12 of the Directive, which is covered by provisions in the Swedish criminal code on company fines and forfeiture.[109] Legal persons cannot be charged for a crime or face criminal sanctions according to Swedish law.[110]

B. Are Irregular Migrant Workers Entitled to Statutory Labour Law Rights and Pay?

The transposition of the Sanctions Directive into Swedish law shed light on the question of whether and to what extent irregular migrant workers are subjects of Swedish labour law.[111] This issue had hardly been discussed before that. The Labour Court had considered the status of irregular migrant workers once, in 1979, when it concluded that an employer could not be liable for a violation of the Employment Protection Act for dismissing a foreign worker who lacked

[104] Legislative Bill 2017/18:176, 16 et seq.
[105] See www.regeringen.se/artiklar/2020/09/prisbasbelopp-for-2021-faststallt/ [last accessed 1 April 2022].
[106] Aliens Act (2005:716), ch 20, s 15 and Legislative Bill 2012/13: 123, 51 ff and 129 ff.
[107] Aliens Act (2005:716), ch 20, ss 16–17 and Legislative Bill 2012/13: 123, 51 ff and 129 ff.
[108] Legislative Bill 2012/13:125, 56–59 and 69.
[109] ibid, 73 et seq.
[110] ibid, 75.
[111] Government Inquiry Report, SOU 2010:63, 170–195.

a work permit. The Labour Court's reasoning was that, because it is a criminal offence to employ a foreign worker without a work permit, the employer could not be sanctioned for dismissing such a person. The requirement of just cause for dismissal was overridden by the provisions of the Aliens Act.[112]

Two questions were key in the debate that was triggered by the Sanctions Directive. First, are protective labour law provisions, like the Employment Protection Act (1982:80), the Annual Leave Act (1977:480), the Working Hours Act (1982;673) and the Wage Guarantee Act (1992:497), applicable to foreign workers working without the necessary work permit? Second, does a foreign worker's right to a wage in accordance with the employment contract depend on whether they have the necessary work permit?

As to the first, qualifying as an employee is usually the 'entry ticket' to coverage by Swedish labour law.[113] Nevertheless, during the transposition process of the Sanctions Directive, a government-appointed inquiry concluded that it was not possible to give a general answer to the question of whether irregular migrant workers were covered by labour law. Instead, the question had to be decided by reference to the *aim* of the particular statutory provision. Only three labour laws were discussed – the Annual Leave Act (1977:480), the Working Hours Act (1982:673) and the Occupational Health and Safety Act (1977:1160) – and all three were considered to be applicable to irregular workers.[114] However, when the government itself was considering this proposal, it was not ready to go that far. Instead, in the Bill implementing the Sanctions Directive, it claimed that only *fundamental* protective labour law and occupational health and safety rules could, to a broad extent, be applied to irregular workers.[115] The government accepted that the human right of freedom of association applied irrespective of the legal status of the migrant, but did not specify which other provisions they considered would extend to such workers. However, since then, at least two district courts have clarified that the Annual Leave Act is applicable also to workers lacking the necessary permits.[116]

The Sanctions Directive provides for an important right, namely the right to back payments – in other words, outstanding remuneration has to be paid.[117]

[112] Labour Court Judgment AD (1979) 90, concerning Employment Protection Act (1982:80) s 7.

[113] P Herzfeld Olsson and E Sjödin 'The Fissured Workplace: Some Contemporary Challenges in Sweden' (2015) 37 *Comparative Labor Law and Policy Journal* 143, 148 et seq.

[114] Government Inquiry Report, SOU 2010:63, 182.

[115] Legislative Bill 2012/13:124, 24. For a discussion, see A Inghammar, 'The Employment Contract Revisited. Undocumented Migrant Workers and the Intersection between International Standards, Immigration Policy and Employment Law' (2010) 12 *European Journal of Migration and Law* 193, 203 et seq.

[116] Judgment District Court Södertörns Tingsrätt T 10750-18, 2019-10-14 (leave to appeal was denied) and District Court Solna Tingsrätt, T 7211-29, 2021-05-07 (leave to appeal pending at time of writing).

[117] Sanctions Directive, Art 6.

In a dispute, unless either of the parties can prove otherwise, the agreed level of remuneration is presumed to have been at least as high as the wage provided for by applicable laws on minimum wages, by collective agreements or in accordance with established practice in the relevant occupational sector. For this purpose, the duration of the employment relationship is presumed to have been at least three months, unless either party proves otherwise.[118]

In Swedish law, the question of whether an employment contract concluded in violation of the Aliens Act is void is decided on a case-by-case basis. Swedish law does not have any general provisions stating that a legal act is void if it violates the law. Nullity can instead be based on general principles of law. Whether an agreement violating the law should be void, despite the fact that it is not prescribed by the particular law, depends on whether the law violated is based on considerations that make nullity appropriate. That must be decided on a case-by-case basis, taking into account the aim of the provision, the need for a sanction like nullity and the different consequences such a sanction will lead to, in particular for joint parties in good faith.[119] However, if it is found to be void none of the parties must gain from that fact.[120] The last principle was established by the Supreme Court in a dispute about a real estate contract, but the government found it reasonable to assume that it can be applied also to employment contracts, meaning that an employer must be obliged to pay wages for conducted work irrespective of whether the contract would be void because the worker does not have the right to be in Sweden or does not have a work permit.[121] However, in order to ensure that the principle required by the Sanctions Directive was sufficiently clear to the parties concerned, a new law was enacted.[122] This law makes it clear that a foreigner without a right to be in Sweden has a right to wages and other remuneration for work done.[123] No time limit applies in this introductory provision.

However, this new law only applies when the employer has not conducted the prescribed check of a foreign worker's status.[124] This aspect highlights the punitive aspect of this provision.[125] It is more about punishing employers for not ensuring that a worker is not irregular, than ensuring that irregular workers get paid for work done. If the employer has conducted the necessary check, the migrant worker does not acquire the right to back payments according to

[118] For a critical evaluation of this provision see, E Dewhurst, 'The Right of Irregular Immigrants to Back Pay' in Costello and Freedland (n 1) 228 and 237.

[119] Legislative Bill 2012/13:125, 80 referring to the Swedish Supreme Court, judgment 27 February 1997 (NJA 1997, s 93).

[120] Swedish Supreme Court, judgment 11 December 1987, NJA 1987, s 845 II.

[121] Legislative Bill 2012/13:125, 80.

[122] ibid, 81.

[123] Act (2013:644) on the right to wages and other remuneration for work carried out by a foreigner who has no right to stay in Sweden, s 4.

[124] ibid, s 1.

[125] N Selberg, 'Åtgärder mot dem som tillgodogjort sig papperslösas arbete: nya principer i arbetsrättens sanktionssystem?', in B Nyström, Ö Edström and J Malmberg (eds), *Nedslag i den nya arbetsrätten* (Malmö, Liber, 2012) 88.

this law. The general Swedish principles of law presented above could instead be invoked in such situations. However, it has turned out that this new law can play a crucial role in safeguarding outstanding payments for irregular workers. At least two cases have been brought to court and the plaintiffs have in both these cases been awarded outstanding payments.[126] The presumptions prescribed by the Directive played a decisive role. In the first case, the defendant agreed that the plaintiff had worked for three months. The plaintiff however claimed that they had been working for a longer period than three months which was not considered confirmed by the court.[127] In the other case, both the employment as such and the period was contested by the defendant. In that case the court considered it confirmed that work had been conducted and used the presumptions to establish that the employment had lasted for three months full time work as the plaintiff could not confirm otherwise. The plaintiff claimed that the wage agreed was a somewhat lower than the level prescribed by the applicable collective agreements and the District Court found the claimed level to be the confirmed level.[128]

If a collective agreement applies in the workplace the general assumption is that irregular workers will be covered by it to the same extent as resident workers.[129] If no collective agreement applies in the workplace, it is the worker who is responsible for identifying the relevant collective agreement or custom on which the presumed remuneration should be based.[130] The cases discussed above illustrate the responsibility of the plaintiff in this regard. The concept of 'minimum wage' is supposed to correspond to the same concept as in the Swedish Posted Workers Act (1999:678).[131] The result is that irregular migrant workers may end up being paid less than resident workers, at least in the construction sector (see the discussion in section IV above). However, the transposition of the 2018 revisions of the Posted Workers Directive in principle removes such wage gaps.[132]

C. New Monitoring and Enforcement Mechanisms

The Sanctions Directive provides for specific inspections 'to control employment of illegally staying third-country nationals'.[133] These inspections are to be based on risk assessments, and should be carried out in sectors where the risks of employment of illegally staying third-country nationals are particularly

[126] Judgment District Court Södertörns Tingsrätt T 10750-18, 2019-10.14 (leave to appeal denied); Judgement District Court Solna Tingsrätt, T 7211-29, 2021-05-07 (outcome in appeal case pending at time of writing).

[127] Judgment District Court Södertörns Tingsrätt T 10750-18, 2019-10.14 (leave to appeal denied).

[128] Judgement District Court Solna Tingsrätt, T 7211-29, 2021-05-07 (outcome in appeal case pending at time of writing).

[129] Government Inquiry Report, SOU 2010:63, 183 et seq; Legislative Bill 2012/13:125, 81.

[130] Legislative Bill 2012/13:125, 81.

[131] ibid, 120–21; Legislative Bill 2009/10:48. Measures in the light of the *Laval* judgment.

[132] See the discussion in section IV of this chapter.

[133] Sanctions Directive, s 14.

high. In Sweden, the border police carry out these risk assessments and inspections.[134] The sectors identified as most prone to such risks are hospitality, parts of retail, and services such as hairdressers and beauty salons.[135] The construction industry, cleaning industry, car workshops and car service, the transport industry, green industry and health and welfare sector were also considered to be risk sectors in 2020.[136] The border police cooperate with other agencies, such as the Tax Authority and the Work Environment Authority, in accordance with a government instruction to coordinate their work against fraud and other violations of the law in working life.[137] The intensity of the raids carried out within this framework has increased over time and a high number of irregular migrant workers without the necessary permits have been found. In most cases, irregular workers have been detained and, where possible, have been repatriated.[138] Many of these workers were paid wages far below the norm in the relevant sectors, and violations of the Occupational Health and Safety Act and Working Time Acts were also detected.[139] The authorities only have limited capacity to act on those findings. The police can investigate if the crimes of human trafficking or human exploitation are at stake. But the threshold for these crimes is rather high.[140] The Work Environment Authority can act on flaws related to the regulation of occupational health and safety and working time. Investigating violations of working time is very resource consuming and the authorities have asked for 'expanded supervision' for example for the restaurant industry where they suspect that many violations take place.[141]

[134] Legislative Bill 2012/12:125, 115; Ordinance with Instructions for the Policy Authority (2014:1102) s 19.

[135] Legislative Bill 2017/18:176, 4, 8.

[136] Status Report 2020, For the inter-agency work against fraud, rule violations and crime in working life.

[137] Government, 'Uppdrag om metodutveckling för myndighetsbaserad kontroll för att motverka fusk, regelöverträdelser och brottslighet i arbetslivet', Government decision of 18 December 2017. A new government instruction was adopted in 2021: www.regeringen.se/48e884/contentassets/245746d49deb414eb93f6f2a4e839aa4/uppdrag-om-fortsatt-myndighetssamverkan-for-att-motverka-fuskregelovertradelser-och-brottslighet-i-arbetslivet.pdf [last accessed 1 April 2022]. The result of this work is communicated on the website of the Work Environment Authority: www.av.se/arbetsmiljoarbete-och-inspektioner/inspektioner-utredningar-och-kontroller/myndighetssamverkan-mot-arbetslivskriminalitet/?hl=arbetslivskriminalitet [last accessed 1 April 2022].

[138] Reports from the Police Authority and The Work Environment Authority: *Polisen, Farlig arbetsmiljö och svartjobb på bilverkstäder och biltvättar* (17 February 2021); *Polisen, Farlig arbetsmiljö och olaglig arbetskraft på byggen* (28 April 2021); *Arbetsmiljöverket, Farlig arbetsmiljö och illegal arbetskraft i flera branscher* (12 February 2020). See also the media report: M Martelleur, Polisinsats mot illegal arbetskraft, *ATL*, 28 June 2021.

[139] T Nandorf, 'Razzior avslöjar hänsynslöst utnyttjande av papperslösa', *Dagens Nyheter*, 4 September 2018 and 'Arbetsmiljöverket, Ökad risk för arbetslivskriminalitet under pandemin', 4 February 2021.

[140] E Sjödin, 'Criminalisation as a Response to Low Wages and Labour Market Exploitation in Sweden' (2021) 12 *European Labour Law Journal* 529. However, the Supreme Court for the first time found an employer guilty of the crime of human exploitation on 15 February 2022, B 1770-21. The plaintiffs had temporary residence permits and the question whether they had a right to work or not in Sweden was not dealt with. The case was not initiated by any inspections.

[141] Status Report 2020, For the inter-agency work against fraud, rule violations and crime in working time, 29.

However, the inspections do lead to prosecutions on other grounds. In one case it turned out that 21 workers in a demolition company lacked the necessary permit to work. The employer was sentenced to pay 1,500,000 SEK in administrative fines.[142]

In order to prevent employment that violates the Aliens Act by increasing the number of inspections, since 1 July 2018 the border police have had the power to make unannounced inspections, even when they do not have specific reason to suspect irregularities.[143] The government's justification for these measures was the risk some workers face of exploitation and of being left outside the safety net provided by statutory employment and working conditions.[144] It also raised the argument that employing workers on low wages and in very poor working conditions, made possible by the fact that they are in Sweden illegally, creates unfair competition.[145]

The first of these arguments must be considered especially weak. An increase in inspections is unlikely to improve the situation of illegally resident workers. In fact, more inspections may well make it more difficult for such workers to *find* work, but they will not ensure that they receive a decent wage or can assert the protection provided for by labour law. In any case, it is very unlikely that irregular migrant workers will make such claims, fearing expulsion as a consequence.[146] Since 2018 the authorities have been conducting over 4,500 inspections to combat work life criminality.[147] The creativity in letting no irregular worker escape the controls is high. For example, drones have been used to identify fleeing workers.[148] Inspections, however, have been severely affected by the pandemic. It has been more difficult to conduct inspections and at the same time the risks for work life criminality were also considered likely to increase during the pandemic.[149] The upcoming plans for future inspections must take these aspects into account.

The Sanctions Directive also includes provisions aimed at increasing a worker's chances of enforcing outstanding wages. During the transposition process, provisions facilitating worker complaints were considered to be already present in the Swedish system.[150] Among other things, irregular workers in a dispute

[142] District Court Södertörn Tingsrätt, 2020-09-21, B 3702-20.

[143] Legislative Bill 2017/18:176, 14. The proposal was adopted by the Riksdag (rskr. 2017/18:348) and entered into force 1 July 2018.

[144] ibid, 11.

[145] ibid, 12.

[146] Lund (n 3); Söderqvist (n 3) 23; For an international outlook see: M Bell, 'Irregular Migrants: Beyond the Limits of Solidarity?' in M Ross and Y Borgmann-Prebil (eds), *Promoting Solidarity in the European Union* (Oxford, Oxford University Press, 2010) 164; ILO General Survey, *Promoting Fair Migration* (2016) 148.

[147] Polisen, 'Farlig arbetsmiljö och olaglig arbetskraft på byggen', 28 April 2021 available at polisen.se/aktuellt/nyheter/2021/april/farlig-arbetsmiljo-och-olaglig-arbetskraft-pa-byggen/ [last accessed 1 April 2022].

[148] C Niklasson, 'Här är polisens nya vapen mot flyende byggjobbare', Byggarb.se, 16 April 2021.

[149] ibid.

[150] Sanctions Directive, Art 13 and Legislative Bill 2012/13:125, 89.

can be represented by a third party and a fast-track process can be applied by the Swedish Enforcement Authority when demanding an injunction to pay outstanding wages in case the claim is not disputed.[151] No particular action has been taken to target irregular workers.

A further provision prescribes chain liability in subcontracting: that is, the contractor of whom an employer is a direct subcontractor may be liable to pay the back payments required by the Directive in place of the employer.[152] It is, however, possible for the contractor to escape this responsibility by undertaking due diligence obligations, as defined by national law. When this provision was transposed into Swedish labour law, it was the first time that the principle of main contractor liability had been accepted. The due diligence provision in the law is rather vague: if a contractor has adopted reasonable control measures and does not realise or does not have reasonable cause to realise that the employer employs one or more foreigners with no right to stay in Sweden, they cannot be held liable for a subcontractor's debts.[153] The control measures demanded will be decided on a case-by-case basis.[154] The government asserts that stricter demands can be made when a company hires a subcontractor for the first time. More thorough checks should be made when a subcontractor offers an exceptionally low price. In sectors in which foreigners without the right to stay in Sweden are more prevalent tougher demands can be made.[155] Through the introduction of this subcontractor liability provision irregular migrant workers were, at least in this respect, put in a stronger position than any other worker under Swedish law.[156]

VI. CONCLUDING REMARKS

The Swedish system provides strong protection for workers who are trade union members and covered by a collective agreement. For workers who are not, which is often the case for labour migrants, the situation is very different.[157] It is clear that the three categories of labour migrants discussed in this chapter are subject to exploitation. When the legislator has considered how to address this problem, however, or has been forced to reconsider regulations governing labour migrants in response to EU developments, the desire to keep the Swedish labour law model intact, and to find solutions within its framework, has dominated the discussion.[158]

[151] Legislative Bill 2012/2013:125, 89–91.
[152] Sanctions Directive, Art 8.
[153] SFS 2013:644, s 7.
[154] Legislative Bill 2012/13:125, 111.
[155] ibid.
[156] Inghammar (n 115) 213 et seq.
[157] The Swedish National Audit Office, *Government Initiatives to combat labour exploitation, Regulations, inspections, information and support to victims*, RIR 2020:27 (Stockholm, 2020); SOU 2021:88.
[158] See, eg, Government Inquiry Report, SOU 2008:123, 241 et seq.

Proposals for a statutory minimum wage, statutory extension of collective agreements and monitoring of employment conditions by the authorities have been firmly rejected on the basis that they would be alien to the Swedish labour law model.[159] Other measures have been taken nevertheless. But what has been the effect of these measures to overcome the challenges involved in safeguarding decent working conditions for labour migrants?

The legislator's commitment to the three groups clearly differs. The aims behind the provisions on irregular workers, to prevent and combat illegal migration, explain why the current unsatisfactory situation will continue. There is no commitment to provide irregular workers with decent working conditions. The measures that have been taken – the right to outstanding remuneration and subcontractor liability – are driven by EU law and are only in exceptional cases likely to lead to improved conditions, as the risk of being discovered and expelled is ever present for such workers. No public authority is given the task of monitoring and enforcing their working conditions. At least it would be a step forward if workers were made aware of their right to outstanding wages when the increased inspections uncover violations of the Aliens Act. The question is, who should initiate and pursue such claims and pay the costs related to them? If a worker is not a trade union member such disputes can be very expensive and few other supportive actors are available. The two cases mentioned above were pursued by a single lawyer who has taken on the task of helping irregular migrants. This is a promising step and hopefully this case law will help other actors to enforce rights to outstanding wages.

Collective agreements are the key to decent working conditions in Swedish law. Measures to increase the salience of collective agreements for labour migrants have been taken with regard to third-country workers and intra-EU posted workers. With regard to third-country workers, measures are taken to enforce the employment condition's related requirements in the Aliens Act. However, the reference to collective agreements in the Aliens Act does not generate any enforceable rights at all for third-country workers. For a long time, nothing was done to ensure that these workers would have a chance to enforce the labour rights they are entitled to. Now that the proposal to require an employment contract has been adopted, it may at least give the labour migrant a legal basis for enforcing a decent wage. An additional way could be to amend the sanctions system related to work permit violations. The aim behind the existing sanction system is rather to protect national workers from unfair competition. More has to be done to create incentives for employers to apply decent working conditions.

When it comes to promoting services and intra-EU posted workers, however, everything is different: only limited rights are guaranteed, but everything possible is being done at the Swedish level to make these rights a reality. The usual respect shown to the Swedish model has, to a certain degree, been set aside and something completely new has taken shape. Even so, these changes will not disrupt

[159] See, eg, Government Inquiry Reports 2008:123, 250 et seq; SOU 2015:83, 251.

the autonomy of the labour market parties. Indeed, these measures strengthen them, in particular the trade unions, but refrain from any form of state interference. Autonomy is retained as far as EU law permits. The trade unions can use the new posting collective agreement to combat unfair competition in the Swedish labour market: for example, they can claim damages if the collective agreement is not complied with. Such damages go to the trade union, however; no damages or unpaid wages will be provided for the posted worker unless they make an individual claim. The rights of unorganised intra-EU posted workers in collective agreements are, however, enforceable, in contrast to those of other unorganised workers. The extent to which these measures will help posted workers claim their rights is uncertain, though, especially as employment protection will be governed by domestic law. How the prohibition against reprisals will work in this context is also difficult to say. But the measures do give the trade unions means to ensure that at least a certain minimum level of working conditions is reached in the workplace. This outcome of course requires that the trade unions succeed in concluding the prescribed collective agreements, and not only with the large companies posting workers to Sweden.

In all cases except for third-country workers the provisions establishing the rights of labour migrant groups are driven by EU law. The Swedish legislator seems uninterested in this issue. One explanation is that problems in the labour market are supposed to be solved by the autonomous labour market parties. It is, however, difficult for these parties to adopt suitable measures to convince these workers to become trade union members and make up for the migration risks these workers face when claiming labour rights.[160]

This fragmented picture is unsatisfactory in many ways. It is a challenge for the Swedish model to deliver in relation to temporary labour migrants as most labour migrants operate outside the structures of the Swedish labour law model. As long as labour migrants' assertions of their rights jeopardise their presence in the Swedish labour market they are unlikely to pursue them. It has rightly been concluded that a key to change would be 'an inclusive trade union strategy towards migrant workers'.[161] The argument is based on the assumption that migrant workers will otherwise 'remain vulnerable to labour market exploitation and precariousness' in sectors outside the coverage of collective agreements.[162] A public monitoring body could be another solution. Measures to guarantee the integrity of such a body in relation to migration law must in any case be taken. While there is no body, private or public, taking responsibility for safeguarding migrant workers' working conditions a parallel labour market prone to exploitation is likely to continue to exist.

[160] SOU 2021:88, 172 et seq.

[161] C Woolfson, J Fudge and C Thörnqvist, 'Migrants Precarity and Future Challenges to Labour Standards in Sweden' (2014) 35 *Economic and Industrial Democracy* 710.

[162] ibid.

3

Exploitation Based on Migrant Status in the United States: Current Trends and Historical Roots

MARIA ONTIVEROS

I. INTRODUCTION

NON-CITIZEN, IMMIGRANT WORKERS have always formed a core of the United States (US) workforce. At the same time, they have been among the most vulnerable and exploited workers. In the antebellum, European indentured labourers and African slaves supported the economy of the North and the South, while lacking the ability to quit, or to control their own labour. After the turn of the nineteenth century, European immigrants laboured in industrial sweatshops while slaves and their descendants lacked citizenship and worked in semi-free systems, including share cropping and debt bondage. From the mid nineteenth to the mid twentieth century, Asian immigrants built the railroads and harvested the nation's produce, while being denied the rights of citizenship and eventually being subject to deportation and internment. The last half-century has witnessed significant immigration from Mexico and Latin America, including groups of undocumented immigrants who have been subject to low pay and abusive working conditions. At the same time, more highly-skilled immigrant workers have come to the US from countries such as the Philippines and India to fill jobs ranging from nursing and home health care to engineering and systems analysis. These so-called 'guest workers' often work at pay levels below the domestic workforce, lack the ability to quit without being deported or incurring large amounts of debt, and frequently suffer workplace abuse and harassment.

This chapter examines the contemporary situation of non-citizen immigrant workers in the US, grounding that examination in an understanding of its historical antecedents. The first section discusses the past and present use of non-citizen, migrant workers in the US, starting with chattel slavery and continuing to the contemporary use of visa workers in industries ranging from agriculture to computer programming. The second section examines the formal legal workplace protections for non-citizen workers, as well as the ways in which the formal rules fail to adequately protect these workers. It concludes that, while these workers are formally covered by the laws guaranteeing basic workplace standards, in practice they lack effective remedies due to the structure of the law and problems in enforcement. They are also deterred from filing claims due to fear of removal.[1] This latter phenomenon occurs, at least in part, because US law, while prohibiting discrimination based on national origin and race, does not prohibit discrimination based on migration or citizenship status. The analytical difficulty in maintaining this distinction has recently been challenged by two separate lines of cases discussed in the chapter. Finally, the third part of this chapter steps back to draw broader lessons by connecting the current exploitation facing non-citizen workers in the US to the historical treatment of non-citizen workers, and to the themes of exit, voice and access to domestic labour markets found in scholarly work dealing with migrant workers in other countries.

II. NON-CITIZEN WORKERS IN THE UNITED STATES: PAST AND PRESENT

Before describing the contours of the current migrant workforce in the US, this section gives a brief history of the use of non-citizen workers.

A. The History of Non-Citizen Workers in the United States: From Slavery to Braceros

Many people cite the Naturalization Act of 1790, which allowed certain free, white immigrants of good character to naturalise and become citizens, as the first US immigration law.[2] Others look to the Immigration Act of 1882,[3] the Chinese Exclusion Act of 1882[4] and the Alien Contract Labor Laws of 1885[5] and 1887[6] as the first true immigration laws, because they regulated who could immigrate into the US.

Recently, though, scholars have started to recognise the African slave trade and its corresponding forced migration and relocation of hundreds of thousands of labourers into the US as that country's first true immigration system.[7]

[1] The term 'removal' is used to denote the situation where an individual is expelled from a country for lack of immigration status. In the US, this situation is generally called deportation.

[2] Naturalization Act of 1790, c 3, s 1, 1 Stat. 103, 103 (repealed 1795).

[3] Immigration Act of 1882, c 376, 22 Stat. 214 (repealed 1966).

[4] Chinese Exclusion Act of 1882, Pub. L. No. 47-126, 22 Stat. 58 (repealed 1943).

[5] Act of February 26, 1885, c 164, 23 Stat. 332 (amended 1887).

[6] Act of February 23, 1887, c 220, 24 Stat. 414 (repealed 1952).

[7] RV Magee, 'Slavery as Immigration?' (2009) 44 *University of San Francisco Law Review* 273; LK Buckner Inniss, 'Tricky Magic: Blacks as Immigrants and the Paradox of Foreignness' (1999) 49 *DePaul Law Review* 85.

Antebellum chattel slavery was, among other things, an abusive system that exploited non-citizen, immigrant labour. In particular, three key aspects of chattel slavery made it an abusive labour system: the inability of slaves to quit or stop working for the slave owner; the inability of slaves to advocate for better workplace conditions through collective action or in the courts; and the fact that the slave owner, and not the slave, owned and controlled the slave's labour. These practices are critical because vestiges of them continued beyond the period of chattel slavery and remain in place even today.

Chattel slaves were not free to quit or stop working for the slave owner; separation occurred only through sale to another owner or manumission.[8] Chattel slavery was abolished in 1865 when the Thirteenth Amendment to the US was ratified, stating that 'neither slavery nor involuntary servitude … shall exist in the United States'.[9] Following abolition, however, many southern states passed laws, known as 'black codes' that restricted the ability of freed slaves to quit employment.[10] For example, South Carolina prohibited freed men from working in a variety of settings, such as skilled trades and store ownership, without the approval of a judge or payment of a large fee. Other states prohibited a new employer from 'enticing' or hiring a freed man from another employer, thus eliminating the opportunity to quit and take another job. Still others passed apprenticeship laws that allowed whites to place the children of freed men deemed unfit into forced labour, until the children became adults.[11]

The right to quit was also severely restricted by the use of other 'black codes' that created a system of debt bondage, often referred to as convict leasing.[12] Southern states criminalised minor offences, such as loitering, and prosecuted freed men for breaching these. Some convicts were required to perform work directly for the states on chain gangs, but the labour of a convict could also be purchased from the state, and the convict held to a term of bondage until their sentence was served or fine paid off.

In the early part of the twentieth century, US courts began to strike down these arrangements.[13] In *Bailey v Alabama* decided in 1910, the US Supreme Court found these practices illegal, and stated that 'compulsory service to secure the payment of a debt' was prohibited.[14] It held that the state 'may not compel one man to labour for another in payment of a debt, by punishing him as a

[8] S Plass, 'Private Dispute Resolution and the Future of Institutional Workplace' (2010) 54 *Howard Law Journal* 45, 51–52.

[9] US CONST. amend. XIII, § 1.

[10] B Azmy, 'Unshackling the Thirteenth Amendment: Modern Slavery and a Reconstructed Civil Rights Agenda' (2002) 71 *Fordham Law Review* 981, 1015.

[11] ibid.

[12] ibid, 1026–27.

[13] These arrangements were challenged under a statute passed pursuant to the Thirteenth Amendment, the Peonage Abolition Act of 1867, c 187, 14 Stat. 546. See, eg, 42 USC § 1994 (2018) (civil provision); 18 USC § 1581 (criminal provision).

[14] 219 US 219 (1910).

criminal if he does not perform the service or pay his debt'.[15] Similarly, the ability of individuals to purchase convict labour was struck down in *US v Reynolds* in 1914.[16] The system was found to violate the Thirteenth Amendment because the contract for labour 'must be kept, under pain of re-arrest, and another similar proceeding for its violation, and perhaps another and another. Thus, under pain of recurring prosecutions, the convict may be kept at labour, to satisfy the demands of his employer.'[17]

In reaching these conclusions, both *Bailey* and *Reynolds* focused on the idea that restricting the ability to quit or requiring service in payment of a debt violated the Thirteenth Amendment, because a person's labour is special and distinct, and is protected by the anti-slavery mandate. It stated that the purpose is to ensure free labour because 'there is no more important concern than to safeguard the freedom of labour upon which alone can enduring prosperity be based'.[18] In *Bailey*, it explained that 'The act of Congress, nullifying all state laws by which it should be attempted to enforce the "service or labor" … in liquidation of any debt or obligations … necessarily embraces all legislation which seeks to compel the service or labor by making it a crime to refuse or fail to perform [labor.].'[19]

Despite the holding in *Reynolds*, the practice of purchase of convict labour persisted. In 1944, the US Supreme Court struck down a similar system that criminalised fraud in relation to an employment contract, and thus linked the requirement to pay a fine, or else to perform work, to compelled labour.[20] In *Pollock*, the Court explained that the practice of compelled labour also violated the Thirteenth Amendment because it destroyed the floor for free labour. It reasoned as follows:

> The undoubted aim of the Thirteenth Amendment as implemented by the Antipeonage Act was not merely to end slavery but to maintain a system of completely free and voluntary labor throughout the United States … In general, the defense against oppressive hours, pay, working conditions or treatment is the right to change employers. When the master can compel and the laborer cannot escape the obligation to go on, there is no power below to redress and no incentive above to relieve a harsh overlordship or unwholesome conditions of work. Resulting depression of working conditions and living standards affects not only the laborer under the system, but every other with whom his labor comes in competition.[21]

This trilogy of cases implied twin purposes, then, to the prohibition of restrictions on the right to quit: the unique nature and sanctity of human labour, and the effect that involuntary servitude has on participants in the free labour market.

[15] ibid, 243–44.
[16] 235 US 133 (1914).
[17] ibid, 149.
[18] *Bailey* (n 14) 245.
[19] ibid, 243–44.
[20] *Pollock v Williams*, 322 US 4 (1944).
[21] ibid, 17–18.

A second, independent way in which slavery oppressed labour was the slaves' inability to improve their conditions through traditional methods, such as use of the legal system or collective action. In one of the earliest cases concerning the legal definition of slavery, *State v Mann* in 1839, the court emphasised that because a master must have total control over a slave, a slave lacks any legal recourse for injury inflicted upon him by his master.[22] Having just the status as property, they were legally unable to sue to improve their conditions. Similarly, in *Dred Scott v Sandford* in 1836 the US Supreme Court found that even a former slave did not have the right to sue in the federal court because he was not a citizen.[23] Since slaves lacked the status of human beings, and even freed slaves lacked the status of citizens, they were unable to work through the political or civil system to improve their workplace conditions or to advocate for changes in society. During slavery, slaves were unable to effectively advocate through the use of collective action, except in ways, such as slow downs, which could be made to appear as if they were still working within the control of their masters.[24] Following emancipation and into the twentieth century, blacks were excluded from burgeoning trade union movements until the passage of antidiscrimination laws halted this practice.[25] Thus, this group lacked the rights of citizens or workers to try to improve their working conditions.[26]

A final way in which the system of chattel slavery oppressed labour rights was that the slave owners, and not their slaves, owned the labour of the slaves. During the antebellum slave period, each state had laws or 'slave codes' that regulated slavery in the American South.[27] These codes gave slave owners the right to control the labour of their slaves because, in addition to owning the slave, they also owned the labour of the slave. So, for example, the slave owner could assign a slave to work for someone else and collect payment in exchange for their labour. In addition, the codes gave slave owners the right to control, forbid or profit from any independent entrepreneurial work done by slaves.[28] Some slaves tended a garden and sold the food at a local market, while others might work as a blacksmith on Sundays or mend and sew clothes for others, at night, in exchange for money. The slave owner could dictate whether this work could be done, and where it could be done, and could demand a percentage of

[22] 13 NC (2 Dev.) 263 (1829).

[23] 60 US 393 (1856).

[24] J Pope, 'Why is There no Socialism in the United States? Law and the Racial Divide in the American Working Class, 1676–1964' (2016) 94 *Texas Law Review* 1555, 1563–67.

[25] ibid.

[26] M Ontiveros, 'Immigrant Workers' Rights in a Post-*Hoffman* World – Organizing around the Thirteenth Amendment' (2004) 18 *Georgetown Immigration Law Journal* 651, 672; M Ontiveros, 'H-1B Visas, Outsourcing and Body Shops: A Continuum of Exploitation for High Tech Workers' (2017) 38 *Berkeley Journal of Employment and Labor Law* 1, 27.

[27] For a thorough discussion of slave codes, see KM Stampp, *The Peculiar Institution: Slavery in the Ante-bellum South* (Vintage Books, 1989).

[28] VV Palmer, 'The Customs of Slavery: The War Without Arms' (2006) 48 *American Journal of Legal History* 177.

the money earned. These practices ended with abolition, but the 'black codes' replaced them as an alternative method of owning or controlling the labour of freed blacks.

Although chattel slavery was the first instance of the exploitive use of non-citizen, immigrant labour in the US, it was not the last. Throughout the nation's history, agricultural work has been performed by a series of non-citizen immigrant workers who have toiled in abusive work situations and who have been deported or disposed of when they tried to assert their rights and improve their conditions.[29] When Spanish missionaries arrived in the 1700s, they brought indigenous Mexicans to work in and around the missions as chattel slaves, with no labour, human, civil or citizenship rights. After these workers perished, the missionaries replaced them with members of indigenous California tribes, whom they kept in slave-like conditions, with families separated and forced to work. They were locked in their dormitories, kept under constant surveillance, and forcibly returned, beaten or killed if they tried to escape.[30] These indigenous slaves were technically freed in 1826, but a system of laws similar to the black codes allowed them to be sold into bonded labour after being convicted of committing petty crimes; required them to work; restricted their ability to change jobs; and allowed any farmer needing labour to petition a judge to indenture them. Like the indigenous Mexicans who preceded them, the indigenous Californians perished under this system, with the indigenous population dropping from a high of 700,000 to only 15,000 at the end of the Mission era.[31]

Between approximately 1850 and 1945, non-citizen immigrant workers from Asia, first from China and then from Japan, laboured in the fields, helped build railroads and participated in other manual labour with few civil or labour rights.[32] Asians were not allowed to naturalise and become citizens until 1952. In addition, family formation was discouraged, and land ownership was prohibited. Many of the Chinese immigrants arrived with debt that bound them to Chinese labour bosses, and failure to follow restrictive laws would result in imprisonment, hard labour and deportation. The Japanese immigrants initially fared better and practised some labour activism; however, that activism was quashed through immigration control. During World War II, the US Government imprisoned Japanese immigrants in internment camps and stripped them of their property. Like previous incarnations of agricultural workers, these non-citizen immigrant workers were brought to the US to work in agriculture in

[29] M Ontiveros, 'Noncitizen Immigrant Labor and the Thirteenth Amendment: Challenging Guest Worker Programs' (2007) 38 *University of Toledo Law Review* 923, 931–37; M Ontiveros, 'Immigrant Workers and the Thirteenth Amendment' in A Tsesis (ed), *The Promises of Liberty* (New York, Columbia University Press, 2010) 283–85.

[30] RS Street, *Beasts of the Field: A Narrative History of California Farmworkers 1769–1913* (Stanford, Stanford University Press, 2004) 25–75.

[31] GT Luna, 'Gold, Souls and Wandering Clerics: California Missions, Native Californians and LatCrit Theory' (2000) 33 *U.C. Davis Law Review* 921, 941.

[32] Ontiveros (n 29) 933–36; Ontiveros (n 29) 284.

disempowered labour relationships and without the citizenship rights necessary to improve their situation.

During the twentieth century, immigrants from Mexico began arriving in large numbers to work the fields. Between 1920 and 1940, those who arrived outside of the formal legal process were easily exploitable because they were subject to detention and removal.[33] Between 1942 and 1964, non-citizen immigrant workers from Mexico arrived pursuant to a treaty establishing the Bracero Program. Under that Program, these 'braceros' worked for low wages without the ability to leave or change employers, were not given enough hours to earn a subsistence wage, and were subject to deductions from their meagre pay checks for room and board, as well as non-existent services and retirement benefits.[34] The abuses were so bad that the government official in charge of the Program called it 'legalized slavery'.[35]

The exploitation of non-citizen immigrants labouring in agriculture echoed many of the same abusive labour conditions as those found in chattel slavery. Their ability to quit was severely restricted by physical restraints, law and threats of deportation. Their labour and job placements were controlled by others, and they were unable to organise to improve their working conditions, either because of their social isolation or because attempts to organise resulted in deportation. This history provides the context for understanding the contemporary situation of non-citizen immigrant workers in the US. (The specific ways in which these three restrictions operate to constrain the contemporary immigrant workforce are detailed in the final section of this chapter.)

B. The Current Situation for Non-Citizen Workers in the United States

This section will discuss all non-citizen workers, regardless of whether they are technically migrants, who enter the US temporarily with the intention of leaving, or immigrants, who enter the US with the intention of relocating there permanently. When studying the contemporary immigrant workforce in the US, it is difficult however to determine whether the person is a migrant worker who is coming to the US for a limited period of time with the intention of returning home or an immigrant worker who wants to permanently relocate to the country. On the one hand, many workers who enter the US on 'guest worker' visas will eventually seek citizenship. On the other hand, even those individuals who are categorised as 'legal permanent residents' may still be removed from the country.

[33] MM Ngai, *Impossible Subjects: Illegal Aliens and the Making of Modern America* (Princeton, Princeton University Press, 2004) 130–35.

[34] M Ontiveros (n 29) 936–37.

[35] L Majka and T Majka, *Farm Workers, Agribusiness and the State* (Philadelphia, Temple University Press, 1982) 136.

The US continues to rely heavily on non-citizen workers in its labour force. Approximately one out of every six workers (17.1 per cent) in the country – 27.6 million – is an individual not born in the US.[36] This population includes both citizens and non-citizens – though it is very difficult to ascertain how many are which. The non-citizen workforce in the US may be categorised into authorised workers, who have the legal right to live and work in the country, and unauthorised workers, who do not. These categories are now considered in turn.

i. Authorised Workers

Two different programmes allow non-citizens to live and work in the US: one programme designed for long-term, permanent immigrants and a second designed for temporary migrants or 'guest workers'.[37] The legal permanent resident programme issues so-called 'green cards' to certain immigrants who have the ongoing right to reside and work in the US.[38] These renewable cards, typically issued for ten years, can be given to relatives of US citizens, to certain refugees or asylees, and to certain guest workers sponsored by an employer. An employer that wishes to sponsor an employee for permanent resident status must apply and state that they have an intent to permanently employ that individual. For current guest workers, this application typically takes place after several years on the job, and the process of obtaining a green card may take several years. Once an individual is a legal permanent resident for at least three years (but typically five years), they may apply for citizenship through the naturalisation process. Unlike a guest worker, once a worker obtains a green card, they can no longer be deported simply for separating from an employer.[39] They can quit or be fired and still legally remain in the US. However, there are other grounds for deportation, including commission of a crime, becoming a public charge, leaving the country for an extended period of time, and failure to establish a permanent residence.[40]

The US developed its 'guest worker' or non-immigrant visa programme to bring workers from abroad to fill jobs in various industries for a temporary period of time. The most common types of visas are the H-1B used for highly skilled, often technical, workers such as computer professionals, engineers and nurses; the H-2A used for agricultural workers; the H-2B used for

[36] D DeSilver, *Immigrants Don't Make Up a Majority of Workers in Any U.S. Industry* (Pew Research Center, 2017) available at www.pewresearch.org/fact-tank/2017/03/16/immigrants-dont-make-up-a-majority-of-workers-in-any-u-s-industry [last accessed 18 March 2022].

[37] ibid, 182.

[38] These cards are issued under a complex quota system, that includes variables such as family relationship, country of nationality, refugee or asylee status, and occupation.

[39] See the discussion in M Ontiveros, 'Migrant Labour in the United States: Working Beneath the Floor for Free Labour?' in C Costello and M Freedland (eds), *Migrants at Work* (Oxford, Oxford University Press, 2014) 180, 182–83.

[40] 8 USC § 1227 (2018).

non-agricultural labourers; and the J-1 or B-1 visas for nannies or other domestic help.[41] Although the specific terms of each visa vary somewhat, they share some broad parameters in terms of how they work. Each year, the government establishes a set number of visas to issue in each category. For example, the government issues approximately 85,000 H-1B visas a year. These visas are in high demand by employers, who must apply for them, entering a lottery if necessary. In order to receive a visa, the employer must demonstrate that they have a need for the worker and that employing the worker will not adversely affect domestic workers.[42] Some visa categories require it to be shown that the employer has been unable to find a worker in the US to fill the position, while others do not.

Once the employer has been issued a visa, they may hire a worker from outside the US and have them begin work. The visa is typically valid for a limited period of time. For example, the H-2A visa is generally issued for one year, while the H-1B is issued for three years.[43] The visas can usually be extended by the employer for an additional time period, upon a sufficient showing of need, although typically there are cumulative time limits for any individual worker (three years for the H-2A workers, six years for the H-1B workers). At the conclusion of this cumulative time period, the worker must either leave the country. or become a legal permanent resident. One of the most significant aspects of the programme is that if the worker separates from employment with that employer, either because they quit or because their employment is terminated, then the worker must leave the US. The worker becomes removable because they are no longer authorised to be in the country. Just as importantly, the visa programme is structured so that the visa is applied for, given to, held by and controlled by the employer, not the employee.

The structure of the guest worker programme has led to a variety of problems for workers. At the lower end of the economic spectrum, farm workers on the H-2A programme face problems such as low pay, wage theft, poor conditions, and the inability to complain for fear of being discharged and deported.[44]

[41] M Ontiveros, 'A Strategic Plan for Using the Thirteenth Amendment to Protect Immigrant Worker's (2012) 27 *Wisconsin Law Journal, Gender and Society* 133, 138; D Costa and J Rosenbaum, 'Temporary Foreign Workers by the Numbers 2' (Economic Policy Institute 2017) available at www.epi.org/publication/temporary-foreign-workers-by-the-numbers-new-estimates-by-visa-classification/ [last accessed 18 March 2022].

[42] Domestic workers have argued that visa workers adversely affect the domestic workforce by taking jobs through subcontracting and offshoring of work; by lowering wages; and through the preference for younger workers. These challenges have been filed in court and in administrative departments. They have met with little success. See Ontiveros (n 39) 17–18, 29–30.

[43] Ontiveros (n 26) 9.

[44] Ontiveros (n 29) 937–38; AV Cortes, 'The H-2A Farmworker: The Latest Incantation of the Judicially Handicapped and Why the Use of Mediation to Resolve Employment Disputes Will Improve Their Rights' (2007) 21 *Ohio State Journal of Dispute Resolution* 409, 415–21; AK Guernsey, 'Double Denial: How Both the DOL and Organized Labor Fail Domestic Agricultural Workers in the Face of H-2A' (2007) 93 *Iowa Law Review* 277, 291–99.

In addition, lack of knowledge of the legal system and language difficulties make it difficult for these workers to enforce their labour rights. Finally, both H-2A agricultural workers and H-2B labourers face extensive restrictions on their ability to access the legal system because of restrictions placed on legal service providers and limitations in the statute.[45]

Even highly skilled technical workers on H-1B visas are subject to abusive employment situations, spanning a continuum of exploitation, depending upon the worker's situation.[46] The H-1B visa workers who are treated the best work directly for the company that applied for and holds the visa. These workers almost all work long hours for wages below those paid to non-visa workers.[47] They are unable to complain about the conditions because they fear deportation. In addition, they are often socially and culturally isolated, living in insular communities, unable to become fully integrated into mainstream society. They often come without their families because their family members are generally not given the right to work in the US and are prohibited from accessing social assistance. They also lack the political rights of citizens. Therefore, they are unable to advocate for changes in the workplace or through the political process.

Other H-1B workers face more difficulty when they do not work directly for the employer who holds their visa.[48] In these situations, the visa holder acts as a labour agency that directs where the visa worker will be assigned, and the worker is usually obliged to work in a series of short-term placements. Although it is prohibited by statute, the worker will often be required to wait, unpaid, for a work assignment. During these times, the worker may be housed in an overcrowded apartment and charged excessive rent. Since the labour agency is the official employer, it controls the worker's pay check and may engage in wage theft. These employers may also engage in other illegal and abusive practices. For instance, they may charge the worker for the costs of the visas, often saddling the worker with a large debt that needs to be paid off upon arrival in the US. Contracts with this type of employer also sometimes include large liquidated damages clauses requiring that the worker pay a large sum if they quit work before the end of the contract term. These fees may range from $5,000 to $30,000 and often prevent the worker from leaving an abusive work situation. Section III of this chapter examines why these illegal or abusive practices remain prevalent.

[45] M Holley, 'Disadvantaged by Design: How the Law Inhibits Agricultural Guest Workers from Enforcing Their Rights' (2001) 18 *Hofstra Labor and Employee Law Journal* 575, 597–616 (H-2A limitations); Ontiveros (n 29) 283 (H-2B limitations).

[46] Ontiveros (n 26) 9–14.

[47] ibid 11–14.

[48] ibid 19–23.

ii. Unauthorised Workers

In 2015, approximately 11 million unauthorised immigrants (or 3.4 per cent of the total US population) called the US home.[49] The large majority (66 per cent) of the unauthorised adults have lived in the country for more than a decade, and a rising number (40 per cent) live with their US-born minor or adult children.[50] About half of them are from Mexico, with growing percentages from Asia and Central America.[51] Sixty per cent of unauthorised immigrants live in five states: California, Texas, Florida, New York, New Jersey and Illinois.[52]

Within the workforce, one in 20 workers (5 per cent or 8 million individuals) are unauthorised.[53] Although they do not have the legal right to live and work in the country, they make up a significant portion of drywallers (31 per cent), agricultural workers (30 per cent), plasterers/stucco masons (36 per cent), sewing machine operators (23 per cent) and housekeepers (24 per cent).[54] The overall percentage of unauthorised workers has remained stable for the past decade.[55]

Employers are prohibited from hiring unauthorised workers, and the law requires that employers have each new employee complete a form verifying their legal right to work in the US. Unauthorised workers continue to labour in the workforce, however, because such workers may use forged documents, or valid documents that belong to someone else. Alternatively, employers may simply ignore the requirement, knowing that the likelihood of being discovered is relatively small, or because they determine that the fines associated with violations are outweighed by the benefits of employing this workforce.[56]

III. WORKPLACE PROTECTIONS FOR NON-CITIZEN WORKERS

Both authorised and unauthorised non-citizen immigrant workers in the US are formally protected by a wide variety of laws, including both laws that cover all workers in the country and laws that have been passed specifically to protect them. Unfortunately, many of these laws are plagued by enforcement

[49] J Passel and D Cohn, *As Mexican Share Declined, US Unauthorized Immigrant Population Fell in 2015 Below Recession Level* (Pew Research Center, 2017) available at www.pewresearch.org/fact-tank/2017/04/25/as-mexican-share-declined-u-s-unauthorized-immigrant-population-fell-in-2015-below-recession-level/ [last accessed 18 March 2022].

[50] ibid.

[51] J Passel and D Cohn, *Overall Number of US Unauthorized Immigrants Holds Steady Since 2009* (Pew Research Center, 2016) available at www.pewhispanic.org/2016/09/20/overall-number-of-u-s-unauthorized-immigrants-holds-steady-since-2009/ [last accessed 18 March 2022].

[52] ibid.

[53] JM Krogstad, J Passel and D Cohn, *5 Facts About Illegal Immigration in the US* (Pew Research Center, 2017) available at www.pewresearch.org/fact-tank/2017/04/27/5-facts-about-illegal-immigration-in-the-u-s/ [last accessed 18 March 2022].

[54] DeSilver (n 36).

[55] ibid.

[56] M Ontiveros (n 39) 183.

problems. Additionally, there is a deep theoretical problem at the core of the US legal approach to treating immigrant workers. Although federal law prohibits discrimination based on race and national origin, it does not prohibit discrimination based on citizenship or migrant status, because it views that as analytically distinct. Fortunately, recent developments have started to chip away at this theoretical roadblock.

A. Generally Applicable Workplace Protections

The US has a variety of statutes protecting workplace standards. The major ones include a requirement of a minimum wage and a premium wage rate for overtime hours.[57] Employees are entitled to a safe workplace and must be provided unpaid family and medical leave.[58] Federal statutes also protect the rights of employees to engage in concerted activity for mutual aid and protection, and to bargain collectively through an appropriate union representative.[59] Finally, under federal law, employers may not discriminate in hiring, firing or the terms and conditions of employment, or allow harassment on the basis of race, colour, sex, religion, national origin, age or disability.[60] These rights and protections apply to both authorised and unauthorised workers, because they accrue from the status of being an employee or worker and are not affected by the immigration status of the worker.

Although all workers are formally protected by these statutes, differences emerge between groups in relation to enforcement and remedies. With respect to enforcement, unauthorised workers are much less likely to seek protection because they fear being discovered and deported.[61] Under-enforcement also occurs because of language and cultural barriers. These barriers include lack of knowledge of their legal rights; inability to complain because the employer is in a race-privileged position; and the hesitancy of complaining about co-workers or supervisors with whom the worker may have a kinship relationship or strong community tie in the home country.[62] Finally, many administrative agencies charged with enforcing these laws lack bilingual staff and bicultural training.[63]

In addition, the agricultural and domestic service industries, which employ many unauthorised immigrants, are excluded from some of these protections.[64]

[57] Fair Labour Standards 1938.

[58] Occupational Safety and Health Act 1970 and Family and Medical Leave Act 1993.

[59] National Labor Relations Act 1935.

[60] Civil Rights Act 1964 (Title VII), Age Discrimination in Employment Act 1967, and Americans with Disabilities Act 1991.

[61] ML Ontiveros, 'Female Immigrant Workers and the Law' in DS Cobble (ed), *The Sex of Class* (New York, Ithaca, ILR Press, 2007) 235, 240–41.

[62] ibid 243.

[63] ibid 244.

[64] ibid 238–40.

Neither of these occupations is covered by the National Labor Relations Act,[65] so those types of workers do not have a protected right to engage in collective action, and may be fired if they try to form a union. The agricultural industry is also exempt from the standard wage and overtime laws. The domestic services industry escapes enforcement of many of the protections because the employers are so small that they fall below the statutory minima, or because they categorise their workers as independent contractors instead of employees.

With respect to remedies, those available to unauthorised workers vary depending upon the statute violated and the harms claimed. In the seminal US Supreme Court case, *Hoffman Plastic Compounds, Inc. v National Labor Relations Board*, the plaintiff was fired for participating in a union organising campaign.[66] The administrative agency charged with enforcing the statute, the National Labor Relations Board, ordered the plaintiff to be reinstated and to be paid backpay – ie, the amount that the employee would have earned had he not been illegally discharged, for the period following the discharge until the decision in the case. These two remedies are typically awarded to an employee for violations of the right to engage in collective activity. The Supreme Court overturned the finding of the NLRB and found that unauthorised workers could not be reinstated because they did not have the legal right to work in the US. In addition, the Court said that the NLRB overstepped their authority when they awarded backpay. It reasoned that, since the employee did not have the right to work during the backpay period under immigration law, the Board's order interfered with immigration policy by implying that such work would have been allowable and should be compensated.

Since *Hoffman*, most courts have taken a similar approach to violations of the antidiscrimination statutes.[67] Unauthorised plaintiffs who are successful in these cases are generally not eligible to be reinstated or to receive backpay. On the other hand, courts have taken a different approach in cases where unauthorised plaintiffs have proved violations of state or federal wage and hour laws.[68] In these cases, employers have either underpaid workers (paying them below the minimum hourly wage) or failed to pay them a premium rate for overtime hours. In the most egregious cases, some employers have refused to pay workers at all the hours worked. In these cases, courts have generally awarded the unpaid wages, as well as statutory penalties, to unauthorised plaintiffs. Courts view these cases as analytically distinct, because the employees actually worked these hours and the employers benefited from the labour.

[65] National Labor Relations Act, 29 USC § 152(3) (2018).
[66] 535 US 137 (2002).
[67] M Ontiveros (n 29) 656–57.
[68] ibid; see also *Lucas v Jerusalem Cafe*, 721 F.3d 927 (8th Cir. 2013).

B. Laws Specific to Non-Citizen Workers

In addition to the laws of general applicability, three important laws apply specifically to immigrant workers: the rules in the statutes establishing guest work visas;[69] the Immigration Reform and Control Act of 1986;[70] and the Trafficking Victims Protection Act.[71]

i. Visa Rules

The statute that established the guest worker visa programme provides specific protections for visa workers.[72] It provides that visa workers must not be required to pay for a visa;[73] must be paid a prevailing wage;[74] must be paid for all the time that they are in the US, even if the assignment has not yet started;[75] and, must not be penalised for leaving the assignment before the end of the visa period.[76]

Unfortunately, in practice, employers have developed ways to circumvent some of these protections while still technically complying with the law. Prevailing wage requirements can be manipulated to pay the least possible, by the way the job classification and geographic location of the job are defined, as well as by the choice of wage survey used by the employer.[77] In addition, since the statute allows an employer to charge liquidated damages to cover actual costs incurred when an employee leaves work before the end of the visa's term, it may be very difficult for employees to prove that that amount charged is an illegal penalty, so that they may still be unable to leave before the end of a contract term. For example, in *Panwar v Access Therapies, Inc.*,[78] the court upheld a liquidated damages charge of $20,000 because the employer put forward evidence of the costs incurred when an employee quit, and the employee could not prove that the charges were 'greatly disproportionate' to the losses. Even though this amount was equivalent to five years' salary in Mr Panwar's home country, making it very difficult for Panwar to quit his employment, the court found the contract term to be legal and enforceable. When other employees see these contract terms being

[69] Temporary Employment of Foreign Workers in the United States, 20 CFR §§ 655.700–655.1319 (2017).

[70] Immigration Reform and Control Act of 1986, Pub. L. No. 99-603, 100 Stat. 3359 (codified as amended in scattered sections of 8 USC).

[71] Trafficking Victims Protection Act of 2000, Pub. L. No. 106-386, 114 Stat. 1464, 1466–91 (codified as amended in scattered sections of 8, 18 and 22 USC).

[72] Temporary Employment of Foreign Workers in the United States, 20 CFR §§ 655.700–655.1319 (2017).

[73] 20 CFR § 655.731(c)(10)(ii) (2017).

[74] 20 CFR § 655.731(a) (2017).

[75] 20 CFR § 655.731(c)(6)(i)–(ii) (2017).

[76] 20 CFR § 655.731(c)(10)(i)(A) (2017).

[77] Ontiveros (n 26) 11–13.

[78] *Panwar v Access Therapies, Inc.*, No. 1:12-CV-00619-TWP, 2015 WL 1396599, at *4 (S.D. Ind. Mar. 25, 2015), appeal dismissed (24 Nov 2015).

enforced, they may become fearful about leaving their employment, even if it is an abusive or exploitive situation.

In other cases, employers, especially labour agencies, do not comply with these rules. Common violations of the laws include failure to provide work for the time stated in the visa application and refusal to pay for time while the employee waits for a work assignment; charging employees for a visa; charging employees an excessive amount for housing and other expenses; and, underpaying employees.[79] Employers are able to evade enforcement of the statute because employees do not know their rights; employee claims must go through an elaborate administrative process before they can go to court; and, administrative agencies have been limited in their ability to bring civil and criminal cases.[80]

ii. The Immigration Reform and Control Act of 1986

The Immigration Reform and Control Act of 1986 (IRCA) established the basic framework for regulation of undocumented workers in the US.[81] The law prohibits employers from knowingly employing unauthorised workers.[82] In order to accomplish that goal, the law requires employers to have every new employee verify that they have the legal authorisation to work in the US.[83] Employees typically provide proof of citizenship (eg, a passport) or a document proving identification (eg, a driver's licence) and a document proving work authorization (eg, a green card).[84] When the law was enacted, workers' advocates feared that this requirement would result in discrimination against those who looked like they might not be citizens. So, the law provided that employers must accept any documents that look reasonably genuine and cannot request specific types of documents.[85] This allows employers to show compliance with the law, even if they are hiring people that they know are providing false documents.[86]

IRCA also contains protection against discrimination in two ways. First, it extends protection against discrimination based on national origin to small employers (those who employ between 4 and 14 employees) that are not covered

[79] Ontiveros (n 26) 20–23.

[80] ibid 28–35. If alleging a violation of the visa statute, the employee must file a claim with an administrative agency. That decision is next reviewed by an administrative appeals board. Only then may an employee turn to a federal court to have their rights adjudicated. The courts have limited the ability of federal agencies to bring complaints and have routinely dismissed criminal charges brought by governmental agencies.

[81] Immigration Reform and Control Act of 1986 (IRCA 1986), Pub. L. No. 99-603, 100 Stat. 3359 (codified as amended in scattered sections of 8 and 42 USC); M Ontiveros, 'To Help Those Most in Need: Undocumented Workers' Rights and Remedies Under Title VII' (1993–94) 20 *New York University Law Review and Social Change* 607, 612.

[82] IRCA 1986 § 274A(a)(1)(A) (codified in 8 USC § 1324a (2018)).

[83] IRCA 1986 § 274A(b) (codified in 8 USC § 1324a(b) (2018)).

[84] IRCA 1986 § 274A(b)(1)(B)–(D) (codified in 8 USC § 1324a(b)(1)(B)–(D) (2018)).

[85] IRCA 1986 § 274A(b) (codified in 8 USC § 1324a(b) (2018)).

[86] Ontiveros (n 81) 609.

by other non-discrimination laws.[87] IRCA also includes a provision that prohibits discrimination based on citizenship.[88] However, this protection has significant limitations. First, it only applies to discrimination in hiring and discharge.[89] It does not include discrimination in other terms and conditions of employment, so that harassment based on migrant status is not covered, and neither is discrimination in compensation rates or scheduling. More importantly, it only protects those who are currently citizens or those who are 'intending citizens'.[90] In order to be an intending citizen, an individual must be in the process of applying for citizenship and must have started that application process at the earliest possible opportunity.[91] If an individual is not a citizen or an 'intending citizen', IRCA does not prohibit citizen-based discrimination.

iii. Anti-Trafficking Laws: Forced Labour and Involuntary Servitude

The US also has a set of laws designed to prohibit workers from being brought into the country in coercive labour relationships. The Trafficking Victim's Protective Act (TVPA), passed under Congressional authority found in the Thirteenth Amendment, prohibits obtaining labour through the use of force for purposes of involuntary servitude, peonage, debt bondage or slavery.[92] For the purposes of the statute, forced labour or involuntary servitude includes labour obtained through 'serious harm' or 'threats of serious harm,' as well as 'abuse or threatened abuse of law or legal process'. Significantly, 'serious harm' has been found to include serious financial harm, while 'abuse of … legal process' has been found to include abuse of the immigration process.

Visa workers have used the TVPA to show forced labour through abuse of the legal process, and through threats of serious financial harm. For example, in *Nunag-Tanedo v East Baton Rouge Parish School Board*, the court found that threats of deportation and confiscation of travel documents used by the employer to coerce employees to continue working for them constituted abuse of legal process for purposes of the TVPA.[93] In that case, the employer also charged the employees a $5,000 fee for a visa and told the workers that they would forfeit the fee, unless they either continued to work in an abusive situation or paid an additional $10,000 plus the costs to travel. The court found that the employees 'felt that they had to comply with [the] Recruiter Defendants' demands since they needed to work in the United States to repay their debt[s]'

[87] IRCA 1986 § 274B(a)(1)(A) (codified in 42 USC § 2000e-2(a)(1)–(2) (2018)). The other laws only apply to employers with 15 or more employees.
[88] Ontiveros (n 81) 613.
[89] IRCA 1986 § 274B(a)(1) (codified in 8 USC § 1324b(a)(1) (2018)).
[90] IRCA 1986 § 274B(a)(1)(B) (codified in 8 USC § 1324b(a)(3)(A)–(B) (2018)).
[91] IRCA 1986 § 274B(a)(3)(B)(i)–(ii) (codified in 8 USC § 1324b(a)(3)(B)(i)–(ii) (2018)).
[92] Victims of Trafficking and Protection Act of 2000, Pub. L. No. 106-386, 114 Stat. 1464, 1466-91 (codified as amended at 22 USC sections 2152d, 7101–7112 (2012)).
[93] 790 F.Supp.2d 1134, 1144–47 (C.D.Cal. 2011).

and that this constituted a threat of serious harm under the statute. Although the TVPA can be used to protect non-citizen immigrant workers, some decisions, such as *Panwar*, have found that a charge which can be justified as reasonable liquidated damages cannot be found to violate the TVPA.[94]

C. The Theoretical Problem: The Relationship between Discrimination Based on Citizenship Status and Discrimination Based on National Origin

Non-citizen immigrant workers seek protection in the patchwork of laws described above because of a problem at the core of US employment law. Although Title VII of the Civil Rights Act 1964 prohibits discrimination in employment on the basis of national origin, it does not prohibit discrimination on the basis of immigration status. If the law did prohibit discrimination on the basis of immigration status, the employees could challenge the abusive practices directly. However, in a case decided almost 50 years ago, the US Supreme Court held that discrimination based on citizenship status is analytically distinct from discrimination based on national origin and so not prohibited under federal non-discrimination law. This analytical distinction, which has always been suspect, has recently begun to unravel in two separate lines of cases.

In *Espinoza v Farah Mfg.*, decided in 1973, the employer refused to hire a Mexican immigrant with the legal right to work in the US because she was not a US citizen.[95] She sued alleging discrimination based on national origin. Under US law, a plaintiff can prove discrimination directly by showing that the employer intentionally discriminated on a prohibited basis, or indirectly by showing that the employer used a neutral practice that has a disparate impact on a protected group and that cannot be justified as a business necessity. The court found no intentional discrimination based on national origin in a citizens-only policy because people not born in the US could become citizens through naturalisation. The employee also argued that the policy would have a disparate impact on those not born in the US and would therefore have a disparate impact based on national origin. Rather than looking at whether a citizens-only rule would, in general, have a disparate impact on people from a national origin other than the US (which it would), the court found no disparate impact violation because of the large number of workers of Mexican origin employed by Farah. The case created a bright line rule that discrimination based on citizenship or immigration status was allowable because it was an employment decision based on a reason independent from national origin.

Recently, two lines of cases have started to challenge this bright line rule. In the first, courts have upheld both disparate treatment and disparate impact claims

[94] *Panwar v Access Therapies, Inc.*, No. 1:12-CV-00619-TWP, 2015 WL 1396599 (S.D. Ind. Mar. 25, 2015), appeal dismissed (25 Nov 2015).

[95] 414 US 86 (1973).

brought by US employees displaced by H-1B workers. In a disparate treatment case, the court held that the employer could not establish that the use of visa programmes is 'non-discriminatory by definition', or that plaintiffs could never show they had been discriminated against as a result of this business practice.[96] In a disparate impact case, the court found that the defendant's practice of

> growing their US offices by setting visa quotas for additional South Asian workers, budgeting for the associated expenses of securing the visas, and filling employment vacancies by assisting persons of the South Asian race to enter the country to work in the defendants' US offices', constituted a specific and particular employment practice for purposes of Title VII, which resulted in a disparate impact on Caucasian Americans.[97]

These cases are important because they allow plaintiffs to use the immigration system as a focus for defining 'national origin' discrimination. That is a significant step away from the bright line rule established in *Espinoza*.

The second line of cases are being brought by the US Equal Employment Opportunity Commission (EEOC) to protect trafficked workers. The EEOC only has jurisdiction to bring cases under specific non-discrimination statutes, such as Title VII; thus, it may only prosecute claims based on categories, including national origin, that are found in the statute. It does not have independent jurisdiction to bring claims for other types of discrimination, such as discrimination based on immigration status. The EEOC has explained and justified the cases being brought on behalf of trafficked workers by stating as follows:

> The EEOC enforces the law against treating workers differently based on their **national origin**. (Human trafficking thrives on exploiting the vulnerability of **immigrant workers** and often targets specific national origins, based on stereotypes about who best performs certain jobs or is less likely or able to complain about exploitation.)
>
> There are forms of labor exploitation that do not fall within the statutory definition of human trafficking, but which are every bit as severe and which often involve elements of **employment discrimination**. In those "less than trafficking" cases, the EEOC's role becomes particularly important, as it may be the only federal agency with jurisdiction over the employers' exploitation of workers.[98]

In one recent EEOC case, the allegations focused on trafficking and exploitation as a result of immigrant status, rather than just the national origin of the employees. The EEOC sought to protect Thai H-2B workers who had been held against their will, who had had their passports confiscated, who had been forced to work without pay, and who had been confined to cramped apartments without any electricity, water, or gas. In addition, the employer told the workers that

[96] *Heldt v Tata Consultancy Services*, 132 F.Supp.3d 1185, 1189 (N.D.Cal.2015).
[97] *Koehler v Infosys Techs., Ltd.*, 107 F.Supp.3d 940, 944 (E.D.Wis.2015).
[98] www.eeoc.gov/eeoc/publications/brochure-human_trafficking.cfm (emphasis in original) [last accessed 18 March 2022].

they would call the police to arrest them if they tried to leave, and that they were not allowed to leave until they repaid huge fees owed to the recruiting company.[99]

The EEOC linked these conditions to national origin discrimination by stating that

> Trafficking cases often involve discrimination on the basis of national origin or race. Even when employees are legally brought into this country, employers may discriminate on the basis of national origin or race through the use of force, fraud, or coercion. This discrimination may include harassment and setting different terms and conditions of employment.[100]

In these cases, the underlying cause of the exploitation is the immigration system, coupled with the national origin of the plaintiffs.

These two lines of cases challenge the bright line rule that discrimination based on citizenship or migration status is not prohibited national origin discrimination. If this rule were abandoned or the law changed to include citizenship or migration status as a protected trait, then non-citizen immigrant workers could directly challenge abusive workplace conditions caused by their status.

IV. CONNECTING THE CURRENT TREATMENT OF NON-CITIZEN LABOUR TO HISTORY

The current treatment of non-citizen workers in the US cannot be studied in isolation. Put in historical perspective, it can be understood to echo the exploitation found in the systems of unfree labour practised in the US in previous eras. This section draws these connections, to show how certain types of labour migration policies create systems that contain vestiges of unfree labour, and discusses their relationship to issues raised by scholars studying labour migration programmes across the globe.

A. Involuntary Servitude, Debt Bondage and Exit

As discussed in section I of this chapter, chattel slaves, their descendants, and other immigrant workers historically lacked the ability to quit employment and remained in forms of involuntary servitude, including debt bondage and convict leasing. Unfortunately, vestiges of this practice remain when visa workers may not quit their employment because they have to pay off large sums of money to the employers that hold their visas. Although these sums may sometimes be

[99] US Equal Employment Opportunity Commission, EEOC Resolves Slavery and Human Trafficking Suit Against Trans Bay Steel for an Estimated $1 million, 2006 WL 3587411 (E.E.O.C.) 8 December 2006.

[100] www.eeoc.gov/eeoc/interagency/trafficking.cfm [last accessed 18 March 2022].

legally categorised and upheld as liquidated damages, that characterisation does not alter the fact that workers must continue to labour because they have no practical way to pay off the debt. Just like the workers held in debt bondage, visa workers are tied to an employer, cannot quit, and must pay off the debt through their labour. As such, the practice is reminiscent of debt bondage and creates a system of unfree labour, as understood in *Bailey* and *Reynolds*.

A softer form of involuntary servitude is experienced by visa workers who cannot quit because they fear removal. The negative consequences of removal are especially severe for H-1A and H-1B workers, because they may have to spend time in a deportation processing centre on the way out of the country, and, if they choose to return illegally, face dangers ranging from financial exploitation to sexual abuse or even death.[101] When workers cannot quit because of large liquidated damages or the fear of removal, they are forced to continue to work. This compulsion has many of the same negative effects of involuntary servitude. In particular, the inability to quit pulls down the working conditions of free, non-visa workers which was identified by the US Supreme Court in *Pollock* as one of the major policy reasons for eliminating slavery and involuntary servitude.[102]

In the international comparative literature on labour migration policies, many scholars highlight the ability of workers to 'exit' as a key indicator of whether the policy can be defended. Exit is the freedom to change jobs in order to find better work opportunities, wages and conditions.[103] In this way, it parallels the discussion of involuntary servitude and the ability to quit in the US. Zou explains that temporary migrant work programmes limit the ability to exit when they include visas that are tied to specific employers, when a migrant must repay large amounts of debt incurred in the visa process before they can leave, and even when the work alternatives available in the migrant's home country are severely limited.[104] She argues that the provision of exit (as well as voice) provide a normative platform to address the most problematic features of temporary migrant work programmes. This approach to exit can be applied to critique the programmes in the US.

B. Lack of Citizenship, Limitations on Workplace Protest and Voice

Since slaves were not considered human beings or citizens, they were unable to advocate for better workplace conditions through the courts or the political process. They were also excluded from collective action and were unable to participate in workplace protests, out of fear of physical punishment. As non-citizen immigrant workers, agricultural workers were also unable to

[101] Ontiveros (n 29) 928.
[102] Ontiveros (n 39) 180 and 191.
[103] AO Hirschman, *Exit, Voice and Loyalty* (Boston, MA, Harvard University Press, 1970).
[104] Chapter 12 in this volume.

participate in the political process. Efforts to organise or improve their workplace conditions were restricted by law and often led to their deportation.

Vestiges of these limitations exist today in the experiences of current authorised and unauthorised workers. As non-citizens without the legal right to be in the US, the ability of unauthorised workers to litigate in court or to protest at the workplace is severely constrained, because they fear deportation. Further, they have limited incentives to protest because their remedies are limited by the *Hoffman* decision. Authorised visa workers are also constrained in their willingness to complain because, as one commentator explained, H-1B 'visa holders, by the very nature of their situation as workers dependent upon employers for the right to remain in the country – either permanently or temporarily – remain less likely to protest against unfair working conditions than their counterparts with permanent resident status'.[105] Since both these types of workers lack citizenship rights, they cannot influence society through the political process, and end up vulnerable to the political process and the power exercised by other interest groups that can and do influence the political agenda and public policy.[106]

In the international comparative literature, the concept of voice represents the ability to speak up in order to try to make change in an organisation.[107] Within the workplace, voice takes the form of using individual and collective, formal and informal channels including collective bargaining and internal grievance procedures.[108] It may also take the form of filing lawsuits or being a whistleblower.[109] Voice is most effective when it is exercised collectively and may only be effective when effective enforcement mechanisms exist to react to the complaints. Zou argues that provision of an effective voice mechanism, coupled with exit opportunities, can ensure that temporary migrant work programmes adequately protect migrant workers.[110] In the US, the requirement for voice can only be met if non-citizen immigrant workers are given the ability to influence the political process, the ability to fully participate in workplace protests including the ability to file lawsuits, and the ability to have these protections effectively enforced.

C. Ownership of Labour and Access to Labour Markets

The guest worker visa rules also echo the type of ownership and control of another person's labour that was found in the antebellum slave codes. The company

[105] TH Goodsell, 'On the Continued Need for H-1B Reform: A Partial, Statutory Suggestion to Protect Foreign and US Workers' (2007) 21 *Brigham Young University Journal of Public Law* 153, 172.

[106] S Underwood, 'Achieving the American Daydream: The Social, Economic, and Political Inequalities Experienced by Temporary Workers Under the H-1B Visa Program' (2001) 15 *Georgetown Immigration Law Journal* 727, 740.

[107] Hirschman (n 103) 30.

[108] Zou (n 104).

[109] I Solanke, 'Black Women Workers and Discrimination' in Costello and Freedland (n 39) 306–9.

[110] Zou (n 104).

that applies for and is awarded a visa owns and controls the labour of the person that it hires to fill the visa. It *exclusively* controls when, where, for whom and for how much the immigrant can work. If the immigrant refuses that work, they must leave the country. Since a visa is granted for a specific job for a specific company, the immigrant must work exclusively for that employer and may not change jobs or even accept outside work because any other employer would not have a visa allowing the immigrant to work in the US. When the visa holder is a subcontracting company or labour agency, the agency determines when, where and for whom the immigrant works. The company also controls the amount of money earned by the immigrant, as well as whether a company may reassign or sublease the employee. In this way, the employee does not control his or her own labour; it is owned by the visa holder in a manner with parallels to slave ownership.[111]

In the US, this arrangement is unique to the visa system. Although an employer may direct its workforce and tell an employee where and when to work, there are significant differences. A non-visa employee is always free to quit without having to pay a large liquidated damages fee and without having to leave the country. More importantly, free non-visa employees are allowed to take additional jobs without interference from their employer. There may be some limits on outside work if there is a valid noncompetition clause, but these are limited to situations where an employee working for a competitor could damage the employer. Perhaps the closest situation are temporary agencies that assign workers to different job sites and employers for short term assignments. In that situation, the temporary agency controls when, where and for whom the employee works, as well as the wage. However, the employee is always free to decline an assignment and, most significantly, can look for and accept work at other employers at the same time. Neither an employer nor a temporary agency owns or controls the labour of the employee outside of immediate work relationship.

The key distinction, then, is whether and to what extent the employee has access to enter the labour market and to participate freely in it. Visa workers do not have access because the visa holder owns and controls their labour. Other workers in the US, however, have full access to the labour market without the control of any other employer.

Other countries must also address the extent to which international migrants have free access to the labour market. Within the EU, free mobility of labour should assure that workers have full access to labour markets. On the other hand, posted workers may not have access to labour markets in other countries outside of their work assignment. Similarly, service providers who bring a workforce to another country might limit the ability of workers to access the labour market. So-called ghost enterprises and staffing agencies present similar problems. The issue that must be explored in these situations is the extent to which

[111] Ontiveros (n 26) 26.

access to the free labour market can be limited before the situation becomes oppressive or a system of unfree labour.

V. CONCLUSION

The US has a very large, non-citizen immigrant workforce that includes both authorised and unauthorised workers. This large number is not surprising because the US has a long history of using non-citizen immigrant workers. Starting with chattel slavery and continuing with a series of other immigration programmes, the non-citizen workers have laboured in disadvantaged and exploitive conditions. This chapter has shown how the current limitations and exploitive conditions faced by non-citizen immigrant workers in the US echo the very same limitations that defined the unfree labour situations of chattel slaves, black workers in the American south and agricultural workers. A comparison with the theories of exit, voice and access to labour markets show that the issues raised in this chapter that apply to the non-citizen workers in the US also apply to temporary migrant worker programmes studied throughout the world.

4

Is There a Welcoming Culture for Migrant Workers in the German Labour Market?

OLAF DEINERT

I. INTRODUCTION

'*WILLKOMMENSKULTUR*' – IN English, a 'welcoming culture' – describes a positive attitude towards migrants. It is a famous phrase in public debate in Germany, which came to prominence during the refugee crisis of 2015–2016. While some commentators had the opinion that refugees too were welcome, out of respect for human rights and human dignity, others took the opposite view, convinced that the country could not host so many refugees, and came to use the term 'welcoming culture' in a sarcastic way. These different understanding of the term are paradigmatic of shifting views within German society concerning migrants.[1]

This chapter evaluates how far migrants who want to work, or who actually work, are 'welcome' in the German labour market.[2] In the German language, the term *Arbeitsmigration* normally focuses on the labour market situation of people who enter the territory for a longer period, and who take up residence in order to work. Accordingly, this chapter will focus primarily on migration with the intention of longer-term residence, including by those who exercise EU rights of free movement and by refugees. The concept of 'migrant workers' may also be understood in a wider sense, to include posted workers. That, however, goes beyond the jurisprudence of the Court of Justice of the EU, according to which posted workers do not enjoy freedom of movement, as they do not gain

[1] For an overview of the debates and shifting attitudes see Bertelsmann Stiftung, *Willkommenskultur zwischen Stabilität und Aufbruch* (2022) available at www.bertelsmann-stiftung.de/de/publikationen/publikation/did/willkommenskultur-zwischen-stabilitaet-und-aufbruch-all [last accessed 1 April 2022].

[2] For a discussion of social security and tax law, see C Schubert and L Schmitt, 'The German Regulations on Labour Migration and the Impact of the EU Directives on Labour Migration' in P Herzfeld-Olsson (ed), *National Effects of the Implementation of EU Directives on Labour Migration from Third Countries* (Alphen aan den Rijn, Wolters Kluwer, 2016) 35 and 55–58.

access to the labour market of the host country.[3] Nevertheless, in line with the broader understanding, the chapter will include a discussion of the labour law position of posted workers in Germany.

After providing a brief sketch of the evolution of migration routes and policy since the Second World War, the rest of the chapter addresses in turn the current legal framework on work by foreign nationals, the labour law approach to migrant workers who work lawfully, the position of posted workers, and that of migrant workers in an irregular situation. It will become clear that labour law essentially provides equal treatment rights, yet the formal equal treatment of workers will not lead to equality. Interpreting contractual obligations in the light of the fundamental rights of migrant workers could be a way to overcome this deficiency.

II. MIGRATION AND THE LABOUR MARKET SINCE 1945

In the years immediately after World War II, the economy of the young Federal Republic of Germany needed migrant labour, which initially came from the recruitment of war refugees from the former eastern parts of Germany. The appearance of an 'economic wonder' led to demand for foreign workers, especially for unqualified workers in unattractive jobs, sometimes with dangerous working conditions. That led to the conclusion of recruitment agreements in the 1950s and 1960s with Italy, Greece, Spain, Turkey, Morocco, Portugal, Tunisia and Yugoslavia, which introduced the first wave of migration by so-called guest workers. In 1969–1970, migration reached a peak: from September 1969 to September 1970, 447,500 migrant workers came into the country.[4] During the same period, the western German labour market also hosted migrants from East Germany (GDR), and emigrants from former eastern territories of Germany as a late consequence of the war.

In the 1970s, economic recession was the origin of a long-lasting labour market crisis, which would be overcome only in the 2010s. Parliament reacted from the beginning of the crisis with a new form of labour market governance, the so-called 'recruitment stop' in 1973,[5] and a policy of promoting return migration. The idea of controlling migration to protect labour market interests re-appeared. It was still possible to get an individual work permit, but that was now made conditional upon the lack of resident workers for the job. These measures did not however lead to disappearance of the migrant workers who came before the 'stop'. It came to be recognised that the former recruitment policy was mistaken, insofar as it had not been accompanied by a clear concept of integration.[6] The older policy had been based upon the idea that

[3] Case C-113/89 *Rush Portuguesa* [1990] ECR I-1417, recital 14.

[4] Bundesanstalt für Arbeit, *Ausländische Arbeitnehmer 1970* (Nürnberg, 1971) 3.

[5] Erlass des Bundesministers für Arbeit und Sozialordnung (Decree of the Minister for Labour and Social Affairs), 23 November 1973.

[6] E Eichenhofer, 'Solidarität und die Geschichte der Anwerbeabkommen – von Sündenfällen und Lernschritten' in K Barwig, S Beichel-Benedetti and G Brinkmann (eds), *Solidarität: Hohenheimer Tage zum Ausländerrecht 2012* (Baden-Baden, Nomos Verlag, 2013) 26, 30.

guest workers would only come and work for a definite period, and then return to their home countries. In reality, many migrant workers remained for lengthy periods, or permanently, even after legislation in 1983 promoting their return if they were unemployed.[7]

In the policy sphere, a key moment was an independent commission on migration under the former President of Parliament, Rita Süßmuth, which reported in 2001.[8] Its conclusion was that Germany needed to find a position as an immigration country, with a set of rules concerning both immigration policy and integration. The same conclusion would also be reached by Parliament. The Bundestag adopted the Immigration Act (*Zuwanderungsgesetz*) in 2004, which aimed at combining traditional labour market migration policy with the idea of integration of migrants in society.[9]

In contrast, in 2006, the then German Minister for Internal Affairs, Wolfgang Schäuble, declared that 'Germany is no immigration country!', and launched an intense political debate. While this slogan seemed to be in line with the legal framework of aliens law, it contrasted with the factual situation. As can be seen from Table 1, in the years that followed, more than half a million foreign migrants a year took up residence in Germany, and from 2013 the number increased above one million a year.[10]

Table 1 Immigration to Germany, 2007–2015

Year	Immigrants	Net migration
1991	925,345	602,523
1992	1,211,348	782,071
1993	989,847	462,096
1994	777,516	314,998
1995	792,701	397,935
1996	707,954	282,197
1997	615,298	93,664
1998	605,500	47,098
1999	673,873	201,975
2000	649,249	167,120

(continued)

[7] Gesetz zur Förderung der Rückkehrbereitschaft von Ausländern, 28 November 1983 (1983 *Bundesgesetzblatt* I 1377).

[8] Unabhängige Kommission Zuwanderung, *Zuwanderung Gestalten, Integration Fördern* (Berlin, 2001).

[9] 2004 *Bundesgesetzblatt* I 1950. The change took effect from 30 July 2004.

[10] Bundesamt für Migration und Flüchtlinge, *Migrationsbericht 2015* (December 2016), 30. This report follows the United Nations norm of counting those who intend to change their country of residence for at least one year.

Table 1 *(Continued)*

Year	Immigrants	Net migration
2001	685,259	272,723
2002	658,341	219,288
2003	601,759	142,645
2004	602,182	82,543
2005	579,301	78,953
2006	558,467	22,791
2007	574,752	43,912
2008	573,815	55,743
2009	606,314	12,782
2010	683,530	127,677
2011	841,695	279,330
2012	965,908	368,945
2013	1,108,068	428,607
2014	1,342,529	550,483
2015	2,016,241	1,139,403

In 2015, more than 20 per cent of the population were foreign or descendants of foreigners, two-thirds of whom were migrants themselves, and one-third of whom had been born in Germany.[11]

For most of the post-war period, the movement of workers within the EU was not seen as a source of serious labour market problems or unemployment in Germany. That would however change from 2010 onwards. Migration from the southern Member States grew as a result of the economic crisis, while increasing numbers of workers came from central and eastern Member States after the end of the transitional periods for freedom of movement.[12]

Of course, migration does not take place only for labour market reasons, but is often an escape route from poverty, war or persecution for political, religious or ethnic reasons. Nevertheless, the economic system has to cope with this kind of immigration and the growth of the workforce too. In this regard, a major challenge for West Germany had resulted from German reunification in 1990, because all the German inhabitants of the former East Germany were entitled to freedom of movement, according to Article 11 of the Basic Law (*Grundgesetz* – GG). Furthermore, some 2 million *Aussiedler* – ethnic Germans from the former

[11] Die Beauftragte der Bundesregierung für Migration, Flüchtlinge und Integration, *Teilhabe, Chancengleichheit und Rechtsentwicklung in der Einwanderungsgesellschaft Deutschland* (December 2016) 18–19.

[12] W Geis and H-P Klös, 'Migration und Integration: Wo steht Deutschland?' [2013] *Sozialer Fortschritt* 2, 3.

eastern territories who were eligible for German citizenship – moved to the Federal Republic after the collapse of the former eastern bloc.[13]

Asylum is a further source of immigration and an important principle in the Federal Republic's constitutional order. One of the results of the experiences of the Nazi period was that the constitutional assembly in 1949 adopted a strong human right of asylum, without any preconditions other than political persecution (former Article 16(2), sentence 2 of the Basic Law). After a large number of refugees arrived (especially from the territories of former Yugoslavia) in the early 1990s, the human right of asylum was amended in 1993.[14] Since then, a person may not enjoy the constitutional right of asylum if they are the national of a designated safe country of origin, or have travelled from an EU Member State or other safe third country. Because all German neighbouring countries are considered safe, the effect of this change was that the only way to claim asylum in Germany was to arrive by air. Due to this, the number of asylum seekers declined dramatically as table 2 indicates.

Table 2 Number of first applications for asylum, 1991–1995[15]

Year	First applications for asylum
1991	256,112
1992	438,191
1993	322,599
1994	127,210
1995	127,937

Another peak of migration was reached during the refugee crisis of 2015–16. From this period onwards, a crucial test for home affairs policy was to address the nationalistic, xenophobic and racist tendencies of sections of the population. The question of an upper limit of number of refugees and subsidiary protected people was discussed in the political arena, and was one of the main issues in the national election campaign in 2017 – even though the fundamental human right admits of no such restriction. The refugee flows were reduced from their peak after political deals with Turkey in late 2015 and early 2016. The number of first applications for asylum in Germany, which had reached 441,899 in 2015 and 722,370 in 2016, fell to 198,317 in 2017 and 151,944 in the first 11 months of 2018.[16]

[13] E Bund, M Kohls and S Worbs, 'Zuwanderung und Integration von (Spät-)Aussiedlern in Deutschland' [2014] *Zeitschrift für Ausländerrecht* 349 et seq.

[14] Gesetz zur Änderung des Grundgesetzes, 1993 *Bundesgesetzblatt* I 1002.

[15] Number of first asylum application in Germany from 1991–2019 available at www.de.statista.com [last accessed 1 April 2022].

[16] Bundesamt für Migration du Flüchtlinge, *Aktuelle Zahlen zu Asyl November 2018*, 4.

Notwithstanding these decreases in the number of asylum seekers, a large number of refugees will remain in the country in the coming years. Between 2015 and November 2018, more than 830,000 persons were recognised as refugees or as persons entitled to subsidiary protection in Germany.[17] According to the research institute of the Federal Employment Agency, the unemployment rate of foreigners from war and crisis countries was 41.1 per cent in January 2018.[18] It forecasts that the unemployment rate of these refugees will increase during the next few years, as more of them become entitled to work. It has been argued that their successful labour market integration will depend on language courses, educational training, placement services, and the willingness of enterprises to employ refugees.

The slogan of 'no immigration country' seems to contrast with the policy of the former German Chancellor Angela Merkel, whose statement '*Wir schaffen das*!' ('We will manage!') was understood by some people as an invitation to immigration by refugees. It should be stressed however that the logic of the 'welcoming culture' does not mean that all immigrants, irrespective of their reasons for migration, are entitled to residence and employment, notwithstanding that the last reform of labour migration law through the 'skilled workers immigration law' (*Fachkräfteeinwanderungsgesetz*)[19] explicitly recognised a need for labour market migration. The 'welcoming culture' is rather a label for the aim of integrating foreign nationals into the society and economy in a better way than was the case under the recruitment agreements of the 1950s and 1960s. The rest of the chapter will evaluate whether aliens law and labour law in Germany succeed in this goal in relation to the labour market.

III. LABOUR MIGRATION POLICY

A. Residence and Employment Permits

The Act on the Residence, Economic Activity and Integration of Foreigners in the Federal Territory (*Aufenthaltsgesetz*, or *AufenthG*, here termed the 'Residence Act') regulates the entry to German territory of those who are not EEA or Swiss nationals, for the purposes of residence and access to the labour market.[20] Foreigners require a 'residence title' in order to enter and to stay in the territory.[21] The Foreigners' Authority (the *Ausländerbehörde*) is responsible for issuing residence titles.[22] The grant of a residence title depends on the

[17] ibid, 10.
[18] Institut für Arbeitsmarkt- und Berufsforschung, *Zuwanderungsmonitor Februar 2018*, 3.
[19] Fachkräfteeinwanderungsgesetz, 2019 *Bundesgesetzblatt* I 1307.
[20] For an English translation, see www.gesetze-im-internet.de/englisch_aufenthg/englisch_aufenthg.html [last accessed 1 April 2022].
[21] Section 4 *AufenthG*.
[22] Section 5 *AufenthG*.

individual meeting several general preconditions, including secure subsistence and possession of a valid passport. In addition, the issuing of a residence permit presupposes that the foreigner has entered the country with the necessary visa.

Under the Residence Act, the standard position is that an individual is entitled to engage in economic activity unless that is prohibited and the foreigner lacks an express permission.[23] It is also provided that the admission of foreign employees depends on the needs of the German economy.[24] A residence title with permission to take up employment requires the approval of the Federal Employment Agency (*Bundesagentur für Arbeit*, or BA).[25] It follows from these rules that foreigners may get a single permit for residence and employment, as required by Directive 2011/98/EU.[26]

The starting point of the Residence Act provisions is that German nationals enjoy priority in access to the labour market if they are not professionally trained. There are though two large groups of foreigners who in most cases have an entitlement to residence and to unrestricted access to the labour market: EU, other EEA and Swiss citizens who enjoy freedom of movement, and persons entitled to international protection, together with certain family members in either case. As these rights are laid down in EU law, these groups enjoy subjective rights which may not be derogated from by the national Parliament.[27] These groups are considered next, before outlining the rules for asylum applicants and refugees.

B. Freedom of Movement under EU Law

Nationals of other EU Member States, of other EEA states, and of Switzerland, are entitled to the free movement of workers, according to Article 45 TFEU. It follows that Germany is not in general able to exclude nationals of these states and their qualifying family members from the labour market, and that there is no labour market test in their case.

These legal rights are reflected in the Act on Freedom of Movement (*Freizügigkeitsgesetz/EU*, or *FreizügG/EU*.) According to it, citizens of these states, and their qualifying family members, are entitled to enter the federal territory, and to take up residence, in order to work.[28] Citizens of those states are also permitted to search for employment for up to six months, or for a longer

[23] Section 4a(1) *AufenthG*.

[24] Section 18 *AufenthG*.

[25] Section 39 *AufenthG*.

[26] Directive 2011/98/EU on a single application procedure for a single permit for third-country nationals to reside and work in the territory of a Member State and on a common set of rights for third-country workers legally residing in a Member State [2011] OJ L343/1. For details of its implementation in Germany, see Schubert and Schmitt (n 2) 59–61.

[27] See A Kufer, 'Wohin steuert die Zuwanderungssteuerung?' [2015] *Zeitschrift für Ausländerrecht* 262, 265.

[28] Section 2(1) *FreizügG/EU*.

period if they hold a realistic prospect of employment.[29] Under these provisions, some 75 per cent of immigrants in Germany enjoy the fundamental freedom of movement of workers.

After 1 May 2011, when the transitional period for the freedom of movement of workers from the eight central and eastern European countries that joined the EU in 2004 came to an end, migration from these states increased remarkably. The same was the case for Bulgaria and Romania when transitional measures for nationals of those states ceased on 31 December 2013 although migration from these countries happened also before in remarkable numbers. Restrictions for Croatian nationals were lifted on 30 June 2015.

Table 3 EU-11 immigration to Germany, 2007–2015[30]

	2007	2008	2009	2010	2011	2012	2013	2014	2015
Estonia	969	621	842	1,110	1,419	1,290	1,336	1,120	991
Latvia	1,737	2,066	4,896	7,485	10,034	9,212	8,403	7,457	6,608
Lithuania	44,075	3,453	4,647	6,134	10,075	10,226	9,271	8,584	9,798
Poland	140,870	119,867	112,027	115,587	164,705	177,758	190,424	192,172	190,834
Slovakia	9,505	8,749	8,499	8,590	12,224	13,892	15,038	15,518	14,541
Slovenia	1,200	1,218	1,242	1,591	2,486	3,592	4,331	4,515	4,754
Czech Republic	6,651	6,309	5,924	6,063	8,255	9,221	9,963	10,776	10,974
Hungary	22,175	25,151	25,270	29,286	41,132	54,491	59,995	58,779	58,096
Romania	43,894	48,225	57,273	75,531	97,518	120,524	139,487	198,705	221,405
Bulgaria	20,919	24,093	29,221	39,844	52,417	60,209	60,896	80,069	86,274
Croatia							25,772	46,090	60,980
total	291,995	239,752	249,841	291,221	400,265	460,415	524,916	623,785	665,255

Although many people were afraid of a rise of unemployment in the German labour market as a result of the EU enlargements, the unemployment rate did not increase. For example, while the unemployment rate in October 2009 was 7.7 per cent, it had decreased to 7.0 per cent in October 2011, and was only 5.7 per cent in August 2017.[31]

C. Residence and Employment Permits for Asylum Applicants and Refugees

Applicants for asylum have no right to work, but may be entitled to permission to remain pending the asylum decision, under the terms of the Asylum Act

[29] Section 2(2) (1a) *FreizügG/EU*.
[30] Data from Bundesamt für Migration und Flüchtlinge, *Migrationsbericht*, various years.
[31] Information from the *Monatsbericht der BA* for October 2009, October 2011 and August 2017.

(*Asylgesetz – AsylG*).[32] As long as they are obliged to live in a reception centre for asylum seekers – something which may last up to six months[33] – they are not allowed to work. In other cases, after three months of legal residence an asylum applicant may – at the discretion of the Federal Employment Agency – be granted an entitlement to work.[34] The possibility to be granted permission to work is however excluded in the case of applicants for asylum who are nationals of a country of origin deemed safe.

Politically persecuted persons enjoy the fundamental right to asylum according to Article 16a of the Basic Law. People who are in the federal territory for reasons of individual persecution with respect to race, religion, nationality, political conviction or membership of a certain social group are protected in a similar way, because they are protected under the Refugee Convention. Both groups of persons will, after recognition as refugees, be granted a temporary residence permit for three years, which allows them to work.[35] This permit, and the right to take employment, correspond to the requirements of the EU Qualification Directive.[36] Foreigners who are threatened by the death penalty or execution, by torture or inhuman or degrading treatment or punishment, or by serious and individual threat to their life or person by reason of indiscriminate violence in a situation of international or internal armed conflict, are entitled to subsidiary protection under the Asylum Act.[37] They too will obtain a residence permit that allows them to work, with the only difference that the Foreigners' Authority may initially grant the permit for only one year, after which it may be prolonged for periods of two years.[38] These provisions concerning subsidiary protection are again in line with the Qualification Directive.[39] In all these cases, residence permits will be issued without the need to obtain the consent of the Federal Employment Agency. Finally, after five years' legal residence, refugees and beneficiaries of subsidiary protection may claim a permanent settlement permit.[40]

Individuals who claim constitutional asylum, refugee status or subsidiary protection, but who are unsuccessful, are obliged to leave the country.[41] The authorities will not however remove a person in a case of a danger to their life or freedom, and will suspend removal in the case of impossibility for factual or

[32] Section 55 *AsylG*. An English translation of the Act is available at www.gesetze-im-internet.de/englisch_asylvfg/index.html [last accessed 1 April 2022]. For a discussion, see C Janda, '"We asked for workers …", Legal Rules on Temporary Labor Migration in the European Union and in Germany' [2017] *Comparative Labor Law and Policy Journal* 143, 158–60.

[33] Section 47 *AsylG*.

[34] Section 61(2) *AsylG*.

[35] Sections 25 and 26 *AufenthG*.

[36] Articles 24 and 26 of the Directive 2011/5/EU on standards for the qualification of third-country nationals or stateless persons as beneficiaries of international protection [2011] OJ L337/9.

[37] Section 4 *AsylG*.

[38] Section 26(1) *AufenthG*.

[39] See Art 24(2), Directive 2011/5/EU.

[40] These are issued in accordance with ss 9 and 26(4) *AufenthG*.

[41] Section 50 *AufenthG*.

legal reasons.[42] The latter category may be granted entitlement to work (only) with the consent of the Federal Employment Agency, in accordance with the standard labour market rules.[43] This means that they have only subordinate access to the labour market.

D. Residence Titles which Permit Third-Country Nationals to Take Up Employment

Although a residence title permits work if not otherwise stated,[44] in most cases a permission by the Foreigner's Authority is necessary. As a general rule, the Residence Act stipulates that the foreigners' authority may issue a residence permit which permits employment only with the consent of the Federal Employment Agency.[45] The exceptions are mainly for highly skilled employees, such as graduates, researchers or company executives. The rules in section 18b and the following sections of the *AufenthG* concerning highly qualified persons were introduced in 2008 by the Labour Migration Governance Act (*Arbeitsmigrationssteuerungsgesetz*).[46] These go beyond the EU Blue Card Directive, in order to address the need for skilled workers in the national economy.[47] According to these rules a residence permit may be granted without the consent of the Federal Employment Agency if that is foreseen in an intergovernmental agreement or if it has been determined by statutory instrument and if integration into the way of life in the Federal Republic, and the foreigner's subsistence without state assistance, are assured. Part 4 of Chapter 2 regulates the details of skilled workers immigration, especially for high-skilled workers, graduates, executives and other specialists for the enterprises and scientists.

A residence permit for the purpose of employment may not be issued for an occupation that does not require vocational training, unless that is foreseen in an international agreement, or by a federal ministerial order.[48] Where the Foreigners' Authority issues a residence permit with the consent of the Federal Employment Agency (ie, the 'normal' case), consent should be given only after two tests have been met.[49] The first is a priority check: there must be: (a) no negative consequences for the labour market of the employment of foreigners; and (b) no worker available who is German, a foreign national with the same right to take up employment under national law, or a person who is entitled

[42] Sections 60 and 60a *AufenthG*.
[43] Sections 18 and the following and 39 *AufenthG*.
[44] Section 4a *AufenthG*.
[45] Section 18 *AufenthG*.
[46] From 20 December 2008, 2008 *Bundesgesetzblatt* I 2846.
[47] M Strunden and M Schubert, 'Deutschland gibt sich Blue Card "Plus" – EU-Richtlinie genutzt für Meilenstein der Arbeitsmigration' [2012] *Zeitschrift für Ausländerrecht* 270.
[48] See section 19c *AufenthG*.
[49] Section 39(3) *AufenthG*.

to preferential access to the labour market according to EU law. The second is an equivalence check: the employee must not be employed on less favourable labour terms than comparable German workers. This precondition applies also to skilled workers according to section 39 *AufenthG*. It is noteworthy that this obligation has only a public law dimension and does not permit civil law claims by employees.[50] If the employee is not treated equally, the Federal Employment Agency may revoke its consent, and the Foreigners' Authority may then revoke the residence title.[51]

There are also rules concerning access to the labour market in specific situations. For example, nationals of Albania, Bosnia and Herzegovina, Macedonia, Montenegro, Serbia and Kosovo may obtain a residence permit for any kind of work, provided that they apply for permission at German consulates in their countries of origin, and have not received benefits as asylum applicants in Germany during the previous 24 months.[52] This rule, which expires at the end of 2023, is intended to prevent people from applying for asylum without any realistic prospect of success, by offering them the chance of 'regular' access to the labour market, and so one cannot say that this is really an example of a welcoming culture.

IV. THE LABOUR LAW APPROACH TO MIGRANT WORKERS

A. When Does German Labour Law Apply?

In most cases, foreign nationals and migrant workers working in Germany will carry out their work under German law. According to the Rome I Regulation, the law of the state where the employee normally performs their work is applicable.[53] Although a choice of law by the parties is possible, that may not lead to the loss by the employee of any protection afforded by the law which would have been applicable without such a choice. Therefore, the provisions of German labour law which are indispensable are applicable where the foreign/ migrant worker 'habitually' works in or from Germany.[54] If a foreign/ migrant worker works under a foreign law – because they do not habitually work in or from Germany – the Rome I Regulation nevertheless requires that 'overriding mandatory rules' must be observed.[55]

The list of those overriding mandatory rules is set out in section 2 of the Posted Workers Act (*Arbeitnehmerentsendegesetz – AEntG*), which is the measure

[50] See O Deinert, 'Migration und Arbeitsrecht' [2018] *Zeitschrift für Arbeitsrecht* 17, 32.
[51] Sections 41 and 52(2) *AufenthG*.
[52] Section 26(2) *BeschV*.
[53] Regulation 593/2008 on the law applicable to contractual obligations (Rome I) [2008] OJ L177/6, Art 8.
[54] ibid, Art 8(2).
[55] ibid, Art 9.

corresponding to the Posted Workers Directive 1996 in Germany.[56] The list covers in particular minimum remuneration, paid annual leave, health and safety, antidiscrimination law, and the protection of groups with disadvantages such as pregnant workers and children.[57] The German Posted Workers Act goes beyond the Directive, however, in that its application is not limited to workers who are transferred in the context of the free movement of services within the single market. Laws about this 'hard core' of working conditions are always applicable as internationally mandatory rules if work is carried out in Germany, for every worker, whether German, EU/EEA/Swiss, or third-country-nationals.

B. Recruitment

A question that may arise during a recruitment process concerns the entitlement of a person to work. As the employer is under a public law duty not to accept work from a foreigner who lacks entitlement to work,[58] the employer has an interest in knowing the immigration status of a potential employee. Therefore, the employer can ask the applicant if they have a legal right to work. If the applicant does not have a right to work, but pretends to do so, the employer may later challenge the contract because of fraud.[59] Nevertheless, according to case law, the employer loses the entitlement to challenge the contract if the initial misrepresentation has lost its significance for the employment relationship – for example, if the employee later obtained a residence permit allowing them to work, and subsequently worked for a long period without any breach of their obligations under immigration law.[60]

The employer has the possibility to avoid these legal problems by checking the individual's documents. Every foreigner with a regular legal status has, or may obtain, a document that includes information on their work entitlement, and any limits to it. While there is no legal rule obliging the employer to ask anyone for documents proving their legal status, an employer risks the imposition of a fine, up to €5,000, if they recruit a foreigner without a right to work.

It does not appear to be discriminatory to ask only some applicants for documents. That is because a residence permit with entitlement to work is a genuine and determining occupational requirement for the purposes of the Equal Treatment Act (*Allgemeines Gleichbehandlungsgesetz*, or *AGG*).[61] Asking

[56] *Gesetz über zwingende Arbeitsbedingungen bei grenzüberschreitenden Dienstleistungen* (*Arbeitnehmerentsendegesetz*), 1996 *Bundesgesetzblatt* I 227 and Directive 96/71/EC concerning the posting of workers in the framework of the provision of services [1997] OJ L18/1.

[57] Section 2 *AEntG*.

[58] Section 404 para 2, n° 3 Social Code III and s 4a, para 5(1) *AufenthG*.

[59] J Schubert, 'Flüchtlinge und Arbeitsrecht' [2015] *Arbeit und Recht* 430, 436.

[60] BAG (Federal Labour Court), 2 AZR 184/69, 12 February 1970, *Arbeitsrechtliche Praxis* § 123 BGB no 17.

[61] Section 8 *AGG*.

only migrants for a residence permit is, as such, not discrimination. However, an inconsistent treatment of applicants may be a fact from which a presumption follows that there has been discrimination in the employer's decision not to engage a particular worker, which would lead to a reverse burden of proof for a claim under the *AGG*.[62] In short, employer checks have high importance in public law but less influence on civil law obligations towards the employee.[63]

C. The Equal Treatment of Foreign Workers

The Federal Republic is bound by many international treaty provisions that require the equal treatment of migrants, including ILO Convention No 111 on discrimination in employment, and the right to 'just and favourable conditions of work' in Article 7 of the International Covenant on Economic, Social and Cultural Rights.[64] It is also bound by the requirement of equal treatment for third-country workers, including in working conditions, in the Single Permit Directive.[65] While setting benchmarks, these instruments do not however affect the labour relationship in themselves. Similarly, the prohibition in Article 3(3) of the *Grundgesetz* on discrimination, including on the grounds of race, language, homeland or origin, has only indirect effects in private law relations.[66] Exceptionally, the requirements of equal treatment of EU migrant workers in Article 45(2) TFEU and Regulation 492/2011 on the freedom of movement for workers, are enforceable within the labour relationship.[67]

For the reasons explained in section IV.A, the substantive German labour law provisions will apply to most migrant workers. At the same time, hardly any specific rules for foreign workers exist.[68] From a formal point of view, foreign workers normally enjoy the same working conditions as German workers. While the doctrine of private autonomy does not prevent the less favourable treatment of foreign workers in comparison to German workers, according to the case law of the Federal Labour Court (*Bundesarbeitsgericht*, or *BAG*), the employer is

[62] Section 22 *AGG*.

[63] For the different position in British law, see B Ryan, 'Employer Checks of Immigration Status and Employment Law' in C Costello and M Freedland (eds), *Migrants at Work* (Oxford, Oxford University Press, 2014).

[64] For an overview of the position in international law see B Ryan and V Mantouvalou, 'The Labour and Social Rights of Migrants in International Law' in R Rubio-Marín (ed), *Human Rights and Immigration* (Oxford, Oxford University Press, 2014).

[65] Article 12(1) Directive 2011/98/EU.

[66] See M Sachs, 'Vorbemerkungen zu Abschnitt I' in M Sachs (ed), *Grundgesetz*, 9th edn (München, Beck, 2021) 32.

[67] See Case C-281/98 [2000] *Angonese* ECR I-4139 in relation to the effect of Art 45(2) TFEU, and Arts 7(1) and 7(4) of Regulation 492/2011 on freedom of movement for workers within the Union [2011] OJ L141/1.

[68] An exception is s 16(6) of the Workplace Protection Act (*Arbeitsplatzschutzgesetz*), which protects the employment, during a period of military service, of the nationals of other states party to the European Social Charter.

under a duty of equal treatment.[69] If the employer operates a general scheme – such as in relation to pensions, holiday payments, or Christmas bonuses, they may not treat employees differently, unless there is an objective reason to do so. This is a case law source of law which leads to private law obligations of the employer towards the employee. It is a right to equal treatment, under conditions linked to collective work relationships, for every employee, including migrant workers.

In addition, one purpose of the Equal Treatment Act is to transpose Directive 2000/43/EC, which prohibits discrimination on grounds of racial or ethnic origin, into domestic labour law, on a like-for-like basis.[70] Under that Act, workers are protected against discrimination inter alia in relation to access to employment, recruitment, conditions of employment, and membership of and involvement in workers' organisations.[71] However, only the grounds set out in the Directive are protected in national law, and in particular, German labour law does not contain a prohibition of discrimination for reasons of nationality or national origin.

D. Positive Measures for Linguistic or Other Reasons

A frequent issue in the context of migrant labour is a lack of German language capacity on the part of workers. This question may be illustrated with reference to a 2014 decision of the Federal Labour Court.[72] The employer bargained with the future employee, a Portuguese national, in Portugal, and in Portuguese. Later, he presented a contract in German, which the employee signed, without understanding its content, as he was not able to speak or read the language. The Court held that the employee was, nevertheless, bound by that contract because, according to contract law doctrine, someone who accepts a contract without knowledge of its content declares implicitly that they accept whatever the other party has presented. This decision was the subject of criticism in labour law literature, at least in relation to people from southern or eastern Europe or the Middle East and North Africa because these people were, without any knowledge of the German legal system and language, not really able to take a free decision with respect to the contractual conditions.[73]

In relation to cases such as these, Däubler has offered a discrimination-based analysis. His view is that, if an employer realises that a worker may not understand the contract, but does not give a further explanation or translation, the

[69] BAG, 3 AZR 173/92, judgment of 28 July 1992, (1993) *Neue Zeitschrift für Arbeitsrecht* 215.

[70] Council Directive 2000/43/EC implementing the principle of equal treatment between persons irrespective of racial or ethnic origin [2000] OJ L180/22.

[71] Section 2 *AGG*.

[72] BAG, 5 AZR 252/12 (B), judgment of 19 March 2014, *Arbeitsrechtliche Praxis* § 130 BGB no 26.

[73] Schubert (n 59) 435.

employer discriminates indirectly against a potential employee on grounds of ethnic origin.[74] If that is correct, the employee could claim restitution – which means treating the contract as if it had not been concluded – and financial compensation.

One difficulty with that approach is that there is no prohibition of discrimination for reasons of nationality or national origin in domestic law. Differences of treatment for these reasons are often discussed instead as involving discriminations on grounds of ethnic origin. It is far from certain however that people of a given nationality, or speaking a given language, share an ethnicity.

Moreover, it is worth asking what the prohibition of discrimination includes. Is it merely the prohibition of different treatment for specified reasons, without taking different situations into account? Or, does it extend to positive measures? Although the EU anti-discrimination directives *permit* positive action, there are no provisions with *obligations* for employers, other than to have reasonable accommodation for disabled persons.[75] Such positive measures are not foreseen by German law in other contexts either.[76]

On this view, a worker may not claim specific rights to recognise their different situation.[77] An employer may not however ignore differences between national and migrant workers, simply by treating them formally in an equal way. That would not be to take the fundamental freedoms seriously enough. In German doctrine and case law, questions concerning reasonable accommodation are more usually discussed in the context of rights of freedom than in the context of rights to equality. The overall theory is that the fundamental freedoms set out in the human rights chapter of the Basic Law set benchmarks for the whole legal order, which the courts must take into account when they have a discretion of interpretation.[78] This leads to the result that many problems that could have been discussed under an equality law approach are solved under a fundamental freedom approach. This became clear in the past mostly with respect to questions of freedom of religion. For example, the Federal Labour Court decided that wearing a headscarf for reasons of religion was not a reason for dismissal, where that did not automatically lead to serious economic or technical problems in the enterprise.[79]

[74] W Däubler, *Das Arbeitsrecht 2* (Reinbek bei Hamburg, Rowohlt, 2009) paras 1681 et seq.

[75] See Art 5 of Directive 2000/78/EC establishing a general framework for equal treatment in employment and occupation [2000] OJ L303/16.

[76] G Thüsing, in F J Säcker, R Rixecker, H Oetker and B Limperg (eds), *Münchener Kommentar zum BGB* vol 1, 9th edn (München, Beck, 2021) § 1 AGG para 11. The only positive obligations for employers can be found in s 81 (4) Social Code IX on specific duties of employers towards disabled employees.

[77] P Hanau, 'Das Allgemeine Gleichbehandlungsgesetz (arbeitsrechtlicher Teil) zwischen Bagatellisierung und Dramatisierung' [2006] *Zeitschrift für Wirtschaftsrecht* 2189, 2191.

[78] Thüsing (n 76), § 3 AGG, para 50; C Brors, in W Däubler and T Beck (eds), *Allgemeines Gleichbehandlungsgesetz*, 5th edn (Baden-Baden, Nomos, 2022) § 8, para 43; W Däubler, in W Däubler and T Beck (eds), *Allgemeines Gleichbehandlungsgesetz*, 5th edn (Baden-Baden, Nomos, 2013) Introduction, para 55.

[79] BAG, 2 AZR 472/01, judgment of 10 October 2002, (2003) *Neue Zeitschrift für Arbeitsrecht* 483, 486; see also BVerfG (Federal Constitutional Court), 1 BvR 792/03, judgment of 20 July 2003, (2003) *Neue Zeitschrift für Arbeitsrecht* 959, 960.

The employer must also offer another task that the employee could perform, without conflicting with their religion – for example, in the case of a Muslim employee who refused to work in a shop serving alcohol.[80] In the same way, the employer is obliged, following a balancing of interests, to organise the working process in such a way that Muslim workers can pray during working time.[81] A Jewish employee may also claim Saturdays free for religious reasons, if this does not interfere with serious employer's interests.[82] The German courts' more favourable case law for employees is compatible with EU antidiscrimination law which sets only minimum standards according to the CJEU case law.[83]

This fundamental freedoms approach offers a more convincing route to critique of the decision in the Portuguese case referred to above. The Court there failed to take into account that freedom of contract, which is guaranteed by Article 12 of the Constitution as a part of the freedom of profession,[84] has limits where the full freedom of one contracting party is not guaranteed. Under such conditions, autonomy turns into constraint. Therefore, it follows from the human right of one contracting party that the state, ie, the courts, has a positive obligation to facilitate the exercise of this right by restricting the same right (freedom of contract) of the other contracting party, ie, the employer.

E. Termination of the Contract

In considering the termination of employment, the possibility to dismiss someone who lacks permission to work will be discussed below in the context of migrants in an irregular situation (section V). Here, the focus is on other possible reasons for dismissal that may affect migrants in particular.

The nationality of an employee cannot be a justified reason for an individual dismissal, either under the Dismissal Protection Act (*Kündigungsschutzgeset*, or *KSchG*) concerning ordinary dismissals with a notice period, or under the Civil Code (*Bürgerliches Gesetzbuch*, or *BGB)* provision for summary dismissals for serious reasons.[85] In the case of dismissal for economic reasons, the employer has to choose among employees based on social criteria (age, seniority, maintenance obligations and disability).[86] The Federal Labour Court has ruled that

[80] BAG, 2 AZR 636/09, judgment of 24 February 2011, (2011) *Neue Zeitschrift für Arbeitsrecht* 1087.

[81] LAG Hamm (District Labour Court Hamm), 5 Sa 1782/01, judgment of 18 January 2002, (2002) *Neue Zeitschrift für Arbeitsrecht* 675; LAG Hamm, 5 Sa 1582/01, judgment of 26 February 2002, (2002) *Neue Zeitschrift für Arbeitsrecht* 1090.

[82] LAG Schleswig-Holstein (District Labour Court Schleswig-Holstein), 4 Sa 120/05, judgment of 22 June 2005, (2005) *Arbeit und Recht* 382.

[83] Case C-804/18 and others WABE [2021] ECLI:EU:C:2021:594.

[84] See, eg, JA Kämmerer in I von Münch and P Kunig (eds), *Grundgesetz*, 7th edn (München, Beck, 2021) Art 12, para 54.

[85] In relation to the latter, see s 626 *BGB*.

[86] Section 1(3) *KSchG*.

these social criteria are exhaustively set out by the Dismissal Protection Act, so that a choice based on nationality is precluded.[87] Accordingly, foreign workers enjoy the right to equal treatment with Germans in the case of dismissals for economic reasons.

A separate issue which may arise is that an employee, due to limitations on their language ability, may be considered unable to perform their work effectively. If the employee has been unable to perform their work from *the beginning* of the contract, then the employer may challenge the contract – ie, treat it as null and void after a declaration – on the grounds that the employee is under an unwritten duty to make known all barriers to the fulfilment of the contract. If, however, the employee lacks language skills only *later*, because the employer's requirements have altered – eg due to changed customer structure – that may justify a termination of contract for individual reasons. In these cases, prior to dismissal, the employer would have to check whether the employment relationship could continue after reasonable education or training measures were provided. In the scenario posited here, the question would be whether the employee would be able to perform work after an appropriate language course.

Similar questions arise when the employer is considering dismissal for economic reasons. In those cases, the employer has to check whether they can employ the worker in another job after reasonable measures of requalification. The requirements of any new job are in principle within the discretion of the employer.[88] What though if an employer creates a reason for not continuing the employment relationship by defining certain language conditions for the alternative job? On this point, we may look to the position of the Federal Labour Court when there is an individual dismissal for personal reasons. If the employer has re-defined the job requirements, and this leads indirectly to a reason for dismissal, the freedom of the employer to organise the establishment is limited, and the courts will check whether the new set of requirements are reasonable.[89] This limitation to the employer's free determination of job requirements should apply in the same way to economic dismissals.[90] The employer cannot therefore dismiss an employee who could perform other work by referring to a lack of language requirements, unless those requirements are reasonable ones.

F. The Role of Collective Actors

If an employee performs their work under German labour law, they benefit from the rights laid down in a collective agreement, because the agreement is part of

[87] BAG, 2 AZR 276/06, judgment of 31 May 2007, (2008) *Neue Zeitschrift für Arbeitsrecht* 33.
[88] BAG, 2 AZR 721/12, judgment of 29 August 2013, *Arbeitsrechtliche Praxis* § 1 KSchG 1969 Personenbedingte Kündigung no 37.
[89] BAG, 2 AZR 1111/06, judgment of 10 July 2008, (2009) *Neue Zeitschrift für Arbeitsrecht* 312.
[90] Deinert (n 50) 39.

the applicable law.[91] The main obstacle in this connection is that a foreign worker might not be a member of the trade union. According to sections 3 and 4 of the Collective Agreements Act (*Tarifvertragsgesetz – TVG*), trade union membership is normally a precondition for the applicability of a collective agreement, unless there is a generally binding declaration under section 5 of that Act.

The provisions of the Equal Treatment Act continue to apply to the content of collective agreements, ie, these ought not to discriminate against foreign workers. However, this seems to be merely a theoretical question, as there are no known cases of agreements that expressly discriminate on this basis. Similarly, while one could imagine that collective agreements contain clauses that cause indirect discrimination, the case law of recent years shows no evidence of that. The challenge for collective negotiations is rather positive action, aimed at the development of an integration policy for foreigners. The collective parties may for instance create specific rules for the education and training of migrant workers, or provisions for promoting the compatibility of religious obligations with working obligations.

Foreign workers also benefit from protection under the Works Constitution Act (*Betriebsverfassungsgesetz, BetrVG*), which regulates works council elections by the workers in establishments with at least five workers. Works councils are representatives of the whole workforce, with the task of promoting workers' interests. They examine compliance with worker protection legislation, exercise information and consultation rights, and have co-determination rights in relation to certain personnel and social matters. Following private international law principles, the Works Constitution Act is applicable to an employer's establishment located in the federal territory, and therefore to any individual migrant worker who belongs to such an establishment.[92] If someone is integrated in the operation and under the managerial power of such an establishment, then he belongs to the workforce. This extends to workers who have no direct contractual relation to the establishment, such as agency workers.[93] There are no restrictions as to the duration of such integration into the workforce. As long as the worker is part of the workforce the works council will represent them. Accordingly, a works council will represent such a migrant worker, the worker may vote in a works council election, and they may be elected as works council member.[94] Under section 2(5) of the Elections Order for Works Councils (*Wahlordnung*, or *WO*), the electoral board must ensure that workers who are not able to speak German are informed in an appropriate way of the electoral procedure. A violation of this provision may lead to a successful challenge to the election, unless the failure could not have had any influence on its result.[95]

[91] O Deinert, *Internationales Arbeitsrecht* (Tübingen, Mohr Siebeck, 2012) § 15, para 50.
[92] ibid, § 17, paras 10 et seq and paras 31 et seq, and references therein.
[93] BAG, 7 ABR 2/15, judgment of 24 August 2016, (2017) *Neue Zeitschrift für Arbeitsrecht* 269.
[94] BAG, 7 ABR 5/04, judgment of 13 October 2004, (2005) *Der Betrieb* 675, 676.
[95] ibid.

According to the Works Constitution Act, management and the works council are obliged to respect the principle of equal treatment in the enterprise.[96] This rule is of central importance for worker participation. The employer and the works council have to observe this obligation in every situation, including exercising co-determination rights, or the conclusion of works agreements (which may impose automatically effective rights and duties on the employees and the employer). This provision goes beyond the anti-discrimination provision in the Equal Treatment Act, in that it covers aspects of a person's origins other than their ethnicity, and also covers worker nationality.

Moreover, the legal tasks of the works council include the following: 'to promote the integration of foreign workers in the establishment, and to further understanding between them and their German colleagues, and to request activities to combat racism and xenophobia in the establishment'.[97] (The last element, concerning racism and xenophobia, was added by an amendment in 2001.[98]) To that end, it is expressly provided in the Works Constitution Act that measures to promote the integration of foreign employees, and to combat racism and xenophobia in the establishment, may be the subject of works agreements.[99] Management and the works council may conclude works agreements for example on information measures for all parts of the workforce, or measures promoting mutual understanding, or on the possibility for foreign workers to learn the German language.

In addition to the integration task set out above, a works council must actively combat racial or ethnic harassment.[100] It follows that it must address any xenophobic behaviour on the part of any worker. In serious, repeated cases, the works council may request the transfer or dismissal of the employee concerned.[101] If the employer refuses, the works council may bring an action to the labour court in order to oblige the employer to act. Similarly, if the employer wishes to hire someone, but the works council fears racist or xenophobic activities by that person, it may reject them.[102] In that case, the employer is not allowed to employ the worker unless they successfully obtain the approval of the local labour court. A labour court then has to check *ex officio* as a matter of fact that the fear is justified.

According to a survey of 500 enterprises in Berlin in 2008, 43 per cent of works councils actively upheld the interests of migrant workers in their establishments.[103] In nearly three-quarters of enterprises with a works council,

[96] Section 75(1) *BetrVG*.

[97] Section 80(1) *BetrVG*. Translation taken from www.gesetze-im-internet.de/englisch_betrvg/ [last accessed 1 April 2022].

[98] *Gesetz zur Reform des Betriebsverfassungsgesetzes*, 2001 *Bundesgesetzblatt* I 1852.

[99] Section 88(4) *BetrVG*.

[100] Section 80 para 1, no 7 *BetrVG*.

[101] Section 104 *BetrVG*.

[102] Section 99(2)(6) *BetrVG*.

[103] V Anders, R Ortlieb, H Pantelmann, D Reim, B Sieben and S Stein, *Diversity und Diversity Management in Berliner Unternehmen* (München, Hampp, 2008) 44.

there were works agreements concerning equality and anti-discrimination.[104] A working group on equal opportunities existed however in only 14 per cent of the enterprises, and in only four per cent had management and labour agreed on diversity management programs.[105] It is thought that in most cases, these works agreements aim at combating racism through memoranda addressed to people both inside and outside the enterprise.[106] While the content of works agreements varies, frequent subjects include equal opportunities in the recruitment process, the promotion of education, recognition of foreign qualifications, combating exploitation, and the definition of responsibilities of the parties.[107]

V. THE LABOUR LAW STATUS OF POSTED WORKERS

In common with other countries, Germany has faced the problem – especially in the construction industry – that enterprises based in other states post their workers to its territory in order to perform services contracts, after competing with lower labour costs under the applicable law of the contract. According to the private international law system of the Rome Convention – now, Article 8 of the Rome I Regulation – the law of the habitual place of work applies, even in cases of temporary employment abroad ('*lex loci laboris*' principle). As a result, posting employers were not obliged to grant German labour conditions to their posted workers, and could instead respect only their (less costly) national labour conditions.

In response to this phenomenon, Germany passed the Act on Posting of Workers in 1996, just before the Posted Workers Directive was adopted by the EU. The Posting Act sets out rules making the hard core of working conditions, specified in the Posted Workers Directive, mandatory internationally. These conditions of the German *lex fori* become applicable irrespective of the law that otherwise governs the employment relationship. One of the main issues which presented itself in Germany at that time was the lack of national minimum wage legislation. In line with the Posted Workers Directive, the Posting Act permitted minimum wages defined in a collective agreement in the construction sector to be generally binding, with an internationally mandatory character.[108] Posted workers became entitled to these minimum wages, irrespective of the law applicable to their contract. Collective agreements on annual leave in the construction sector may also be declared generally binding, with an internationally mandatory

[104] ibid 45.
[105] ibid.
[106] M Dälken, *Beschäftigte mit Migrationshintergrund integrieren – Beispiele guter Praxis* (Düsseldorf, Setzkasten, 2015) 5.
[107] ibid.
[108] The power to make collective agreement generally binding is in s 5 of the Act on Collective Agreements (*Tarifvertragsgesetz – TVG*).

character. That permitted posted workers and their employers to join a joint solidarity system for holidays in the construction sector in Germany, if they were not included in such a system in their home country.

The Posting Act aimed at combating the risk of unemployment of German resident workers in the construction sector which resulted from unfair competition based on working conditions. The Act furthermore aimed at protecting the system of collective bargaining.[109] In a subsequent case, the CJEU would hold that the Act was a justified restriction on the freedom of the posting employers to provide services, because it aimed at the protection of the workers.[110] It would also find the extension of the joint holiday scheme to posted workers and their employers compatible with the employer's freedom to provide services.[111]

The Posting Act was seen as a first step to a minimum wage in Germany. For that reason, the national employers' association – the *Bundesvereinigung der Deutschen Arbeitgeberverbände*, or *BDA* – prevented the trade union and employers' organisation in the construction sector from having a generally binding declaration of their collective agreement on minimum wages. It did so by withholding its agreement in the national committee (the *Tarifausschuss*) whose approval is needed for a generally binding declaration. In 1998, Parliament therefore adopted an amendment that allowed such minimum wages to be made generally binding by governmental regulation, without the consent of the national committee.[112] That legislation permitted the first sectoral minimum wages in Germany applicable to both resident workers and posted workers.

These developments linked to the construction sector might lead to the conclusion that the main purpose of the national minimum wage, which was created in 2014 by the Minimum Wage Act (*Mindestlohngesetz – MiLoG*), was the protection of posted workers.[113] The opposite was in fact the case: the protection of posted workers became the blueprint for a national minimum wage system. In the political sphere, a national minimum wage was widely discussed, and was called for especially by the trade unions.[114] Initially, however, in 2009, the conservative-liberal government under Chancellor Merkel agreed only to a system of minimum wages in specific sectors. Under an amendment to the Posting Act, it became possible to set minimum wages for a given sector, if there was a generally binding collective agreement which a government

[109] Government's draft, explanatory memorandum, 1995 *Bundesrats-Drucksache* 523.

[110] Case C-164/99 *Portugaia Construções* [2002] ECR I-787.

[111] Case C49/98 and others *Finalarte* [2001] ECR I-7831.

[112] Gesetz zu Korrekturen in der Sozialversicherung und zur Sicherung der Arbeitnehmerrechte, 1998 *Bundesgesetzblatt* I 3843.

[113] Gesetz zur Regelung eines allgemeinen Mindestlohns (Mindestlohngesetz – MiLoG) from 11 August 2014, 2014 *Bundesgesetzblatt* 1348.

[114] See for the history O Deinert and M Kittner, 'Die Arbeitsrechtliche Bilanz der Großen Koalition 2005–2009' [2009] *Recht der Arbeit* 265, 274–75.

regulation made generally applicable.[115] The same reform saw provision made for sectors where the parties who concluded a collective agreement on minimum wages were not representative: there, a minimum wage could be created under the Minimum Working Conditions Act (*Mindestarbeitsbedingungengesetz – MiArbG*).[116] In line with these changes, the official title of the legislation was changed to state that it was an Act on the Working Conditions of Posted and Domestic Workers. That concept was not altered when Parliament later adopted the Minimum Wage Act, which created a minimum wage for all sectors which could not be undercut by sectoral minimum wages. In 2020, the *AEntG* was amended in order to transpose the Revised Posted Workers Directive.[117]

The philosophy of protecting German industry and the German labour market from unfair competition based on undercutting has also been reflected in legislation at the regional level ('*Länder*'). That legislation has laid down that public construction contracts may only be concluded if the tenderer declares that they comply with the collective agreements at the construction site, irrespective of whether they are applicable in the employment relationship or not. As the obligation to respect collective agreements which have not been declared generally binding is not foreseen in the Posted Workers Directive, it was not surprising that the CJEU held in *Rüffert* in 2008 that Lower Saxony legislation of this type was incompatible with the freedom to provide services of the posting employers.[118] Some *Länder* reacted by adopting their own legislation setting out minimum wages for public contracts. In relation to those, the CJEU ruled in the *Bundesdruckerei* case in 2014 that it was incompatible with the fundamental freedoms for the tenderer to be obliged to pay such a minimum wage to *all* their employees, including those who worked in their home state, and to ensure that contractors did the same.[119] However, in *RegioPost* it held that these minimum wages were in conformity with the fundamental freedoms, if they applied (only) to all workers who performed their work in the German *territory* in question.[120]

In summary, we may conclude that posted workers are only 'welcome' if their employer grants a minimum of working conditions to avoid unfair completion.

[115] Gesetz über zwingende Arbeitsbedingungen für grenzüberschreitend entsandte und für regelmäßig im Inland beschäftigte Arbeitnehmer und Arbeitnehmerinnen, 2009 *Bundesgesetzbatt* I 799.

[116] Gesetz über die Festsetzung von Mindestarbeitsbedingungen from 11 January 1952, as amended (2009 *Bundesgesetzbatt* I 818).

[117] See Directive (EU) 2018/957 of the European Parliament and of the Council of 28 June 2018 amending Directive 96/71/EC concerning the posting of workers in the framework of the provision of services [2018] OJ L173/16 and Gesetz zur Umsetzung der Richtlinie (EU) 2018/957 des Europäischen Parlaments und des Rates vom 28. Juni 2018 zur Änderung der Richtlinie 96/71/EG über die Entsendung von Arbeitnehmern im Rahmen der Erbringung von Dienstleistungen, 2020 *Bundesgesetzblatt* I 1657.

[118] Case C-346/06 *Rüffert* [2008] ECR I-1989.

[119] Case C-549/13 *Bundesdruckerei* [2014] ECL:EU:C:2014:2235.

[120] Case C-115/14 *RegioPost* [2015] ECLI:EU:C:2015:760.

VI. THE STATUS OF MIGRANT WORKERS IN AN IRREGULAR SITUATION

A. Labour Law

If an employee lacks an entitlement to work, the position under the contract of employment remains to be determined. In a decision in 1969, the Federal Labour Court had decided that in that case the contract was null and void.[121] From 1976, however, it took the opposite approach, and stressed that only the actual work of the foreign worker was prohibited, and that neither searching for a job, nor concluding a contract of employment was unlawful in itself.[122] Therefore, the legality of a contract could not depend upon the existence of a public law entitlement, and there was no contractual difference between a worker who never had an entitlement to work, and one who lost the entitlement after starting employment. More recently, when transposing the Employer Sanctions Directive (Directive 2009/52), Parliament adopted section 98a(1) of the Residence Act, according to which an employee is entitled to the remuneration agreed in the contract of employment.[123] With this provision, the legislator accepted the case law according to which the contract of employment is not null and void, but is valid in the same way as others.[124]

Nevertheless, the worker's lack of a public law entitlement does impose obstacles to contractual performance which have private law consequences. Under public law, the employer may not accept the work of the employee, and the Foreigners' Authority may impose a fine upon the employer for a violation of this prohibition.[125] It has been taken to follow from this prohibition that the worker is not entitled to carry out their work.[126] Accordingly, the worker is not entitled to payment when the employer refuses to accept their work for this reason.[127]

If, notwithstanding the prohibition upon work, the parties fulfil the contract, then the doctrine of wrongful contracts of employment is applicable.[128]

[121] BAG, 5 AZR 256/68 from 30 May 1969, *Arbeitsrechtliche Praxis* § 35 AVAVG no 4.

[122] BAG, 3 AZR 66/75 from 19 January 1977, *Arbeitsrechtliche Praxis* § 19 AFG no 3; BAG, 2 AZR 423/75 from 13 January 1977, *Arbeitsrechtliche Praxis* § 19 AFG no 2, with observations from Engels; BAG, 3 AZR 716/75 from 16 December 1976, *Arbeitsrechtliche Praxis* § 19 AFG no 4.

[123] Directive 2009/52/EC providing for minimum standards on sanctions and measures against employers of illegally staying third-country nationals [2009] OJ L168/ 24.

[124] Government's justification, *Bundesrats-Drucksache* 210/11, 75; B Huber, 'Das Arbeitsrecht der illegal beschäftigen Drittstaatsangehörigen' [2012] *Neue Zeitschrift für Arbeitsrecht* 477, 478.

[125] Section 404(2)(3) *Sozialgesetzbuch III* (Social Code III). For a discussion of public law enforcement see Schubert and Schmitt (n 2) 50–52.

[126] E Eichenhofer, 'Arbeitsrechtliche Folgen der Arbeit ohne Arbeitserlaubnis' [1987] *Neue Zeitschrift für Arbeitsrecht* 732, 733; I Kanalan, 'Die illegale Beschäftigung im deutschen Arbeits- und Sozialrecht unter Berücksichtigung von Fragen der sozialen Sicherung' in A Fischer-Lescano, E Kocher and G Nassibi (eds), *Arbeit in der Illegalität* (Frankfurt am Main, Campus, 2012) 91, 93.

[127] C Lewek, 'Arbeitsrechte für Menschen ohne Papiere in Deutschland' in Fischer-Lescano et al (n 126) 182, 187.

[128] P Hanau, 'Das Verhältnis von Arbeitsvertrag, Arbeitserlaubnis und Aufenthaltserlaubnis ausländischer Arbeitnehmer' in F Gamillscheg (ed), *Festschrift 25 Jahre Bundesarbeitsgericht* (München, Beck, 1979) 169, 184 et seq; *cf* also E Eichenhofer, 'Arbeitsrechtliche Folgen der Arbeit

This means that both parties have to conduct themselves as if there had not been a barrier to carrying out the work in the past. In particular, the worker may claim remuneration for the work done, and periods working under the contract count as service in the enterprise, eg, for qualifying periods for unfair dismissal protection. For the future, however, from a private law perspective, both sides may reject performance by the other party.

This principle has been accepted as regards remuneration by Parliament in the implementation of the Employer Sanctions Directive in 2011.[129] The Residence Act now sets out the presumption that the parties had agreed upon the customary amount of remuneration, though either may prove that they agreed to higher or lower wages.[130] Furthermore – in line with the Directive – the law presumes that the worker carried out the work for at least three months, though again the parties may prove otherwise.[131] The content of this provision indicates that the legislator wanted to regulate the entitlements of the employee in cases of illegal work in Germany, irrespective of the law applicable to the contract, ie, these are internationally mandatory rules within the meaning of Article 9 of the Rome I Regulation.[132]

Article 6(1)(c) of the Employer Sanctions Directive stipulates that the employer has to bear the costs of transfer of remuneration to a state of origin to which an employee has returned (or has been returned). Although Parliament has not transposed this rule, one could argue that the employer is obliged to pay the costs of international transfer of payment by interpreting section 670 of the Civil Code on reimbursement of expenses in the light of the Directive.[133] In specific cases, the same legal consequence could result from the rules on delay in the Civil Code.[134]

In line with the requirements of the Directive, all those in the contracting chain are responsible for payments like a guarantor.[135] Nevertheless, contractors may avoid liability if they can prove that they exercised due diligence that the employer had not hired workers who lacked authorisation. This kind of chain liability as an instrument of protecting exploited workers has precedents in German labour law, in the case of posted workers, and in the case of failure to pay the national minimum wage.[136]

ohne Arbeitserlaubnis' [1987] *Neue Zeitschrift für Arbeitsrecht* 732, 733; N McHardy, 'Das Recht der Illegalen' [1994] *Recht der Arbeit* 93, 99.

[129] Government's justification, *Bundesrats-Drucksache* 210/11, 76.

[130] Section 98a(2) *AufenthG*.

[131] E Kocher and G Nassibi, 'Eine erste Einschätzung der Neuregelung in § 98 a AufenthG' in Fischer-Lescano et al (n 126), 137; W Breidenbach, in W Kluth and A Heusch (eds), *Beck Online Kommentar Ausländerrecht* (2021), § 98a AufenthG, para 1.

[132] Deinert (n 91), § 11, para 15.

[133] For a contrary position, see S Wunderle in J Bergmann and K Dienelt (eds), *Ausländerrecht* 13th edn (München, Beck, 2020) § 98a AufenthG, para 8.

[134] See S Keßler in R Hofmann (eds), *Ausländerrecht* 2nd edn (Baden-Baden, Nomos, 2016) § 98a AufenthG, para 7.

[135] Section 98a(3) *AufenthG*.

[136] Section 14 *AEntG* and s 3 *MiLoG*.

Section 98a of the Residence Act only covers remuneration for work, and says nothing about payment for periods of non-work which are unrelated to the lack of entitlement to work. If a worker who lacked entitlement to work did not work because of illness, they are entitled to payment under section 3 of the Act on Continued Remuneration (*Entgeltfortzahlungsgesetz*, or *EntgeltFZG*).[137] The provision for payment in section 18 of the Act on Protection of Pregnant Workers and Young Mothers (*Mutterschutzgesetz*, or *MuschG*), and for paid annual leave under the Act on Paid Annual Leave (*Bundesurlaubsgesetz*, or *BUrlG*), should be interpreted in the same way.[138] In the latter case, if the employer decides to terminate the contract without giving the employee the opportunity to take paid leave, compensation must be paid for the lost holidays.

The rules on entitlement to wages in the case of illegal work are not however important in the practice of the labour courts. One reason is likely to be that labour and social courts are covered by section 87(2) of the Residence Act, which obliges public authorities and courts to inform the Foreigners' Authority if they acquire knowledge of a person lacking a residence permit.[139] As a result, foreign workers do not enjoy effective remedies.[140] This legal position is also arguably a violation of the Sanctions Directive.

When a residence permit with permission to work is cancelled, the Federal Labour Court has held that the employer may terminate the contract only when an entitlement has been definitively refused by the Foreigners' Authority.[141] The employer will have to observe any specific dismissal protection which is applicable – for example in the case of works council members or pregnant women. Any other preconditions to the legality of the dismissal will apply, such as the need to consult the works council.[142]

Nor is it possible for the employer to conclude a fixed-term contract which will end when a residence permit finishes. The legal context is that Parliament has implemented the fixed-term contracts Directive (Directive 1999/70) inter alia through a requirement that there be a reasonable ground for any limitation as to time.[143] The Act codified the earlier case law of the Federal Labour Court which prevented bypassing dismissal protection and therefore stated that an employment contract could only be entered into for a fixed-term period if there was an objective reason for doing so. The Federal Labour Court has decided that there

[137] P Hanau, 'Das Verhältnis von Arbeitsvertrag, Arbeitserlaubnis und Aufenthaltserlaubnis ausländischer Arbeitnehmer' in F Gamillscheg (ed) *Festschrift 25 Jahre Bundesarbeitsgericht* (München, Beck, 1979) 169, 186.

[138] Kanalan (n 126) 95 and 7.

[139] ibid, 101; Lewek (n 127) 191 et seq.

[140] C Lewek (n 17), 181, 113; T Tschenker, 'Arbeit ohne Lohn' [2015] *Forum Recht* 8, 10–11.

[141] BAG 3 AZR 66/75, judgment of 19 January 1977, *Arbeitsrechtliche Praxis* § 19 AFG no 3.

[142] J Schubert, 'Flüchtlinge und Arbeitsrecht' [2015] *Arbeit und Recht* 430, 436.

[143] Directive 1999/70/EC concerning the framework agreement on fixed-term work [1999] OJ L174/43, and the Act on Part Time and Fixed-Term Contracts (*Teilzeit- und Befristungsgesetz – TzBfG*) 21 December 2000, (2000 *Bundesgesetzblatt* I 1966), s 14, para 1.

is a reasonable ground for a fixed-term contract only when, from the beginning of the contract, it is clear that the foreigners' authority will not prolong the residence permit.[144] Otherwise, it would be unfair to conclude a fixed-term contract, as there could not be a justified expectation that it would be impossible to carry out work in the future.

B. Social Security Law

For the full picture concerning workers without an entitlement to work, the position in social security law may be summarised briefly. If foreigners in an irregular situation have performed work, they are, generally speaking, protected by the social security systems. These systems are based on the fact that someone is 'occupied' under the direction of another person, which means that they actually carry out work, irrespective of their labour law status.[145] The only precondition is that the work is carried out in the national territory.[146] Workers without status are protected where the employer has registered the employment correctly, and has paid the required social security contributions. They are also protected if the employer breached their notification duties, and/or did not pay the social security contributions: by law, workers are covered by the social security systems simply by being employed.[147]

If they carry out work, foreigners in an irregular situation are therefore covered by health insurance, nursing care insurance and accident insurance. In the case of the pensions insurance system, they may only claim benefits where the employer paid the contributions.[148] That said, according to the doctrine of insurance by law, the employer is in any case under a duty to pay the contributions to the pensions scheme. If the employer does not, this will be treated merely as a case of delay, and the employee will get their entitlements if the employer subsequently pays the contributions.

Foreigners without legal residence are also entitled to unemployment insurance if they have carried out work. Here, however, the factual problem arises that entitlements are conditional upon availability on the labour market, which is normally not the case if the employee is not entitled to work under public law.[149] Availability will though be accepted if the foreigner has a good chance to get a residence permit if he finds a job.[150]

[144] BAG, 7 AZR 863/98 from 12 January 2000, (2000) *Neue Zeitschrift für Arbeitsrecht* 722.

[145] Section 7(4) *SGB IV* – Social Code IV.

[146] Section 3 No 1 *SGB IV*.

[147] See E Eichenhofer, 'Arbeits-, aufenthalts- und sozialrechtlicher Schutz illegaler Einwanderer' [2007] *Informationsbrief Ausländerrecht* 229, 231.

[148] Section 63 *SGB VI*.

[149] Section 138(1) No 3 *SGB III*.

[150] *BSG* (Federal Social Court), B 11 AL 75/98 R, 26 March 1998.

Protection by the social security systems is only one side of the coin. On the other side is the question whether contributions have to be paid for the period of work. In line with the requirements of the Sanctions Directive, German social law provides that employment for remuneration is presumed to have been for at least three months, unless the parties prove otherwise.[151] Moreover, the employer owes contribution payments as a debt to the social security providers for at least this period.[152] While the employee has to pay their half of the contributions, the employer may only claim the employee's share through a deduction from wages.[153] If the employer has failed to make deductions then the same rule applies as where work is 'regular': the employer may make the deductions only on the occasion of the next three payments. If no further payments take place – as is common where the illegal employment of foreigners is discovered – the employer has no possibility to deduct the employee's share of the contributions.

VII. CONCLUSION

To return to the question posed at the outset, within immigration law there is far from a welcoming culture in Germany. The Federal Republic respects the fundamental freedom of movement of workers within the EU, and the human rights of refugees. Generally, access to the labour market for others is possible only after a priority check and an equivalence check. As in other EU countries, a welcoming culture exists only for highly skilled workers.

On the other hand, we may say that there is a welcoming culture towards migrant workers who are already in the country. Parliament has adopted a number of measures for integrating migrants into society and the labour market. Labour law, however, tends only to guarantee the equal treatment of foreign workers, both through general equality law and in the law on the works constitution. Furthermore, the legal position of migrant workers with an irregular status is generally protected in labour law. Specific rights with respect to the different situation of migrant workers may also be recognised, but only after a balancing of interests, taking into account the fundamental rights of the employer and of the employee.

It would in particular be mistaken to conclude that the legislator has done more for migrant workers with an irregular status then for other migrant workers. In the end, the legislation aims at a clear-cut distinction between the illegality of the work on the one hand, and the equal contractual situation of the workers on the other. We may summarise that foreign workers with an irregular status are not welcome, but that the state wants to treat them fairly.

[151] Section 7(4) *SGB IV*. See J Berchtold, 'Illegale Ausländerbeschäftigung nach der Neufassung von § 7 SGB IV' [2012] *Neue Zeitschrift für Sozialrecht* 481 et seq.
[152] Section 28e *SGB IV*.
[153] Section 28g *SGB IV*.

Finally, the answer to the question of whether there is a welcoming culture in German labour law depends to a significant degree on the activities of the social partners. Their big challenges in this area are to create rules for the integration of foreign workers and to combat racism and xenophobia at the workplace. The more they achieve in this field, the more the enterprises, the resident workforce and migrant workers stand to gain.

5

'Wanderer, the Road is Made by Walking': The Long, Hard Road Towards Equality for Migrants in Employment in Spain

FERRAN CAMAS RODA

I. INTRODUCTION

The title of this chapter is inspired by a poem by the Spanish poet, Antonio Machado, which goes as follows:

> Wanderer, your footsteps are the road
> and nothing else;
> wanderer, there is no road,
> the road is made by walking.
> Walking makes the road,
> and on glancing back,
> one sees the road
> that will never be trod again.
> Wanderer, there is no road,
> just waves in the sea.[1]

The words 'Wanderer, there is no road, the road is made by walking', aptly describe the long journey, full of obstacles, which migrants coming to Spain to work have to overcome, in order to achieve full equality and freedom from discrimination in the workplace.

The chapter will focus on the main barriers to employment and to equal treatment with Spanish nationals that immigrant workers face in the employment sphere. The immigrants referred to are exclusively non-EU nationals, in other words, third-country nationals. This group includes not only those who

[1] A Machado, 'Proverbios y cantares XXIX' [Proverbs and Songs 29], *Campos de Castilla* (1912); translation: Betty Jean Craige in *Selected Poems of Antonio Machado* (Baton Rouge, Louisiana State University Press, 1979).

have obtained residence and work permits to settle and work in Spain, but also those who are actually working, having entered the country without obtaining authorisation, or whose legal status does not entitle them to work.[2]

II. EQUAL ACCESS TO EMPLOYMENT FOR FOREIGN WORKERS

The starting point in relation to the rights and responsibilities of non-EU Community citizens in Spain is Article 13.1 of the Spanish Constitution, which stipulates that aliens shall enjoy the fundamental rights and liberties protected by the Constitution 'under the terms to be laid down by treaties and the law'. A first reading of the supreme Spanish law implies that rights such as equal treatment and non-discrimination are not accorded directly to aliens, but only insofar as those rights are recognised under the law that serves to regulate their situation. As was pointed out by the Constitutional Court (*Tribunal Constitucional*) in Decision 107/1984 of 23 November 1984, the text of the Constitution makes no mention of a general principle of equality between Spanish nationals and aliens and, therefore, 'equality or inequality in the entitlement to and exercise of rights will depend, as laid down in the Constitution itself, on the free will of the Treaty or the law'. (Legal foundation 3). Following that logic, the Constitutional Court concluded that there was not a constitutional right to equal treatment for aliens in access to employment, since the right to work is only recognised for Spanish nationals. This means that a non-EU migrant worker not yet in Spain cannot demand equal treatment with a Spanish national to enter Spain and gain access to employment. To do so, the non-EU worker would previously need to have obtained authorisation from the state to live and work in Spain.

The legal provisions regulating the right to employment and social security for aliens are contained in Organic Law 4/2000 of 11 January 2000 on the Rights and Freedoms of Foreigners in Spain, and their Social Integration.[3] Article 10.1 of this Law lays down that 'foreign nationals who possess all the necessary requirements specified in this Organic Law, and in measures implementing it, shall have the right to engage in remunerated activities, on the basis of self-employment or otherwise, as well as access to the social security system, in conformity with applicable legislation'. As a result, only foreigners who have been authorised to come to Spain to work can enjoy the right to take up employment, whether in the public or private sector – as employees, never as civil servants – on equal terms with Spanish nationals.

Making equality in access to employment conditional on prior authorisation to reside and work is the first demonstration of inequality between aliens and

[2] After this chapter had been prepared, the Spanish Government adopted regulations to speed up recognition of foreign educational qualifications, to make it easier for irregular migrants to obtain residence permits in Spain, and to grant powers to the Spanish government to attract migrant workers to specific sectors. These reforms are noted in footnotes below.

[3] *Ley Orgánica 4/2000 sobre derechos y libertades de los extranjeros en España y su integración social.*

Spanish nationals, who are protected under the law. A second demonstration of differential treatment is the fact that aliens seeking to work in Spain will only be granted residence and work permits if they successfully pass through a 'filter', namely, the 'national employment situation', laid down in Organic Law 4/2000. This means that foreigners can come to Spain to work if there are no Spanish nationals – or EU citizens or other documented migrants – to fill job vacancies in Spain.

The national employment policy assumes preference for nationals in filling job vacancies in Spain. It must be added that the economic recession and the resulting loss in jobs that has taken place in Spain since 2008, has meant that the channels to accept migrant workers in Spain have literally been closed, since job vacancies have been filled by nationals by virtue of the legal preference granted to them. Besides general legislation, Spanish laws adopted in recent years have facilitated entry to Spain only for reasons of economic interest or talent: that is, by the highly qualified, investors, entrepreneurs, researchers or workers who are transferred within the same business group.[4]

Nonetheless, the challenges facing Spain today and in the future might lead the Spanish Government to reconsider a policy that makes the entry of migrants seeking employment and wishing to improve their quality of life, practically impossible to achieve. Special attention should be paid to the constant trickle of irregular migrants (mainly for economic reasons) crossing the Mediterranean from Africa to Spain and Europe since the beginning of the twenty-first century. A significant increase has been detected in recent years: in 2017, 21,971 irregular immigrants were reported entering the coasts of the Iberian Peninsula, the Balearic Islands, the Canary Islands, Ceuta and Melilla (the latter two cities on the African continent) by sea. In 2018, the number of entries had already reached 57,498, which prompted special attention from the European Commission in its 2018 Communication from the Commission to the European Parliament, the European Council and the Council: *Managing Migration in all its aspects: Progress under the European Agenda on Migration*.[5] After these years, and among other factors, the collaboration mechanisms agreed between the Spanish Government and Morocco in migration control led to a gradual stabilisation of the number of arrivals by boat, which stood at 32,875 people in 2021.[6] The causes that led to these migration movements also remain unchanged. These include income inequalities between one side of the Mediterranean and the other, differences in social, political and economic

[4] See in particular, Law 14/2013 of 27 September, concerning support for entrepreneurs (*Ley 14/2013 de apoyo a los emprendedores y su internacionalización*).

[5] In January 2019, the European Commission reported that the Mediterranean route to Europe had moved to the western Mediterranean (ie to the Spanish beaches) with more than 57,000 irregular entries in 2018: Communication from the European Commission: 'La gestión de la migración en todos sus aspectos: avances en el marco de la Agenda Europea de Migración' 4 de diciembre de 2018, COM (2018) 798 Final.

[6] These data can be consulted on the Spanish Ministry of the Interior website: www.interior.gob.es/es/prensa/balances-e-informes/2022 [last accessed 20 May 2022].

development in areas such as the Maghreb, or the difficulties of sending countries to absorb their rapidly growing populations. These are factors that should be taken into account when current immigration policies – which promote regular migration only to a limited degree – are being reassessed. These policies should also take the labour market conditions in Spain into account. Significant imbalances clearly exist, such as the progressive ageing of the population and the related failure to maintain social protection schemes, or to fill job vacancies.

Two other legal instruments also distance foreign workers from obtaining full equal treatment with respect to national workers. First, the Law stipulates that foreigners coming to Spain with a residence permit can only enter employment if they 'have the training, and where applicable, the professional qualifications legally required to exercise their profession'.[7] As a result, in order to be employed in Spain, migrant workers are legally required to provide proof of 'professional qualifications', while migrants entering self-employment must provide proof of specific qualifications for the profession they wish to pursue. In both cases, the granting of residence and work permits hinges on having the appropriate qualifications, and having them recognised.

Difficulties have been detected worldwide regarding the failure of immigrants to utilise their education and work skills due precisely to obstacles encountered in the transferability of competencies at international level.[8] The lack of equivalence or recognition of academic and professional qualifications is a serious obstacle in the recognition of the proven work experience and qualifications of migrant workers.[9]

On the other hand, a presumption exists that, under labour law, the employer is free to consider the workers' qualifications in relation to the work to be done. Even though foreigners may have specific qualifications, they are not necessarily employed in jobs for which they are qualified, leading them in many cases to situations of under-employment, in which they are clearly over-qualified for the work they do. To avoid this, legal measures should be adopted to enable foreigners in Spain to accredit their professional qualifications more quickly, but also to prevent migrant worker concentration in unskilled jobs, in keeping with the principle of non-discrimination in the workplace. For example, in September 2017, the Autonomous Government of Catalonia launched the so-called *Citizenship and Migration Plan 2017–2020*, in which strategic programmes promoting the inclusion of all citizens, regardless of origin, is planned.[10] The recognition of

[7] Article 64 of Royal Decree 557/2011, approving the Regulation of Organic Law 4/2000.

[8] OECD, ILO and World Bank, *The Contribution of Labour Mobility to Economic Growth*, 2015 Joint Report, available at www.oecd.org/g20/topics/employment-and-social-policy/The-Contribution-of-Labour-Mobility-to-Growth.pdf [last accessed 24 March 2022] 19.

[9] Given the urgency of these problems, the Spanish Government approved a regulation in 2022 to facilitate recognition of university degrees obtained in other countries: see Royal Decree 889/2022 of 18 October 2022.

[10] Generalitat de Catalunya, *Pla de Ciutadania i de les Migracions 2017–2020*, treballiaferssocials.gencat.cat/ca/ambits_tematics/immigracio/politiques_i_plans_dactuacio/pla_2017_2020/ [last accessed 24 March 2022].

migrants' professional qualifications and degrees is addressed in one of these programmes. The Plan is aimed at providing support through a specialised service, to help users register their academic qualifications with the state educational authorities.

Second, under Spanish law, employers are assigned a significant role in the phase of access to employment of foreigners in Spain. Employers have to follow the specific Public Services Employment procedures to hire Spanish nationals (or EU citizens or resident foreigners) in preference to foreigners from outside Spain. Then, once a lack of native workers for a post has been confirmed, and the migrant worker has been authorised to come to Spain, the law stipulates that 'the effectiveness of the initial authorisation to live and work will be subject to the worker being registered in the Social Security system'.[11] Consequently, the authorisation only comes into effect when the worker is registered in the Social Security system by the employer. Employers have three months from the migrant's legal date of entry to do so. This regulation is aimed at ensuring that foreigners entering Spain to take up employment have really been hired by their employer, thus preventing fraud. However, the enforcement of the authorisation to work and to legally provide labour services is left in the hands of the employer. Thus, foreign workers may suffer the consequences if employers fail to comply with their obligation to make the foreigner's work permit effective. It appears desirable that measures be adopted to prevent the situation of migrant workers from becoming irregular for reasons that may be attributed to the employers' failure to discharge their obligations. If employers fail to register a worker in the Social Security system, they are subject to punishment.

Naturally, if employers do not register foreign workers, but still employ foreigners coming to Spain to occupy a job vacancy, they will also be committing a second infringement of the law; that is, employing a foreigner in an irregular situation. This is precisely because, by failing to register the foreigner with the Social Security system, the initially granted work authorisation has not become legally effective.

The statistics on foreigners in Spain, show that in 2016, the foreign population was 9.92 per cent (4.6 million) of the total population (46.6 million).[12] This was a fall of some 19.7 per cent from the peak of 5.75 million in 2011.[13] This data should however be viewed in context. The outflow of foreigners from Spain came to an end in 2016. Since then, a resurgence of immigration to Spain has been detected on a scale not seen since 2009. A total of 354,000 migrants, mainly from Morocco (30,000), Romania (29,000), and Colombia and Venezuela (16,000 each) have entered Spain.[14] Nonetheless, the foreign population has

[11] Article 36.2 of Organic Law 4/2000.

[12] Observatorio de las Ocupaciones del Sector Público Estatal, *Observatorio de las Ocupaciones: Informe del Mercado de Trabajo de los Extranjeros Estatal Datos 2018*), www.sepe.es/contenidos/observatorio/mercado_trabajo/3066-2.pdf [last accessed 24 March 2022] 12. For these purposes, a person counts as 'foreign' if they do not possess Spanish nationality.

[13] ibid, 12.

[14] OECD, *International Migration Outlook 2018* (Paris, OECD Publishing, 2018).

remained stable, with 4,572,055 foreigners living in Spain on 1 January 2018.[15] As for the population registered in the Social Security system, on 1 January 2019, the percentage of affiliated foreign workers was 10.45 per cent of the total affiliated working population (18,819,300) with an upward trend since 2016 (9.92 per cent). According to the 2017 data, the largest number of foreign affiliates were from Romania (17.36 per cent), Morocco (12.70 per cent) and China (5.59 per cent).[16] The service sector currently employs the vast majority of registered foreign workers (73.69 per cent). The main professional activities in which foreign workers are engaged are the hotel industry, wholesale and retail trade, vehicle repair, administration, construction and the manufacturing industry.[17]

In relation to unemployment rates, statistics published during the recent years of economic recession reveal a higher unemployment rate among migrant workers compared to Spanish nationals (approximately 14 per cent more unemployment among foreign workers compared to national workers). Even though there has been a revival of the economy and a certain downward trend in unemployment levels, in January 2017 the unemployment rate for foreign workers was 23.6 per cent, eight percentage points higher than for Spanish national workers (15.6 per cent).[18]

This situation could be due to the fact that the group of foreign workers is over-represented in the areas of activity most sensitive to the economic cycle (construction and services). This group is either made up of low-skilled labour, or it tends to be framed within the most vulnerable socioeconomic categories.[19] In fact, after 2007, the construction and services sectors were the most affected by the economic recession – especially the construction sector due to the collapse of the housing market. Yet, several reports of interest on this issue have shown that the impact of unemployment was unequal during the economic recession. On the one hand, migrant workers lost more employment than native workers. In four years of recession (2008–2011), 2.2 million jobs were lost: 11.5 per cent by natives, 15 per cent by migrants from Latin America and the rest of Europe, and 21 per cent by migrants from Africa. Not only that, but unemployment rates show that native workers have always had greater job opportunities and their advantage over migrant workers widened during the recession (from 4 to 12 percentage points between 2007 and 2011).[20]

[15] Instituto Nacional de Estadística, 25 de junio de 2018 available at www.ine.es/prensa/cp_e2018_p.pdf [last accessed 24 March 2022].

[16] Observatorio de las Ocupaciones del Sector Público Estatal, *Observatorio de las Ocupaciones: Informe del Mercado de Trabajo de los Extranjeros Estatal Datos 2018*, 2018, 12.

[17] ibid, 12.

[18] Instituto Nacional de Estadística, *Encuesta de Población Activa: Cuarto trimestre de 2017* (January 2018) available at www.ine.es/daco/daco42/daco4211/epa0417.pdf [last accessed 24 March 2022].

[19] Carmen Grau Pineda. 'El impacto de la crisis económica sobre la gestión de los flujos migratorios laborales en España'. *Temas laborales, núm. 109/2011* 73–110.

[20] Colectivo IOÉ, *Impactos de la crisis sobre la población inmigrante* (Colectivo Ioé, Estudio promovido por la Organización Internacional para las Migraciones, 2012) available at www.colectivoioe.org/uploads/0bae582aa3b0842a9eaf50cde16f4f97d9527bcb.pdf [last accessed 24 March 2022] 5.

At the peak of the recession, job loss among foreign workers occurred in both the regulated and informal sectors. However, it is important to note that among Spanish native workers, 12 per cent of those who lost jobs were working in the underground (or informal) economy, while this figure rose to 53 per cent among foreign workers. Consequently, over half the jobs lost by foreign workers during the recession were not covered by the social security system.[21] This social and economic trend might suggest that the upturn of the economy and the labour market could be leading to an increase in informal employment and in jobs held by foreign workers, whether documented or undocumented. This last group comprises not only immigrants who have never obtained authorisation to work in Spain, but also those who came to Spain with a temporary work permit and, on losing their jobs, are no longer authorised to work. Under Spanish Law, an extension for the initial temporary work permit is subject to proof provided by the migrant worker of a valid employment contract. If workers lose their jobs, they must provide proof of a minimum period of work before the extension of the work permit, and demonstrate that they are actively seeking employment. Against the backdrop of the economic recession, not only did many foreign workers lose their jobs, but they were also unable to provide proof of current employment in order to have their permits extended.

It is arguable that a further factor explaining the persistently higher level of unemployment among migrants compared to national workers is the existence of discrimination towards immigrants in employment on the grounds of ethnicity, culture or religion. A 2018 Ministry of Labour, Migration and Social Security report revealed that, according to surveys conducted among youth in Spain (whether children of migrants or not), discrimination against immigrants does indeed exist in Spain, and has an important impact on access to employment.[22] It is therefore necessary to highlight legal measures taken in Spain to combat discrimination towards immigrants in access to employment.

The starting point is the legislation dealing with employment policies, mainly Royal Legislative Decree 3/2015 (Employment Act or *Ley de Empleo*[23]), in which the labour market integration of immigrants occupies an important place. This law guarantees foreigners effective equality of opportunities and non-discrimination in access to employment, and in the actions taken to achieve employment, but they are subject to the terms of the laws governing the rights and freedoms of non-EU nationals. Non-EU nationals may therefore benefit from the measures set out in the Employment Act, provided they have a residence permit.

[21] ibid, 71.

[22] Observatorio Español del Racismo y la Xenofobia (OBERAX) del Ministerio de Trabajo, Migraciones y Seguridad Social, *La integración de los hijos de inmigrantes en el mercado laboral*, 2018 available at www.mitramiss.gob.es/oberaxe/ficheros/documentos/integracion_hijos_inmigrantes.pdf [last accessed 24 March 2022] 10.

[23] Royal Legislative Decree 3/2015 replaced the original Law on Employment (Law 56/2003, of 16 December 2003), although it did not introduce changes regarding the 2003 Law.

In order to benefit from measures to promote employment opportunities, non-EU nationals must be registered as job seekers with the relevant public services. In accordance with the ministerial decrees currently in force, the registration of foreigners as job seekers in public employment services and public and/or private recruitment agencies places them on an equal footing with other job seekers. They can therefore benefit from employment mediation; that is, from the work of the public employment services and private placement agencies to match the demands of the workers seeking employment with job offers, as well as from job promotion and employability enhancement schemes that are provided by those services. Generally speaking, however, undocumented migrants are unable to benefit from employment measures since, precisely because they lack work and residence permits, they are not entitled to register with public employment services.

Under Spanish employment legislation, immigrants are contemplated as a priority group to benefit from employment promotion measures, in order to guarantee their labour market integration.[24] Article 30 of the Employment Act provides for the adoption by the Spanish Government and the Autonomous Communities of specific programmes intended to promote employment among groups 'with particular difficulties in their labour market integration'. Special mention is made of young people, particularly those with educational deficits, women, the long-term unemployed, the over 45-year-olds, people with family commitments, people with disabilities or at risk of social exclusion, and finally 'immigrants, in compliance with immigration law'. This is the main basis for the adoption of programmes specifically designed to promote employment among the immigrant population. The strategy underlying current legislation is aimed at creating selective employment policies, targeting specific groups who experience greater difficulties in labour market integration, such as immigrants, rather than the unemployed in general.[25]

In Spain, the autonomous communities, which have competence in active employment policies, can play an important role in promoting labour market integration. Accordingly, the Autonomous Community of Catalonia adopted the Citizenship and Migration Plan 2017–2020 with several programmes aimed at encouraging the social inclusion of all persons regardless of their origin. One of the programmes is directed at enhancing migrants' competencies, skills and abilities to improve their chances of finding quality employment. Another programme is aimed at preventing authorised migrants from becoming undocumented due to job loss (ie, they fail to extend work and residence

[24] E Rojo Torrecilla, F Camas Roda and I Camós Victoria, *Dictamen sobre la incidència de la normativa reguladora dels drets i deures dels immigrants en l'elaboració i organització de les polítiques actives i passives d'ocupació* (Barcelona, Servei d'Ocupació de Catalunya, 2005) 58.

[25] See O Molina Hermosilla and C Molina Navarrete, 'Más acá y más allá del trabajo: comentario a la Ley 56/2003 de empleo' (2004) 251 *Revista de Trabajo y Seguridad Social. Centro de Estudios Financieros* 42.

permits because they are unable to find work). To this end, agreements or plans have been promoted with the support of social organisations to facilitate the re-integration of migrants into the labour market. At the same time, the creation of an institution has been called for 'to manage the supply and demand of domestic services and to permit their regularisation'.[26]

III. EQUALITY IN EMPLOYMENT

Social indicators in Spain reveal differences in working conditions between foreign and national workers. There is evidence, for example, that foreign workers more frequently work more than 40 hours a week than Spanish workers, especially because they are generally employed in jobs with long working hours, such as domestic work and the building and hospitality sectors.[27] Migrant workers also have a higher rate of accidents at work. A study on this specific issue conducted in 2008 found that the incidence rate[28] of work-related accidents was 6,567.2 a year for foreign workers, as compared to 4,889.3 a year for Spanish workers.[29] Moreover, the incidence of workplace fatalities was 7.6 per year for foreign workers compared to 4.8 a year for national workers. Finally, it should be mentioned that, according to the International Labour Organisation study *The Migrant Pay Gap: Understanding Wage Differences between Migrants and Nationals*, in high-income countries, migrant workers earn around 12.6 per cent less on average than nationals – Spain being one of the 10 countries with the highest wage gap – concluding that behind which may lie factors of discrimination.[30] Finally, it should be noted that migrant workers were one of the groups that suffered most from the impact of the COVID-19 pandemic, in the form of contract terminations, such as, for example, migrant women mainly working in domestic service.

[26] See *Pla de ciutadania i de les migracions* 2017–2020 available at: dixit.gencat.cat/web/.content/home/04recursos/02publicacions/02publicacions_de_bsf/05_immigracio/pla_ciutadania_migracions_2017_2020/pla_ciutadania_migracions_2017_2020.pdf [last accessed 20 May 2022].

[27] See J Aragón Medina, A Martínez Poza, J Cruces Aguilera and F Rocha Sánchez, *La integración laboral de las personas inmigrantes en España. Una aproximación al empleo y las condiciones de trabajo* (Madrid, Fundación 1º de Mayo, 2010) 113.

[28] The incidence rate or index represents the number of work-related accidents that took place with the average number of people exposed to risk in the reference period (specifically, we are referring here to 2008). For more information on how to calculate the incidence rate or index, you can consult the National Institute for Safety and Hygiene at Work website: calculadores.insht.es:86/Accidentesdetrabajo/Introducción.aspx [last accessed 24 March 2022].

[29] C González Través, M Zimmermann Verdejo, M Victoria La Orden Rivera and C Díaz Aramburu, *Condiciones laborales y siniestralidad laboral en el colectivo de trabajadores* (Madrid, Instituto Nacional de Seguridad e Higiene en el Trabajo, 2008) available at: www.oect.es/Observatorio/Contenidos/InformesPropios/Desarrollados/Ficheros/Informe%20siniestralidad%20inmigrantes.pdf [last accessed 24 March 2022].

[30] See this 2020 study by the International Labour Organisation available at: www.ilo.org/wcmsp5/groups/public/---ed_protect/---protrav/---migrant/documents/publication/wcms_763798.pdf [last accessed 20 May 2022].

To address these issues, it is essential not only to recognise the principle of non-discrimination, but also to establish measures to ensure its implementation. One of the competences attributed to the public authorities by Organic Law 4/2000 is the implementation of the principle of equal treatment for non-nationals in employment and social security.[31] As a result, at a legal level, the Workers' Statute Act (*Ley del Estatuto de los Trabajadores*) provides that any work-related regulatory standards, collective bargaining clauses, individual agreements and unilateral employer actions regarding pay, working hours and other labour-related conditions that lead directly or indirectly to unfavourable treatment or discrimination towards workers on the grounds of 'origin, including racial or ethnic origin', are null and void.[32] To this precept must be added the commitments derived from Spain's ratification of the International Labour Organisation's Convention 111 of 1958 on discrimination in employment and occupation, which includes national descent and social origin as a factor of discrimination. Crucially, for our purposes, the notion of 'origin' set out in the Workers' Statute Act is applied to foreign workers who are not nationals of an EU Member State. The question is what scope the 'origin' factor has as a prohibited ground of discrimination: we can be sure that it covers discrimination on the grounds of racial or ethnic origin; and we can also affirm that the notion of origin covers national origin in the specific scope of application of labour relations regulated by the Workers' Statute Law. In this sense, a foreign worker with a residence and work permit could allege discrimination on grounds of national origin in relation to their working conditions, since in this area provided for in the Workers' Statute Law the prohibition of discrimination on grounds of national origin also includes foreigners who have obtained the relevant authorisation to reside and work.[33] It must be noted that the mentioned precept of the Workers' Statute Act stems from Law 62/2003,[34] which transposed EU Directive 2000/43 concerning the principle of equal treatment between persons irrespective of racial or ethnic origin. This Directive states in its preamble that it 'does not cover differences of treatment based on nationality and is without prejudice to provisions governing the entry and residence of third-country nationals and their access to employment and to occupation'. In other words, depending on the Member State, nationality cannot be claimed by the foreigner as grounds for discrimination when gaining access to employment, or in the exercise of their

[31] Organic Law 4/2000, Art 2.

[32] Royal Decree 2/2015 approving the consolidated text of the Statute of Workers, Art 17.

[33] See F Camas Roda and C López Roca, 'La influencia en el ámbito jurídico español de la prohibición de discriminación por motivos de nacionalidad, raza u origen étnico regulada en el ordenamiento europeo e internacional', in A Ballester (ed), *La transposición del principio antidiscriminatorio comunitario al ordenamiento jurídico laboral español*, (Valencia, Editorial Tirant lo Blanc, 2010).

[34] Law 62/2003 on fiscal, administrative and social measures. This has recently been complemented by Law 15/2022, entitled 'Comprehensive law for equal treatment and non-discrimination', which recognises the right to equality of all persons, whether legally resident in Spain or not.

work. As we have seen, third-country nationals wishing to enter Spain to work do not benefit from the principle of equality with Spanish nationals (at least, not until they have obtained authorisation to reside and work). If they fail to obtain authorisation, yet continue to work in Spain, they are unable to claim national origin discrimination in their workplace (since they are de facto not entitled to work). As we will see later, they can claim equal working conditions to Spanish national workers, but by other legal means. Nonetheless, as I see it, foreigners who are legally authorised to reside and work can defend themselves from any discrimination on the grounds of national origin under the concept of 'origin', provided for under the Workers' Statute Act, which assumes that Spanish Law will not only respect Directive 2000/43, but enhance it in this particular point.

In order to achieve equal treatment and the prohibition of discrimination against immigrants, certain actions should be taken under Law 62/2003. These include corporate equality plans, promoting equality in collective bargaining between employers and union representatives, as well as adopting corporate diversity plans. These actions should always be conducted from the perspective of social dialogue between employers and workers.

The adoption by Catalonia of legal initiatives aimed at encouraging employers to implement diversity schemes is noteworthy. Act 10/2010 on the Reception of Immigrants and Returnees to Catalonia includes a provision assigning responsibility for promoting non-discrimination measures in relation to immigrants in the workplace to the Catalan Administration. According to Article 16(2) of this Act, 'such measures should be taken with the participation of workers' representatives'. This should be interpreted as meaning that the measures adopted by employers with the help of initiatives driven by the Administration of the Generalitat (Catalan Government), and laid down in the Article, must count on the workers' participation. These measures adopted by employers with the participation of the workers' representatives should cover both access to employment and the establishment of working conditions under applicable labour legislation. Under Article 16(3), these measures may include the promotion of diversity management programmes, to achieve the cultural and organisational changes that may be generated by the presence of immigrant workers, and financial, commercial, labour, welfare and similar measures to promote equality among workers, whatever their nationality, in each company (or organisation) and its social community. The Act also establishes that collective bargaining and company agreements may contain clauses designed to further these various measures. These measures are likely to be more effective in preventing any kind of discrimination if immigrant workers are involved in planning them (especially as workers' representatives).[35]

[35] F Camas Roda, *Trabajo decente e inmigrantes en España. Un estudio sobre los derechos laborales de los trabajadores migrantes y del objetivo internacional del trabajo decente* (Barcelona, Huygens Editorial, 2016) 109.

Some Catalan companies have negotiated diversity agreements with workers' representatives regarding the interests or needs of migrant workers, including those related to religious faith.[36] These agreements are aimed at addressing issues related to working hours, such as leave to observe religious festivals or compassionate leave to visit sick relatives in the migrant's country of origin. Nonetheless, and as a general rule, leave-granting depends on the employer's decision based on whether it is feasible for that organisation.

IV. UNDOCUMENTED MIGRANT WORKERS: SCOPE OF LABOUR AND SOCIAL SECURITY RIGHTS

It is difficult to establish the number of undocumented migrants – ie, persons without a residence permit – who are living in Spain. One estimate is that there were over one million in 2010.[37] Given its probable scale, specific measures should be adopted to reduce the impact on Spanish society and the labour market. For example, as mentioned previously, reforms to extend permits should be adopted so that migrants with temporary residence permits do not forfeit the chance for permit renewal by becoming unemployed. Here, the application of labour and social security legislation to undocumented migrant workers is addressed, in order to identify adjustments to ensure respect for their rights, not just as migrants, but as workers.

The right of undocumented migrants to work – in other words, the right to engage in a remunerated activity as either an employee or a self-employed person – is not recognised by either the Spanish Constitution or Organic Law 4/2000. Nor is their right to social security protection recognised under Spanish legislation. The fact that they are not entitled to these rights prevents them from working in the same conditions as Spanish nationals.

Moreover, Spain is not a party to the International Labour Organisation Migrant Workers (Supplementary Provisions) Convention (N° 143, 1975), which requires respect for the fundamental human rights of all migrant workers. It is understood that undocumented workers are covered by this provision. At the same time, Article 9 of the Convention requires that migrant workers whose situation cannot be regularised are accorded equal treatment in rights relating to remuneration, social security and other benefits arising out of past employment. Although this precept protects the recognition of certain rights for undocumented workers in relation to previous employment, it does not seek to accord equal treatment to workers in an irregular situation.[38]

[36] See, eg, some agreements adopted since 2010 in the abattoir in Girona, the Diversity Agreement adopted by the Majestic Hotel in Barcelona, and also by Mantylim, Ferroberica or ABD.

[37] J Cerezo Mariscal, *Praxis de la inmigración irregular en la España del siglo XXI* (Madrid, Ministerio de Empleo y Seguridad Social, 2010) 317.

[38] See F Camas Roda, *Trabajo decente e inmigrantes en España* (Barcelona, Editorial Huygens, 2016). The 2016 International Labour Organisation report *Promoting fair migration: General*

Nor has Spain ratified the 1990 United Nations Convention on the Rights of Migrant Workers. That Convention recognises labour rights that extend beyond human rights, and acknowledges the right to equality in working conditions and in relation to Social Security. As laid down in the Convention Preamble itself, undocumented migrant workers are frequently employed under less favourable working conditions than other workers. If fundamental human rights were recognised for all, the practice of employing migrant workers who are in an irregular situation would tend to be discouraged.

Even though these international standards have not been ratified by Spain, undocumented immigrants have come to have their rights recognised. The origins of that recognition lie in the reform of Organic Law 4/2000 by Organic Law 8/2000. This second law had excluded undocumented migrants from entitlement to many rights, including the right to assembly and association, trade union freedom, the right to strike, the right to education, the right to free legal aid, and the right to family reunification. All of these rights were made conditional on possession of legal authorisation to live in Spain.

A first indication that the Law modifying Organic Law 4/2000 could be considered unconstitutional came from the ILO Committee on Freedom of Association in March 2002, in response to a complaint lodged by the Spanish UGT (Unión General de Trabajadores). The UGT objected to the fact that, in the case of migrant workers, exercising the right to association was subject to obtaining legal authorisation to live in Spain under Spanish law. In response, the Committee on Freedom of Association concluded that this was contrary to Article 2 of ILO Convention 87 under which workers 'without distinction' have the right to join organisations of their own choosing.[39]

Within Spain, the Constitutional Court rulings N° 236/2007 of 7 November 2007 and N° 259/2007 of 19 December 2007 overturned most of the regulations in the reform introduced by Organic Law 8/2000 with regard to restricting the rights of immigrants in an irregular situation.[40] These rulings derived from several challenges to the reforms, which claimed that exceptions regarding undocumented migrants violated the Constitution, particularly as it should be interpreted in compliance with the Universal Declaration of Human Rights and international agreements ratified by Spain. Consequently, migrants should enjoy the fundamental rights provided for in the Constitution in equal conditions with Spanish nationals, despite being in an irregular situation.

Survey concerning the migrant workers instruments, states that the objective of Article 9 is to ensure that migrant workers in an irregular situation are not deprived of any of the work-related rights corresponding to the job done (see paras 277 to 300).

[39] *Spain* (Case No 2121) (23 March 2001) Report of the Committee on Freedom of Association No 327, paras 561–562.

[40] The Constitutional Court invalidated the regulations of Organic Law 4/2000 that excluded undocumented workers from exercising their right to freedom of association, education, and legal aid, but not the right to family reunification, to which foreigners with a residence permit are entitled.

In these rulings, the Court held that undocumented migrants could not be excluded from enjoying those rights most closely linked to human dignity. This legal foundation, based on human dignity, was used by the Court to acknowledge certain work-related rights for undocumented immigrants; namely, the right to freedom of association and the right to strike. With regard to the former, the Court noted that the Universal Declaration of Human Rights, the International Covenant on Civil and Political Rights, and the European Convention on Human Rights recognised the right to freedom of association of 'all persons' in the defence of their interests. On these grounds, not only was freedom of association granted to workers who were authorised to work and to hold a valid work contract, but to everyone who worked. Thus, it was logical to acknowledge this particular right for immigrants who were not authorised to stay or work in Spain, but who could join trade unions to defend their interests, among which might be precisely the fight to regulate their legal status. This same premise was used to recognise the right to strike of undocumented migrant workers.

Under the law, undocumented migrants are not entitled to work and, therefore, face administrative sanctions if they do. Articles 53 and 55 of Organic Law 4/2000 provide that foreigners working in Spain without legal authorisation are liable to a fine of between €501 and €10,000.

Despite this prohibition on work, certain labour rights are contemplated for the undocumented migrant who has been employed. In Article 36(5) of Organic Law 4/2000 lays down that 'The lack of a work or residence permit … shall not invalidate the contract of employment with respect to the rights of the foreign worker.' In other words, the Law recognises that, despite being undocumented, the contract that the foreigner has entered into with the employer is valid as far as work-related rights are concerned. Consequently, the labour rights of undocumented migrants who are employed must be respected, in line with their status as workers. Although not expressly laid down in Article 36.5 of Organic Law 4/2000, in my opinion, foreign workers are in a position of equality with respect to other workers, specifically in relation to their rights at work. Undocumented foreign workers must have the same working conditions as other workers, whether these are established in the legislation or in collective agreements.[41]

One of the working conditions provided for by law that has led to the most difficulty of interpretation in Spain concerns the dismissal of an undocumented migrant worker by an employer. Generally speaking, if the employer dismisses a worker solely because they are in an irregular situation, and identifies no other

[41] M I Ramos Quintana, 'El trabajo de los inmigrantes extracomunitarios: situaciones administrativas y posición jurídica', in Asociación Española de Derecho del Trabajo y de la Seguridad Social, *Derechos y libertades de los extranjeros en España*, (Tomo I, XII Congreso Nacional de Derecho del Trabajo y de la Seguridad Social. Informes y Estudios, Edita Gobierno de Cantabria, 2003) 489 et seq.

legal justification for the dismissal, the dismissal is considered invalid[42] by the Spanish courts.[43] The standard implication of such a finding is that the employer can choose either to re-hire the dismissed worker, or to pay compensation. In this scenario, however, because undocumented workers cannot (usually) return to their former employment, they are entitled to receive the legally established compensation in cases of unfair dismissal.[44]

As we have seen, foreign workers in an irregular situation do have rights regarding dismissal. However, debate in Spain currently surrounds the issue of foreigners who were initially entitled to work and were, therefore, employed, but whose legal status later changed (for example, because their work permit could not be renewed). As a result, their employer decided to dismiss them on the grounds that they were undocumented workers. From the outset, if workers lose their legal residence or work status, the employer cannot terminate their work contract based on these grounds (which are not specifically regulated under Spanish Law as grounds for dismissal). Therefore, the dismissal would be considered unlawful. In this case, the employer would be bound to pay the compensation due to prevent the practice of social dumping and unjust enrichment on the part of the employer.[45] In conclusion, undocumented migrant workers, including those who are unable to renew the residence permit, are protected by labour rights, including dismissal rights.

Yet, the question raised in the case of foreign workers who have not been able to renew their work permit is: what legal grounds can be applied to make dismissal lawful?

One recent subject of case law has concerned foreign workers who previously held residence and work permits, but who unexpectedly lost their entitlement, and were then dismissed by their employer. This type of situation was addressed in ruling 955/2016 of the Spanish Supreme Court (*Tribunal Supremo*) on 16 November 2016. In this case, a migrant worker's request for renewal of her residence and work permit was refused by the Spanish Administration, and resulted in the termination of employment by her employer. The grounds for dismissal alleged by the employer were that one of the conditions agreed upon in the employment contract was permit renewal and that because the worker had failed to fulfil that obligation the contract could be terminated. If this argument were successful, the employer would also have been spared compensation payments for dismissal. The first court to deal with this matter ruled that the

[42] LA Triguero Martínez, 'El trabajo de los extranjeros en situación irregular: la extinción del contrato y otros problemas sociales' (2017) 36 *Trabajo y Derecho* 10–11.

[43] This is for example contrary to the default position in the UK, where the illegality doctrine is considered an obstacle preventing foreign workers from lodging an appeal for unfair dismissal in such a case. See B Ryan, 'Employer Checks of Immigration Status and Employment Law', in C Costello and M Freedland (eds), *Migrants at Work* (Oxford, Oxford University Press, 2014). See also the judgment in *Kelly v University of Southampton* (2007) UKEAT/0295/07/ZT.

[44] Triguero Martínez (n 40).

[45] ibid.

worker's dismissal had been unfair and that she was entitled to compensation. The employer appealed to the Supreme Court, which confirmed the lower court's decision. It first noted that including a condition of contract termination based on one circumstance (non-renewal of work and residence permits) was abusive, as that was in no way influenced by the worker's behaviour. It would appear to follow that conditions for contract termination based on non-renewal of work and residence permits by migrant workers cannot be introduced into the employment contract. The Court did observe that 'there was no doubt that loss of authorisation to work in Spain prevented the foreigner's employment contract from being continued', and it recognised that this was a case in which the reasons for terminating the employment contract were beyond the employer's control. Nevertheless, the Court took the view that Spanish legislation sought to provide a degree of protection to workers whose contract had been terminated for legal reasons, and it held that that protection ought to be guaranteed to all foreign workers, including those who lacked authorisation.

The key question is whether there are grounds that could be used by the employer to fairly dismiss a foreign worker who has lost the right of residence and to work. It could be argued that the only grounds that employers could rely upon to dismiss a migrant worker who is no longer authorised to work are 'objective causes' for dismissal – that is, reasons outside the control of either the employer or employee. In the Workers' Statute Act, objective causes for dismissal not only include corporate crises but also the failure of the worker to adapt to technical modifications at work, or incompetence on the part of the worker, revealed (or occurring) after actually being hired by the company. In my opinion, the company could claim sudden incompetence as grounds for dismissal for undocumented workers who have lost their legal residence status. Yet, if the worker were dismissed for this reason, even though the dismissal could be termed fair or lawful, the employer would also be responsible for the payment of compensation imposed by the law in the case of dismissals for objective reasons.

The right of undocumented migrant workers to the effective protection of their health and safety should also be recognised, not least because they often experience illegal or abusive conditions in employment, showing a blatant disregard for their health and safety. The link between Article 36(5) of Organic Law 4/2000 and the 1995 Occupational Health and Safety Act, recognising the right to physical integrity and an adequate health and hygiene policy at work, is an important legal principle. From my point of view, the application of laws to protect the health and safety of undocumented migrant workers at work cannot be questioned, since, as we have previously seen, if undocumented foreigners are working, the labour rights derived from their employment contract are considered legally applicable. The employer's responsibility to ensure the worker's health and safety is also included here.

Undocumented workers are not protected by social security law, because of the terms of Article 14 of Organic Law 4/2000. However, if migrants in an irregular situation are employed, Article 36(5) of the Organic Law states that they are entitled to any benefits contemplated by international agreements for the protection of workers, as long as these are compatible with their situation. The benefits in question include those relating to occupational hazards – ie, social security benefits received by workers as compensation for accidents at work or occupational diseases contracted in the exercise of their profession.[46] Article 36(5) of Organic Law 4/2000 expressly denies undocumented migrant workers the right to unemployment benefit, however.

Nonetheless, a major change has taken place in Spanish legislation concerning the right of undocumented foreigners to healthcare. Undocumented workers were ineligible for healthcare under Law 16/2013 relating to the national health system.[47] Foreign workers were allowed access to the Spanish National Health System on payment of the corresponding insurance fee. Nonetheless, under Law 16/2013 foreigners in an irregular situation were entitled to receive free healthcare only in the following circumstances: (a) emergency care for a serious illness or accident, until discharged; and (b) pregnancy, birth and postpartum care. The Law also stipulated that, in all cases, foreign nationals under 18 years of age may receive healthcare under the same conditions as Spanish nationals.[48]

The general exclusion of undocumented migrants from access to healthcare was the subject of a legal challenge brought before the Constitutional Court, which was rejected in rulings 139/2016 of 21 July 2016 and 134/2017 of 16 November 2017. The arguments given by the Constitutional Court for its conclusion included the preservation of constitutionally protected goods or interests 'such as the maintenance of the public health system at a time of complex economic issues'. The rulings also added that the distinction between foreigners who legally reside in the country and those who do not is proportionate, and 'complies with international requirements in the matter'. This restrictive, non-universal approach to the right to healthcare, undertaken by the legislature, and accepted by the Constitutional Court, is however open to criticism due to the consequences that it might have. For example, migrants might not go to a medical centre because they would have to pay to see a doctor (which, in turn, could also result in the spread of infection to the people around them). Also questionable is the fact that a right such as the right to free healthcare is dependent on a foreigner's residence status.

[46] For a detailed study of this judgment, see the Doctoral Thesis of Professor Mercedes Martínez Aso, *La eficacia de la protección del Derecho a la Seguridad y Salud en el trabajo de los trabajadores extranjeros, ya citada* (presentada en el programa de Doctorado de Turismo, Derecho y Empresa de la Universidad de Girona en 2013) available at www.tdx.cat/handle/10803/124038 [last accessed 24 March 2022].

[47] Law 16/2003 on the Cohesion and Quality of the National Health System (*Ley 16/2003 de cohesión y calidad del Sistema Nacional de Salud*).

[48] This provision means that Spanish Law is in line with international requirements. See in particular the interpretation of Article 17 of the European Social Charter (Revised) by the European Committee of Social Rights in Complaint 14/2003, *International Federation of Human Rights Leagues (FIDH) v France* (3 November 2004), available at docs.escr-net.org/usr_doc/Committee_Social_Rights_Decision_Merits.pdf [last accessed 24 March 2022].

Nonetheless, this situation has changed with the adoption of Royal Decree law 7/2018, of 27 July, on Universal Access to the National Health System, which modified the 2013 Royal Decree, and which guarantees the right of undocumented foreigners to health protection and free health care. The preamble of this Law lays down that:

> access to the National Health System is a fundamental right of every individual. Guaranteeing the exercise of said right and the effective health protection of citizens is of even greater importance when those who are deprived of normal healthcare are especially vulnerable groups threatened by social exclusion, as is the case of the foreign population that is neither registered nor authorised to live in Spain.

The main issue in the recognition of labour rights to which undocumented migrant workers are entitled, is the difficulty in having these rights enforced. In these cases, undocumented workers must report their employer, either to the courts or to the labour authorities (in particular, the Inspection of Labour and Social Security). In so doing, they would put themselves at risk of losing their jobs. They are also at risk of being prosecuted for not being legally authorised to work, which may lead not only to financial sanctions, but even removal from the territory.

These same consequences are also a risk in cases in which undocumented migrant workers apply for status regularisation for work reasons. According to the law (Article 124 Royal Decree 557/2011, approving the Regulation of Organic Law 4/2000), there are two main ways to regularise undocumented foreigners' situation if they are working: by claiming so-called work reasons, or social reasons (it is also possible to claim family reasons, but in this case, being employed is not a requirement).[49] In the first case, for work reasons, if foreigners have resided in Spain for two years, and present a judicial order or a work inspection certificate to the effect that they are working, they may be granted the appropriate work permit. In effect, foreign workers are obliged to report the employers hiring them in order to obtain this order or inspection certificate.

As for social reasons, if undocumented foreigners have been living in Spain for three years and provide proof that they have had an employment relationship for at least one year, they can request regularisation by submitting the appropriate documentation to the relevant government authorities, but without having to report their employer.

Applications alleging work reasons have been marginal compared to the other two routes to regularisation (social and family reasons).[50] In my opinion,

[49] The possibility for migrants to regularise their irregular situation if they undertake training for employment was added by Royal Decree 629/2022 of 26 July 2022.

[50] Studies carried out have shown that between 2006 and 2014, applications alleging work reasons only represented 1.66% of the almost 750,000 applications alleging social or family reasons. See J M Cerezo Mariscal, *Praxis de la inmigración irregular en la España del siglo XXI* (Edita Subdirección General de Información Administrativa y Publicaciones del Ministerio de Empleo y Seguridad Social, 2016) 317–19.

this is due to several factors. First, the lack of information that many migrants have in relation to this legal concept, and second, the nature of the requirements that must be activated to achieve regularisation in this way; namely, the obligation to report their employer either to the labour courts or to a labour relations inspector. Undocumented foreigners may be afraid to do so since these institutions are able to check their intervention and activate it, not only for the facts reported by them but also for their own situation as unauthorised foreigners, with the negative consequences that this may have for them personally.[51]

Rights protection for migrant workers in an irregular situation, whether seeking to regularise their status for work reasons, report situations of abuse, or gain entitlement to the same working conditions under law as Spanish workers, would be greatly facilitated if a 'firewall' were adopted. This would guarantee their right to lodge complaints before the courts or labour authorities without fear of being arrested and/or removed by the immigration authorities.[52] If a foreigner in an irregular situation is prosecuted for bringing a complaint to the labour authorities or making a judicial complaint to demand work-related rights, their right to access to justice (or effective legal protection) is arguably being violated. The solution is a protocol agreed to by the appropriate authorities in order for complaints by migrant workers in an irregular situation to be addressed properly. Only the record or acknowledgement of facts, and not the individual's administrative status, would be controlled or judged. Migrant workers should be made sufficiently aware of such a protocol or procedure so that they are not discouraged from claiming their labour rights.

Special attention should also be paid to possible collaboration between institutions involved in deterring the informal economy and undeclared employment – that is, the Inspection of Labour, trade unions, labour and social security authorities, and social organisations who work with the immigrant population. Not only should there be awareness-raising campaigns, but also these organisations should seek out situations in which undocumented migrant workers are employed in undeclared work, to support them in the process of filing a complaint.[53]

[51] The recent Royal Decree 629/2022 of 26 July 2022 has facilitated the use of regularisation for work reasons. The foreign national is no longer required to denounce their employer, and to prove irregular work, but must instead prove that they had regular employment in Spain at some point in time. The possibility of denunciation of the employer, leading to the grant of a residence and work permit, is provided for in exceptional circumstances.

[52] On the notion of a firewall, see S Olney and R Cholewinski, 'Migrant Workers and the Right to Non-discrimination and Equality' in Costello and Freedland (n 41) 276.

[53] For example, Barcelona City Council has adopted a specific plan regarding foreigners in an irregular situation: *Mesura de govern per afavorir l'accés a la regularitat i prevenir la irregularitat sobrevinguda* (2017) available at www.bcn.cat/novaciutadania/pdf/mgrregularitat.pdf [last accessed 24 March 2022]. One of its objectives is to increase collaboration with stakeholders, such as trade unions, the Labour Inspectorate and Spain's National Police Illegal Immigration Network and False Document Unit (UCRIF) in order to promote employment integration.

V. CONCLUSION

This chapter has focused on obstacles faced by migrant workers, whatever their legal status, to gain access to employment in Spain, and to enjoy equal working conditions with regard to national workers.

First, the main problem for foreigners coming to work in Spain is what may be termed the 'filter', based on the national employment situation, which, to a large extent, prevents migrants (especially those who lack economic resources) from working in Spain. Challenges, such as an increasingly ageing population, or migratory pressures on Spain's Mediterranean coast, are also relevant factors when considering labour and immigration policy changes.

Further questions that need to be addressed regarding third-country nationals seeking employment in Spain are that even if they overcome the filter of the national employment situation, their own situation is still conditioned by work and residence authorisation being dependent on the employer registering the foreign worker with the Social Security administration, by the lack of international recognition of professional qualifications between countries, and by migrant under-employment. The need to adopt employment policies specifically directed at the immigrant population should also be highlighted, as should the need to undertake equality initiatives at the workplace in which migrant workers themselves can take part.

It is significant that unemployment rates continue to be higher among migrants who are legally authorised to reside and work in Spain than among Spanish nationals, which could be construed as a situation of discrimination within the employment sphere. Differences in working conditions between migrants and nationals should be addressed by guaranteeing the effective application of the principle of equality and non-discrimination.

In the case of undocumented migrant workers, the right to equal treatment has not been fully recognised, even if certain basic rights, derived from the inherent dignity of the human person, have. This incompleteness has at the same time been mitigated by the legal recognition that, in the event of working, undocumented migrants, like the rest of workers, cannot be deprived of their labour rights, including rights regarding dismissal. Equality of treatment does, however, lead to serious enforcement issues, as undocumented workers may be prevented from claiming their rights for fear of being penalised due to their legal status in the country of residence.

Finally, I would merely like to underline that the main concern of the public authorities in immigration matters is focused on the migratory pressures of undocumented migrants following the western Mediterranean route to enter Europe, as mentioned in this paper. In my view, instruments should be adopted to provide legal routes for migration, especially economic migration, but this issue would warrant another publication.

Part II

Countering Exploitation

6

Labour's Recourse? Legal Protections and Remedies for Migrant Workers in Canada

SARAH MARSDEN*

I. INTRODUCTION

MIGRANT WORKERS IN Canada face a variety of rights shortfalls and workplace issues, including reduced wages, health and safety risks, unlawfully long working hours, racial discrimination, sexual harassment and assault, and difficulty in unionising.[1] The power disparity between worker and employer is amplified for migrant workers, and especially so for those with a closed work permit, for which the worker relies on the endorsement of an employer to maintain their immigration status. Workers in this situation are understandably reluctant to seek redress for workplace harms. While there are multiple remedial options available to migrant workers, the structure of federal immigration law, and in particular the strong role of private employers in the provision of work permits, shapes both the needs of workers and the ways in which the law responds. Employment standards and other laws that regulate the workplace do not expressly exclude any migrant workers, whether authorised or unauthorised, and some laws go further, aiming to protect migrant workers specifically. Both categories of law have the potential to address migrant workers' concerns, but neither address the fundamental inequality that arises from the allocation of permanent migration status to some workers and not others. The employment experience of migrant workers is marked by particular forms of vulnerability arising from the institutionalisation of non-permanent status,

* The author wishes to thank Sarah Yorston for her able research assistance with revisions to this chapter.

[1] See, eg, L Goldring and P Landolt, *Producing and Negotiating Non-citizenship: Precarious Legal Status in Canada* (Toronto, University of Toronto Press, 2013); P Lenard and C Straehle, *Legislated Inequality: Temporary Labour Migration in Canada* (Montreal, McGill-Queen's Press-MQUP, 2012); IU Syed, 'Labor Exploitation and Health Inequities Among Market Migrants: A Political Economy Perspective' (2016) 17 *Journal of International Migration and Integration* 449.

including differential access to social benefits.[2] The situation is also complicated by the interaction of federal and provincial law, as well as by the heightened power of employers and the absence of labour mobility, particularly for those with a closed work permit.[3]

Canada's Constitution divides powers between the federal government and the provinces, creating complexity at the intersection of migration and labour law and policy. Immigration is an area of shared jurisdiction, but federal law has primacy, which means that laws regulating borders, permanent and temporary admission, and immigration enforcement, are within federal jurisdiction.[4] The regulation of labour migration by federal authorities includes the labour authorisation process, through which employers obtain permission to hire temporary foreign workers, as well as the power to issue work permits. The provinces do however have a role in the selection of permanent immigrants.[5] In contrast, employment standards, human rights, and the law relating to labour unions fall primarily within the jurisdiction of the provinces.

In this chapter, I consider in detail the potential of multiple aspects of Canadian law to address the workplace problems that many migrant workers face. The chapter aims to provide an overview of the legal avenues available to migrant workers in Canada with regard to the regulation of working life. It considers the effectiveness of the legal frameworks in providing redress for workers and deterrence of harmful action on the part of employers. Specifically, it will consider migrant workers' rights in federal employment and immigration law, provincial employment standards and human rights, common law employment remedies, and through labour unionisation.[6] Migrant workers as a group encounter particular challenges which are distinct from those faced by workers more generally. By focusing on the law through the lens of migrant workers' concerns and the reception of their claims in courts and tribunals, this chapter concludes by identifying the features most likely to enable positive change in migrants' working lives.

The chapter first provides a brief background account of the legal structure of migrant work schemes in the context of Canadian immigration

[2] M Sargeant and E Tucker, 'Layers of Vulnerability in Occupational Safety and Health for Migrant Workers: Case Studies from Canada and the UK' (2009) 2 *Policy and Practice in Health and Safety* 51; K Priebisch and J Hennebry, 'Temporary Migration, Chronic Effects: The Health of International Migrant Workers in Canada' (2011) 183 *Canadian Medical Association Journal* 1033.

[3] J Fudge and F MacPhail, 'The Temporary Foreign Worker Program in Canada: Low-Skilled Workers as an Extreme Form of Flexible Labour' (2009) 31 *Comparative Labour Law and Policy Journal* 11.

[4] Constitution Act 1867 (UK) 30 & 31 Vict c 3, reprinted in RSC 1985 App II No 5, s 95.

[5] Immigration and Refugee Protection Act SC 2001 c 27, ss 8, 9.

[6] Workers' compensation law and constitutional law are not canvassed in this chapter, but see Sargeant and Tucker (n 2) and C Dauvergne, 'How the Charter has Failed Non-citizens in Canada: Reviewing Thirty Years of Supreme Court of Canada Jurisprudence' (2013) 58 *McGill Law Journal/Revue de droit de McGill* 663.

law, and an outline of the challenges and barriers faced by migrant workers in Canada. With a view to mapping the various aspects of Canadian law which could address the exploitation of migrant workers, it will then turn to the statutory regulation of employers of migrant workers through federal insurance and tax law and through immigration law. It follows with an examination of migrant workers' avenues of recourse through employment standards, anti-discrimination law, and common law remedies in employment, as well as touching briefly on collective action through unionisation. It concludes that, while imperfect, recent developments in several of these avenues show promise in terms of moving toward greater protection of migrant workers' rights.

II. MIGRANT WORKERS IN CANADA

In Canada's taxonomy of immigration status, there is a clear line between permanent status and everything else: in immigration law, each person is classified as either a citizen, a status Indian, a permanent resident, or a foreign national. While permanent residents are also nationals of foreign countries, the term 'foreign national' in Canadian law refers exclusively to people who have neither citizenship nor permanent resident status. All but foreign nationals have a right to enter and remain in Canada.[7] Foreign nationals can be granted permission to work and reside temporarily in Canada, and thereby to become holders of work permits. (Individuals with non-permanent status who are engaged in the labour force in Canada are referred to here as 'migrant workers' regardless of whether they are authorised or unauthorised.[8])

The total labour force in Canada in 2019 was 20.2 million people, of whom just over 19 million were employed full-time or part time.[9] In the Canadian immigration system, permanent residents have the right to enter and reside in Canada, and can move freely within the labour market, but migrant workers rely on work permits that determine the conditions and duration of their labour market engagement. The number of migrant workers entering Canada outstrips the number of permanent economic class migrants. In 2018, Canada issued a total of 338,635 temporary work permits, not including work permits

[7] Immigration and Refugee Protection Act SC 2001 c 27, ss 19(1)–(2).

[8] It is beyond the scope of this chapter to consider the engagement of permanent immigrants in Canada. For a detailed treatment of this issue, see, eg, GE Galabuzi, *Canada's Economic Apartheid: The Social Exclusion of Racialized Groups in the New Century* (Toronto, Canadian Scholars' Press, 2006) and N Lightman and LG Gingrich, 'The Intersecting Dynamics of Social Exclusion: Age, Gender, Race and Immigrant Status in Canada's Labour Market' (2012) 44 *Canadian Ethnic Studies* 121.

[9] Statistics Canada, 'Labour Force Characteristics by Age and Sex – Seasonally Adjusted' (2019) www.statcan.gc.ca [last accessed 25 March 2022].

issued for humanitarian and compassionate reasons.[10] The same year, Canada admitted a total of 186,090 foreign nationals as permanent residents in economic classes.[11]

There are several paths to economic permanent residence in Canada. These are: points-based 'Federal Skilled Worker' and 'Federal Skilled Trade' classes; provincial nominee classes; Canadian Experience class based on skilled work experience in Canada; self-employed class, limited to those with experience in world-class cultural or athletic activities or experience managing farms; caregiving streams for domestic workers who have worked in Canada (previously live-in caregivers); and the Start-up (entrepreneur) Visa Program.[12]

Work permits in Canada fall into two categories. 'Closed' work permits are limited to a specific employer and occupation for the duration of the permit. Workers with these permits cannot freely circulate in the labour market, and, if they wish to change employer or position, must obtain a new work permit, a process which depends on finding a new employer who is willing to undergo an onerous bureaucratic process. This category includes large-scale programmes for agricultural workers and domestic workers, as well as work in any sector for which an employer has demonstrated a specific labour market shortage. Men outnumber women in this programme as well: of those in Canada at the end of 2017, just under 34 per cent were women.[13] Of total workers in this category as of the end of 2017, 47 per cent were 'high skilled' and 53 per cent were 'low skilled'. Of male workers, 54 per cent were 'high skilled' and 46 per cent were 'low skilled'. Women are over-represented in work classified as 'low skilled': 33 per cent were 'high skilled' and 67 per cent were 'low skilled'.[14] In this category, the main countries of origin for workers in 2017 were Mexico, Jamaica, and the Philippines.[15] In the case of agricultural workers, the nationality of workers is specified, as Canada has agricultural work agreements with Mexico

[10] IRCC, 'Temporary Residents: Temporary Foreign Worker Program (TFWP) and International Mobility Program (IMP) Work Permit Holders – Monthly IRCC Updates', sum of 2018 annual total from tables IRCC_M_TR-0004_E and IRCC_M_TR-0008_E available at open.canada.ca/data/en/dataset/360024f2-17e9-4558-bfc1-3616485d65b9 [last accessed 25 March 2022].

[11] IRCC, 'Permanent Residents: Monthly IRCC Updates', sum of 2018 annual total of Economy Category from each province and territory, from table IRCC_M_PRadmiss_0001_E.xls available at open.canada.ca/data/en/dataset/f7e5498e-0ad8-4417-85c9-9b8aff9b9eda [last accessed 25 March 2022].

[12] IRCC, 'Statistics and Open Data: Facts and Figures 2016: Immigration Overview – Permanent Residents – Annual IRCC updates' available at open.canada.ca/ [last accessed 25 March 2022].

[13] IRCC, 'Temporary Foreign Worker Program work permit holders with a valid permit on December 31st by gender and age, 1997 to 2017' available at open.canada.ca/data/en/dataset/2bf9f856-20fe-4644-bf74-c8e45b3d94bd [last accessed 25 March 2022].

[14] IRCC, 'Temporary Foreign Worker Program work permit holders with a valid permit on December 31st by gender and occupational skill level, 2008 to 2017' available at open.canada.ca/data/en/dataset/2bf9f856-20fe-4644-bf74-c8e45b3d94bd [last accessed 25 March 2022].

[15] IRCC, 'Temporary Foreign Worker Program work permit holders by top 50 countries of citizenship and sign year,' available at open.canada.ca/data/en/dataset/2bf9f856-20fe-4644-bf74-c8e45b3d94bd [last accessed 25 March 2022].

and the Caribbean. In all other sectors, closed work permits are available to nationals of any country, although concentrations exist, such as women from the Philippines working as caregivers.[16]

'Open' work permits enable migrant workers to circulate in Canada's labour market for the duration of their authorised stay, and are usually issued for policy reasons, without the need for a labour market test, unlike closed work permits. For example, open work permits are issued to students during their studies and after their graduation from a Canadian programme, to working holidaymakers, to spouses of certain closed work permit holders and to refugee claimants. As of the end of 2017, this group made up 68 per cent of total entries of authorised foreign workers.[17] Government data do not record the skill level of this group, and they are permitted to work in most labour segments. The top five source countries for this group, in order, are India, China, the US, France, and Australia,[18] and men outnumber women in the programme, making up 58 per cent in 2017.[19]

The distinction between 'low-skilled' and 'high-skilled' work is determinative of specific rights and entitlements under federal immigration law. 'Low-skilled' migrant workers are less likely to obtain permanent residence. Most categories of economic permanent residence require the applicant to have a period of experience in 'high-skilled' work.[20] Those whose work is classified as 'low-skilled' will qualify for permanent residence only if they are captured by periodic and changing provincial selection programmes. For example, one such programme in British Columbia allows employers to sponsor 'low-skilled' workers, but only in listed long-haul trucking, food processing, and tourism jobs. The primary exception to this is the caregiving stream (previously the 'Live-in Caregiver Program'), in which the 'low-skilled' work of domestic caregiving can be used to qualify for permanent residence.[21]

Those whose work is classified as 'high skilled' are also able to obtain open work permits for their spouses, enabling their spouse to enter, reside, and work

[16] RK Brickner and C Straehle, 'The Missing Link: Gender, Immigration Policy, and the Live-in Caregiver Program in Canada' (2010) 29 *Policy and Society* 309.

[17] IRCC, 'Temporary Foreign Worker Program work permit holders by top 50 countries of citizenship and sign year' available at open.canada.ca/data/en/dataset/2bf9f856-20fe-4644-bf74-c8e45b3d94bd; 'International Mobility Program work permit holders with a valid permit on December 31st by program, 2008 to 2017' available at open.canada.ca/data/en/dataset/2bf9f856-20fe-4644-bf74-c8e45b3d94bd [both last accessed 25 March 2022].

[18] IRCC, 'International Mobility Program work permit holders with a valid permit on December 31st by top 50 countries of citizenship, 2008 to 2017' available at open.canada.ca/data/en/dataset/2bf9f856-20fe-4644-bf74-c8e45b3d94bd [last accessed 25 March 2022].

[19] IRCC, 'IMP work permit holders by top 20 citizenship, sign year' available at open.canada.ca [last accessed 25 March 2022].

[20] Immigration and Refugee Protection Regulations SOR 2002/227, ss 75(2)(a), 87.1(2).

[21] IRCC, 'Caring for children and caring for people with high medical needs' available at www.cic.gc.ca/english/resources/tools/perm/econ/children-med/index.asp [last accessed 25 March 2022].

in Canada. 'Low-skilled' workers do not share this entitlement. They are entitled to spousal work permits where they have been subject to provincial nomination. Otherwise their spouses must go through the work permit and labour justification process separately, which is often not a realistic option and may lead to family separation, sometimes for years.[22]

There are also individuals in an unauthorised position, because they have overstayed their permits, worked beyond the terms of their permits, or they are in Canada completely without status. There are no reliable numbers to describe the unauthorised migrant population: entry into Canada is well controlled, and Canada does not yet use exit control. There are also no current, reliable data on the number of people who enter Canada without authorisation. In 2006, estimates of undocumented migrants ranged from 50,000–200,000.[23] Commentators have noted that Canada's immigration system tends to destabilise migration status, through unintentional loss or institutional features beyond the control of individuals. Such institutional features include lack of recourse after sponsorship breakdown, complex refugee determination processes, and the difficulty of finding an employer to go through the labour market justification process if workers lose their initial job (which is tied to their work permit).[24]

III. STATUTES REGULATING EMPLOYERS

Much of the law that governs employment in Canada is statute-based. Statutes and regulations in the federal jurisdiction set out standards, penalties, and remedies in multiple areas relevant to the employment of migrant workers, including tax law, insurance law, and immigration law. These include measures to regulate employer compliance through administrative penalties, such as fines and removal of privileges. Many statutory schemes also include regulatory offence provisions, under which a person or corporation may be formally charged and prosecuted.

This section relies on statutory and regulatory texts, interpretive decisions by tribunals and courts, and the responses of government agencies to requests by the author under freedom of information legislation. It provides a map of the regulation of employers including, where available, data to show how these laws are used in practice.

[22] G Pratt, 'From Registered Nurse to Registered Nanny, Discursive Geographies of Filipina Domestic Workers in Vancouver, B.C.' (1999) 75 *Economic Geography* 215.

[23] D Tilson, *Temporary Foreign Workers and Nonstatus Workers* (Ottawa, Library of Parliament, 2009) 65.

[24] L Goldring, 'Institutionalizing Precarious Migratory Status in Canada' (2009) 13 *Citizenship Studies* 239.

A. Employer Checks of the Right to Work

In Canadian law, there are multiple statutory avenues which deter employers from employing migrant workers in an irregular capacity, whether because the work itself is informal, or because the migrant worker does not have authorisation to work. For the purposes of this chapter, employment insurance and tax law have been grouped together as one form of regulation, and immigration law as a second form of regulation.

First, under insurance and tax law, individuals must have a Social Insurance Number (SIN) in order to work in Canada. This requirement applies equally to citizens, permanent residents, and non-permanent migrants. Permanent SINs are available to citizens and permanent residents of Canada. Migrant workers who hold work permits are also able to obtain a temporary SIN based on the expiry date of their work permit.[25] Those whose migration status has expired, or who otherwise require but do not hold a work permit, are unable to obtain a SIN. Employers are required to obtain a SIN from every worker within three days of the commencement of employment, and if they are unable to determine the worker's SIN, they are obliged to report this to federal authorities responsible for labour (ie, not the immigration authorities).[26] Employers are required to collect employment insurance contributions from all workers at the point of pay, and may be subject to regulatory offences if they do not.[27] It is an offence for any person (including both workers and employers) to wilfully evade compliance with these requirements.[28] However, the federal prosecution services reported zero prosecutions under this Act between 1 June 2007 and 24 August 2017.[29]

Workers are also required under federal income tax law to file tax returns, and employers are obliged to collect and remit taxes. As with the employment insurance laws, failure to meet these requirements could engage regulatory offence provisions.[30] As in employment insurance law, there is an offence provision in income tax law for 'wilful evasion' of compliance or the payment of taxes. The federal prosecution service discloses an average of 102 annual prosecutions under this general 'wilful evasion' provision from 2007 to 2017.[31] As they represent total prosecutions under this section, it is impossible to determine whether any of these relate to the requirement to obtain a SIN, or are specific to migrant workers.

[25] Immigration and Refugee Protection Act SC 2001 c 27 (IRPA), s 90.
[26] Employment Insurance Regulations SOR/96-332 (EI Regs), ss 89(2), 89(5).
[27] Employment Insurance Act SC 1996 c 23 (EI Act), ss 82, 106.
[28] ibid, s 106(4)(d).
[29] Response A-2017-00016 provided to the author in response to a request under the Freedom of Information and Protection of Privacy Act, 1.
[30] ITA, s 239(1)(d).
[31] Response A-2017-00016 provided to the author in response to a request under the Freedom of Information and Protection of Privacy Act, 1.

Second, turning to immigration law, it is a regulatory offence under federal immigration law for an employer to hire a worker who is not authorised to work in Canada.[32] This offence has been in force since 2002. Prior to 2002, there was a general offence provision for individuals remaining in Canada without authorisation or misleading immigration officers, as well as an 'aiding and abetting' provision, but no specific offence for employing an unauthorised foreign national.[33] Only a few prosecutions have resulted in published judicial decisions. In a Manitoba sentencing hearing for an employer convicted of employing six unauthorised migrant workers, the Manitoba Court of Appeal noted that by employing people without a work permit, the employer was unlawfully giving himself a marketplace advantage; in that case, the employer was sentenced to a fine of $15,000, probation, and 50 hours of community service.[34] In a 2016 sentencing decision, the British Columbia Supreme Court found that continuing to employ a caregiver without status was contrary to the public interest, as it deprived the caregiver of protections commonly available to other workers, and circumvented immigration laws concerning the issuance of work permits. The employer was sentenced to three months' imprisonment, nine months' probation, and 25 hours of community service.[35]

In a recent British Columbia case, two separate general offence provisions from the federal immigration statute were applied in the migrant work context. One was section 127 of the Immigration and Refugee Protection Act, which inter alia makes it an offence to: 'directly or indirectly misrepresent or withhold material facts relating to a relevant matter that induces or could induce an error in the administration of this Act'.[36] The other was section 124(1)(a) of the same Act, which makes it an offence where a person inter alia 'fails to comply with a condition or other obligation imposed under this Act'.[37] In *R v Harlens Trucking Ltd*, a trucking company hired 79 migrant workers after obtaining labour market impact assessments based on an offered wage of $23.50 per hour.[38] Once the workers arrived, the employer paid them on a mileage basis instead, in keeping with industry practice, at 0.40 per mile driven, and workers signed contracts agreeing to this pay method. In its accounting and pay stubs, the employer retroactively reduced the 'hours worked' so as to make it appear as though $23.50 per hour was being paid. This resulted in a shortfall of $352,001.83 in workers' pay. Counsel for the employer argued at trial that the workers were not in a vulnerable position because they were paid according to industry standard and agreed to the change in pay structure, that they benefited from their employment, and

[32] IRPA, s 124(1)(c).
[33] Immigration Act 1976–77 c 52, s 94.
[34] *R v Choi (J.W.)* 2013 MBCA 75.
[35] *R v Orr* 2016 BCSC 2064.
[36] Immigration and Refugee Protection Act SC 2001 c 27 (IRPA), s 127.
[37] IRPA, s 124(1)(a).
[38] *R v Harlens Trucking Ltd.*, 2018 BCSC 1171.

that they eventually had the chance to apply for permanent residence. The trial judge rejected this argument and held that the workers did suffer from an imbalance of power because their status relied on the employer, as they would not have had access to a work permit without the employer's support.[39] On appeal, this reasoning was upheld, and the employer was given a suspended sentence and two years' probation, a restitution order of $352,001.83 in accordance with the wage shortfall, and a fine of $10,000.[40]

Under federal immigration law, workers can also be prosecuted for working without authorisation, including working for employers or in jobs not specified on the permit, as well as working without a permit (as an aspect of general non-compliance).[41] Federal statistics suggest that workers are much more likely to be subject to removal from Canada than to criminal prosecution – and foreign nationals are also subject to removal much more frequently than employers are subject to charge or prosecution.[42] The federal prosecution service discloses an average of 85 prosecutions annually for non-compliance under this section for all of Canada.[43] In British Columbia alone, the Canada Border Services Agency confirms a range of 1,318 to 2,567 annual removals for non-compliance (from 2001 to 2016), of which a subset would be related to working without a permit.[44]

B. Employment Standards Compliance under Federal Immigration Law

Until recently, the federal government disclaimed any responsibility for monitoring or enforcing workplace rights for migrant workers who had entered Canada through federal programmes, on the basis that these labour issues were within the jurisdiction of the provinces. In 2015, however, the federal legislature integrated provincial employment standards as a required component of employer compliance, through changes to the Immigration and Refugee Protection Regulations.

These changes set out conditions that employers must meet in order to continue employing migrant workers, both those they actually employ, and future prospective workers, of which three are especially relevant here. First, employers are required to comply with both federal and provincial employment laws as a condition of hiring migrant workers. While the provincial laws are

[39] ibid, para 31.

[40] ibid, para 43.

[41] IRPA, s 124(1)(a).

[42] Response CBSA A-2016-10534 provided to the author in response to a request under the Freedom of Information and Protection of Privacy Act.

[43] Response PPSC A-2017-00016 provided to the author in response to a request under the Freedom of Information and Protection of Privacy Act.

[44] Response BCSA A-2016-10534 provided to the author in response to a request under the Freedom of Information and Protection of Privacy Act. The CBSA dataset does not break down types of noncompliance.

binding on employers in any case, these laws tie them to the federal immigration power in a new way. Under the previous regime, a worker's complaint under provincial employment law would have had no impact on the employer's capacity to hire migrant workers under federal law. Now, breach of provincial law can trigger federal employer compliance steps. Second, employers are required to comply with the terms of job offers made to migrant workers.[45] Third, employers must 'make reasonable efforts to provide a workplace that is free of abuse'.[46] 'Abuse' is defined in the Regulations as: (a) physical abuse, including assault and forcible confinement; (b) sexual abuse, including sexual contact without consent; (c) psychological abuse, including threats and intimidation; and (d) financial abuse, including fraud and extortion.[47]

As regards enforcement, the regulations empower both the immigration authorities and Economic and Social Development Canada – the federal authority responsible for labour benefits such as employment insurance, and federal labour standards – to conduct compliance reviews and investigations, and to issue penalties. The new regulations also set out a system of penalties for employers, organised by way of a 'points' system, in which the severity and frequency of violations are expressed by a number of points, and penalties assessed accordingly.[48] Certain factors increase the number of points, including the type of condition breached and the frequency of violations. More points are attached to situations where the violation involved abuse of a worker, where the employer derived competitive advantage from the breach, or where the employer did not make reasonable efforts to minimise or prevent the breach from recurring. An employer may face fines of up to $100,000 per violation and may be barred from employing migrant workers for a number of years, or permanently.[49]

If an employer is barred from employing migrant workers, this has a consequence for the workers as well, as their permits are tied to a specific employer. If the employer is no longer permitted to employ migrant workers, the workers will be unable to work lawfully unless and until they are able to obtain a work permit for a new employer, who must undergo a labour market justification process which can take months. Workers with valid work permits may remain in Canada, but cannot work other than as specified by their permit.[50] Needless to stay, remaining in Canada without being able to work lawfully puts migrant workers in a difficult position of choosing between unemployment and unlawful employment while they seek a new employer. Workers may also fall out of status entirely if a new employer does not undergo the labour market justification

[45] IRPR, ss 209.2, 209.3.

[46] ibid, ss 209.2, 209.3.

[47] ibid, s 196.2.

[48] ibid, Sch 2.

[49] ibid, Sch 2. Note that an employer must accrue repeat violations to receive enough 'points' to merit a $100,000 penalty for a subsequent violation.

[50] IRPR, ss 183(1)(b), 183(3), 183(4).

process before the expiry of the workers' permit, because their status ends when the permit ends.[51] The new regulations do not provide protection or compensation for workers employed by barred employers. The absence of protection for workers fails to take account of the reliance of migrant workers on their employers, and may therefore serve as a disincentive to reporting workplace abuses.

The Regulations include a due diligence defence for employers, by which an employer can justify a failure to comply where any of the following conditions exist:

(a) a change in federal or provincial law;
(b) a change to collective agreement terms;[52]
(c) the implementation of measures by the employer in response to a dramatic change in economic conditions that directly affected the business of the employer, provided that the measures were not directed disproportionately at foreign nationals employed by the employer;
(d) an error in interpretation made in good faith by the employer with respect to its obligations to a foreign national, if the employer subsequently provided compensation – or where it was not possible to provide compensation, made sufficient efforts to do so – to all foreign nationals who suffered a disadvantage as a result of the error;
(e) an unintentional accounting or administrative error made by the employer, if the employer subsequently provided compensation – or where it was not possible to provide compensation, made sufficient efforts to do so – to all foreign nationals who suffered a disadvantage as a result of the error;
(f) circumstances similar to those set out in paragraphs (a) to (e); or
(g) force majeure.[53]

At the time of writing, there has only been one example of judicial consideration of these provisions. In the *Farms* case, a federal inspector had determined that an agricultural employer was in breach of multiple requirements, including that the workers were made to work seven days a week, were not paid according to the terms of their contract, faced unauthorised deductions and were not paid on time.[54] In upholding the investigator's decision on these issues, the Federal Court made clear that the regulatory defences for employers are to be interpreted strictly, given the underlying purpose of protecting migrant workers.[55]

The defence provisions available to employers are, however, problematic from the perspective of workers, even if interpreted strictly. While the employers have an obligation to make 'reasonable efforts' to ensure that a workplace is

[51] ibid, s 183(4).

[52] There is no analogous provision under which migrant workers could be protected due to collective agreement changes affecting their employment or causing a breach of immigration law.

[53] IRPR, ss 209.2(3), 209.3(3), 203 (1.1).

[54] *Farms v Canada (Employment and Social Development)*, 2017 FC 302.

[55] ibid.

free of abuse, they are enabled to defend measures that breach this requirement on the basis of economic circumstances, as long as migrant workers, as a group, did not suffer disproportionately from the measures taken by the employer. On the face of this provision, if there is a serious economic change and the employer fails to make reasonable efforts to maintain a workplace free of abuse, the employer would have a complete defence. Similarly, where a workforce is made up exclusively of migrant workers, it is impossible to demonstrate that migrants suffer disproportionately, because there is no other group with which to compare them.

These regulations represent the federal government's first attempt at a comprehensive employer compliance structure dealing specifically with migrant workers. While investigations under these regulations number in the thousands annually, few result in penalties or suspensions of employers from hiring migrant workers.[56] The immigration department publicises the names of all employers who have faced any kind of penalty.[57] Between 1 December 2015 and August 2017, a total of 50 employers had been penalised under this stronger regulatory scheme. Of these, 24 were issued a two-year ban on hiring migrant workers, and 26 were given monetary penalties ranging from $500 to $54,000 (with the majority being $2,000 or under).[58]

IV. PROVINCIAL EMPLOYMENT STANDARDS LAW

For the majority of workers in Canada, the regulation of employment standards is within provincial jurisdiction.[59] Employment standards relate to minimum wages, hours of work and leave, notice and basis for termination, advertising of work, recruitment practices, and provide frameworks for complaints, enforcement, and appeals. A small minority of provinces have legislation dealing specifically with foreign workers, and these statutes will be reviewed here before turning to general employment standards.

In the case of general employment standards, the law is similar across Canada's 13 provinces and territories, and for the purposes of this chapter I will draw mainly on the examples of Ontario and British Columbia.[60] In both,

[56] Response A-2017-00510 ESDC provided in response to the author's *Access to Information Act* request provided August 2017.

[57] IRCC, 'Employers Who Have Been Non-compliant' available at www.cic.gc.ca/english/work/list.asp [last accessed 25 March 2022].

[58] ibid.

[59] The exception to this is workers who work in federally regulated industries, such as railways and postal delivery.

[60] For an overview of employment standards across Canada, see J Willows and S Schetagne, *Mapping Basic Working Conditions in Employment Standards Across Canada – 2011/2012* (Ottawa, Canadian Labour Congress, 2012).

general employment standards laws do not distinguish between workers on the basis of migration status: a citizen, an authorised migrant worker, and an unauthorised migrant worker are all 'workers' under these laws. Because the definition is without reference to immigration status, undocumented workers are included so long as they meet the general requirements, as has been confirmed in several cases cited below. While this is not as strong as a formal 'firewall' between the laws governing migration status and those dealing with employment rights, it at least serves to allow those workers who are able to claim their rights to be considered on par with citizen workers.[61] While migrant workers are not excluded as such from employment standards, some will be excluded due to the type of work they do. The most notable example of this is with regard to farmworkers, who comprise a significant proportion of migrant workers under the Seasonal Agricultural Worker Program and the agricultural stream of the Temporary Foreign Work Program, but who have fewer legal protections than other workers in both Ontario and British Columbia.

A. Legislation Specific to Foreign Workers

Four provinces have legislation designed to address the employment of migrant workers specifically. A first example is the Manitoba Worker Recruitment and Protection Act, which requires any employer wishing to hire a foreign worker to be licensed by the provincial government, and provides that a licence may be refused if 'having regard to the past conduct of the applicant, there are reasonable grounds to believe that the applicant will not act in accordance with law, or with integrity, honesty or in the public interest, while carrying out the activities for which the licence is required'.[62] That Act also prohibits charging recruitment fees or business costs to foreign workers, and requires employers to meet the conditions to which they agreed in obtaining federal labour market authorisation to hire the worker.[63]

The Saskatchewan Foreign Worker Recruitment and Immigration Services Act requires recruiters of foreign workers to obtain a provincial licence, and employers of foreign workers to hold a provincial certificate of registration.[64] Both may be refused on grounds similar to those in the Manitoba legislation. The Saskatchewan Act has a uniquely broad definition of 'foreign worker', which includes foreign nationals seeking employment, and therefore potentially

[61] For a detailed argument in support of a legislated 'firewall' between immigration status and other benefits, see JH Carens, 'The Rights of Irregular Migrants' (2008) 22 *Ethics & International Affairs* 163.

[62] The Worker Recruitment and Protection Act, CCSM c W197, s 9(1)(c).

[63] ibid, ss 15(4), 16 and 17.

[64] The Foreign Worker Recruitment and Immigration Services Act, SS 2013 c F-18.1, ss 8(2), 16.

includes undocumented or irregular workers. It also prohibits recruiters, employers, and immigration consultants from doing any of the following:

(a) to produce or distribute false or misleading information;
(b) to take possession of or retain a foreign national's passport or other official documents or property;
(c) to misrepresent employment opportunities, including misrepresentation respecting position, duties, length of employment, wages and benefits or other terms of employment;
(d) to threaten deportation or other action for which there is no lawful cause; to contact a foreign national or a foreign national's family or friends after being requested not to do so by the foreign national;
(e) to take action against or threaten to take action against a person for participating in an investigation or proceeding by any government or law enforcement agency or for making a complaint to any government or law enforcement agency; or
(f) to take unfair advantage of a foreign national's trust or exploit a foreign national's fear or lack of experience or knowledge.[65]

Ontario also has an employment standards law specific to migrant workers, the Employment Protections For Foreign Nationals Act (EPFNA).[66] This Act prohibits employers and recruiters from charging fees to workers for recruitment, prohibits employer reprisal against workers for inquiries and complaints to the Employment Standards Branch which administers the Act, prohibits employers from taking documents such as passports from a worker, and requires employers to provide written rights materials to a worker in an appropriate language, if the worker does not speak English. There is a reverse onus in the case of a reprisal complaint – once a violation is alleged against an employer, the burden shifts to the employer to refute the allegation. The Act provides a complaint mechanism, investigative powers for employment standards officers, and financial penalties and regulatory offence provisions for employers and recruiters. Unauthorised workers appear not to be included under the Ontario EPFNA as it requires that a person be 'performing or seeking work pursuant to an immigration program'.[67] The Act is though used relatively rarely: between 2010 and 2017, there were an average of only 43 claims per year.[68] In one case, a migrant live-in caregiver

[65] ibid, s 22.

[66] See also similar legislation in Manitoba and Saskatchewan namely The Worker Recruitment and Protection Act CCSM c W197, The Foreign Worker Recruitment and Immigration Services Regulations RRS c F-18.1, Reg 1.

[67] Employment Protection for Foreign Nationals Act (Live-in Caregivers and Others) SO 2009 c 32 (EPFNA), s 3.

[68] 'Annual Totals: EPFNA Claims and Inspections' provided July 2017 in response to author's request under the Ontario Freedom of Information and Protection of Privacy Act.

successfully used the EPFNA for an order to repay unlawful recruitment fees of $4,500.[69] In another, the employer of a restaurant worker was found to have breached requirements concerning wages, unpaid termination pay, vacation days, and employer reprisals, and the worker received an order for reinstatement, compensation for lost wages, and compensation for pain and suffering as his dignity was impaired in the manner of dismissal.[70] Several other migrant workers have received out-of-court settlements subsequent to complaints against corporate and individual respondents, though the terms of these are not publicly available.[71]

Most recently, British Columbia has enacted the Temporary Foreign Worker Protection Act, which mandates the licensing of recruiters of migrant workers and registration of employers. This Act also prohibits recruiters and employers from disseminating false information, holding workers' documents (eg passport), charging fees to workers, misrepresenting the terms of employment, threatening deportation, and reprisal for workers' complaints. The Director of Employment Standards is empowered to enforce these standards by way of inspection and disclosure powers, and has the capacity to recover fees owing to workers. Breach of the Act can also amount to an offence punishable by fine or up to one year of imprisonment.[72]

B. General Employment Standards in Ontario and British Columbia

Ontario's Employment Standards Act provides protection for the basic employment rights of all workers. Those rights include a minimum wage, a worker's right to refuse excess hours, breaks, overtime pay, statutory holidays, vacation pay, gender equality in pay, and notice of termination or pay in lieu thereof. Enforcement mechanisms under the Act include a prohibition on reprisals by employers, powers of investigation, orders for compensation and reinstatement, and offence provisions. Farmworkers (harvesting labourers), including those under agricultural migrant work programmes, are exempt from the general standards concerning minimum wage, breaks, and overtime pay. They may be paid by piece rate, and the piece rate payments must amount to at least the minimum wage, unless it is the case that workers are paid a piece rate sufficient to ensure that minimum wage would be met with 'reasonable effort'.[73]

[69] *Erazo v Amah International Inc*, 2014 CanLII 23658 (ON LRB).

[70] *Uttam Thapa v Suisha Gardens Limited* 2016 CanLII 28492.

[71] *Erazo v Amah International Inc*, *Lofranco v Omni Personnel and Immigration Agency Ltd.* 2014 CanLII 32096, *Bruni v Roselada* 2010 CanLII 61185 (ON LRB), *Aziqa Masih v Benedict John* 2017 CanLII 26390 (ON LRB).

[72] Temporary Foreign Worker Protection Act, SBC 2018 c 45, ss 3, 10, 20–21, 41, 80.

[73] Exemptions, Special Rules and Establishment of Minimum Wage (Exemption Reg) O Reg 285/01, ss 24–27.

Homeworkers, including migrant domestic workers, are entitled to 10 per cent more than the minimum hourly rate for workers in general.[74] It appears that unauthorised migrant workers are included within the regular Employment Standards Act so long as they met the definition of 'employee'.

Public records disclose several thousand investigations annually under the Ontario Act, as well as hundreds of annual convictions resulting in fines to employers.[75] The top reasons for employer convictions are holiday pay, excess hours of work, failure to keep records, and vacation pay. An example from a reported case shows a migrant caregiver obtaining an order for payment of regular and overtime wages, holiday and vacation pay, termination pay, and the return of unauthorised deductions.[76]

In British Columbia, unlike in Ontario, there is no legislation dealing specifically with migrant workers. The British Columbia Employment Standards Act has a broad definition of 'employee' which does not distinguish between citizen and migrant workers, and includes both authorised and unauthorised migrant workers. A number of tribunal decisions from British Columbia specifically consider the applicability of this legislation to unauthorised migrant workers. In one, a group of agricultural workers applied to the Employment Standards Tribunal for wages for work that was non-agricultural, and thus unauthorised under their work permits. The Tribunal found that the workers' compliance with the federal migration programme was irrelevant to its determination on wages, and that the workers were entitled to have their wages paid because what they were doing was clearly 'work'.[77] Similarly, the Tribunal heard the case of a pre-school teacher whose permit had expired, but whom the employer invited back to work as an unpaid 'volunteer' while she was out of status. The Tribunal rejected the employer's argument that the worker was not entitled to the protection of the Employment Standards Act because she was not working under a legal permit. It confirmed that, even without status, the worker was an 'employee' within the meaning of the Act and entitled to its protections.[78]

The British Columbia Act also provides protections for overtime pay, basic holidays and leave, minimum wages, breaks, and termination pay to compensate for length of service. While it does not include the right to refuse excess hours, it does prohibit 'excessive hours or hours detrimental to the employee's health or safety'.[79] The Act contains similar enforcement mechanisms to the Ontario Act. Farmworkers are excluded from provisions governing hours of work, breaks,

[74] ibid, s 5(1).

[75] Ministry of Labour, 'Prosecution and Conviction Statistics' available at www.labour.gov.on.ca/english/es/pubs/enforcement/convictions.php [last accessed 25 March 2022]. These statistics do not specify the number of convictions pertaining specifically to migrant workers.

[76] *Leys v Likhanga*, 2012 CanLII 29267 (ON LRB).

[77] *BC EST #D061/12.*

[78] *BC EST # D087/14.*

[79] Employment Standards Act RSBC 1996 c 113 (ESA), s 39.

and overtime, and instead are given a piece rate which must result in at least the minimum wage hourly (but with no entitlement to overtime or breaks).[80] Employers must register workers in private residences.[81] The Act also prohibits employers from charging fees from requesting, charging, or receiving payment from any worker for employment opportunities.[82]

A group of migrant live-in caregivers successfully used this regime to recover fees charged unlawfully by a nanny agency, which had implicitly included job-finding fees in its service agreement with them. The agency was required to repay fees to the workers in the amount of $25,987, and a single $500 fine was imposed, and these decisions were upheld by the Supreme Court of British Columbia on judicial review.[83] In 2012, 64 migrant agricultural workers used this regime to receive a total of $49,672.07 in unpaid wages, with interest, from their employer, who also received two fines of $500 each.[84]

In British Columbia, the Employment Standards Branch is active in investigations, conducting several thousand per year, and issuing over a thousand penalties a year on average. However, it does not track the migration status of workers; it is therefore impossible to know the extent to which migrant workers make use of this process. The Branch includes a team specific to farm labour compliance, in which migrant labour is prevalent, and reports several dozen contravention orders on average per year, but this team does not capture data on migrant workers specifically. No prosecutions for breaches of regulatory offences have been reported under this Act for the past five years.[85]

V. ANTI-DISCRIMINATION LAW

Human rights law in Canada is regulated by each individual jurisdiction – each province and territory has its own human rights statute, and there is a federal code as well. Most workers and employers are subject to provincial human rights law, as the federal code applies to a limited subset of workers. Canada's federal Canadian Human Rights Act applies only to workers in the federal jurisdiction, such as federal government employees, the national postal service, and aviation and railway workers. This Act does not define 'employee', and in theory would not exclude unauthorised migrant workers, but in practice it is highly unlikely that they would be employed in the federal sectors to which the Act applies.

[80] Employment Standards Regulation BC Reg 396/95 (ESR), s 18.

[81] ESA, s 15.

[82] ibid, s 10.

[83] *Prince George Nannies and Caregivers Ltd. v British Columbia (Employment Standards Tribunal)*, 2010 BCSC 883.

[84] *BC EST #D061/12*.

[85] Response LBR-2017-72206 provided on 31 July 2017 to a request under the Freedom of Information and Protection of Privacy Act.

Compared to employment standards, human rights laws provide a broader range of remedies, including significant compensatory remedies. Moreover, these provincial statutes apply equally to all workers, regardless of migration status. Although human rights decisions made by a tribunal are not binding on subsequent tribunals or courts, they have persuasive value across jurisdictions. Remedial options available to human rights tribunals include compensation for injury to dignity, payment of lost wages, job reinstatement, and orders to the employer to cease the contravention and to change its policies.

All human rights legislation in Canada prohibits discrimination by employers based on specified grounds, which usually include such grounds as sex, gender identity or expression, sexual orientation, race, colour, ancestry, place of origin, disability, and age.[86] Employers are prohibited from discriminating on prohibited grounds in wages, hiring practices, and conditions of work. The utility of human rights law to resolve workplace problems for migrant workers is though limited to those matters which can be framed as discriminatory on the basis of these listed grounds. Of particular relevance here is the 'place of origin' ground, which has been defined in case law to encompass place of birth, including country of birth, and can include being born in a particular group of countries.[87] It has also been held to be broader than simply 'place of birth', and to include, for example, discrimination on the basis of where a person obtained their professional credentials.[88]

Immigration status is not protected as such in any Canadian jurisdiction. Furthermore, the Federal Court of Appeal has rejected the argument that 'migration status' is an analogous ground of discrimination under the Canadian Charter of Rights and Freedoms.[89] Poor treatment on the basis of migration status, even when it is racialising, does not fit within these human rights concepts. Consider for example a construction site which employs Canadian people of Mexican origin, as well as Colombian and Mexican authorised and unauthorised migrant workers. If the employer pays the Colombian workers more than then Mexican workers, it commits a human rights violation. If it pays the Mexican migrant workers less than the Canadian workers of Mexican origin, it would be discriminating on the basis of nationality, albeit not race or ethnicity. If, however, it pays all migrant workers less than all Canadian workers, there would be no easy fit within human rights law, because 'migration status'

[86] See, eg, British Columbia Human Rights Code RSBC 1996 c 210, s 11. Ontario's *Human Rights Code* additionally prohibits discrimination based on ethnic origin, creed, and citizenship. In all jurisdictions, employers may defend discrimination claims by establishing that the distinction in question is a bona fide occupational requirement. For a comprehensive overview of human rights law across Canada, see RW Zinn and PP Brethour, *The Law of Human Rights in Canada: Practice and Procedure* (Canada Law Book, 1996).

[87] *Bitonti et al v The College of Physicians and Surgeons of BC et al* 1999 BCHRT 63 148.

[88] *Mihaly v Assn. of Professional Engineers, Geologists and Geophysicists of Alberta* 2014 AHRC 1.

[89] *Toussaint v The Attorney General of Canada*, 2010 FC 810, leave to appeal to the Supreme Court of Canada dismissed.

is not a protected ground. The same conclusion would apply if unauthorised migrant workers were paid less than authorised migrant workers, unless the two groups were also distinct from each other on the basis of race, nationality, or another enumerated ground.

Despite these limitations, human rights law provides viable remedies to migrant workers where their complaints can be framed within existing grounds of protection. Furthermore, recent cases include an analysis of the particular vulnerability of migration workers which, while not amounting to formal protection on the basis of immigration status per se, allow tribunals to consider the role of non-permanent migration status in amplifying the risk to workers. Tribunals appear willing to consider human rights claims regardless of status irregularities of the worker, which makes them a potential venue for both authorised and undocumented migrant workers.[90]

One of the first cases to explicitly consider the human rights claims of migrant workers – and to use 'place of origin' discrimination – was *SELI*, decided by the British Columbia Human Rights Tribunal in 2008.[91] In that case, a construction employer site provided different wages and working conditions to two different groups of foreign workers: one of eastern European origin, the other of Latin American origin. The employer argued that its differential wage policy constituted a 'bona fide occupational requirement', as the wages offered varied with the economic position of the country of origin so as to be better than local wages in the particular country in question. Thus, it argued, higher wages were required to recruit workers from European countries in which wages were higher as compared to local wages in Latin America. The tribunal rejected this argument, finding that:

> In effect, the application of SELI's actual international compensation practices to the Latin Americans employed by them on the Canada Line project was to take advantage of the existing disadvantaged position of these workers, who are from poorer countries, and to perpetuate that disadvantage, and to do so while they were living and working within the province of British Columbia. As such, the application of those practices in British Columbia perpetuated, compounded and entrenched existing patterns of inequality.[92]

The tribunal found that these workers had experienced employer discrimination based on 'a constellation of identifiable characteristics related to the grounds of race, colour, ancestry and place of origin'.[93] The Latin American workers were successful and obtained orders for the cessation of the employer's practices, back wages to compensate for the wage differential, and damages for injury to dignity.[94]

[90] *Bolcato v Magranite Industry* 2017 BCHRT 54 [6].
[91] *C.S.W.U. Local 1611 v SELI Canada and others* (No. 8) (SELI), 2008 BCHRT 436.
[92] ibid, [489].
[93] ibid, [248].
[94] ibid, [529].

In a more recent decision, the Ontario Human Rights Tribunal considered a complaint of sexual assault and harassment by two Mexican women workers at a fish processing plant. It is significant that the tribunal specifically considered their status as migrant workers in assessing appropriate remedies. It found that the employer had used threats to return the workers to Mexico to enforce sexual demands on the workers, and explicitly considered the impact of the federal work permit system on workers' labour vulnerability:

> While theoretically possible to transfer employment to another employer while in Canada, there are significant barriers that make this practically impossible or at least very difficult. As a result, a migrant worker like O.P.T. tends to be reliant upon the employment relationship with the designated employer to a degree that is not experienced by Canadian workers. Migrant workers like O.P.T. live under the ever-present threat of having their designated employer decide to end the employment relationship, for which they require no reason and for which there is no appeal or review, and being 'repatriated' to their home country and thereby losing the significant economic and financial advantages of their Canadian employment upon which they and their families depend.[95]

This worker was awarded $150,000 in damages for injury to dignity – one of the largest human rights awards in Canadian history. Subsequent to that decision, the Ontario Human Rights Tribunal considered the 'foreign worker status' of an applicant as a factor increasing monetary damages.[96]

Human rights tribunals have also protected domestic workers and agricultural workers, who are among the most vulnerable workers in Canada. In 2013, the Ontario Human Rights Tribunal heard a claim from a migrant agricultural worker whose employment had been terminated, and who had been repatriated, after complaining to the employer about racial slurs on his jobsite.[97] The Tribunal received expert academic evidence on the unique vulnerabilities of migrant workers and the connection between fear of deportation and workers' reluctance to report workplace concerns. It found that the employer had discriminated on the basis of race, colour, ancestry, ethnic origin and place of origin in making the comments, and that the employer had retaliated against the worker for having complained about a human rights issue by terminating the worker's position. The tribunal awarded lost wages plus $3,000 for injury to dignity.

A 2015 British Columbia case considered the situation of an undocumented caregiver from the Philippines. The complainant had accompanied her employers to Canada after working as a caregiver for their children in Hong Kong in exploitative conditions. The employers pressured the caregiver to come to Canada, and did not secure a work permit, relying instead on a tourist visa

[95] *O.P.T. v Presteve Foods Ltd.*, 2015 HRTO 675, [216].
[96] *Ben Saad v 1544982 Ontario Inc.*, 2017 HRTO 1.
[97] *Monrose v Double Diamond Acres Limited* 2013 HRTO 1273.

for her. The Tribunal heard evidence that this worker was subjected to sexual assault and other abuse by her employer, had inadequate food and housing, and was subject to an extreme degree of control and isolation, working illegally long hours for little pay. It considered expert evidence on the stereotypes and prejudices that are often applied to Filipina domestic workers, and applied an intersectional approach to find that the employer's treatment amounted to discrimination on the basis of age, sex, family status, colour, ancestry and place of origin.[98] The tribunal awarded lost wages and $50,000 for injury to dignity.[99]

VI. COMMON LAW REMEDIES

For many workers in Canada, and particularly for higher-earning workers, the most financially substantial remedies are not those available through tribunals and regulatory structures, but those available at common law. Common law remedies hold particular potential for migrant workers who have been dismissed from employment, for example for fixed-term migrant workers, or where there are situations of consequential economic loss specific to labour migration, such as repatriation costs or other costs flowing from an absence of labour mobility. As with Canadian workers, migrant workers have access to larger damages awards through common law than through employment standards tribunals. While there is no aspect of contractual remedy that deals specifically with structural vulnerabilities, damages for breach of fiduciary duty have been adjudicated for migrant workers in exploitative situations in which the employer has an implied or express undertaking to act in their interests. While neither of these causes of action allows courts to exercise regulatory control over employers, the size and scope of remedies, including the potential for punitive damages, may provide an indirect deterrent. The potential for migrant workers to rely upon contract law and to claim breach of fiduciary duty are considered in turn in this section.

A. Breach of Contract

Workers can use the common law to enforce the express terms of written employment contracts, as well as their implied terms. Primary among the latter is the requirement for reasonable notice of termination, or payment in lieu thereof. Ongoing employees who are terminated can also pursue an action for wrongful dismissal, and if successful, courts award damages based on a reasonable notice period. However, many migrant workers are not ongoing employees – especially

[98] *PN v FR and another (No. 2)*, 2015 BCHRT 60 [92].
[99] ibid, [137].

those hired on closed work permits, who are often on a fixed-term contract, or a series of fixed-term contracts. If their contract is prematurely terminated, they can seek damages for the remaining duration of the contract.[100] For example, in *Tigchelaar*, a group of migrant agricultural workers' employments were terminated partway through their fixed-term contracts, and they were repatriated to Mexico. The workers commenced an action in wrongful dismissal and subsequently settled with the employer out of court on undisclosed terms.[101]

The availability of remedies to unauthorised migrant workers could be limited by way of the doctrine of illegality, according to which a worker's lack of migration status renders their employment contract void. The doctrine of illegality has not yet been applied in common law employment cases in Canada with regard to undocumented workers. This doctrine has though been applied narrowly in other contexts. In *Still v MNR*, the Federal Court of Appeal considered the case of an undocumented housekeeper who had applied for unemployment insurance benefits based on time worked while out of status. The Court of Appeal found that any analysis of the doctrine of illegality should consider public policy, including both the purposes of immigration law and the purposes of the statute in question. The Court of Appeal made clear that the worker's knowledge and behaviour could be considered in this policy analysis; for Ms Still, the fact that she unknowingly fell out of status in 'good faith' was relevant to the Court's refusal to apply the doctrine. It distinguished her situation from that of 'those cases where a person gains entry to this country through stealth or deception'.[102]

In contract cases, there is also the potential for claims on the basis of documented psychological harm, and for consequential economic loss – for example, the loss of expected employment insurance benefits for a seasonal worker.[103] Punitive damages may also be awarded against an employer, where a worker can show that the employer engaged in malicious conduct amounting to an independent actionable wrong.[104]

Courts also consider migrant workers' particular vulnerabilities in decision-making. In one example, a live-in caregiver whose employer controlled her bank account successfully argued that her claim was not discoverable until she regained control of the account years later, and realised that she had been underpaid wages. The court extended the statutory limitation period for her claim. The plaintiff had worked for the employer for nine years and was awarded 10 months' salary in lieu of reasonable notice, in addition to compensation for

[100] *Howard v Benson Group Inc. (The Benson Group Inc.)* 2016 ONCA 256.

[101] *Tigchelaar Berry Farms v Espinoza* 2013 ONSC 1506.

[102] *Still v M.N.R.* [1998] 1 FCR 549, para 53. See also *Decision No. 1896/15 2016* ONWSIAT 51. For a comparative discussion of the use of the doctrine of illegality in the UK, the US, and Canada, see LA Bihari, 'Clashing Laws: Exploring the Employment Rights of Undocumented Migrants' (2011) 69 *University of Toronto Faculty Law Review* 9.

[103] *Jean v Pêcheries Roger L. Ltée* 2010 NBCA 10.

[104] *Boucher v Wal-Mart Canada Corp.* 2014 ONCA 419.

underpayments and for failure to pay overtime.[105] In another live-in caregiver case, the worker was treated as an ongoing employee on the basis that her employment relationship was indefinite, even though she had a term-based work permit – ie, an implicit assumption was made that the work permit would have been extended. The court in that case extended the period of reasonable notice required due to the lack of availability of similar employment.[106]

Employers are also able to sue workers – including migrant workers – at common law for breach of contract. While the threat of a lawsuit from one's employer might be particularly intimidating for migrant workers, such claims by employers are viewed sceptically by courts, and there is room for the fashioning of remedies in favour of the worker, rather than the employer. For example, in a case in Alberta, an employer attempted to recover damages from a migrant caregiver for having ended her work term early.[107] In that case, the worker had sustained an ankle injury, and was medically unable to work, but resigned when the employer continued to request that she carry out her duties. The Provincial Court of Alberta treated the employer's insistence on the worker's performance of duties while injured as a repudiatory breach amounting to constructive dismissal. The judgment also specified that in any case the employer should not be able to recover recruitment and transportation fees from the worker. While this reasoning would apply to any worker, regardless of migration status, migrant workers are far more likely that others to have employer-paid transportation and recruitment costs.[108]

B. Breach of Fiduciary Duty

Employment relationships are not prima facie of a fiduciary nature, but may instead be designated as such on an ad hoc basis. Even where there is a clear power-dependency relationship favouring the employer, to be considered a fiduciary relationship, there must also be an express or implied undertaking that the employer (fiduciary) will act in the best interests of the worker.[109] However, where there is evidence of such an undertaking, there is a potential remedy for breach of fiduciary duty, if there is also exploitation, such as through excessive hours, lack of pay, coercion, and isolation of the worker. For example, in the case of *Mustaji v Tjin*, the British Columbia Supreme Court considered the situation of a domestic worker, finding that the employer had failed to remit mandatory deductions, that the worker had been subjected to extremely long

[105] *Fernandes v Goveas* 2016 ONSC 1992.
[106] *Pascua v Khul-Schachter* 2013 CanLII 47860.
[107] *Ludwig v Bergonio*, 2013 ABPC 367.
[108] ibid.
[109] *Perez v Galambos* 2009 SCC 48.

hours, including unpaid overtime, and that the employer kept her in a situation of fear and isolation in which she was unable to negotiate her conditions of employment. The trial court applied the test of whether 'given all the surrounding circumstances, one party could reasonably have expected that the other party would act in the former's best interests with respect to the subject matter at issue', considering, inter alia, 'discretion, influence, vulnerability, and trust'.[110] It found that the employers

> had the opportunity to exercise power or discretion over the affairs of the plaintiff, were capable of using that power or discretion without the plaintiff's knowledge or consent so as to affect her legal and practical interests, and that the plaintiff was especially vulnerable to the defendants' exercise of that discretion or control.[111]

The court distinguished this as an ad hoc fiduciary relationship because, unlike a doctor-patient or analogous relationship, the inherent purpose of the relationship was not 'to compel the defendants to act in the plaintiff's interests', but rather was 'essentially contractual'[112] with individual features giving rise to a specific instance of a fiduciary relationship. In addition to awarding damages for breach of contract for unpaid wages and deductions, the trial judge awarded exemplary and punitive damages for breach of fiduciary duty in the amount of $175,000 (in 1995).[113] A more recent decision confirms the principles enunciated in *Mustaji*, while holding that the power disparity engendered by the structure of the foreign worker programme itself will be insufficient to establish a fiduciary relationship, where the employer does not exercise control over the affairs of the worker.[114]

The necessity of proving the individual instance of fiduciary adds an evidentiary burden but is not necessarily a bar to collective action by workers. In 2012, in *Dominguez v Northland Properties Corporation*, the British Columbia Supreme Court certified Canada's first class action for migrant workers.[115] A group of migrant workers who had come to Canada to work for the Denny's restaurant chain were made to pay thousands of dollars to recruiters to secure their jobs, were not given the full-time hours they were promised, and were not paid overtime, or their airfares, as required under their contract. The Court certified the workers' class action for breach of contract and also for breach of fiduciary duty – not as a categorical fiduciary relationship, but as an individual, fact-based instance of such a relationship. It found that the

[110] *Mustaji v Tjin*, [1995] B.C.J. No. 39, para 19.
[111] ibid, para 27.
[112] ibid, para 29.
[113] ibid, upheld in *Mustaji v Tjin*,1996 CanLII 1907 (BCCA).
[114] *Nishina v Azuma Foods (Canada) Ltd*. 2010 BCSC 502. Note that even in the absence of a fiduciary duty, punitive damages may be awarded where the employer breaches the obligation of fair dealing and good faith in the manner of dismissal.
[115] *Dominguez v Northland Properties Corp*. 2012 BCSC 328.

workers' closed permits created vulnerability, forming the basis for a potential claim in breach of fiduciary duty. The path thus was cleared for the workers to argue for damages both on the basis of their employment contract, and on the basis of the extra-contractual features which arose due to the nature of the temporary foreign work programme under which they came to Canada. The case was eventually settled, with the terms including entitlement to payment for full-time hours (even when the workers were assigned fewer hours), overtime payment for overtime hours, compensation for fees paid by workers to a recruiter, as well as *cy près* payments to charities serving migrant workers and children.[116]

VII. COLLECTIVE LABOUR RIGHTS

In the private sector, where the vast majority of migrant workers are employed, unionisation rates are low and decreasing; the overall private sector unionisation rate in Canada was 15.8 per cent in 2018.[117] However, there are some recent examples of the unionisation of migrant workers, and of attention to their particular needs. In 2010, the United Food and Commercial Workers obtained conditional certification of a bargaining unit comprised entirely of migrant farm workers in British Columbia.[118] In 2015, the British Columbia Labour Board refused to grant decertification in this case, finding that 'the true wishes of the employees are unlikely to be disclosed by the vote due to improper interference by Mexican officials responsible for administering the [Seasonal Agricultural Workers' Program]'.[119] In Alberta, a branch (local 1118) of the same union negotiated a collective agreement clause in 2011 requiring the employer to support the permanent residence applications of all of its migrant workers, to provide information on immigration requirements, and to offer English language classes.[120]

While it is evident from these examples that unionisation is possible, and its benefits made available to some migrant workers, others have less access to these protections. Notably, in Ontario, the province with the largest number of

[116] ibid.

[117] Statistics Canada, Table 14-10-0070-01, 'Union Coverage by Industry, annual (x 1,000)' available at www150.statcan.gc.ca/t1/tbl1/en/tv.action?pid=1410007001 [last accessed 25 March 2022].

[118] *Sidhu & Sons Nursery Ltd. v United Food and Commercial Workers International Union, Local 1518* BCLRB B26/2010 (Leave for Reconsideration denied in No. B64/2010).

[119] *BC LRB No B56/2014*, para 95. The admissibility of evidence of the conduct of Mexican consular officials was contested by the Government of Mexico as far as the British Columbia Court of Appeal, which ruled the evidence admissible. See *United Mexican States v British Columbia (Labour Relations Board)*, 2015 BCCA 32.

[120] Collective Agreement between Olymel and UFCW Local 1118 available at work.alberta.ca/apps/cba/docs/50289-2011-02-01-2016-01-31-CBA-redact.pdf [last accessed 25 March 2022].

agricultural migrant workers in Canada, agricultural workers are governed by a separate labour statute with limited rights relative to other workers. While this exclusion does not specifically mention migrant workers, agricultural work is by far the largest single sector in which migrant workers are hired in Canada, and the numbers are growing: in 2017, the most recent year for which full data are available, a total of 48,185 migrant workers entered Canada for agricultural work, which is almost double the number recorded in 2006.[121] The complete exclusion of farmworkers from laws protecting unionisation and collective bargaining in Ontario was found to be unconstitutional by the Supreme Court of Canada in 2001.[122] The Ontario Government responded with the Agricultural Employees Protection Act 2002, which provided farmworkers with the right to form or join an 'employees' association', to assemble, and to make representations to their employers. Unlike standard labour legislation, it does not expressly protect the right to good faith bargaining, the right for workers to have their representations heard by the employer, the right to exclusive representation by an organisation representing workers' collective interests, or the right to strike in the case of bargaining failure. This Act too was challenged on constitutional grounds, with the Supreme Court of Canada upholding it by a narrow margin. The majority found that the constitutional right to freedom of association includes collective bargaining, with minimum requirements of good faith bargaining and a meaningful process for workers, but that a particular process (such as that contained in standard labour laws) is not the only means by which this right can be protected by legislatures. It found that the Agricultural Employees Protection Act met the constitutional minimum despite providing significantly fewer protections on the assumption that a duty to bargain in good faith was an implied duty in the legislation.[123] Since coming into force in 2003, there have been no reported decisions based on farmworker complaints under this legislation.

VIII. CONCLUSION

In Canada, formal equality is extended to migrant workers through the universal applicability of employment standards and common law remedies to all workers. Substantive equality, however, demands attention to the circumstances of migrant workers, including the impact of differential migration status created through immigration law. The resulting vulnerability of workers could be

[121] IRCC, 'Canada-Temporary Foreign Worker Program (TFWP) work permit holders by province/territory' (Table TR-0010) available at open.canada.ca [last accessed 25 March 2022].

[122] *Dunmore v Ontario (Attorney General)*, [2001] 3 SCR 1016.

[123] *Ontario (Attorney General) v Fraser* 2011 SCC 20. For a detailed treatment of this case, see F Faraday, J Fudge and E Tucker, *Constitutional Labour Rights in Canada: Farm Workers and the Fraser Case* (Toronto, Irwin, 2012).

addressed directly through the abolition of temporary status, and the provision of permanent status to all those who enter Canada to work. Given Canada's longstanding reliance on migrant labour with temporary migration status, however, it is unlikely that migration law will be restructured in this way.

Assuming no change in underlying immigration law, steps toward substantive equality for migrant workers in Canada could be pursued through critical attention to legal rights and remedial options, in order to respond to the endemic rights and standards shortfalls migrant workers face. Whether through regulatory structures or the common law, remedies are more likely to provide meaningful redress if they explicitly take account of the underlying structural features which shape the vulnerability of migrant workers relative to citizen workers. While systems and precedents based on the experiences of citizen workers are unlikely to provide an adequate response, cases fought and won by migrant workers show increased responsiveness in the law and can serve as signposts for further improvement. Specifically, the creation of provincial legislation designed to protect foreign workers, such as exists in Ontario, Manitoba, and Saskatchewan, plays both a normative and a practical role and could be implemented across Canada. Whether through the creation of specific legislation or the amendment of general employment standards laws, this example could be followed by increasing the compensatory and deterrent approaches which are specific to migrant workers – for example, heightened penalties where the complaint involves a migrant worker, restitution as a remedial option, or extra compensation where a worker faces migration consequences as a result of the employer's breach. Similarly, labour codes could include amendments to add protections specific to the organisation of migrant workers, such as express inclusion of migrant workers in the definition of 'employee', or through specific reference to coercion or exploitation on the basis of migration status, such as threatening deportation, in the prohibition of unfair labour practices. While any such measures would be limited by provinces' lack of ability to actually extend or confer migration status, they could be tied in with provincial selection programmes, in which the provinces' endorsement of migrants renders them eligible for permanent residence at the federal level.

The increasingly sophisticated analysis of migrant workers' vulnerability in anti-discrimination claims before human rights tribunals holds promise in that venue, as well, and shows the potential for expansive advocacy, even without legislative change. Including migration status as a listed ground of protection would strengthen the potential of human rights legislation to protect migrant workers against discrimination by employers. Common law cases concerning the employment relationship, including both wrongful dismissal and actions on the basis of breach of fiduciary duty likewise provide a solid framework for further advocacy. As is the case with low-wage citizen workers, lack of access to courts creates a barrier both to an adequate remedy and to the development of the common law to robustly consider migrant worker issues. Courts have however been willing to consider the particular vulnerabilities of migrant workers by addressing labour mobility issues, and by recognising situations of extreme power imbalance in which a fiduciary relationship can be said to arise.

The new regulatory innovations making employers' compliance with provincial standards a condition of their ability to hire migrant workers also holds promise. This approach may fail to meet their full potential while it lacks protections for workers who report their employers, or who are put out of work due to employer-based sanctions. Compliance regimes should provide for and assess penalties which provide an effective deterrent. For corporate employers, paying a \$500 or \$1,000 fine may not provide deterrence, but larger fines, prosecutions, or penalties affecting the business licensing of the employer may be more effective. Employer sanctions should always take into account the potential effect on workers and provide associated protections, such as clear and publicised 'firewalls' between employment standards laws and immigration status determination. As Bridget Anderson has noted, however, a firewall is much more effective if it operates in conjunction with the provision of labour mobility to migrant workers on par with citizens.[124] The absence of such protections in the new compliance regulations under immigration law may well undermine the efficacy of what would otherwise be a robust instrument for employer compliance because workers are likely to face immigration consequences for the wrongs of their employer.

In both compensatory and compliance-based measures, lawmakers and courts should follow the developments that recognise the particular situation of migrant workers, and could thereby correct the longstanding construction of migrant workers as simply commodified labour; by picking up these more hopeful threads, they can continue to build on an approach in which the rights and interests of migrant workers are protected.

[124] B Anderson, 'Migrants and Work-related Rights' (2008) 22 *Ethics & International Affairs* 199, 202.

7

Exploitation of Unauthorised Migrant Workers in Australia: Access to the Protection of Employment Law

LAURIE BERG AND BASSINA FARBENBLUM

I. INTRODUCTION

UNAUTHORISED WORKERS ARE notoriously susceptible to exploitative working conditions across the western world.[1] However, western legal systems differ markedly in their approach to according labour rights to this vulnerable group of workers. There are still great divergences when it comes to enforcement of labour standards for unauthorised work, and in the extent to which, when these migrants are exploited at work, they can access government assistance and recover their wages.

This chapter examines the work experiences of migrants engaging in unauthorised work in Australia. These workers include individuals who have overstayed their visa, and those who have worked in breach of their visa conditions. The latter include tourists, and international students who have exceeded the number of work hours permitted under their visa.[2] The chapter explores the legislative framework and the unsettled body of case law concerning the entitlement of unauthorised workers to basic employment protections.[3] It also reviews

[1] Although the term 'illegal worker' is used by the Department of Home Affairs (DHA), and is often found in the Australian media, this chapter uses the term 'unauthorised migrant worker'. This term acknowledges that some permission (to remain or to work or both) has been withheld. But it also suggests the possibility of change of status, and in particular the ability of a government authority (whether the department or parliament) to effect that change.

[2] L Berg, *Migrant Rights at Work: Law's Precariousness at the Intersection of Immigration and Labour* (Oxfordshire, Routledge, 2016) 150–55.

[3] In Australia, labour law (also known as employment or industrial relations law) is extremely complex. It contains rights and obligations for workers and employers in a range of different instruments, including a mix of federal, state and territory statutes and regulations, industry-based awards authorised by tribunals which have the force of legislation, registered enterprise agreements setting out conditions in a business, and common law principles, especially those related to contracts of employment. As this chapter deals with underpayments of minimum wage, it considers primarily the Fair Work Act 2009 (Cth) and its interaction with contract law and the Migration Act 1958 (Cth).

a range of government policies and attitudes which have historically prioritised immigration compliance goals over the enforcement of labour rights for these migrant workers. Finally, it considers the extent to which exploited unauthorised workers are able to access assistance from Australia's federal labour inspectorate, the Fair Work Ombudsman (FWO), and recover their wages in practice.[4]

This study draws on the authors' broader empirical research on access to justice for temporary and unauthorised workers in Australia. This included field research conducted between 2016 and 2017 in Sydney, Melbourne, Brisbane, Adelaide and Canberra, involving six focus groups with 26 temporary migrants in Sydney, Melbourne and Brisbane, and 36 interviews with a range of stakeholders involving government agencies, legal service providers, advocates, unions, and five temporary migrants.[5] Together with Stephen Clibborn, the authors also conducted the National Temporary Migrant Work Survey in 2016, which yielded 4,322 responses from individuals who have worked on a temporary visa in Australia, including 281 who had engaged in unauthorised work in breach of their visa conditions.[6] That survey was distributed to temporary migrant workers via social media and email lists of unions and service-providers, and asked participants about the wages and other conditions in their lowest paid job in Australia, as well as a range of questions about their experiences, perceptions and knowledge of their rights at work.

Our analysis reveals a lack of clarity as to the protections accorded to unauthorised work under the Fair Work Act 2009 (Cth), which is the statutory framework underpinning Australia's minimum employment laws and agency bodies. In addition, there appears to be a practice among government agencies in Australia of differential treatment of the two subsets of unauthorised workers: those, including international students, who work in breach of temporary visas authorising work (likely the vast majority), and those working in breach of visas that do not permit work, or who work having overstayed a valid visa. In relation to the first group, the immigration authorities appear to be more willing to overlook breaches of work-related visa conditions in exercising discretion not to cancel visas and initiate removal from Australia. The same discretion does not seem to be accorded to unauthorised workers who do not hold visas

[4] For detailed discussion of other temporary migrant workers' access to employment protections and recovery of wages in Australia, see: Berg (n 2); L Berg, S Dehm and A Vogl, 'Refugees and Asylum Seekers as Workers: Radical Temporariness and Labour Exploitation in Australia' (2022) 45 *University of New South Wales Law Journal* 35; A Reilly, L Berg, J Howe and B Farbenblum, 'Understanding International Students' Professed Satisfaction with Underpaid Work in Australia' (2020) 46 *Monash University Law Review* 50; J Howe, L Berg and B Farbenblum, 'Unfair Dismissal Law and Temporary Migrant Labour in Australia' (2018) 46 *Federal Law Review* 19; B Farbenblum and L Berg, 'Migrant Workers' Access to Remedy for Exploitation in Australia: The Role of the National Fair Work Ombudsman' (2017) 23 *Australian Journal of Human Rights* 310 and UNSW Human Rights Law Clinic, *Temporary Migrant Workers in Australia* (Issues Paper, 15 October 2015).

[5] References to interviews and focus groups in subsequent footnotes are to this field research.

[6] L Berg and B Farbenblum, *Wage Theft in Australia: Findings of the National Temporary Migrant Work Survey* (2017) 46.

with work rights. Further, in response to intense media coverage of systemic underpayment of international students, and given the very large numbers of international students who have traditionally studied and worked in Australia, the FWO appears to be more willing to deliberately involve them in its investigations and provide them with targeted assistance to recover unpaid wages. However, in keeping with Australia's long-standing deference to immigration compliance, there is no comprehensive or predictable protection against visa cancellation for students who have breached their work-related visa condition and seek the assistance of the labour regulator.

Indeed, serious barriers remain to unauthorised workers in Australia recovering their wages in practice. We therefore conclude this chapter with suggested regulatory reforms. These include legislative action to ensure the validity of employment contracts of those engaging in unauthorised work and an enforceable firewall regarding immigration status to decrease unauthorised workers' fear of detection when seeking FWO assistance.

II. THE CONTOURS OF UNAUTHORISED WORK IN AUSTRALIA

There are good reasons to think that unauthorised migrant labour in Australia occurs on a far more limited scale than elsewhere in the world. This is primarily because both Australia's geographic isolation and lack of contiguous land borders prevent clandestine entry, and facilitate the strict monitoring of arrivals and departures by means of a universal visa system. Australia's own Auditor-General has concluded that the country's immigration compliance arrangements are 'arguably the most effective of any country in the world'.[7] These compliance systems mean that the numbers of migrants who are present without a right to remain are small but known. By contrast, the extent of visa-holders working in contravention of their particular visa conditions is 'not well understood'.[8] A government-commissioned review of unauthorised migrant labour in Australia in 2011 posited that roughly 100,000 people may work without permission in Australia at any one time, or around 0.8 per cent of the Australian workforce.[9]

[7] Australian National Audit Office, *Onshore Compliance – Visa Overstayers and Non-Citizens Working Illegally: Department of Immigration and Multicultural and Indigenous Affairs* (the Auditor-General Audit Report No 2, 2004–05) 20.

[8] Australian National Audit Office, *Managing Compliance with Visa Conditions: Department of Immigration and Border Protection* (Auditor-General, ANAO Report No 13, 2015–16) 8.

[9] S Howells, *Report of the 2010 Review of the Migration Amendment (Employer Sanctions) Act 2007* (Cth of Australia, 2011) 12. This rudimentary estimation was based on adding the 53,900 non-citizens in Australia at that time having overstayed their visa (recorded in the Department of Immigration and Citizenship *Annual Report 2019–10*) to the unknown number of non-citizens working in breach of visa conditions which 'it is not possible to determine or even estimate' (at 26).

A. Who are Unauthorised Workers in Australia?

The first group of unauthorised workers are those who are present without a visa. Since all non-citizens in Australia require a visa in order to lawfully remain, and virtually no one has ever entered Australia without detection, these unauthorised migrants are all overstayers. There may be anywhere from 60,000 to 100,000 undocumented workers in Australia.[10] The Department of Home Affairs (DHA) estimated that there were 62,900 visa overstayers as at 30 June 2018. In most cases, these visa holders entered Australia on a subclass 600 visitor visa and applied for an asylum visa once onshore.[11] This produces a ratio of unlawful non-citizens to total population in Australia of about 1:450, compared to the ratio of 1:29 in the US, where there were an estimated 11 million undocumented migrants in 2016,[12] or 1:100 in the UK, where the number of unauthorised residents in 2007 was estimated at 618,000.[13] According to statistics released by the DHA in 2014, the largest proportions of overstayers were from China (12.3 per cnet), Malaysia (10.2 per cent), the US (8.3 per cent), the UK (6 per cent), and India (5.5 per cent).[14] It has been estimated that, as of 2015, 25 per cent of overstayers had overstayed their visa by between 5 and 15 years, and a further 28 per cent had overstayed by 15 years or more.[15]

The remaining unauthorised workers are made up of two groups of visa-holders who engage in work contrary to their visa conditions. One such group comprises individuals who are working while holding a visa that prohibits work entirely. These are largely tourists, but may also be asylum seekers who arrived by boat without authorisation, and who have ultimately, after a long period in immigration detention, been offered temporary bridging visas without work rights.

The other group are those who are working contrary to work limitations on their visas. The pool of temporary visa-holders with restricted work authorisation in Australia has grown dramatically since the 1990s. While Australia has

[10] J Azarias, R Nettle and J Williams (National Agricultural Labour Advisory Committee), 'National Agricultural Workforce Strategy: Learning to Excel (Department of Agriculture, Water and the Environment' (Cth), December 2020) 206; Department of Immigration and Border Protection (Cth), BE17/172 – 'Visa Overstays for the Financial Year – Programme 1.2: Border Management (Budget Estimates Hearing, Question Taken on Notice', 22 May 2017).

[11] Department of Home Affairs (Cth), Incoming Government Brief (2019) 172. The Department of Home Affairs (DHA) is Australia's federal agency responsible for federal law enforcement, national security, immigration and border-related functions. It was preceded by the Department of Immigration and Border Protection (DIBP), which operated between 2013 and 2017.

[12] J Passel and D'Vera Cohn, 'Overall Number of US Unauthorised Immigrants Holds Steady Since 2009' (Pew Hispanic Centre, September 2016) available at www.pewresearch.org/hispanic/2016/09/20/overall-number-of-u-s-unauthorized-immigrants-holds-steady-since-2009/ [last accessed 24 March 2022].

[13] I Gordon, K Scanlon, T Travers and C ME Whitehead, *Economic Impact on the London and UK Economy of an Earned Regularisation of Irregular Migrants to the UK* (Greater London Authority, GLA Economics, 2009) 48.

[14] DIBP, *Australia's Migration Trends 2012–13* (2014) 78.

[15] Australian National Audit Office (n 7) 22.

historically prioritised permanent residence, from 2000 the net migration gain from long-term temporary movement exceeded that from permanent movement, effecting a transformational shift to temporary migration.[16] If we exclude New Zealanders, whose work rights are unrestricted, as of 2016, there were over 878,000 temporary migrants with work rights in Australia, comprising 11 per cent of the Australian labour market.[17]

For decades, international students have been the largest group of temporary visa-holders in Australia with work entitlements. The number of international students in Australia fell dramatically during the period when Australia's national borders were closed to all temporary visa holders (between 20 March 2020 and 1 December 2021) in response to COVID-19. However, prior to the pandemic, international students had surged: in 2018 there were more than 525,000 the number of international students in Australia.[18] Over one-third were from China (20 per cent) or India (15 per cent).[19] Prior to the COVID border closures, Australia was the third most popular destination for international students after the US and UK, although international students comprised a far greater proportion of the Australian population than its competitors.[20] Indeed, it was predicted, in the years before COVID, that Australia would soon overtake the UK in terms of actual numbers of incoming students.[21]

As funding for the higher education sector has become increasingly reliant on international student fees,[22] there is a significant incentive and effort across government to maintain a positive image of international students' experience in Australia. While some international students may come from wealthy families, this is not the case for many of them. In one survey, around half of international undergraduate students were worried about their financial situation and one in seven regularly went without food or other necessities because they could not afford them.[23] A large subgroup is undertaking short English language or

[16] P Mares, *Not Quite Australia: How Temporary Migration is Changing the Nation* (Melbourne, Text Publishing, 2016); G Hugo, 'A New Paradigm of International Migration: Implications for Migration Policy and Planning in Australia', Information and Research Services, Parliamentary Library, Research Paper No 10, 2003–04, March 2004.

[17] Senate Education and Employment References Committee, *A National Disgrace: The Exploitation of Temporary Work Visa Holders* (March 2016) 15; DIBP, *Temporary Entrants and New Zealand Citizens in Australia: As at 31 December 2016* (2016) 3.

[18] N Robinson, 'Australia Hosting Unprecedented Numbers of International Students', *ABC News*, 18 April 2018.

[19] DHA, *Student Visa and Temporary Graduate Visa Program Bi-Annual Report* (ending at 31 December 2017) 11.

[20] 'UK Slipping Behind Australia in International Education' *University World News*, Issue No 515, 19 July 2018.

[21] ibid.

[22] A Norton and I Cherastidtham, *Mapping Australian Higher Education 2018* (Grattan Institute Report No 18-11, September 18) 45–46.

[23] Universities Australia, *2017 Universities Australia Student Finances Survey* (August 2018) 13.

vocational courses.[24] As workers, their circumstances may be such that they are more like archetypal vulnerable migrant workers than they at first appear.[25] The National Temporary Migrant Work Survey found that a quarter of all international students earned half the minimum wage or less in their lowest paid job in Australia.[26]

Because of the large numbers of international students in Australia, and the financial pressures on them, international students have traditionally also been the group of temporary visa holders most likely to be working in Australia contrary to their visa conditions. These visas permit a mandatory maximum of 40 hours' work per fortnight while the student's course is in session, and the same limitation also applies to their partners on secondary visas. Many students may be working more hours than permitted to service significant debts to finance their studies. For others, unlawfully low pay rates may lead them to work more hours than permitted.[27] Others may overshoot their work cap by a small amount, or on isolated occasions, and may do so unintentionally or without realising it has happened.[28] Changed visa settings during the years following the onset of COVID diminished the size of this population of unauthorised workers, although these policy changes are likely to be temporary. In an effort to address labour shortages in the context of national border closures, the government relaxed this 40 hour work restriction in March 2020 for international students working in certain essential industries including supermarkets, aged care providers and healthcare. In 2021, this dispensation was extended to all international students working in any industry.[29] However, this temporary relaxation of the work restrictions was likely to be reinstated in 2023.

A number of other visa-holders may become unauthorised workers by virtue of the structure of their temporary visas, albeit that the numbers are likely to be small. One such group is young Working Holiday Makers, whose work is restricted to no more than six months with any one employer (except in certain exceptional cases). Another is temporary skilled visas that only permit work in the sponsored occupation at a salary at the market rate, and at a salary at least as high as the minimum specified amount. (These were known as 457 visas until

[24] 14% of enrolments in May 2018 were in English language courses and 26% were in vocational education and training: Department of Education and Training, *International Student Data: Monthly Summary* (May 2018).

[25] A Reilly, 'Protecting Vulnerable Migrant Workers: The Case of International Students' (2012) 25 *Australian Journal of Labour Law* 181.

[26] Berg and Farbenblum (n 5) 6.

[27] Reilly (n 24) 188.

[28] In some reported cases the breaches are extremely marginal: see, eg, *090314* [2010] MRTA 522, where the visa-holder breached condition 8105 in only one instance, which involved a choice between covering an absent employee's shift or losing his job.

[29] 'Temporary relaxation of working hours for student visa holders', Department of Home Affairs (Webpage) immi.homeaffairs.gov.au/visas/getting-a-visa/visa-listing/student-500/temporary-relaxation-of-working-hours-for-student-visa-holders [last accessed 27 May 2022].

March 2018, when they were replaced with the Temporary Skill Shortage ('TSS') visa scheme.)

Consequently, the population of unauthorised workers is highly varied in Australia. On the one hand, are those who have overstayed a visa, often a tourist visa. Many of these will have deep roots in the community, having lived in Australia for many years, and they may be living with their families, contributing to the community, and working informally. Their circumstances are particularly precarious because they lack the legal authority to remain in Australia at all. A historically larger group have been international students who work (or have worked) more than the 40 hours per fortnight permitted to them. These may in some ways have more privileged circumstances: they are not in Australia illegally, are likely to have private health insurance and may have families back home providing some financial support for their stay.[30] We shall see below that, increasingly, these quite diverse populations of workers are subject to different treatment both in law and at a policy level.

B. The Immigration Regulatory Framework Governing Unauthorised Work

The legal treatment of unauthorised work under the Migration Act is similar for all migrant workers. In Australia the ever-present status of 'deportability'[31] for overstayers is particularly acute because of the country's rigid and punitive approach to immigration regulation and enforcement, justifiably described as a 'culture of control'.[32] On expiration of a visa, if the migrant is not eligible for any other visa, they become an 'unlawful non-citizen'. Unlawful non-citizens in Australia are *automatically* subject to mandatory detention and removal *as soon as practicable* without the judicial oversight or bureaucratic discretion which exist in other jurisdictions.[33] A small empirical study commissioned by the Immigration Department has found that this threat of detention may be an even greater concern for unauthorised workers than the prospect of removal.[34]

Those visa-holders who work contrary to visa restrictions similarly fear detection of their unauthorised work, as DHA decision-makers are accorded

[30] S Robertson, *Transnational Student-Migrants and the State: The Education-Migration Nexus* (Basingstoke, Palgrave Macmillan, 2013).

[31] N De Genova, 'Migrant 'Illegality' and Deportability in Everyday Life' (2002) 31 *Annual Review of Anthropology* 419, 419.

[32] K Cronin, 'A Culture of Control: An Overview of Immigration Policy-Making' in J Jupp and M Kabala (eds), *The Politics of Australian Immigration* (Canberra, Australian Government Publishing Service, 1993) 83.

[33] Migration Act 1958, ss 189 and 198. The constitutionality of mandatory detention and removal have been upheld in numerous High Court judgments: *Chu Kheng Lim v Minister for Immigration* [1992] HCA 64; *Al-Kateb v Godwin* [2004] HCA 37.

[34] Hall & Partners Open Mind, *Engagement Strategies Associated with Deterring Illegal Workers* (research report submitted to DIAC, 11 October 2012) 17.

discretion to cancel visas on this basis.[35] Upon visa cancellation, they too face mandatory detention and summary removal. However, in contrast to the gravity of these fears and the severe consequences of visa cancellation, the DHA in fact rarely exercises its visa cancellation power on this basis. For example, the agency has informed the authors that between 1 July 2016 and 30 November 2021, fewer than 62 student visas were cancelled for breach of work rights, and that fewer than 15 visas of students' dependents were cancelled for breach of their identical work rights.[36]

The climate of insecurity in which unauthorised workers live has been intensified, at least symbolically, by the introduction of a number of civil and criminal offences related to unauthorised work. Working without authorisation – whether as an overstayer, or while holding an otherwise valid visa – has been a criminal offence since 1979.[37] This criminal offence is set out in section 235 of the Migration Act 1958 (Cth): we return to the legal implications of this offence in more detail in section III, below. Employers found to have allowed a non-citizen to work in breach of their visa may also face civil and criminal sanctions.[38] Fault-based criminal offences for knowingly or recklessly allowing a non-citizen to work without authorisation were introduced in 2007. In order to create a more graduated employer sanctions scheme, strict liability offences were introduced in 2013 with no-fault civil penalties for those who employ unauthorised workers. However, there is no evidence of investigations or prosecutions of the worker-related offence in Australia, presumably because of the overwhelming policy imperative to remove unauthorised migrants from Australia without delay.[39] Between 2007, when criminal offences related to employers were introduced, and 2013, there were fewer than ten convictions.[40] Although more employers have received lower-tier sanctions – for instance, 150 Illegal Worker Warning Notices were issued to employers in 2020–21 – these sanctions carry no financial penalty.[41] Compared with the financial and social upheaval of summary removal for workers, such sanctions therefore do very little to disrupt the power imbalance within exploitative employment arrangements.[42]

[35] Migration Act 1958, s 116.

[36] DHA, 'Student Visa Cancellations – subclass 500 – by cancellation ground and fin year' released pursuant to authors' Freedom of Information Request 21/12/00662.

[37] Migration Act 1958, s 235. Berg (n 2) 169.

[38] Migration Act 1958, s 245AB.

[39] Private communication between DIBP and Laurie Berg, 19 July 2013.

[40] More recent decisions include: *R v Simonetta* [2017] VCC 2015; *Kartawidjaja v Rowe* [2016] VSC 176.

[41] DHA, *2020–21 Annual Report* (2021) available at www.homeaffairs.gov.au/reports-and-pubs/Annualreports/home-affairs-annual-report-2020-21.pdf [last accessed 8 May 2022].

[42] Migrant Worker Focus Group, Brisbane, 2016; C Hemingway, 'Not Just Work: Ending the Exploitation of Refugee and Migrant Workers' (WEstjustice Employment Law Project, Final Report, November 2016) 9.

C. The Working Conditions of Unauthorised Workers

There is very limited data available on the working conditions of unauthorised workers, due in large part to the hidden nature of this population and their reluctance to seek assistance. As the National Agriculture Workforce Strategy notes, 'undocumented workers are at highest risk of exploitation, due to the fact that they are unlikely to report mistreatment for fear of losing their visa and ability to stay in Australia'.[43] Given the diversity of unauthorised workers in Australia, it is likely that experiences and conditions vary between groups. It is clear from the few government reviews conducted in recent years into unauthorised labour that the ever-present threat of detection and removal leaves all unauthorised workers susceptible to employer exploitation. There is evidence of employers pressuring international students into breaching their work restrictions, then 'blackmailing' them with demands for 'work at reduced wages, breaches of occupational health and safety conditions, even sexual favours'.[44] A government-commissioned report into employer sanctions in 2011 recorded the poor treatment typically experienced by tourist visa-holders and overstayers engaging in unauthorised work:

> [Immigration] officers have encountered dozens of [unauthorised] workers in single rooms and [busloads] of workers who do not appear to know who is employing them, where they are working or staying, who will pay them, whether they are actually entitled to work and what is the proper rate of pay … These workers are particularly vulnerable. They may be underpaid, mislead [sic] about what they are doing, undernourished, beaten and threatened.[45]

The National Temporary Migrant Work Survey 2017, undertaken by the authors with Clibborn, explored the working conditions of different sets of unauthorised workers. It included 281 unauthorised workers, comprising 247 international students who admitted to working more than 20 hours per week in an average week in their lowest-paid job, and 34 individuals who had been tourists when working in their lowest-paid job in Australia. As suggested in previous research on international student vulnerability, these figures are likely to underestimate the unauthorised work among the survey's total 4,322 respondents, since many students are reluctant to report work done in excess of visa conditions, even in an anonymous survey.[46]

[43] National Agricultural Labour Advisory Committee, National Agricultural Workforce Strategy: Learning to Excel (Commonwealth of Australia, December 2020) 190.

[44] M Knight, *Strategic Review of the Student Visa Program 2011 – Report* (Cth of Australia, 30 June 2011) 85.

[45] Howells, (n 8) 56.

[46] S Marginson, C Nyland, E Sawir and H Forbes Mewett, *International Student Security* (Cambridge, Cambridge University Press, 2010).

Within the group of 281 respondents who admitted to engaging in unauthorised work while holding tourist or student visas, a fifth (21 per cent) worked as convenience store or petrol station attendants. This finding accords with a number of recent media exposés of systemic underpayment of international students working in excess of the hours permitted on their visa in these types of premises.[47] The industry with the next highest number of these unauthorised workers (12 per cent) was cleaning, which has also been the subject of investigation in relation to the exploitation of international students.[48] This was followed by retail (8 per cent) and food services (7 per cent), the latter of which is another industry that has been the subject of research into the exploitation of international students.[49]

Figure 1 Occupations with the highest number of international students working more than 20 hours per week and tourists

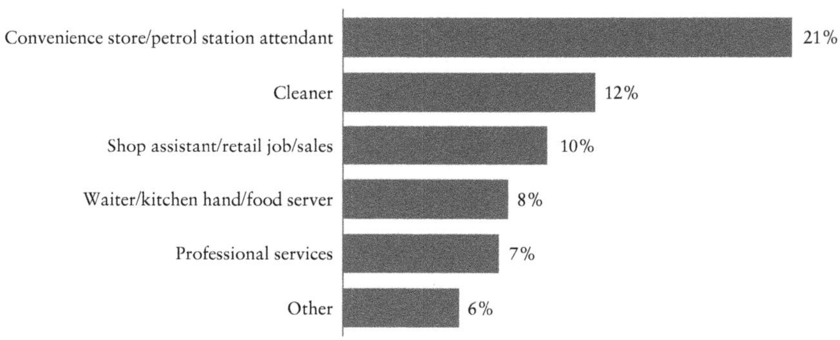

As can be seen in Figure 2 below, these workers were paid substantially less in their lowest paid job than the other temporary visa holders who participated in the survey. Almost half (46 per cent) of the unauthorised workers were paid $12 per hour or less, compared with just over a quarter (28 per cent) of other temporary workers.[50] The difference in wage rates is also striking between

[47] A Ferguson, '7-Eleven: Workers caught in cashback scam' *Sydney Morning Herald*, 8 September 2015; M Christodoulou, 'Caltex audits to date reveal 80 per cent of franchisee petrol stations underpaid staff' *Sydney Morning Herald*, 2 May 2017.

[48] Fair Work Ombudsman 'Statement on outcome of Inquiry into the housekeeping services of 4 and 5-star hotels' (2016) available at www.fairwork.gov.au/about-us/news-and-media-releases/2016-media-releases/may-2016/20160520-hotel-housekeepers-inquiry [last accessed 24 March 2022]; United Voice, *A Dirty Business: The Exploitation of International Students in Melbourne's Office Cleaning Industry* (2013).

[49] I Campbell, M Boese and J-C Tham, 'Inhospitable Workplaces? International Students and Paid Work in Food Services' (2016) 51 *Australian Journal of Social Issues* 279.

[50] It may be added that $12 per hour was probably around half the minimum wage for the job. The minimum statutory wage at the time was $17.70 per hour, and in most cases workers would have been entitled to more under relevant Awards (higher arbitrated minimums in a range of industries). Furthermore, the vast majority of unauthorised migrants worked in casual positions, which attract a 25% loading in lieu of regular hours, paid leave and other entitlements.

the outcomes of more similarly situated workers: students working in breach of visa conditions and students working in compliance with visa conditions. Figure 3 below reveals that while 46 per cent of unauthorised students were paid $12 per hour or less, only 26 per cent of all other international students were paid $12 per hour or less.

Figure 2 Pay in lowest paid job for international students working more than 20 hours per week and tourists (unauthorised) vs. all other visa holders (authorised)

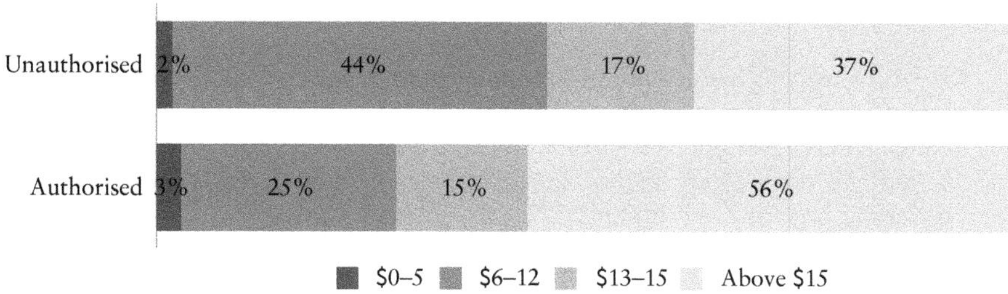

Figure 3 Pay in lowest paid job for international students working more than 20 hours per week vs. international students overall

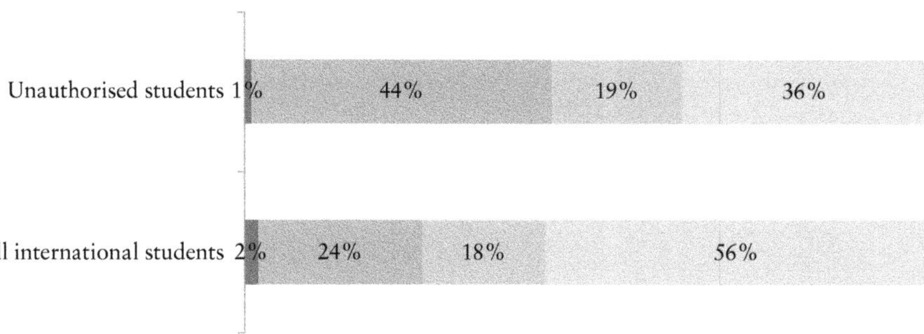

Almost a third (30 per cent) of the respondents who admitted to unauthorised work while holding tourist or student visas were in their lowest-paid job for a year or more, and almost three-quarters (73 per cent) were in their lowest -paid job for four months or more. This suggests that these unauthorised workers often stay in underpaying jobs for significant lengths of time.

In another study published in 2017, Marie Segrave reported on the results of the first detailed empirical examination of the experience of overstayers working in Australia, having interviewed 46 workers who had worked unlawfully. She reported that every participant in her study had experienced non- or low-payment for work, as well as incidences of debt bondage and unauthorised deduction from wages, frequently without explanation.[51] Segrave reports that

[51] M Segrave, *Exploited and illegal: The impact of the absence of protections for unlawful migrant workers in Australia* (The Border Crossing Observatory and the School of Social Sciences Monash University, 2017) 38.

participants either worked without formalised work agreements, or in a web of complex subcontracting arrangements in which workers were uncertain about who was paying or employing them. Workers were generally aware that they were being underpaid, but accepted their position as one of powerlessness.[52] As one worker noted, '[i]t [is] very tough to live in a country like in Australia compared to where we come from … [but] we can't afford to do anything else so we have to just stay … as long as we get something [i.e. some money]. (14 March 2017)'.[53] Other workers reported having to work under degrading and dehumanising conditions. For example one worker stated,

> It's – they treat us like it's not like a human. They treat us like very low, low, low person. It's not come from planet. Maybe some other planet that treat us like – it's saying animals, but they don't treat you like animal, more than like – it's not good …. [but] you don't complain, in case you don't get your job …. Once you complain, you're gone anyway. (18 February 2017, 6 female workers).[54]

In a third study published in 2017, on labour use on Australian farms, researchers found that the horticulture industry had a 'structural reliance' on undocumented workers.[55] This study involved interviews with growers and industry association officials, who reported widespread use of undocumented workers on farms, with evidence that in some instances, workers were encouraged into undocumented work through a complex network of offshore and onshore labour hire and migration agents. The study concluded that undocumented workers were 'the most vulnerable in the horticulture industry'.[56]

It is also clear that during COVID lockdowns in 2020 and 2021, undocumented workers may have become even more vulnerable to exploitation by virtue of decreased mobility while state borders were closed.[57]

III. THE LABOUR ENTITLEMENTS OF UNAUTHORISED WORKERS

There is conflicting Australian authority on the issue of whether unauthorised migrant workers are entitled to employment protections. Analysis of these cases is complicated by the fact that they involve a mix of judicial decisions from courts of different levels in different states along with administrative tribunal decisions. The cases consider a variety of employment protections in different state and federal statutes, as well as the interaction of these with different

[52] ibid 36.
[53] ibid 37.
[54] ibid 34.
[55] J Howe, S Clibborn, A Reilly, D van den Broek and CF Wright, *Towards a Durable Future: Tackling Labour Challenges in the Australian Horticulture Industry* (2017) 35.
[56] ibid 42.
[57] J Howe, 'Out of Limbo and into the Light: A Case for Status Resolution for Undocumented Migrant Workers on Farms' (2021) 43(4) *Sydney Law Review* 433.

versions of statutory offence of unauthorised work set out in the Migration Act over time. There has, however, to date been no consideration of this issue by the High Court of Australia, Australia's highest court of appeal.

This section provides a chronological account of the main case law.[58] We shall see that, in the case of workers' compensation legislation, the pre-eminent approach has been to deny coverage to unauthorised workers, on the basis that their employment contract was void for illegality because it contravened Migration Act offences. However, the approaches which have been taken have been so divergent as to leave the law unsettled, such that a litigant seeking employment entitlements in relation to unauthorised work would lack certainty as to which way their case would be decided.

Both the first and most recent judicial considerations of the work-related rights of unauthorised workers have held that an employment contract performed in breach of the Migration Act is invalid and unenforceable. This means not only that an unauthorised worker would not be entitled to remuneration for work performed under the contract, but also that they would be ineligible for statutory protections under the Fair Work Act, which extend only to employees defined as those who hold valid contracts of employment.[59] In 1994, in *WorkCover Corporation v Da Ping*, the Supreme Court of South Australia denied South Australian workers' compensation protection to an unauthorised worker, Liang Da Ping, a Chinese man, who had injured his right hand while working for San Remo Macaroni Company.[60] In South Australia, the Workers Rehabilitation and Compensation Act 1986 (SA) provided that entitlement to compensation depends on the existence of a valid contract of service.[61] However, Liang Da Ping was working in breach of section 83(2) of the Migration Act, which was in effect from 1979 until 1994, and provided that '[w]here a person who is an illegal entrant performs any work in Australia without permission, in writing, of the Secretary of the Department of Immigration, the person commits an offence'. In relation to the common law principles governing the legality of contracts, the court noted Australian High Court authority that 'the cases are likely to be rare in which a statute prohibits a contract but nevertheless reveals an intention that it should be valid and enforceable'.[62] Applying this jurisprudence to the section 83(2) offence, the South Australian Supreme Court found that the 'act to be performed under the contract [was] the very act forbidden by the statute', which strongly suggested an implication that the prohibition rendered the

[58] For a more detailed discussion of this case law, see Berg (n 2) 170–78.

[59] Fair Work Act 2009, s 11.

[60] (1994) 175 LSJS 469. For excellent reviews of the early case law on unauthorised workers, see R Guthrie, 'Tourists Overstaying Their Welcome: When the Visa Runs Out and the Workers Stay On' (2004) 6 *The Tourism Industry* 1; R Guthrie and M Quinlan, 'The Occupational Safety and Health Rights and Workers' Compensation Entitlements of Illegal Immigrants: An Emerging Challenge' (2005) 3(2) *Policy and Practice in Health and Safety* 69.

[61] Workers Rehabilitation and Compensation Act 1986 (SA), ss 3 and 30(1).

[62] *Yango Pastoral Co Pty Ltd v First Chicago Australia Ltd* (1978) 139 CLR 410, 413.

employment contract void.[63] Consequently, Da Ping was determined not to be a worker for the purposes of the legislation, and had no entitlement to workers' compensation.

Four years later, in *Nonferral (NSW) Pty Ltd v Taufia*, the New South Wales Court of Appeal (the highest court in that state) considered the implications of the section 83(2) offence for workers' compensation coverage in New South Wales legislation, but arrived at the opposite result.[64] Silivenusi Taufia had entered Australia from Tonga in March 1992 on a tourist visa, subsequently overstayed, and began working at the Nonferral aluminium foundry. Shortly after he sustained a leg injury when a block of aluminium fell onto him, Taufia was arrested as an 'illegal entrant' and deported. After the New South Wales Compensation Court awarded him workers' compensation benefits under the Workers Compensation Act 1987 (NSW), his employer appealed to the Court of Appeal. That court focused on two High Court judgments that had been delivered since *Da Ping*, in which the High Court had become somewhat more circumspect about rendering a contract illegal on the basis that its performance breached a statute.[65] The New South Wales Court of Appeal observed that unauthorised work would not invalidate a contract of employment, because it was not necessarily contrary to public policy, nor the intent of the Migration Act at that time, to deny employment entitlements to a worker who has contravened its provisions in relation to unauthorised work.[66]

However, when the issue arose again before the Queensland Court of Appeal (the highest court in that state), in *Australia Meat Holdings v Kazi* in 2004, that Court held that a worker who had engaged in unauthorised work was not entitled to workers' compensation under a Queensland statute.[67] A Bangladeshi man, Mainuddin Kazi, having overstayed a visitor visa, was working at a meat-works when he injured his knee falling over the conveyor belt in the cold store. He received medical treatment for the injury, before ceasing employment in June 2002. His employer sought a declaration that Kazi was not entitled to workers' compensation. In this case, the relevant provision of the Migration Act was the criminal offence in section 235, which had been introduced in 1994, after the facts considered by the New South Wales Court of Appeal in *Nonferral*. The majority of the Queensland Court of Appeal declined to follow the New South Wales Court of Appeal's reasoning, on the basis that, unlike the repealed section 83, section 235 absolutely proscribes work by a migrant contrary to visa conditions. According to the majority, the Act no longer envisages any circumstance in which an unlawful non-citizen may enter into an employment contract, for instance with the permission of the Departmental Secretary.

[63] *Da Ping* (1994) 175 LSJS 469, 473.
[64] (1998) 43 NSWLR 312.
[65] *Nelson v Nelson* (1995) 184 CLR 538; *Fitzgerald v JF Leonhardt Pty Ltd* (1997) 189 CLR 215.
[66] *Nonferral (NSW) Pty Ltd v Taufia* (1998) 43 NSWLR 312.
[67] *Australia Meat Holdings v Kazi* [2004] QCA 147.

Several scholars have submitted that the NSW Court of Appeal's reasoning in *Nonferral* is preferable to that of the Queensland Court of Appeal in *Australia Meat Holdings*.[68] Nevertheless, the Queensland Court of Appeal's approach to invalidity has since been applied by tribunals, in preference to *Nonferral*, even in New South Wales, on the basis that *Australia Meat Holdings* dealt with the current statutory provision, section 235. In 2006, the NSW Workers Compensation Commission found an unauthorised worker's employment contract void pursuant to *Australia Meat Holdings*.[69] (The worker nevertheless received an award of workers' compensation because the NSW legislation granted the Commission a statutory discretion to deem an illegal contract to be legal.) In 2014, the Fair Work Commission (Australia's federal industrial tribunal) applied the Queensland Court of Appeal's decision in *Smallwood v Ergo Asia Pty Ltd* in a different statutory context.[70] It rejected an unfair dismissal application brought by an employer-sponsored migrant worker, on the basis that, contrary to the condition of her 457 visa, she was employed by a labour hire company rather than her sponsor.

The *Australia Meat Holdings* line of reasoning would preclude an undocumented immigrant worker from benefits under minimum wage guarantees, unfair dismissal and anti-bullying provisions under the Fair Work Act. However, several labour law experts have argued that, notwithstanding this precedent, a court could justifiably uphold the enforceability of an unauthorised worker's employment contract, so as not to allow the employer to unjustly avoid its responsibilities under the Fair Work Act.[71] In the more recent case of *Gnych v Polish Club Ltd*, outside the migration context, the High Court considered whether a statutory prohibition should be construed as denying all effect to a particular contract.[72] The Court emphasised that that is not necessarily the case, and that it depends on a careful consideration of the legislative regime. In the course of their joint judgment, French CJ, Kiefel, Keane and Nettle JJ made the following remarks:

> As a matter of legislative construction, the likelihood of adverse consequences for the 'innocent party' to a bargain has been recognised as a consideration which tends against the attribution of an intention to avoid the bargain to the legislature. That consideration is consistent with the general disinclination on the part of the courts to allow a party to a contract to take advantage of its own wrongdoing. There may

[68] S Clibborn, 'Why Undocumented Immigrant Workers Should Have Workplace Rights' [2015] *Economic and Labour Relations Review* 1; R Guthrie and M Quinlan, 'The Occupational Safety and Health Rights and Workers' Compensation Entitlements of Illegal Immigrants: An Emerging Challenge' (2005) 3 *Policy and Practice in Health and Safety* 69.

[69] *Yong Fu Zhang v Mei Hu t/as Eden Furniture and the WorkCover Authority of NSW* [2006] NSWWCCPD 15.

[70] [2014] FWC 964.

[71] A Stewart, S McCrystal and J Howe, submission DR271 responding to Draft Report of the Productivity Commission Inquiry into the Workplace Relations Framework (September 2015) 24.

[72] [2015] HCA 23.

> be cases where the legislation which creates the illegality is sufficiently clear as to overcome that disinclination; but it is hardly surprising that the courts are not astute to ascribe such an intention to the legislature where it is not made manifest by the statutory language.[73]

This observation appears pertinent to the case of an employer who deliberately employs a temporary migrant in breach of their visa conditions, then seeks to rely on that breach to avoid liability for an underpayment of wages or denial of other entitlements under the Fair Work Act.

Indeed, there is another basis upon which a court could justifiably uphold the enforceability of an unauthorised worker's employment contract, notwithstanding breach of section 235. To date, all decisions considering the enforceability of employment contracts which contravene the Migration Act have focused solely on the criminal conduct of the employee in undertaking unauthorised work. None have considered the effect of employer sanctions offences introduced in 2007, which criminalise *employers*' use of labour performed in contravention of the Migration Act.[74] A court which attended to the wrongdoing of both parties to the contract could justifiably uphold the validity of the employment contract.

In fact, the most recent court to consider this issue, the Federal Circuit Court of Australia in 2021, enforced the worker's *Fair Work Act* entitlements notwithstanding their unauthorised work. In *Lal v Biber* (2021), Jeevan Lal was paid less than $8 per hour for cleaning a food factory, and admitted to working more than 40 hours per fortnight in contravention of his student visa condition.[75] The defendant claimed it did not need to pay the $147,900 the worker was owed because the contract was performed in breach of the *Migration Act* and was therefore void for illegality.

The reasoning in this case appeared to turn on the applicant's work rights. The Court found that because the applicant was permitted to work in Australia, and because the initial contract of employment provided for up to 20 hours per week and was within the terms of his visa, the contract itself was found not void for illegality. The Court observed that:

> The clear policy of the *Fair Work Act* is to ensure that all those who work in Australia receive a minimum rate of pay. To limit such protections to Australian citizens would be to create a class of people ripe for exploitation. To fail to ensure that employers fulfil all of the obligations imposed by the *Fair Work Act*, in cases where there are breaches of visa conditions ultimately disadvantages Australian citizens, as it creates an incentive for unscrupulous employers to engage immigrants in breach of the Migration Act, for lower wages than would be payable to Australian workers. If employers must engage all workers at the same minimum rates, then the offences in *Migration Act* create an incentive to only employ workers who are citizens or who have appropriate work rights.

[73] ibid, [45]. See also D Meagher and M Groves (eds), *The Principle of Legality in Australia and New Zealand* (Alexandria NSW, Federation Press, 2017).

[74] Introduced by Migration Amendment (Employer Sanctions) Act 2007 (Cth).

[75] [2021] FCCA 959.

Because this reasoning was so closely tied to the applicant's work rights, there is a question as to whether a similar finding would have been reached if the applicant had not been entitled to work under his visa. Nevertheless, the decision suggests that a court considering an employment contract held by a visa overstayer may now take a different view to the one reached in *Smallwood* and *Australia Meat Holdings*. Challenging these decisions, however, may create a risk that a worker identifies themselves as having undertaken unauthorised work. For that reason, legal services providers advise clients who have engaged in unauthorised work that it is likely a court will not enforce their workplace rights.[76]

Consequently, it would be preferable to put this jurisprudential issue beyond doubt through legislative amendment. Such a legislative amendment could take a number of forms. Section 235 could be amended so as to clarify that commission of this offence does not render protections under other statutes unenforceable.[77] Alternatively, as has been recommended in two government inquiries into migrants and labour law, the Fair Work Act could be amended to clarify that it applies to all workers regardless of immigration status.[78] (The Labor Party, now in Government, previously indicated support for such a reform, to amend the Fair Work Act to clarify its applicability to 'all workers, irrespective of their immigration status'.[79]) Third, a provision of the type found in some workers' compensation statutes could be inserted into the Fair Work Act,[80] to specify that, as a matter of discretion, the illegality of an employment arrangement may be disregarded in any proceedings brought under the Act.[81]

IV. UNAUTHORISED WORKERS' ABILITY TO RECOVER WAGES IN PRACTICE

Having considered unauthorised workers' entitlements to remedies at law, this section now examines these workers' access to these remedies in practice. It outlines the contradictory approaches of different federal government agencies to providing legal and support services to unauthorised workers. On the one hand, border protection officials subject the vast majority of unauthorised workers they encounter to summary removal, with exceptions mainly for the very small numbers whose circumstances amount to suspected human trafficking. On the other, the FWO has prioritised employment protection for unauthorised

[76] Community Legal Centre representative 2016, interview.

[77] See Berg (n 2); Reilly (n 24).

[78] Productivity Commission, Report on Inquiry into Workplace Relations Framework (21 December 2015), Recommendation 29.4; Senate Education and Employment References Committee, above n 16, Recommendation 23. See also Clibborn (n 67) 5.

[79] Proposed s 15A of Fair Work Amendment (Protecting Australian Workers) Bill 2016, introduced into Parliament by the Labor Party, although not passed into law.

[80] See, eg, Workers Compensation Act 1987 (NSW) s 27.

[81] Stewart, McCrystal and Howe (n 3) 25.

workers, espousing the view that all workers in Australia are entitled to protections under the Fair Work Act, notwithstanding the legal authority discussed in the previous section. However, as this section explains, it would appear that both the DHA and the FWO accord differential penalties and protections to subsets of unauthorised workers.

A. Government Policy Towards Unauthorised Workers

In recent years, legislative and policy reforms have strengthened protections for victims of trafficking and forced labour. Australia's laws criminalise slavery – the condition of a person over whom any or all of the powers attaching to the right of ownership are exercised – and slavery-like practices.[82] The offence of forced labour occurs where a person does not consider themselves free to stop working or to leave the place where they work, because of threats, coercion or deception (section 270.6 of the Criminal Code (Cth)). The offence of servitude contains an additional element to forced labour that the person must be significantly deprived of personal freedom in other aspects of their lives not linked to their work (section 270.5 of the Criminal Code). The offence of debt bondage occurs when a person pledges their services as a security for a debt, if the debt is manifestly excessive or the value of the services is not reasonably applied towards reducing the debt (section 271.8 of the Criminal Code). There are additional specific offences for trafficking in persons, which prohibit moving a victim into, out of, or within Australia if that movement occurs because of force, threats or deception for the purpose of exploitation.[83]

An unauthorised migrant worker who has been identified by federal or state/territory police as being a suspected victim of trafficking, slavery or slavery-like practices receives a comprehensive suite of protections. These include authorisation to remain in Australia through a special visa, various social and other support services (including income support, legal advice, counselling and housing assistance), and the prospect of a civil remedy at the conclusion of criminal proceedings.[84] The circumstances of only a tiny number of unauthorised workers would meet the definitions of trafficking, slavery or forced labour in criminal law.

The vast majority of unauthorised workers, whose circumstances do not amount to criminal trafficking or who do not come forward as trafficking victims, are subject to summary removal once detected. They are not proactively referred to the support services set out above, or to legal assistance to enforce any

[82] Divisions 270 and 271 of the Criminal Code. See further Berg (n 2) 225ff.

[83] Divisions 271.2 and 271.3 of the Criminal Code. See further Berg (n 2) 225ff.

[84] F Simmons and J Burn, 'Evaluating Australia's Response to all forms of Trafficking: Towards Rights-centred Reform' (2010) 84 *Australian Law Journal* 71; M Segrave and S Milivojevic, 'Auditing the Australian Response to Trafficking' (2010) 22 *Current Issues in Criminal Justice* 632.

employment rights they may have. A search of the DHA LEGENDcom database reveals no relevant policy or direction requiring the referral of unauthorised workers to the federal labour inspectorate, the FWO, or support services (including to obtain legal advice) prior to removal, or notification to the migrant that they may have an employment claim.[85] Rather, the only reference to employment claims in the context of removal is that '[t]he existence of unresolved claims or complaints should not stop or delay removal'.[86] Indeed, in one case we know of, immigration officials were aware that a labour hire operator withheld payments from unauthorised workers and then reported them, whereupon the officials rapidly removed the workers without payment.[87]

B. The Approach of the Fair Work Ombudsman to Unauthorised Workers

The FWO is an independent statutory body established by the Fair Work Act to educate employees and employers about their employment rights and to ensure compliance with the federal workplace relations system. It has identified overseas workers as particularly vulnerable to exploitation, and in recent years has directed substantial resources to investigating industries and key employers associated with exploitation of migrant workers, including especially temporary visa-holders and permanent residents who are new arrivals. The FWO has expressed its determination 'to use every avenue in addressing exploitation of … migrant workers'.[88] In 2012, it established an Overseas Workers Team of specialist inspectors, which coordinates targeted investigations in industries known to employ high numbers of visa-holders, such as hospitality, horticulture, poultry processing, cleaning, convenience stores and trolley collectors. In 2015, it established a Migrant Worker Strategy and Engagement Branch to coordinate effective compliance, education and engagement activities for visa holders. Between 2014 and 2016, these initiatives, campaigns and inquiries into systemic non-compliance involving migrant workers tripled the wages recovered for migrants.[89] In 2015–16, visa-holders comprised 13 per cent of all formal complainants and were significantly overrepresented in the agency's compliance and enforcement initiatives. In 2015–16, 76 per cent of litigations initiated involved visa-holders, some achieving record-breaking penalties.[90]

[85] LEGENDcom is an electronic database of migration and citizenship legislation and policy documents that is available on a subscription basis, containing statutes, regulations, the Procedures Advice Manual 3 (detailed policy material to assist immigration officials), non-legislative instruments, gazette notices and Migration Series Instructions.

[86] DIBP Procedures Advice Manual 3, 2016 'Removal from Australia'.

[87] Howells (n 8) 57.

[88] ibid 2.

[89] ibid 2.

[90] ibid 1–2, 22.

No information is available on how many of the workers assisted by the FWO may have worked without authorisation. The FWO has expressed the scope of its assistance to unauthorised migrants differently on different occasions. The agency publicly takes the position that, despite the decision of the Fair Work Commission in *Smallwood* and the majority judgment of the Queensland Court of Appeal in *Australia Meat Holdings*, unauthorised workers *are* subject to employment protections afforded by the Fair Work Act, as evidenced by its recognition of jurisdiction with respect to unauthorised work. In a submission to a government inquiry, it stated that:

> it is critical that the Government makes clear to workers, employers and their advisers that the FWO can and does enforce Fair Work laws with respect to all workers, including migrant workers, irrespective of their visa conditions.[91]

Pursuant to this position, the FWO has on numerous occasions pursued employers for contraventions involving unauthorised workers. These workers have included: students who had worked in excess of 40 hours;[92] 457 visa-holders who worked outside their visa conditions;[93] 457 visa-holders whose underpayments breached the terms of their visas;[94] and, a partner visa-holder who worked in excess of the permitted hours.[95] In none of these matters did the employers raise the unenforceability of the employment contract as a defence to the FWO's suits, and so the issue of the applicability of the Fair Work Act to these workers was not tested.

Elsewhere, however, the FWO has referenced a narrower set of workers whom it targets for assistance. For example, the FWO's Overseas Worker team, established in 2012, provides assistance to newly settled residents and 'workers in Australia on temporary visas who have work rights',[96] apparently excluding from its remit workers who have worked while on tourist visas or as overstayers. Indeed, the numerous cases concerning unauthorised work which the FWO has litigated in recent years all appear to have involved recovery of underpayments for students, 457 visa-holders or a partner visa-holder. These cases therefore all involved workers who held visas that permitted work, but who worked in breach of the work limitations in those visas. Of course, it is possible that tourist visa-holders or overstayers have benefited from FWO assistance in matters that have not resulted in litigation. Alternatively, the FWO may have undertaken litigation

[91] FWO, submission responding to Draft Report of the Productivity Commission Inquiry into the Workplace Relations Framework No DR368 (2015), 3.

[92] *FWO v Bosen Pty Ltd* [2011] VMC 21; *FWO v Haider Enterprises Pty Ltd* [2015] FCCA 2113.

[93] *FWO v Taj Palace Tandoori Indian Restaurant Pty Ltd* [2012] FMCA 258.

[94] *FWO v Chia Tung Development Corp Ltd* [2016] FCCA 3457; *FWO v Rubee Enterprises Pty Ltd* [2016] FCCA 3456.

[95] *FWO v Shafi Investments Pty Ltd* [2012] FMCA 1150.

[96] FWO, 'FWO specialist team flies in to gather intelligence on 417 visa-holder wages & conditions', media release, 13 April 2015.

on behalf of tourist visa-holders or overstayers without specifying their visa status.[97]

C. The Impact of Fear of Removal on Access to Assistance from the Fair Work Ombudsman

Fear of detection is likely the overwhelming barrier to unauthorised workers reporting violations of employment standards when they feel aggrieved. The potential costs of complaining about abusive treatment – visa cancellation and removal – are likely to be dramatically higher for this workforce than for all other workers, and have a powerful silencing effect. Segrave found that unauthorised workers in their interviews simply knew not to complain and accepted that being exploited, primarily financially, was an inevitable aspect of this way of life and something about which they could do nothing.[98] As participants in one group interview observed:

> P1: It's just instinct in us. We shouldn't be complaining.P4: [We] just ignore [it]. P5: Just in case we get thrown out. (18 February 2017, 6 female workers).[99]

It does not appear to be unlawful for an employer to prevent a worker from exercising their workplace rights by threatening to report, or actually reporting, their unauthorised status to the immigration authorities.[100] Revealing the employment of unauthorised workers carries little risk for the employer because, as discussed in section II, above, there appears to be limited enforcement of sanctions against employers for employment of an unauthorised worker. Unauthorised workers are aware of this, and of the power imbalance that unauthorised status creates between the worker and their employer. As one worker in the Segrave study observed,

> I think they rip off because they think it's no point even we report to the Government or we report to the awards, rights, they cannot do anything because we don't have legal here, we don't have power to fight with them. (15 February 2017, 2 female workers).[101]

In the context of widespread underpayment of international students working at 7-Eleven, uncovered by an investigative journalist in 2015,[102] a key factor that

[97] For instance, in *FWO v South Jin Pty Ltd (No 2)* [2016] FCA 832, the Federal Court noted that the employer underpaid a large group of trolley collectors, which included international students and tourist visa-holders, but did not state whether the latter group of these workers were the recipients of back payments recovered by the FWO.

[98] Segrave (n 50) 51.

[99] ibid 34.

[100] Fair Work Act 2009, s 342.

[101] Segrave (n 50) 42.

[102] Ferguson (n 46).

deterred workers from reporting their conditions to the FWO was that many had worked more hours than permitted on their visa, and feared visa cancellation and removal. As one former 7-Eleven employee stated to a federal Senate committee inquiry into temporary migrant labour in Australia:

> [t]hey are all scared to stand up because of the [previous] 20 hour [per week] work limit. I believe that if Immigration say in the newspaper that the 20 hour limit does not apply, people will just run in behind it, and you could get thousands of people right now saying, 'Yes, I have been underpaid.[103]

Another former 7-Eleven worker confirmed in an interview with us that 'there's this notion among students that Fair Works [sic] and Immigration work together, so as soon as you get some information to the Fair Works [sic], it's already gone to the Immigration'.[104]

The FWO has stated publicly that it does not require complainants to disclose their immigration status, and does not routinely refer international student visa breaches to the DHA.[105] However, there is nothing preventing the FWO's sharing of information on workers' visa status with the DHA.[106] Indeed, the agency holds various roles in relation to immigration enforcement. These include the FWO's direct involvement in immigration enforcement through its role, since 2012, in monitoring employers' immigration-related sponsorship obligations under the 457 visa scheme (now rebranded as the Temporary Skills Shortage visa scheme).[107] Pursuant to Migration Amendment (Temporary Sponsored Visas) Act 2013 (Cth), Fair Work Inspectors are vested with powers to detect certain breaches of immigration laws, which must be reported to the DHA. Consequently, the FWO is *required* to refer to the DHA any TSS visa-holders who have engaged in unauthorised work. The FWO also has commitments within Taskforce Cadena, which was established by the government in 2015 as a collaboration between the DHA, the Australian Border Force, and the FWO. Taskforce deliverables include joint intelligence, information-sharing and investigative activities between the three agencies, 'ensuring a coordinated, strategic approach is taken to tackling the issue of visa fraud, illegal work and foreign worker exploitation nationally'.[108]

[103] M Rashid Ullat Thodi, Evidence to Education and Employment References Committee, Senate, Melbourne, 24 September 2015, 6.

[104] International student 2016, interview.

[105] N James, Evidence to Education and Employment Legislation Committee, Senate, Canberra, 2 March 2017, 79; Productivity Commission 2015 (n 76) 931.

[106] For a fuller discussion of the use of institutional firewalls to safeguard the rights of irregular migrants, see F Crepeau and B Hastie, 'The Case for 'Firewall' Protections for Irregular Migrants' (2015) 17 *European Journal of Migration and Law* 157; J Carens, 'The Rights of Irregular Migrants' (2008) 22(2) *Ethics and International Affairs* 163.

[107] See J Howe, T Hardy and S Cooney, 'Mandate, Discretion and Professionalism at an Employment Standards Enforcement Agency: An Antipodean Experience' (2013) 35 *Law and Society* 1.

[108] Taskforce Cadena Joint Agency Agreement (2016), 3–4.

For some time, FWO's practice had been to seek DHA assurances against visa cancellation in order to facilitate visa-holders' engagement with the regulator and potential court action.[109] However, the unpredictability of FWO's discretion to seek leniency from the DHA had led legal service providers to recommend that migrant workers do not contact FWO where work had been undertaken in breach of visa conditions.[110] Despite the low likelihood of removal in practice, even a remote possibility has been sufficient to deter unauthorised workers from approaching the regulator.[111] Even workers who are compliant with immigration requirements may be deterred by the possibility that their complaint will trigger the detection of co-workers who may be working in breach of visa conditions ('if I have to go forward and tell them what's happening, I'm going to put everyone into trouble').[112] For these reasons, government reviews and scholars have for many years called for workers' immigration status to be insulated from their labour claims through whistleblower protections[113] and for entitlement to a visa to regularise stay while a labour claim is under determination.[114]

Amidst these calls, in mid-2017, for the first time, a formal arrangement was publicised between the FWO and the DHA regarding the relationship between the two agencies in relation to unauthorised workers. Recognising that fear of visa cancellation impedes migrant workers from approaching the FWO, the two agencies established a new protocol designed to provide protection against removal to certain unauthorised workers, under certain conditions. The FWO announced the following on its website:

> We've set up an arrangement with the Department of Immigration and Border Protection (DIBP) to support and encourage migrant workers to come forward to request our assistance and provide us with any evidence or information about exploitation. This will help us to better understand the issues faced by visa holders and migrant workers so that we can educate employers and employees about entitlements and obligations.
>
> We've come to an agreement with DIBP that a person's temporary visa will not be cancelled if they
>
> - had an entitlement to work as part of their visa
> - believe they have been exploited at work
> - have reported their circumstances to us
> - are actively assisting us in an investigation.

[109] Unite organiser 2016, interview.

[110] Community Legal Centre representative 2016, interview; Pro bono practice in private firm 2016, interview.

[111] International students focus group 2016; Community Legal Centre representative 2016, interview; Jobwatch representative 2016, interview.

[112] Migrant worker 2016, interview.

[113] Productivity Commission (n 76) 915; Berg (n 2) 272; C Wright, S Clibborn, N Piper and N Cini, 'Economic Migration and Australia in the 21st Century', *Lowy Institute Analyses*, 19 October 2016.

[114] Berg (n 2) 277ff; Senate Education and Employment References Committee (n 16) Recommendation 19.

> This applies as long as:
>
> - they commit to abiding by visa conditions in the future
> - there is no other basis for visa cancellation (such as on national security, character, health or fraud grounds).
>
> For temporary visa holders who don't have work entitlements attached to their visa, DIBP will consider the case on its merits.[115]

The protocol therefore extends protections only to visa-holders who have the right to work, and so leaves overstayers and tourist visa-holders unprotected.[116]

For those workers whom the protocol does cover, the dispensation is conditional on the FWO's assessment as to whether the individual is actively assisting it. Thus, it is unclear whether the dispensation could be withheld or revoked if the migrant worker did not wish to participate, or to continue participating, in an investigation, or if the FWO declined to pursue the matter further. It is also unclear whether the protocol gives rise to any rights on the part of a visa-holder, such as a right to appeal a visa cancellation on the basis of unauthorised work. (These concerns may be mitigated by the fact that in practice DHA very rarely cancels a student visa due to a breach of work conditions, as discussed above.)

In principle, the protocol was an innovative approach to migrant worker protection, acknowledging the need for visa safeguards to enable migrant workers to report exploitation. In practice, however, it has had little impact: between 2017 and 2021, it was used by only 77 temporary visa holders.[117]

V. PATHS FORWARD

While it is unlikely that unauthorised workers would rush to seek remedies on a large scale, even if broader protections were instituted, there are several key reforms that would make access to justice for unauthorised workers a clear possibility. These include, first, repealing section 235 of the Migration Act which criminalises unauthorised work, and amending the Fair Work Act to clarify that it applies to all workers regardless of immigration status. Second, whistleblower protections should be introduced. In late 2022, a coalition of 40 civil society organisations called on the new Labor Government to introduce new protections for migrant workers who take action to address exploitation. These include a visa to permit unauthorised workers (and other migrants at the end of their visa) to remain in Australia to pursue a claim and protections against

[115] www.fairwork.gov.au/find-help-for/visa-holders-and-migrants [last accessed 24 March 2022]. The Department of Immigration and Border Protection (DIBP) preceded the DHA and was in operation between 2007 and 2013.

[116] Segrave (n 50).

[117] Information provided by DHA pursuant to Freedom of Information Request FA 21/12/00662, 14 February 2022.

visa cancellation for international students who have breached their visa. These protections would be available where a migrant worker can evidence a meritorious and labour claim over a certain threshold of magnitude. This could include a claim or complaint through a government agency, union action against an employer, or private legal action against the employer in a court or tribunal.[118] Third, and related, a protocol should be instituted within the DHA to ensure referral to the FWO prior to removal of all non-citizens who have engaged in unauthorised work.[119]

The inability or unwillingness of unauthorised workers to complain to the authorities, or to seek employment remedies, makes these workers highly susceptible to exploitation. In order to reduce employer impunity for exploitation of unauthorised workers, the Australian government and Parliament must create legislative and practical pathways for these workers to access employment remedies. That would increase the ability of government agencies to detect and address instances of serious exploitation including situations of forced labour and trafficking that remain unreported. Most importantly, these reforms would enable a number of unauthorised workers to obtain the wages that their employer owed them for the work they have performed.

[118] L Berg, B Farbenblum and S Verma, *Breaking the Silence: A Proposal for Whistleblower Protections to Enable Migrant Workers to Address Exploitation* (Migrant Justice Institute Research and Policy Guide Series, 2022), available at www.migrantjustice.org.

[119] Berg (n 2) 284–85; Productivity Commission (n 76) 931.

8

Blurring Legal Divides: The EU Employer Sanctions Directive and its Implementation in the Netherlands

TESSELTJE DE LANGE*

I. INTRODUCTION

THIS CHAPTER DISCUSSES sanctions against employers for the informal employment of migrants staying irregularly in the EU under the Employer Sanctions Directive 2009/52/EC (hereafter 'ESD' or 'Directive'). The objectives of the Directive are twofold: it offers a framework for curbing informal employment of irregularly staying migrants in the EU, while also aiming to protect irregular migrants who are illegally employed. To these ends, it introduced enforcement tools which relate both to state bodies (fines and other sanctions) and to private actors (chain liability, complaint mechanisms and remuneration claims). The Directive is a unique example of a legal instrument blurring the divide between administrative, criminal, and civil law. In other words, it combines (crim)migration laws with labour laws which protect migrant workers.[1]

The chapter as a whole will investigate how the legal design of employer sanctions and of migrant worker rights in Directive 2009/52 lead (crim)migration and labour law to overlap, and even to a blurring of their boundaries.

* I am grateful to Bernard Ryan for his thoughtful comments on earlier versions of this chapter, and to Giulia Ledda for her research assistance.

[1] 'Crimmigration' is a term used to describe how criminal law and migration law merge: see in general terms M van der Woude, V Barker and J van der Leun, 'Crimmigration in Europe' (2017) 14(1) *European Journal of Criminology* 3, which does not however mention employer sanctions. The American scholarly literature does include employer sanctions in their discussion: see, eg, JP Stumpf, 'The Crimmigration Crisis: Immigrants, Crime, and Sovereign Power' (2006) 367 *American University Law Review* 1689 and KJ Morgan, 'De-magnetizing the Market: European Integration, Employer Sanctions, and the Crackdown on Undeclared Work', in T de Lange, W Maas and A Schrauwen (eds), *Money Matters in Migration: Policy, Participation, and Citizenship* (Cambridge, Cambridge University Press, 2021) 169.

It therefore starts off by theorising blurring of boundaries between administrative law and civil law (including labour law) (section II). That is followed by a discussion of the effectiveness of the Employer Sanctions Directive (section III). The Directive is not thought to have been very successful in achieving its objectives, and in 2021, the European Commission advocated for the effective enforcement of the Directive, while opening up the possibility of a future amendment of the Directive if that proved insufficient.[2]

To show how 'blurring' works in practice, and to consider whether it offers effective enforcement of irregular migrant worker rights, the chapter then investigates the Directive's implementation in the Netherlands (section IV). In general terms, the Netherlands can be seen as an EU Member State which practices strict enforcement against informal, precarious employment.[3] Yet, the Dutch approach to protecting irregular migrant worker rights, as this chapter will illustrate, is stretching and blurring the boundaries between migration law and employment law, to the point that one may lose sight of the bigger picture of protecting migrant workers against precariousness. This bigger picture includes the fact that in some sectors (domestic services, hospitality, construction, and agriculture) employers rely on irregular migrant labour in the absence of feasible legal migration routes into the EU labour markets for low waged labour, while demand is rising. The absence of legal alternatives feeds into labour arrangements which lend themselves to abuse, something the Directive in principle aims to reduce.

The chapter will conclude with a discussion of the blurring of (crim)migration and labour law (section V). It will call for the development of new ethical standards when administrative law is used as an instrument to settle disparities in employment relations, especially when migrant workers are involved. Finally, some thoughts will be offered on how the Directive might be improved, if amendments were to be considered.

For the purposes of this chapter, and following the scope of the Directive, the term 'irregular migrant workers' refers to non-EU nationals staying 'illegally' and without permission to work.[4] This means that non-EU nationals who are

[2] European Commission, Communication on the application of Directive 2009/52/EC of 18 June 2009 providing for minimum standards on sanctions and measures against employers of illegally staying third-country nationals, COM (2021) 592 final.

[3] The Netherlands was one of the initiators, together with the UK, of the letter sent to the President of the Justice and Home Affairs Council of the EU in April 2013, pressing for effective sanctions against EU migrants who supposedly abused the right of freedom of movement.

[4] This also includes non-EU nationals with legal residence in one Member State, but found 'illegally' employed in another Member State, a phenomenon discussed in L Della Torre and T de Lange, 'The "Importance of Staying Put": Third Country Nationals' Limited intra-EU Mobility Rights' (2018) 44 *Journal of Ethnic and Migration Studies* 1409 and in L Berntsen and T de Lange 'Employer Sanctions: Instrument of Labour Market Regulation, Migration Control, and Worker Protection?' in C Rijken and T de Lange (eds), *Towards a Decent Labour Market for Low Waged Migrant Workers* (Amsterdam, Amsterdam University Press, 2018).

authorised to stay but are not permitted to work fall outside the scope of the Directive. The focus is thus on the non-EU nationals who are staying *and* working in the EU without a right to do so, working to make a meagre living at the margins of the informal economy.

II. THEORISING THE BLURRING OF BOUNDARIES

The blurring of the administrate/civil law divide may best be understood by drawing upon a model from a regulation-oriented study.[5] According to that study, blurring of boundaries can operate in the following five ways:

(1) Blurring may occur as between the *roles* of regulatory actors – for example where private-sector actors are involved in regulating instead of only state actors. In our case, that could occur when a legislative body consults unions or employer representatives before setting standards.[6]
(2) Blurring may occur as between the *stages* of regulation, meaning that policy formulation is only a first stage, while implementation (including case law) is the stage where the true intent of the policy comes to the fore. The courts' interpretation of law and policy and their weighing of interests can be seen as both the stage of regulation and that of implementation. The same may be said of the evaluation and possible renegotiation of legal instruments.
(3) *Modes* of regulation may become blurred. This includes the blurring of boundaries between formal laws and self-regulation. For example, codes of conduct and certification are typical examples of private sector self-regulation. Blurring occurs when non-certification has consequences in formal law. A non-certified business may be excluded from certain state-provided benefits, such as expedited procedures for certain permits. Or, businesses fined by the government for illegally employing migrant workers may no longer be eligible for private sector certification.
(4) The *functions* of a regulatory regime may become blurred. Examples of such functions include the setting of standards, monitoring compliance (eg, through reporting obligations), and taking enforcement action against non-compliance through sanctions.
(5) The *structure* of a regulatory regime may become blurred when it no longer belongs to either centralised or decentralised bodies, but mixes this binary divide and allows decentralised actors to act centrally, or to have horizontal

[5] JM Solomon, 'New Governance, Pre-emptive Self-Regulation, and the Blurring of Boundaries in Regulatory Theory and Practice' [2010] *Wisconsin Law Review* 591.

[6] A recent example of such blurring can be found in the revised Blue Card Directive: Directive 2021/1883 on the conditions of entry and residence of third-country nationals for the purpose of highly qualified employment ([2021] OJ L382/1).

> relations with one another. Another blurring of structures is the 'integration of policy domains'.[7] This type of blurring calls in particular for us to look beyond the historically-developed division between administrative law and civil law referred to in the introduction to the chapter.

EU law sets obligations for the Member States, and only to a limited extent does it oblige the Member States to adopt a specific regulatory structure. Therefore, the implementation of EU law may involve the integration of policy domains. For example, the legal position of an irregular migrant is structured through migration law and labour law, but also other domains, such as the right to a bank account under consumer law,[8] or to medical care under human rights law and national health care law. Whether these additional rights are organised as administrative or civil law is part of the national legal *couleur locale*. EU law largely ignores such national divisions between administrative or criminal law sanctions, or between employment law and migration law, when it comes to regulating migrant worker rights. The national regulatory structure can influence – whether positively or negatively – migrant workers' rights at the individual level. Thus, the framework of blurring is appropriate for this study of the regulatory tools for fighting illegal migrant work *and* protecting migrant workers in a precarious position at work, both in the EU and in the Netherlands.

III. THE 'BLURRED' EU EMPLOYER SANCTIONS DIRECTIVE 2009/52

The EU Employer Sanctions Directive 2009/52 obliges EU Member States to prohibit the employment of illegally staying third-country nationals.[9] To uphold that prohibition, Member States must have in place effective, proportionate and dissuasive sanctions of a financial nature against the employer.[10] Member States shall also ensure that the infringement of the prohibition constitutes a *criminal* offence when committed intentionally, when it continues or is persistently repeated, when it concerns a significant number of illegally staying people, when it is accompanied by particularly exploitative working conditions, when the employer knew the migrant to be a victim of trafficking in human beings, or when the infringement concerns a minor.[11]

Otherwise, the Directive is vague as to which field of law employer sanctions must be implemented in, whether administrative law or civil law. Thus, the

[7] O Lobel, 'The Renew Deal: The Fall of Regulation and the Rise of Governance in Contemporary Legal Thought' (2004) 89 *Minnesota Law Review* 342.

[8] T de Lange and E Guild, 'Migrant Financial Inclusion versus the Fight against Money Laundering and Terrorist Financing' in de Lange, Maas and Schrauwen (n 2).

[9] ESD, Art 3.

[10] ibid, Art 5.

[11] ibid, Art 9.

Directive immediately presents a structural blurring of the legal fields and agencies involved.[12] Potential other sanctions include financial penalties which must increase in amount according to the number of illegally employed migrants; and payment of the costs of return of illegally employed migrants who are actually returned.[13] (Member States may instead decide to reflect the average costs of return in financial sanctions.) The provisions on financial sanctions against employers have been implemented in national legislation by all Member States, with differences in the proportionate size of fines, and in the authority in charge of defining the amount of the fine.[14] The clause on costs of return provides for yet another potential structural blurring between government authorities, as the costs of return and the financial sanctions are likely not imposed by the same authorities. Also, Member States may provide for reduced financial sanctions where the employer is a natural person and the irregular migrant is performing, for example, domestic services *and* no particularly exploitative working conditions are involved.[15] This requires the enforcing authority to adjudicate on the working conditions, which implies a blurring of functions as the public officials handling these cases are not necessarily trained to do so.

Further non-criminal measures which can be imposed draw upon a wide range of other legal disciplines, such as exclusion from entitlement to subsidies or recovery of such benefits (the law on subsidies), exclusion from participation in a public contract as defined in Directive 2004/18/EC (public procurement law), temporary or permanent closure of the establishments that have been used to commit the infringement, or temporary or permanent withdrawal of a licence to conduct the business activity in question.[16] The last of these would be covered by administrative law, but the withdrawal would not necessarily be performed by the same authority, which implies more blurring of the legal structures in the Member States. The implementation of the additional measures listed in Article 7 ESD shows great differences in the Member States.[17] Although all Member States have implemented at least one of these administrative measures in their national legislation, only a smaller group of nine Member States[18] have chosen to rely upon all four measures. Only eight Member States have reported to have *applied* at least one of the measures, with the temporary or permanent closure of establishment, and the withdrawal of a licence to operate, the options which are most utilised.

Irrespective of their status under migration law, migrant workers have rights as employees under the Directive. As an employee, a migrant has the right

[12] ibid, Art 10.
[13] ibid, Art 5.
[14] COM (2021) 592 final, 5.
[15] ESD, Art 5(3).
[16] ibid, Art 7.
[17] COM (2021) 592 final, 7.
[18] Germany, Spain, France, Lithuania, Austria, Poland, Romania, Slovakia and Sweden.

to equal wages, holiday allowances, and safe working conditions under the Directive.[19] This was at the time of writing not self-evident in all EU Member States.[20] (In the Netherlands, migration status and worker rights have been disconnected since 1981.[21]) Besides the ESD, other EU labour law Directives can also confer social rights upon irregular migrants. In *Tümer*[22] the Court of Justice held that to ensure that the 'social objectives' of the Insolvency Directive are met (Directive 80/987), Member States were obliged to treat migrant workers equally to national employees if they qualified as employees according to national law. Migrant workers may also fall within the protection of other EU Directives, depending on the scope and/or Member States' legal definitions.

The Directive does not include an obligation to impose a financial sanction on the employer for undercutting the minimum wage (if applicable), or for failing to meet social security or tax obligations, as that would go beyond the scope of migration control. It does though provide tools to increase irregular migrants' agency as workers, hence blurring the *function* of the Directive. To this end, the Member States are required to have an effective complaints procedure in place in cases of labour exploitation and abuse.[23] They must allow migrants to claim outstanding pay with their employer, or with a contractor if they work for a sub-contractor.[24] The salary shall be presumed to have the level of the minimum wage, or the wages set by collective agreements or in accordance with established practice in the relevant occupational sectors, unless either the employer or the employee can prove otherwise.[25] It must also be possible for migrants to claim back payments from abroad, and to receive back payments abroad.[26] Member States may allow third parties to engage in these procedures on behalf of workers, though this has only been implemented by some Member States.[27] Even without third party involvement, the Directive requires Member States to allow illegally employed migrants to bring a claim before a civil court or a labour tribunal, in case of labour rights violations.[28] Finally, the Directive lessens the burden of proof upon irregular migrants, by creating a legal presumption of

[19] On the right to equal wages/holiday allowances, see recital 20 and Art 6 ESD, and on safe working conditions termed 'particularly exploitative working conditions', see recital 22 and Art 2(1)(c) ESD.

[20] E Dewhurst, 'The Right of Irregular Immigrants to Outstanding Remuneration under the EU Sanctions Directive: Rethinking Domestic Labour Policy in a Globalised World' (2011) 13 *European Journal of Migration and Law* 389.

[21] Dutch Supreme Court in civil and criminal cases Hoge Raad, 27 March 1981.

[22] Case C-311/13 *Tümer*, judgment of 5 November 2014.

[23] ESD, Art 13. See further PICUM, *Undocumented Migrant Workers: Guidelines for developing an effective complaints mechanism in cases of labour exploitation or abuse* (2016) and Fundamental Rights Agency, *Protecting Migrants in an Irregular Situation from Labour Exploitation: Role of the Employers Sanctions Directive* (2021),13.

[24] ESD, Arts 6 and 8.

[25] ibid, Art 6(1).

[26] ibid, Arts 6920(a) and 6(4).

[27] ibid, Art 13. See further Fundamental Rights Agency *Protecting Migrants*, Annex II, 1-2. The Netherlands is not among the states that has done so.

[28] ESD, Art 13(1).

employment of at least three months, which becomes relevant once an irregular migrant is mobilising the law against an employer.[29]

The Directive thus has a 'multi-dimensional nature', with effects upon social policy, civil law, criminal law and migration policy, among others.[30] From complaints to court procedures, the Directive covers different stages of rights claims, in an unstructured manner, which involves a kind of 'blurring'. There is also a structural blurring, in that the Directive impacts upon horizontal relations between private actors: the migrant worker and the employer, as well as between the migrant and unions and between employers and contractors. The blurring of functions in the Directive enables the EU legislator to make inroads into social policy, a policy domain it would otherwise not be competent to regulate; blurring provides a solution for what is called the 'social deficit' of the EU.[31] Due to this blurring, the Employer Sanctions Directive is a highly complex instrument, and this complexity is a source of weakness within it.

IV. EMPLOYER SANCTIONS AND IRREGULAR MIGRANT RIGHTS IN THE NETHERLANDS

The Employer Sanctions Directive's complexity also comes to the fore through a case study of the Netherlands. This case presents a variety of specialised laws, different actors and specialised courts hearing complaints over the Directive's actual – though largely unstated – implementation. The relevant public actors are the state institutions in charge of inspections, such as the labour inspectorate, the Minister of Social Affairs and Employment, legislative bodies designing policy tools, operating from within different ministries, and specialised courts. The private actors involved are the migrant workers themselves and labour unions, as well as hiring companies working in a chain, and (understudied) actors such as the national workforce and business competitors.

The Employer Sanctions Directive is implemented in Dutch administrative law in the *Wet arbeid vreemdelingen* (Foreign Nationals Employment Act, hereafter WAV). To a large extent this was a 'tacit' implementation, as the instruments (administrative fines, criminalising, and worker rights) required of the Member States by the Directive were already part of the legal infrastructure designed to fight illegal employment of irregularly staying migrants in the Netherlands. The Minister of Social Affairs and Employment is authorised

[29] ibid, Art 6(3).

[30] E Guild and S Carrera: *An EU Framework on Sanctions against Employers of Irregular Immigrants. Some Reflections on the Scope, Features and Added Value* (CEPS, 2007) 4.

[31] See C Joerges and F Rödl, 'Informal Politics, Formalised Law and the 'Social Deficit' of European Integration: Reflections after the Judgments of the ECJ in Viking and Laval' (2009) 15 *European Law Journal* 1, who use the term social deficit in relation to migration and posting. I expand this notion of a social deficit to cover non-EU national migrant workers remaining illegally.

to impose administrative fines following an infringement report of the Dutch Labour Inspectorate.[32] In addition, the Minister of Justice and Security is authorised to take decisions on (the withdrawal of) migrants' residence permits in cases of illegal employment.[33]

A. Enforcement of the Employer Sanctions

The WAV goes beyond the Directive's obligations in respect of employer sanctions in several respects. It prohibits the illegal employment of irregularly staying migrants, as well as of legally staying migrants without a work permit when required. The legal definition of 'employer' in the WAV is also broader than in standard employment law – something which goes to the heart of the divide between administrative and civil law. The WAV-employer includes anyone – a company, natural person, or governmental organisation – who has a migrant perform a job, however marginal the job, and irrespective of an employment contract or remuneration being paid. Awareness of enabling a migrant to perform the job on their behalf is irrelevant to qualification as a WAV-employer. Moreover, administrative fines may be imposed on all subcontracting parties in a chain, as they all qualify as WAV-employers.[34]

Administrative fines were introduced into law in 2005 to replace criminal penalties, which were found to be ineffective because they were too low to be dissuasive.[35] The standard fine is €8,000 and can increase to up to €16,000 in the case of repeat offences or severe infringements, for instance when a large group of immigrants is involved, or the illegal employment is combined with underpayment of the migrant worker.[36] A non-EU national with legal residence can lose the right to remain in case of illegal employment, and such employment may be a ground for refusal of legal residence permission for irregularly staying persons.[37]

In practice, the Labour Inspectorate learns of WAV infringements through targeted inspections, and through complaints by irregular migrants or third parties, such as (former) colleagues, competitors, the competitors' workers, or labour unions. If a third party complains and the Labour Inspectorate indeed encounters an infringement, the third party may formally request the administration to issue an enforcement order. In practice, third parties sometimes do just that.

[32] WAV, Art 19a.

[33] Dutch Immigration Act, Arts 19 and 18(1)(g).

[34] On this definition, see LE Berntsen and T de Lange. 'Employer Sanctions Instrument of Labour Market Regulation, Migration Control, and Worker Protection?' in de Lange and Rijken (n 5) 218.

[35] PJ Krop, *De Handhaving van het Verbod op Illegale Tewerkstelling* [The Enforcement of the prohibition on illegal employment], (The Hague, BJU 2014).

[36] The administration can also decide to issue a warning before imposing the fine. The results of all inspections are published online resultaten.nlarbeidsinspectie.nl/ [last accessed 31 January 2022].

[37] Dutch Immigration Act, Art 16.

For example, in 2016 labour union Nautilus, operating in the waterborne transport sectors, was granted *locus standi* to challenge the failure of the minister to issue an enforcement order to an employer underpaying non-union member migrant workers.[38] In previous cases, unions had not been granted *locus standi* and could thus not file such a formal request for enforcement.[39] On this occasion the *Raad van State* (the highest administrative court) held that the union had standing because it pooled the individual interests of the affiliated members, and represented a collective interest in maintaining fair working conditions in the maritime sector. By filing an enforcement request with the minister, Nautilus was taking a stand against the underpayment of foreign seamen. As organised protests of that kind were among its core activities, standing was granted.[40]

Employees of a competing business are other private actors who may request formal administrative enforcement. In 2014, Dutch employees of a seagoing tugboat business filed a request with the minister for enforcement of the WAV, because a competitor business was guilty of unfair competition by illegally employing and underpaying its foreign employees. The Dutch employees argued that as a consequence of the lack of a level playing field, they ran the risk of losing their jobs. They too had *locus standi* based on an immediate interest in discouraging the distortion of competition. The *Raad van State* held that their request concerned their fundamental right to employment, and whenever a fundamental right is at stake, *locus standi* is more likely to be recognised.[41]

In both cases, neither the union nor the Dutch workers seem to have tried to protect the migrant workers from losing their jobs, or to help them invoke their right to back payments if they had been underpaid. As far as I am aware, neither of the enforcement requests resulted in any payments to the migrant workers involved, though they each led to administrative sanctions being imposed on the employers for illegally employing migrant workers *and* undercutting wages.

B. Enforcement of Labour Laws

The legal presumption of three months' employment enshrined in Article 6(3) of the Directive is shorter than the period provided for in the Netherlands, as Article 23 WAV establishes a presumption of six months' employment, and thus a right to six months' back pay, unless the employer can prove otherwise.[42] This legal presumption can obviously be helpful for the migrant worker in a

[38] *ABR v S* 5 October 2016, in appeal against Rb Rotterdam 12 June 2016.

[39] District Court Rotterdam 27 March 2014; District Court Rotterdam 12 June 2016, and *ABR v S* 27 March 2014.

[40] *ABR v S* 5 October 2016.

[41] ibid.

[42] T De Lange, 'De verborgen schat van artikel 23 Wav' [the hidden treasure of article 23 WAV] (2011) 4 *Journaal Vreemdelingenrecht*.

labour law procedure against the employer. The obligation to provide for a legal presumption was not new to Dutch law – indeed, Article 6(3) ESD appears to have been a 'transplant' from Dutch law.[43]

The fear of such pay claims is supposed to work as an incentive for employers to refrain from illegally employing migrants for financial benefits.[44] That said, irregularly employed migrant workers in the Netherlands have seldom made use of the civil law procedures at their disposal to claim rights under employment law against an employer. The only case where the legal presumption of Article 23 WAV was invoked successfully concerned an irregular migrant worker illegally employed for some 12–16 hours a day, seven days a week, for €25 per day, at a souvenir shop in Amsterdam, while he slept in a room above the shop.[45] His reliance upon the law began in 2010 with a complaint of human trafficking, which led to a criminal conviction of the store owner. Based on the police reports from the criminal case, which proved that he was seen behind the counter in the shop cleaning up, his employer qualified as an employer under the WAV. That allowed the migrant to invoke the legal presumption of six months in a claim before the labour court. In line with Article 6(1)(a) ESD, he claimed back payment of the usual wages in the sector (which were likely to have been more than the Dutch minimum wage, albeit that a collective agreement did not apply). Without the legal presumption he would have failed to prove his legal entitlements as to pay. His claim of outstanding pay *beyond* the six months was unsuccessful, as the Court held that neither Article 23 WAV, nor Article 6 ESD, supported the argument that the presumption could cover a longer period.

There are two main reasons related to blurring that explain why Article 23 WAV is not invoked more often. First, although eminently well suited to use in employment law procedures, the provision is tucked away in an administrative law act which otherwise defines *employers*' rights and obligations vis-à-vis public authorities. It is thus not widely known by those making or adjudicating upon employment law claims. When implementing the ESD, the Dutch legislator re-drafted Article 23 WAV to make its relevance to employment law explicit, and its paragraph 5 now provides that 'the employment law chamber of the District Court is competent to receive claims based on this article'.[46] Yet, this does not make the clause better known. This legislative approach is an example of a blurred structure, and shows how it can lead to missed opportunities to protect migrant workers' rights.

[43] The clause was implemented in Dutch law in 1995 after the Dutch Social Economic Council advised on such a legal presumption.

[44] The logic of back pay as an instrument of migration control was also central to Case C-311/13 *Tümer*.

[45] District Court Amsterdam 13 May 2014, Section civil law 1398938\CV EXPL 12-37560 (unpublished) and in appeal Court of Appeal (Gerechtshof) Amsterdam 5 April 2016, case number 200.160.819/01 (unpublished).

[46] WAV, Art 23(5), in force since March 2021, *State Gazette* 2012, 143.

A second reason why back payments are infrequent in the Dutch context is that a back payment claim cannot be made by labour unions as third parties. Although this is optional under Article 13 of the Directive, and Dutch unions have at times tried to obtain standing independently of migrants, the Netherlands has not implemented a right for third parties to claim back payments.[47] The claim will always have to be filed by the migrant worker, whether on their own, via a power of attorney, with union support, or otherwise. But if the migrant does not wish to invoke employment law, the Directive and Dutch labour law remain irrelevant.

A further reason that there is little case law on Article 23 WAV is that the clause *has* been used in negotiating back payments outside court.[48] Migrants may also fear repercussions for their immigration status, especially through deportation. If they were convinced that such a risk did not exist, they might come forward more often. In the Dutch context, however, a firewall between labour law claims and migration law enforcement is not by definition secured.[49]

C. Enforcement Through Contractual Provisions

According to Article 8 of the Directive, where a migrant worker is employed by a subcontractor, it is mandatory for Member States to ensure that a claim for outstanding pay may be made against at least one link in the contractual chain. This chain liability has spurred another legal debate in Dutch case law, and further blurring, in that it has brought about private enforcement of contractual provisions between contractors and subsequent subcontractors.[50]

In litigation before the *Hoge Raad*, contractual provisions on the recovery of financial sanctions from subcontractors were found not to be incompatible with the public policy aims at stake in employer sanctions.[51] The Court based its opinion on the rationale behind the broad definition of 'employer' in the WAV, which was that, otherwise, it would be far too easy to get around licensing requirements, and the fines imposed for their violation, by making use of short cuts, front or straw men, or complex (sham) arrangements. Any administrative

[47] T de Lange, *Staat, Markt en Migrant: De Regulering van Arbeidsmigratie naar Nederland 1945–2006* (Den Haag, BJU, 2007), 265.

[48] Reported by Dutch NGO Fair Work (personal communication with the author).

[49] This may be contrasted with ECRI guidelines that urge EU Member States to ensure that no public authority providing services in the field of labour protection and justice is under a reporting duty for immigration control and enforcement purposes: European Commission against Racism and Intolerance, *General Policy Recommendation No. 16 on Safeguarding Irregularly Present Migrants from Discrimination* (2016), point 16.

[50] T de Lange, 'The Privatization of control over Labour Migration in the Netherlands: In Whose Interest?' (2011) 13 *European Journal of Migration and Law* 185.

[51] Supreme Court (Hoge Raad) prejudicial ruling 11 December 2015, followed by Appeal Court ruling of 20 December 2016.

fine is, at the end of the day, unaffected by a recovery clause, and indeed such a clause allows the legislator's intentions to be realised throughout the entire chain: financial gain garnered through illegal employment melts away. The employer at the bottom of the chain has all the more reason to make certain that the terms of the WAV are faithfully followed. Employer sanctions and back payments in a chain, in practice, have made contractors into 'unpaid immigration officers', also blurring their role.[52]

V. CONCLUDING DISCUSSION

In this final section, I discuss whether the blurring between administrative and civil law offers effective protection of irregular migrant worker rights, again focusing on the Dutch context. The short answer is that it does not. A longer version would be that the Directive has contributed little to a decent, dignified, and rights-based life for irregular migrant workers in the Netherlands. From other studies, such as the 2021 FRA report, and the European Commission 2021 communication, we learn that this is not significantly better elsewhere in the EU.

Many international statements call for a labour market which guarantees 'decent' work', which implies that migrant workers are protected against abuse.[53] However, in practice, neither administrative enforcement measures nor contractual enforcement does much good for migrant workers. The blurring of the administrative and civil law instruments is part of the problem, because it creates a legal complexity difficult to navigate, and relevant actors may not even be aware of the options.

One way to raise awareness would be to give administrative courts a more active role in protecting the migrant workers involved, when they decide on the legality of administrative fines for illegal employment. For instance, they could invite migrant workers as third parties to a case, as criminal courts can do with a victim of trafficking. They could grant them a right to award damages to the migrant, as can be done in a criminal case. This would of course require some significant blurring – or even *merging* – into one legal field, going beyond the administrative/civil law divide.

Enforcement through administrative fines and subsequent contractual claims can be seen as the regulator's choice to blur the roles of employers and contractors and to 'contract out' government functions, making employers into immigration officers. The consequence of enforcement may though be that the migrant

[52] A Bloch, L Kumarappan and S Mckay, 'Employer Sanctions: The Impact of Workplace Raids and Fines on Undocumented Migrants and Ethnic Enclave Employers' (2015) 35(1) *Critical Social Policy* 132.

[53] See T de Lange and C Rijken, 'Towards a Decent Labour Market for Low-Waged Migrant Workers: An Introduction' in de Lange and Rijken (n 5) 18–22.

worker loses a (bad) livelihood, and becomes at risk of falling into an even more precarious position. If indeed there is no alternative workforce available, why do employers not do more than just follow their blurred role as immigration officers? Employers and contractors could argue in favour of regularisation, or proper entry schemes for low-waged workers, to secure migrants' access to decent work. Instead, employers who are in a chain where illegal employment takes place contract out their fines, and profit from cheap contracts, made possible thanks to informally employing (irregular) migrants.

Finally, how might the Directive be improved if a recast were to be considered? It is undeniable that a safe environment is required for migrant workers to come forward and claim their rights. But the chances are small that a legal instrument with two such different aims – to punish the employers *and* to offer migrant workers a possibility to claim rights from these employers – offers such a safe environment on the ground. The Dutch case has shown that indeed this combination of aims is not successful. Ultimately, this implies the disentangling the Employer Sanctions Directive into two separate legislative instruments. The rights of irregular migrants could become part of another Directive, such as that on equal rights for legally employed migrant workers (Directive 2011/98/EC). The result would be one Directive on employer sanctions and one clear instrument defining migrant workers' rights.

9

Irregular Migrants and Fundamental Social Rights: The Case of Back-Pay under the English Law on Illegality

ALAN BOGG*

I. INTRODUCTION

THIS CHAPTER EXAMINES the scope to enforce fundamental social rights against the employer under English law where a migrant is engaged in illegal employment. It will focus specifically on the enforcement of back-pay entitlement where the worker has committed the criminal offence of illegal working, as introduced in section 34 of the Immigration Act 2016. Although the chapter focuses on the English law of illegality, the underlying normative themes are universal: where legal rights are violated in circumstances where the claimant is involved in criminality, when should the criminal be entitled to the assistance of a public court to enforce their rights against the wrongdoer? Different legal systems respond to this problem in different ways. However, doctrinal tools that respond to the claimant's criminal conduct are ubiquitous in modern legal systems, and have been central to the developing law on the legal position of migrants engaged in illegal employment.

The second section provides a short overview of the English law on illegality and its recent development in the United Kingdom Supreme Court (UKSC). The third section then proposes a 'constitutionalised' normative framework for the law on illegality as it applies to irregular migrant workers, based upon the constitutional principle of legality. This requires a recognition that irregular migrant workers occupy a position of democratic, social and economic precarity. They are formally excluded from the democratic process in that they do not

* I am sincerely grateful to Serena Crawshay-Williams for valuable research assistance in the preparation of this chapter. I am grateful to Bernard Ryan for valuable criticisms of an earlier draft, and to participants at the workshop held at the University of Leicester. I am also grateful to the Leverhulme Trust for its generous support of my academic work through the Philip Leverhulme Prize.

have a right to vote, and their engagement in civil society organising may result in arrest, detention and deportation. As such, this group is especially vulnerable to majoritarian hostility and bias in the political process, particularly given the vilification of irregular migrants in populist discourses. In these circumstances, the principle of legality would direct the courts to adopt a strict approach to the construction of statutes that purport to cut back the fundamental social rights of such workers. In the fourth section, I propose a legal approach to the fundamental right to back-pay of irregular migrant workers examining the relevant rules in contract and unjust enrichment. In the concluding fifth section, I set out some thoughts on the wider significance of irregular migrants as a distinct constituency in shaping the constitutional theorisation of labour law.

II. THE ILLEGALITY DOCTRINE AND IRREGULAR MIGRANT WORKERS: SOME PRELIMINARIES

In what circumstances should criminals be entitled to enforce their legal rights in a court of law where the legal claim is tainted by their participation in criminal activity? In common law systems, this enquiry is undertaken through the public policy doctrine of illegality. There is however no single common law approach, and indeed a variety of possible approaches are displayed in those systems.[1] Civilian legal systems have also grappled with the problem of illegality using a variety of legal techniques.[2] The 'problem' of illegality may represent a universal feature of legal systems. While the legal responses vary, the necessity for *some* legal response is ubiquitous.

In the English law on employment, the illegality doctrine has been of particular importance in relation to the employment claims of irregular migrants who do not have a right to work. In these circumstances, the migrant worker is very likely to have committed a statutory criminal offence.[3] This situation of illegal working may give rise to a multiplicity of legal claims where the migrant worker seeks to vindicate their fundamental social rights against the employer. They might allege that they have been discriminated against or harassed because of their race or sex; they might allege that they have been unfairly dismissed; or they might allege that they have not received the minimum wage entitlements due to them under the work contract as unpaid wages. Each of these social

[1] See, eg, W Gummow, 'Whither Now Illegality and Statute: An Australian Perspective' and M McInnes, 'Illegality and Canadian Private Law: Hall v Hebert's Legacy' in A Bogg and S Green (eds), *Illegality after Patel v Mirza* (Oxford, Hart Publishing, 2018).

[2] B Häcker, 'The Impact of Illegality and Immorality on Contract and Restitution from a Civilian Angle' in Bogg and Green (n 1).

[3] Recently there has been specific criminalisation of *illegal working*: see Immigration Act 2016, s 34. Prior to this enactment, which specifically nominates the activity of illegal working as the criminal wrong, the irregular migrant would usually have been criminalised under general immigration offences: see, eg, s 24 of the Immigration Act 1971.

rights is protected as a statutory entitlement under English law. How should the courts proceed where they are presented with, on the one hand, statutory criminality under the immigration regime and, on the other hand, the enforcement of fundamental social rights guaranteed by protective employment statutes?

Historically, this legal enquiry was very complex. This complexity arose because there was not a unified approach to fundamental social rights under the illegality doctrine. Instead, English law applied distinct sets of rules depending upon whether the social right protected by statute was characterised by the courts as a 'tort' right, a 'contract' right, or an 'unjust enrichment' right. This reflected the compartmentalised approach to illegality in the general private law.

In relation to discrimination and harassment claims, this social right was generally treated as a tort right.[4] Consequently, it was amenable to the common law rules on illegality as they applied to tort claims. While these tort rules were themselves highly complex, and seemed to vary across different torts, discrimination claims were examined through the concept of 'inextricable link'.[5] Where the tort claim was 'inextricably linked' with the illegality, it would be barred under the illegality doctrine. Otherwise, the tort claim would be permitted. The application of this test suffered from a high degree of unpredictability given the accordion-like quality of 'inextricable link' in different factual scenarios. It also obscured the relevant policy factors and moral judgements that often seemed to underlie these judicial determinations, with 'inextricable link' functioning more as a conclusory label than a predictable tool of legal reasoning.

By contrast, the social right not to be unfairly dismissed was treated as a contract-like right. The rules on contractual illegality were even more labyrinthine, and depended upon whether the relevant illegality was treated as statutory illegality or common law illegality. Under statutory illegality, the statutory offence itself has the effect of prohibiting a category of contracts, either expressly or impliedly.[6] Even where there is no statutory illegality, the contract claim might still have been barred under the common law tests of illegality. This invited a more discretionary enquiry, ascertaining the level of knowledge and participation of the employee in the illegal conduct,[7] the proximity of the illegality to the contract claim, and the seriousness of the illegality.[8]

Finally, the social right to unpaid wages was most likely to be treated as a claim in unjust enrichment in situations where the employment contract itself was unenforceable. Since in many cases the employment contracts of irregular migrants were treated as impliedly prohibited by the immigration offence,[9] there

[4] *Hall v Woolston Hall Leisure Ltd* [2001] 1 WLR 225; *Wijesundera v Heathrow 3PL Logistics Ltd* [2014] ICR 523 (EAT).

[5] *Hounga v Allen* [2012] EWCA Civ 609.

[6] *Zarkasi v Anindita* [2012] ICR 788.

[7] *Hall* (n 4).

[8] *Enfield Technical Services Ltd v Payne*; *Grace v BF Components Ltd* [2008] EWCA Civ 393, [2008] ICR 1423.

[9] *Hounga* (n 5) and Zarkasi (n 6).

could be no contract claim for unpaid wages in an action for debt. However, it might be possible to seek a restitutionary remedy in unjust enrichment through *quantum meruit*. This was treated as subject to the 'reliance' test,[10] such that the claim would be barred if the claimant had to rely on their illegality in order to prove their claim. Like 'inextricable link', the 'reliance' test was rather unpredictable in its application to different sets of facts.

The enforcement of social rights in situations of migration illegality has given rise to some of the sharpest recent controversies in the English common law of employment. The leading case that is still directly on point is *Hounga v Allen*.[11] This involved a tort claim for race discrimination brought by an irregular migrant who had been trafficked into the UK as a minor under an arrangement orchestrated by her employers. She was working illegally and had committed a criminal offence in undertaking work in breach of her visa restrictions. The Supreme Court endorsed a 'balancing' approach in determining the effect of the criminal offence on her tort claim against the employer. According to Lord Wilson, the correct approach was to ask:

> did the award compromise the integrity of the legal system by appearing to encourage those in the situation of Miss Hounga to enter into illegal contracts of employment? … Conversely, would application of the defence of illegality so as to defeat the award compromise the integrity of the legal system by appearing to encourage those in the situation of Mrs Allen to enter into illegal contracts of employment?[12]

On the facts in *Hounga*, the public policy reasons in favour of barring a claim on the grounds of illegality were held to 'scarcely exist'.[13] Lord Wilson also articulated the need to identify and balance any countervailing public policies that favoured upholding the legal claim. In *Hounga*, this was identified as the public policy favouring the protection of victims of human trafficking, which was viewed as having decisive weight in the case.

Hounga was regarded by some commentators as a humane and liberalising judgment that mitigated the harshness of the illegality doctrine as it applied to the fundamental social rights of irregular migrants.[14] However, there were three main problems with the *Hounga* judgment.

First, the judgment applied only to tort claims. Consequently, the harsh and restrictive rules on illegality continued to extinguish her claims in contract.[15] The Supreme Court in *Hounga* did not question that those claims had been correctly rejected or not pursued by the claimant in the lower courts. This led

[10] *Tinsley v Milligan* [1994] AC 340 (HL); *Patel v Mirza* [2014] EWCA Civ 1047, [2015] Ch 271.
[11] *Hounga v Allen* [2014] UKSC 47, [2014] 1 WLR 2889.
[12] ibid, [44].
[13] ibid, [45].
[14] A Bogg and S Green, 'Rights Are Not Just for the Virtuous: What Hounga Means for the Illegality Defence in the Discrimination Torts' (2015) 44 *Industrial Law Journal* 101.
[15] Law Commission, 'Illegality and Employment Law' (February 2005).

to a certain arbitrariness in the treatment of social rights under the illegality doctrine. For example, unfair dismissal was treated as a contract right, even though its remedies could be viewed as tracking a tort rather than a contract measure of damages.[16] Admittedly, there is some difficulty in conceptualising unfair dismissal and the loss of the job as a genuine loss to the claimant where she ought not to have been working in the first place. Still, the contractual characterisation was by no means obvious or straightforward. Another odd distinction is that equal pay would likely be treated as a contract right, whereas sex discrimination was a statutory tort. Yet both these statutory rights would seem to share a common normative foundation in gender equality, despite the possible application of different illegality rules to each claim. It would seem preferable to have a unified approach to social rights, regardless of their technical legal characterisation under English private law. This is because many of the underlying policy issues are common to all these statutory social rights. This was not always reflected in the application of different legal rules.

Second, the recognition of a category of public policy that favoured upholding the legal rights of the claimant was narrowly targeted at protecting the victims of trafficking. While this was understandable given the specific facts in *Hounga*, it was unclear what else might be encompassed in this category of public policy beyond the fundamental right not to be trafficked. In *Hall*, for example, the Court of Appeal recognised that the statutory tort of sex discrimination protected a fundamental human right. This opened the possibility that all irregular migrants, regardless of whether they had been trafficked, might be protected by public policy where they were seeking to enforce their fundamental social rights against the employer. This argument would be particularly strong where those statutory rights were recognised as fundamental rights under international law and binding on the UK under its treaty obligations or customary international law.[17]

Finally, the judgment in *Hounga* was silent on the treatment of statutory illegality. Statutory illegality is concerned with situations where a statutory offence is regarded as prohibiting a class or category of contracts, either expressly or impliedly. Under common law illegality, by contrast, the effects of the illegality on the private law claim are determined by the common law itself. This omission was very important in the context of irregular migrants, because statutory illegality was generally treated as operative where the migrant was working under a personal employment contract without a right to work.

Following *Hounga*, there were conflicting judgments of the Supreme Court on the correct approach to illegality in English law, as to whether a rule-based 'reliance' approach or a balancing approach should be pursued. In *Patel v Mirza*,

[16] H Collins, 'Compensation for Dismissal: In Search of Principle' (2012) 41 *Industrial Law Journal* 208.

[17] *Hounga v Allen* (n 11) [50].

a nine-member panel sought to resolve the conflict.[18] Mr Patel, the claimant, paid sums totalling £620,000 to Mr Mirza, the defendant. This payment was made under an agreement whereby the defendant agreed to use the money to bet on the movement of shares, using inside information. The offence of insider dealing is contrary to section 52 of the Criminal Justice Act 1993. Hence, the agreement between Mr Patel and Mr Mirza was a contract to commit a crime and was itself a criminal conspiracy. When the anticipated information did not materialise, Mr Mirza refused to pay the money back to Mr Patel. Mr Patel sought restitution of the money in a claim for unjust enrichment. The question for the Supreme Court was whether his unjust enrichment claim was barred for public policy under the illegality doctrine.

All the judges agreed that Mr Patel was entitled to restitution of the moneys paid over pursuant to the illegal agreement. A majority of nine Justices of the Supreme Court set down a balancing methodology for approaching the illegality defence in English private law. In this respect, *Patel* can be seen as affirming and building upon the approach in *Hounga*. Leading the majority, Lord Toulson proposed a 'trio of necessary considerations' to be applied as a general test whenever illegality is relevant to a private law claim. Although *Patel* itself concerned an unjust enrichment claim, it must now be regarded as a general test to be applied across the full range of private law rights in tort and contract.[19] The UKSC has confirmed the applicability of the *Patel* approach to tort claims.[20] In *Okedina v Chikale*, Underhill LJ viewed the *Patel* trio of factors as encompassing contract claims in common law illegality.[21] The application of a common normative framework for the illegality defence across all types of legal claim is to be welcomed. It is more likely to lead to predictable and consistent decision-making, and it avoids the arbitrariness of the pre-*Patel* law where outcomes in illegality cases depended heavily on the technical characterisation of the statutory right as a 'contract' or 'tort' claim. It would also seem rather formalistic to confine the scope of *Patel* to unjust enrichment, when the trio was itself based upon authorities in contract[22] and in tort.[23]

In *Henderson*, the UKSC confirmed that there would be no 'year zero', and that existing precedents should continue to be applied where they are consistent with the *Patel* approach: 'Those decisions remain of precedential value unless it can be shown that they are not compatible with the approach set out

[18] *Patel v Mirza* [2016] UKSC 42, [2017] AC 467.

[19] See A Burrows, 'A New Dawn for the Law of Illegality' in Bogg and Green (n 1).

[20] *Stoffel and Co v Grondona* [2020] UKSC 42; [2021] A.C. 540; [2020] 10 WLUK 387; *Henderson v Dorset Healthcare University NHS Foundation Trust* [2020] UKSC 43; [2021] A.C. 563; [2020] 10 WLUK 386.

[21] *Okedina v Chikale* [2019] EWCA Civ 1393.

[22] *ParkingEye Ltd v Somerfield Stores Ltd* [2012] EWCA Civ 1338, [2013] QB 840. For an excellent analysis of contractual illegality after *Patel*, see J O' Sullivan, 'Illegality and Contractual Enforcement after Patel v Mirza', in Bogg and Green (n 1).

[23] *Hounga* (n 11).

in *Patel* in the sense that they cannot stand with the reasoning in *Patel* or were wrongly decided in the light of that reasoning.'[24] In a similar vein, Underhill LJ in *Okedina* considered that the 'broad principles' in the trio did 'not require a reconsideration of how the rule has been applied in the previous case-law except where such an application is inconsistent with those principles'.[25] This integrative approach to existing precedent has recently been applied by Singh LJ in the contract illegality case of *Tracy Robinson v His Highness Sheikh Khalid Bin Saqr Al-Qasimi*.[26]

Lord Toulson's trio consists of the following considerations set out in the pivotal paragraph 101 of the judgment:

> a) considering the underlying purpose of the prohibition which has been transgressed, b) considering conversely any other relevant public policies which may be rendered ineffective or less effective by denial of the claim, and c) keeping in mind the possibility of overkill unless the law is applied with a due sense of proportionality.[27]

The application of the trio must now be considered in the light of post-*Patel* authorities. As discussed, the trio does not obviate the need to consider the pre-*Patel* law on illegality. Rather, and where it is possible to do so, the pre-*Patel* illegality authorities should be understood as laying down intermediate rules, mediating between the general principles in *Patel* and the specific facts in the case. Furthermore, it is also important to adopt a purposive approach to the application of these rules. According to Lord Lloyd-Jones in *Stoffel*, the overarching purpose is to assess whether permitting the legal claim in circumstances of illegality leads to 'incoherent contradiction damaging to the integrity of the legal system'.[28] That is the fundamental point of the illegality doctrine, and it should permeate the legal enquiry and its discrete elements.

The first *Patel* consideration requires the court to identify the relevant offence as a basis for elucidating its statutory purpose, and whether that purpose would be furthered by denying the claim. It should no longer be sufficient to appeal to a general sense of free-floating criminality in examining the effect of illegality on the employee's claim. There is now some guidance in *Stoffel* as to how this should be approached. Lord Lloyd-Jones has suggested that the relevant policies should be considered

> at a relatively high level of generality before considering their application to the situation before the court. In particular, I would not normally expect a court to admit or

[24] *Henderson* (n 20) [77]. In an introductory essay to an earlier edited volume on *Patel*, we used the terminology of 'year zero' to ask whether the existing rules and principles were swept away by *Patel*: see A Bogg and S Green, 'Introduction' in Bogg and Green (n 1), 19. There were a variety of views expressed on the 'year zero' question across different contributions to the edited collection.

[25] *Okedina* (n 21) [62].

[26] [2021] EWCA Civ 862, 2021 WL 02366021.

[27] *Patel* (n 18) [101].

[28] *Stoffel* (n 20) [46].

> to address evidence on matters such as the effectiveness of the criminal law in particular situations or the likely social consequences of permitting a claim in specified circumstances. The essential question is whether to allow the claim would damage the integrity of the legal system.[29]

After *Stoffel*, this first limb invites a broader assessment of the law's general purposes, such as deterrence and legal consistency.[30] This does not preclude an assessment of the purposes of the specific legal prohibition, but the enquiry must not be restricted to that and it must be contextualised within the broader purposes of the illegality doctrine itself.[31]

The second *Patel* consideration builds upon the earlier decision in *Hounga*, where the Supreme Court identified the public policy in favour of protecting the victims of trafficking as supporting the worker's race discrimination claim *despite* the illegality.[32] Again, as in *Hounga*, there is no specific guidance in *Patel* itself as to what else might be encompassed by this category of countervailing public policy. In *Stoffel*, Lord Lloyd-Jones considered that permitting the negligence claim against the solicitors in that case would serve the policy that conveyancing solicitors should perform their legal duties to their clients diligently and effectively.[33] There is now an increasing recognition of the English law's protection of fundamental rights through both statute and common law.[34] This second consideration has the potential to provide a conduit for worker-protective policies to restrain the illegality doctrine where irregular migrants are seeking to enforce fundamental social rights, particularly where those rights are protected under international law. By analogy with *Stoffel*, it is an important public policy that employers should observe their legal duties to workers diligently and effectively, particularly where those duties are correlative to fundamental labour rights protected through legislation. Where denial of enforcement of fundamental rights encourages a culture of impunity in the labour market, especially in an era when labour enforcement is in crisis more generally, this should weigh heavily against permitting the illegality defence to employers.

The final consideration in Lord Toulson's 'trio' is 'proportionality' and the avoidance of 'overkill' in the denial of rights. This goes further than the

[29] ibid [26].

[30] In fact, Lord Lloyd-Jones' reading of the first limb of the trio is aligned with Lord Kerr's view of the matter in *Patel*, where he focused on whether the general purposes of the illegality doctrine were served, rather than the specific purposes of the prohibition itself: *Patel* (n 18) [124].

[31] *Henderson* (n 20) [119].

[32] *Hounga* (n 11).

[33] *Stoffel* (n 20) [32].

[34] See, eg, *R (on the application of UNISON) v Lord Chancellor* [2017] UKSC 51, [2017] 3 WLR 409. For general discussion, see M Elliott, 'Beyond the European Convention: Human Rights and the Common Law' (2015) 68 *Current Legal Problems* 85 and A Bogg, 'Common Law and Statute in the Law of Employment' (2016) 69 *Current Legal Problems* 67, 100.

judgment in *Hounga*, where proportionality was not identified as a freestanding element of the legal test. This was elucidated further by Lord Toulson in *Patel*:

> In considering whether it would be disproportionate to refuse relief to which the claimant would otherwise be entitled, as a matter of public policy, various factors may be relevant ... Potentially relevant factors include the seriousness of the conduct, its centrality to the contract, whether it was intentional and whether there was marked disparity in the parties' respective culpability.[35]

The judgments in *Stoffel* and *Henderson* make clear that the proportionality enquiry need not be undertaken on every occasion where illegality arises for consideration.[36] It is only necessary to do so where the balance of public policies under the first two limbs point towards a denial of the legal claim. This invites an enquiry into whether that denial is disproportionate. Where there is no prospect of the claim being barred by illegality, questions of proportionality are unnecessary. Where proportionality is relevant, this requires a highly particularised engagement with the specific facts of the case.[37] The judicial task is to evaluate whether denial of the claim would be disproportionate. In *Robinson*, for example, there had been a gap of several years between the employee's illegal conduct and the subsequent enforcement of the contractual claims. According to Singh LJ, this temporal dimension was relevant to the proportionality enquiry, which required an assessment of 'all the circumstances, for example the seriousness of the illegality, how long the distance in time, how closely it is connected to the nature of the claim now being made and so on'.[38] On this basis, it was open to the appeal court to decide that barring her claim would be disproportionate, given the lack of temporal proximity between the earlier illegality and the legal claim. This issue of temporal proximity is particularly important in personal employment contracts where the contractual relationship may extend over a significant period of time.

What impact will *Patel* have on the ability of irregular migrant workers to enforce their fundamental social rights? Before answering this question, the chapter will propose a normative framework to guide the application of the *Patel* formula in back-pay cases. The remainder of the chapter will then examine the fundamental social right to back-pay after *Patel*.[39]

[35] *Patel* (n 18) [107].

[36] *Stoffel* (n 20) [26]; *Henderson* (n 20) [123].

[37] *Stoffel* (n 20) [26].

[38] *Robinson* (n 26) [90].

[39] On the right to back-pay as a fundamental social right in international law, see E Dewhurst, 'The Right of Irregular Immigrants to Back Pay: The Spectrum of Protection in International, Regional, and National Legal Systems' in C Costello and M Freedland (eds), *Migrants at Work* (Oxford, Oxford University Press, 2014).

III. THE SOCIAL RIGHTS OF IRREGULAR MIGRANT WORKERS: A NORMATIVE FRAMEWORK

There is a fundamental constitutional dimension to the illegality doctrine where the social rights of irregular migrants are at stake. This public constitutional dimension may be obscured given illegality's basis as a doctrine of private law. On the one hand, recent democratically elected governments in the UK have pursued an aggressive agenda of criminalisation to ensure that migration controls are strictly enforced, most notably in the Immigration Act 2016. Parliament has exercised only weak constraints in this regard, perhaps reflecting the extent of popular democratic support for hostile environment policies. On the other hand, irregular migrant workers represent one of the most vulnerable and disadvantaged groups in the labour market. Such workers are formally excluded from the democratic process in that they do not have a right to vote. Although there are some examples of civil society mobilisation and successful political activism by organised groups of irregular migrant workers,[40] they are, in Jeff King's terms, a group that is 'particularly vulnerable to majoritarian bias or neglect'.[41]

The right to back-pay of irregular migrants has been considered explicitly by the government and by Parliament, and its status as a fundamental social right has been scarcely acknowledged. The UK Government secured an opt-out from the EU Directive on sanctions against employers of illegally staying third-country nationals.[42] The Directive provides under Article 3 that 'Member States shall prohibit the employment of illegally staying third-country nationals.' Alongside the prohibition of illegal employment, Article 6 specifies that

> employers shall be liable to pay any outstanding remuneration to the illegally employed third-country national. The agreed level of remuneration shall be presumed to have been at least as high as the wage provided for by the applicable laws on minimum wages, by collective agreements or in accordance with established practice in the relevant occupational branches.

In a written statement to the House of Commons on 24 May 2011 by Immigration Minister Damian Green MP, the UK Government's refusal to opt in to the Directive was justified in part on the basis that:

> The directive also guaranteed additional rights to illegally-staying employees, including provision of back payments where an employee has earned less than the minimum

[40] B Anderson, 'Mobilizing Migrants, Making Citizens: Migrant Domestic Workers as Political Agents' (2010) 33 *Journal of Ethnic and Racial Studies* 60.

[41] J King, *Judging Social Rights* (Cambridge, Cambridge University Press, 2012) 181.

[42] Council Directive (EC) 2009/52 providing for minimum standards on sanctions and measures against employers of illegally staying third-country nationals [2009] OJ L168/24.

> national wage, which would be difficult to administer and would send the wrong message by rewarding breaches of immigration legislation.[43]

Furthermore, the recently enacted offence of 'illegal working', inserted into the Immigration Act 1971 by the Immigration Act 2016, provides under section 24B (5) that:

> [I]f a person is convicted of an offence under subsection (1) in England and Wales, the prosecutor must consider whether to ask the court to commit the person to the Crown Court under section 70 of the Proceeds of Crime Act 2002 [POCA] (committal with view to confiscation order being considered).

The policy of the legislation is to treat wages earned in the course of illegal employment as 'proceeds of crime' which could be recouped by the state under a confiscation order.[44] The then Immigration Minister, James Brokenshire MP, sought to reassure law-abiding citizens that the UK would no longer be a 'soft touch' for illegal migrants, and the more aggressive use of the Proceeds of Crime Act framework to seize illegal earnings was a crucial element in this punitive public policy.[45]

Given the vulnerability of irregular migrants to majoritarian bias and hostility in the democratic process, any legislative or executive encroachment on their fundamental social rights should attract the most anxious scrutiny by the courts. The relevant constitutional principle is the principle of legality, as formulated by Lord Hoffmann in *ex p Simms*:

> Parliamentary sovereignty means that Parliament can, if it chooses, legislate contrary to fundamental principles of human rights … But the principle of legality means that Parliament must squarely confront what it is doing and accept the political cost. Fundamental rights cannot be overridden by general or ambiguous words. This is because there is too great a risk that the full implications of their unqualified meaning may have passed unnoticed in the democratic process. In the absence of express language or necessary implication to the contrary, the courts therefore presume that even the most general words were intended to be subject to the basic rights of the individual.[46]

Interpreting the *Patel* considerations through the prism of the legality principle gives appropriate recognition to the constitutional character of the enquiry. The enactment of statutory criminal offences criminalising illegal working has

[43] See Home Office, 'EU directive on sanctions against employers of illegally staying third-country nationals' www.gov.uk/government/speeches/eu-directive-on-sanctions-against-employers-of-illegally-staying-third-country-nationals [last accessed 15 March 2022].

[44] Home Office, 'New Action to make Britain a Harder Place for Illegal Migrants', www.gov.uk/government/news/new-action-to-make-britain-a-harder-place-for-illegal-migrants [last accessed 15 March 2022].

[45] ibid: 'A new offence of illegal working will allow wages to be seized as proceeds of crime.'

[46] *R v Secretary of State for the Home Department ex parte Simms* [1999] UKHL 33, [2000] 2 AC 115, 131.

wider ramifications for the migrant worker's social rights under the illegality doctrine. The application of the illegality doctrine could be construed as a form of selective judicial deregulation of social rights. The enforcement of social rights against the employer should not be framed as a pure private law dispute. The social rights protected under employment legislation also have a public dimension.[47] The principle of legality would direct the courts to interpret these criminal offences in a rights-compliant way wherever it was possible to do so. The particular vulnerabilities of this group in the democratic process – a minority that is regularly stigmatised and vilified in public discourse – mean that the courts have an essential role to play in protecting their fundamental rights. The criminal offences introduced in the Immigration Act 2016 already provide for significant punitive sanctions, even without the cascade of further social rights' deprivations that might occur through illegality as a collateral consequence of criminalisation.

IV. THE FUNDAMENTAL SOCIAL RIGHT TO BACK-PAY: THE LEGAL FRAMEWORK AFTER *PATEL*

In assessing whether the irregular migrant has an enforceable right to back-pay after *Patel*, there are two legal bases for such a claim. First, the back-pay may be sought under the contract as a claim in debt against the employer or through the National Minimum Wage Regulations 1999. That will depend upon the contract being enforceable. Prior to *Patel*, the employment contract of irregular migrant workers had generally been treated as prohibited under the doctrine of statutory illegality. It will be necessary to ascertain whether that position has changed after *Patel*. Second, if the contract is prohibited or otherwise unenforceable, the back-pay may be sought through a restitutionary claim in unjust enrichment as a *quantum meruit*. *Patel* liberalised the law on illegality in unjust enrichment for restitutionary claims, and it is likely also to have liberalised the law on *quantum meruit* too.

While *Patel* was not directly concerned with irregular migrants' legal claims, Lord Toulson's judgment reveals a particular sensitivity to this issue. This was reflected in the choice of comparative examples used to support his general approach. Lord Toulson referred approvingly to case law from Canada and the US where the courts have sometimes adopted a protective approach to migrants' legal claims.

The first decision was *Still v Minister of National Revenue*, where the Federal Court of Appeal in Canada balanced the policies underlying the

[47] *UNISON* (n 34) [72]. For further discussion, see A Bogg, 'Labour, Love and Futility: Philosophical Perspectives on Labour Law' (2017) 33 *International Journal of Comparative Labour Law and Industrial Relations* 7.

immigration legislation against the policies underlying the Unemployment Insurance Act 1985.[48] The claimant, although acting in good faith, had been employed without a valid work permit. The Court concluded that it would have been disproportionate to bar her claim for unemployment insurance in these circumstances, effectively treating the 'worker protective' legislative policy underlying the unemployment insurance legislation as overriding any countervailing policy of immigration control.

The second decision was the New York Supreme Court decision in *Nizamuddowlah v Bengal Cabaret Inc*.[49] In circumstances not dissimilar to *Hounga*, the plaintiff was induced to work illegally in the defendant's restaurant, in the expectation that the employer would secure the plaintiff an appropriate visa for him. Eventually, the plaintiff obtained the relevant visa by his own efforts, but in the meantime had not been paid for 20 months. The judge awarded the plaintiff a payment under *quantum meruit*, calculated by reference to the statutory minimum wage. This was upheld by the New York Supreme Court, on the basis that 'deprivation of compensation for labor is not warranted by any public policy consideration involving the immigration statutes'.[50]

Both judgments represent a 'worker-protective' approach to the social rights claims of irregular migrants, and the fact that Lord Toulson relied upon them suggests that such a reading of *Patel* is the correct one. Lord Hoffmann's legality principle could provide a robust constitutional basis for this worker-protective approach.

A. Unpaid Wages, Statutory Illegality and Implied Prohibition of Contracts

Statutory illegality contemplates the situation where a statutory offence, usually involving the imposition of a criminal penalty, has the additional effect of prohibiting a category of contracts. It is the statute itself that gives rise to legal effects on the enforceability of the contract, because those legal effects are treated as attributable to the intention of Parliament.[51] In this respect, statutory illegality should be regarded as conceptually distinct from common law illegality. In common law illegality, the effects of the illegality on the claimant's legal rights are determined by the common law doctrine of public policy. This is so even

[48] *Still v Minister of National Revenue* (1997) 154 DLR (4th) 229; and see Lord Toulson's discussion, *Patel* (n 18) [58]–[61]. It would also appear that there is Australian authority that supports this 'balanced' approach to legislative purposes. For discussion, see A Stewart, A Forsyth, M Irving, R Johnstone and S McCrystal, *Creighton and Stewart's Labour Law*, 6th edn (Annandale, Federation Press, 2016) para 9.40 discussing *Nonferral (NSW) Pty Ltd v Taufia* (1998) 43 NSWLR 312. I am grateful to Andrew Stewart and Tess Hardy for very helpful discussions of the Australian position.

[49] *Nizamuddowlah v Bengal Cabaret Inc* (1977) 399 NYS 2d 854.

[50] *Nizamuddowlah v Bengal Cabaret Inc* (1979) 415 NYS 2d 685 discussed in *Patel* (n 18) [66].

[51] For discussion, see RA Buckley, *Illegality and Public Policy*, 4th edn (London, Sweet and Maxwell, 2017) para 1-11.

where the relevant illegality is based in the violation of a statute, as will often be the case. For example, many cases of revenue fraud might be prosecuted using the general fraud offences in the Fraud Act 2006. As general criminal offences, there is nothing in these crimes that would indicate a *further* legislative intent to prohibit contracts of employment. By contrast, where a criminal offence specifically criminalises the activity of working without a 'right to work', it is easier to infer that the legislature intended thereby to prohibit employment contracts. This is because the very essence of the contract – the work – has been identified as a criminal act by the legislature. The analysis will always depend upon the precise construction of the specific statutory offence.

Where the contract is *expressly* prohibited by statute, the contract is regarded as unenforceable at the suit of either party.[52] Such instances of express prohibition are rare. For express prohibition to be in point, the statute must set out in explicit terms that the contractual right is void or unenforceable.[53] There is also a category of *implied* statutory prohibition. In determining the existence and scope of implied statutory prohibition, the legal enquiry is more complex. The courts have developed principles of statutory construction to determine whether a statutory offence impliedly prohibits a category of contracts, in addition to the criminal penalties imposed for the statutory breach.[54] Even where the contract is impliedly prohibited, the worker's claim in unjust enrichment will still fall to be considered under Lord Toulson's trio of considerations.

There is no suggestion in *Patel* that the category of statutory illegality has been superseded. This acceptance of the continuing role of statutory illegality is reflected in the Supreme Court's discussion of the decision in *Hounga*. Thus, Lord Toulson observed that the claimant in *Hounga* had brought proceedings for unfair dismissal, breach of contract and unpaid wages, and that those claims had been unsuccessful at first instance and in the Employment Appeal Tribunal (EAT).[55] He did not question the correctness of those conclusions on the contract claims, although he indicated his regret that the Court did not have an opportunity to consider an unjust enrichment claim in *quantum meruit* for the services she had provided.[56] Later in the judgment, Lord Toulson reiterated this observation that 'it is perhaps unfortunate that this court did not have the opportunity of considering a claim by Miss Hounga for a quantum meruit'.[57] He did not express any similar reservations about the findings on contract illegality in *Hounga*. In a similar vein, Lord Sumption observed that 'There was no claim under the employment contract itself, which was illegal, but it may well

[52] See, eg, *Re Mahmoud and Ispahani* [1921] 2 KB 716 (CA).
[53] Buckley (n 51) para 1-12.
[54] *Hughes v Asset Managers Plc* [1995] 3 All ER 669 (CA).
[55] *Patel* (n 18) [74].
[56] ibid, [74].
[57] ibid, [119].

be that a claim for a *quantum meruit* for services would have succeeded on the same ground.'[58]

In examining the role of statutory illegality after *Patel*, there are three issues to be considered: (i) are *Hounga* and similar cases to be regarded as true cases of implied statutory prohibition? (ii) Should Lord Toulson's common law 'trio of necessary considerations' inform the future development of the law on implied statutory prohibition? (iii) How should we analyse the criminal offences on illegal working in the Immigration Act 2016 after *Patel*? Each will be taken in turn. The answers will be considered in light of the Court of Appeal judgment in *Okedina v Chikale*, which was the first time that statutory illegality for migrant workers was considered after *Patel*.

i. Are Hounga and Similar Cases to be Regarded as True Cases of Implied Statutory Prohibition?

Some leading commentators have treated *Hounga* as an implied statutory illegality case.[59] That is not however supported by a careful reading of that case. It is certainly true that the Employment Tribunal concluded that, since Hounga's employment contract was tainted with illegality, she was unable to pursue any of the legal claims based upon her contract of employment.[60] In the EAT, there was discussion of the relevant basis for this finding of contractual illegality. The employer had argued that it was a situation where the contract was entered into with the intention of committing an illegal act, whereas the claimant argued that the contract had been illegally performed (but that the claimant had not participated in that illegal performance to a sufficient degree to bar enforcement).[61] So *neither* party had contended that it was an instance of implied statutory prohibition. Although the relevant discussion was rather slender, Silber J regarded it as most likely involving a situation of illegal contractual performance, albeit that the claimant had sufficient knowledge of, and active participation in, that illegal performance.[62] Hence, the EAT did *not* treat the contractual illegality as based upon implied statutory prohibition. The contract claims were in fact disposed of under the common law illegality tests as set down in *Enfield Technical Services v Payne* and *Hall v Woolston Hall Leisure Ltd*.[63] Since the EAT did not identify the relevant statutory offence that had been committed, simply treating it as obvious that the employment was criminal under some or other piece of legislation, it would have been quite wrong to assert that the contract of employment was impliedly prohibited.

[58] ibid, [243].

[59] See, eg, A Burrows, *A Restatement of the English Law of Contract* (Oxford, Oxford University Press, 2016) 222, 235–36. Compare O' Sullivan (n 22) 179–184, where she provides compelling arguments for a rejection of that reading of *Hounga*. The second edition of Burrows' *Restatement*, published in 2020, no longer contains this analysis of *Hounga*.

[60] *Allen v Hounga* [2011] Eq LR 569.

[61] ibid, [33].

[62] ibid.

[63] *Enfield* (n 8); *Hall* (n 4).

By the time the case reached the Supreme Court, the focus had then shifted to her statutory tort claim for race discrimination, and the relevant legal tests for illegality in tort claims. It is surprising, however, given the thinness of the reasoning in the EAT, how the earlier conclusions on the contract claims were treated as obvious legal outcomes by the Supreme Court. Thus, Lord Wilson at least identified the relevant criminal offence, which was set down in section 24(1)(b)(ii) of the Immigration Act 1971. He noted that the defence of illegality had been successful in relation to the contract claims, and that the appeal had proceeded without challenge to those findings. He also observed that the findings on unpaid wages, while also not challenged in the appeal, 'might conceivably have yielded a different conclusion' if the public policy considerations elucidated by him had in fact been applied to an unjust enrichment claim.[64] He did not suggest that the public policy considerations would have yielded a different conclusion had they been applied to her contract claims.

This emerges even more strongly from Lord Hughes' judgment in *Hounga*, where he observed that 'Miss Hounga's contractual claims have rightly not been pursued either in the Court of Appeal or in this court.'[65] This was explained on the basis that her unfair dismissal and breach of contract claims 'depend on a lawfully enforceable contract of employment but her whole employment was forbidden and illegal'.[66] As we have seen, however, the question of statutory illegality was never addressed in the EAT, because it was not treated as relevant to the contractual illegality point.

Other 'right to work' cases have displayed a similarly harsh approach to statutory illegality. For example, in *Zarkasi v Anindita* the claimant was engaged to undertake live-in domestic work for her employer, and entered the UK using a passport acquired fraudulently under a false identity.[67] The claimant brought claims for unfair dismissal and for unlawful deduction from wages, and further alleged that she had been a victim of trafficking. The Employment Tribunal dismissed her claims on the basis of illegality, treating the contract of employment as unenforceable because of implied statutory illegality.[68] It did so without examining the relevant statutory offence at issue, regarding it as sufficient that it was 'common knowledge' that it was a criminal offence to employ an individual without a right to work.[69] This reasoning was upheld by Langstaff J:

> It seems to us clear that if legislation makes a particular form of contract unlawful at the outset and throughout its existence … then the policy is clear. A court should not as a matter of public policy permit any party to enforce a contract that was and

[64] *Hounga* (n 11) [24].
[65] ibid, [54].
[66] ibid, [59].
[67] *Zarkasi* (n 6).
[68] ibid, [11].
[69] See, eg, the Immigration, Asylum and Nationality Act 2006, s 21. It is also a criminal offence for an employee to enter into a contract of employment in these circumstances: see the Immigration Act 1971, s 24(1)(b)(ii), referred to by Lord Wilson in *Hounga* (n 11) [24].

> always has been illegal. To do so would be to give recognition to such a contract as having legal effect, when according to the law it had and should have none. That policy is clear and clearly applicable here ... There is no question here of exercising a discretion ... still less any question of construing a statute. There is no room for holding lawful a contract as a matter of discretion or interpretation where the law must be accepted to be and is before us clear that it is not.[70]

There is nothing 'clear' about the prohibition of the contract in *Zarkasi*. On the contrary, determining whether there is implied prohibition requires careful construal of the terms of the relevant statutory offence. For example, the general immigration offences applying to migrant workers, that preceded the new offences of illegal working in the Immigration Act 2016, made no specific reference to contracts for work. The gist of the offence was to criminalise those who knowingly failed to observe the prescribed conditions of leave to enter or remain in the UK.

In the decision in *Okedina v Chikale*, Underhill LJ considered the pre-*Patel* authorities on statutory illegality. In relation to *Hounga*, there was a welcome recognition that the EAT's reasoning on the claimant's contract claims in that case was focused on common law illegality.[71] Underhill LJ regarded the Supreme Court's reflections on the contract claims to be 'quite abbreviated', given that the appeal was concerned with her tort claim of race discrimination.[72] This was an important advance in getting the law in coherent shape, challenging the assumption that implied statutory illegality is self-evident in illegal migrant cases. This gain in coherence was undermined by Underhill LJ's rather puzzling assertion that the appeal in *Zarkasi* 'was treated throughout as one of common law illegality, and no doubt for that reason no reliance was placed on any particular statutory prohibition: it was clear that the employee's conduct was illegal'.[73]

This reading of *Zarkasi* is difficult to understand. The ET had decided in that case that the claimant was complicit in the circumstances of her illegal employment, and it concluded that the contract was impliedly prohibited.[74] In any event, given her knowledge and complicity, the ET correctly observed that her contract claims would have been barred under common law illegality.[75] The appeal in the EAT was focused entirely on whether there was any scope for recognising an exception to the implied statutory prohibition, on the basis of international law protecting victims of trafficking. The EAT concluded that there was no basis in authority for recognising such a public policy exception. The EAT was therefore focused throughout on the statutory illegality point. Indeed, there was no logical alternative to that approach, for if the contract

[70] *Zarkasi* (n 6) [27].
[71] *Okedina* (n 21) [40].
[72] ibid, [41].
[73] ibid, [39].
[74] *Zarkasi* (n 6) [11].
[75] ibid.

was impliedly prohibited and hence void, the question of common law illegality would not even arise for consideration. The common law point would be otiose if the contract was prohibited as a matter of statute. This confusion is unlikely to assist in the rational development of the law on implied statutory illegality.

ii. How Should the Courts Approach Implied Statutory Prohibition After Patel?

In *Okedina*, the Court of Appeal considered the correct approach to implied statutory prohibition in a situation where the employer had committed a criminal offence under the immigration legislation (specifically section 21 of the Immigration, Asylum and Nationality Act 2006) but the employee was innocent and had not committed a crime. In this respect, the situation of asymmetrical criminality in *Okedina* is somewhat unusual. In cases now falling under the Immigration Act 2016, both parties may have committed criminal offences of illegal employing and illegal working respectively.

According to Underhill LJ, this was not a situation where the contract was impliedly prohibited. The general interpretive approach was to be based upon 'a healthy principle that Courts should be slow to give a statute an effect that is not expressly stated. Parliament should say what it means.'[76] Underhill LJ noted that statutory illegality was a 'blunt instrument', the effect of which was to wipe out the entirety of the rights based upon the contract.[77] Such an implication was neither 'clear' nor 'necessary' in view of the statutory penal regime.[78] This was particularly acute in a situation, such as *Okedina*, where the party seeking to enforce the contractual rights was innocent of wrongdoing. In this way, *Okedina* provides a more exacting approach to implied statutory prohibition than cases like *Zarkasi*.

Interestingly, Underhill LJ also suggested that Lord Toulson's 'trio of necessary considerations' could provide a background framework of interpretive principles to determine the existence and scope of implied statutory prohibition.[79] The use of these interpretive principles in implied statutory prohibition would enable the process of statutory construction to be developed in a transparent way. It would also ensure coherence of illegality across the different types of illegality and legal rights.

There is a need for caution here. The conceptual bases of common law and statutory illegality are distinct, and it is important to keep that demarcation in clear view. Indeed, it is a real strength of *Okedina* that Underhill LJ provided a lucid account of the different legal bases for these types of illegality. According

[76] *Okedina* (n 21) [45].
[77] ibid, [49].
[78] ibid, [46] and [50].
[79] ibid, [58].

to Lord Hamblen in *Henderson*, 'it should be emphasised that *Patel* concerned common law illegality rather than statutory illegality. Where the effects of the illegality are dealt with by statute then the statute should be applied.'[80] However, provided that we understand that these considerations are being developed and applied analogically as *aids to statutory construction*, there may be some value in so doing. Furthermore, the normative rationale of legal consistency and maintaining the 'integrity of the legal system' is also likely to be relevant to statutory illegality. After all, Parliament should not be taken to have legislated so as to *undermine* legal integrity and consistency unless that statutory interpretation is unavoidable. The judge should at least *attempt* to treat different statutes as elements in a coherent and integrated system of law, rather than spasmodic legislative reflexes intervening haphazardly from time to time in the life of the community. With these caveats in mind, how might the *Patel* trio of considerations inform the rational development of the law in implied statutory prohibition cases?

The first element of Lord Toulson's trio is a consideration of the purpose of the prohibition that has been transgressed by the claimant, and whether that purpose would be furthered or undermined by disallowing the legal claim. As Lord Toulson explained, this required a 'purposive' construction of the statute: 'The question whether a statute has the implied effect of nullifying any contract which infringes it requires a purposive construction of the statute.'[81] At the very minimum, this would require the court to identify and consider the relevant statutory provision at issue. Generalised references to free-floating criminality, such as were displayed in *Hounga* and *Zarkasi*, are not sufficient for the task.[82] The reasoning in *Okedina* represents an important advance in implied statutory prohibition, with the court identifying and construing the purpose of the relevant statutory offence.

The second element of Lord Toulson's trio requires a consideration of countervailing public policies that would support upholding the legal claim despite the illegality. In *Hounga*, this was identified as protecting the victims of trafficking. The category should be viewed as encompassing respect for the worker's fundamental social rights as protected under social rights legislation, such as the national minimum wage or working time protections. When construing the statutory purpose, the legality principle in *ex parte Simms* would direct the court to adopt a social rights-compliant interpretation of the relevant legislation where it is possible to do so. This would ensure that the courts hold both sets of

[80] Henderson (n 20) [74].

[81] *Patel* (n 18) [40].

[82] See, eg, *Patel* (n 18) [245]: Lord Sumption described *Hounga* as 'an attempt to bar her claim for unlawful discrimination on account of her participation in her own illegal trafficking'; *cf Hounga* (n 11) [24]: Lord Wilson referred specifically to the relevant illegality as the immigration offence in section 24 of the Immigration Act 1971. This imprecision is not acceptable given that the claimant's legal rights are at stake in the determination.

statutory purposes in view – the restrictive *and* the protective – when undertaking the interpretive exercise under the statutory illegality doctrine. This would also reflect the approach in cases like *Still*.

It would be better to view this as *internal* to the exercise of construing the statutory purpose, as an aspect of the constitutional principle of legality. The court is not 'balancing' different statutes or ranking competing statutory purposes. Instead, *it is construing the statutory prohibition so that it impairs the fundamental right protected under other protective legislation only to the extent strictly necessary in light of the clear wording of that prohibitive statute.* The legality principle in *ex p Simms* is thus concerned to construe parliamentary intention against a background of constitutional principle, treating different statutes as integrated elements of a seamless whole. This is not at all the same thing as negating parliamentary intention or carving out public policy exceptions to statutory prohibitions, as appears to have been assumed in *Zarkasi*.

The third element in the trio is the requirement of proportionality, considering the seriousness of the illegality, relative culpability, the proximity of the illegal conduct to the legal claim, and so forth. This concern with proportionality is reflected in older cases, such as *St John Shipping Co*, where Devlin J observed that:

> [A] court should not hold that any contract or class of contracts is prohibited by statute unless there is a clear implication ... that the statute so intended ... a court ought to be very slow to hold that a statute intends to interfere with the rights and remedies given by the ordinary law of contract.[83]

Since the criminal law already provides for a wide range of severe criminal penalties for immigration offences,[84] alongside the possibility of detention and deportation for migrants, considerations of proportionality would incline strongly against disallowing the claimant's social rights through prohibition. This could even be viewed as a strong presumption against statutory illegality, one that gives way only where the implication is necessary and, in Devlin J's words, 'clear'. This is particularly so where the relevant rights are not merely rights and remedies in the ordinary law of contract, but fundamental social rights protected by legislation. The legality principle would support a strong presumption against prohibition where the effect would be to render the claimant's fundamental social rights unenforceable. Again, Parliament should not be taken to have legislated in a disproportionate way unless this interpretation is compelled by the statutory language of the prohibition.

We must also remember that common law illegality continues to be operative even where the contract is not prohibited. This provides a more flexible

[83] *St John Shipping Corporation v Joseph Rank Ltd* [1957] 1 QB 267 (QB) 288, referred to by Lord Toulson in *Patel* (n 18) [5]–[6].

[84] A Aliverti, 'The Wrongs of Unlawful Immigration' (2017) 11 *Criminal Law and Philosophy* 375.

mechanism for denying specific contractual rights, in circumstances where it is proportionate to do so. In *Robinson*, Singh LJ confirmed that the 'knowledge and participation' test for illegality in contractual performance needs to be applied in light of the *Patel* trio. As such, 'knowledge and participation' should no longer be regarded as a *sufficient* test for the illegality defence in contractual performance cases. It will be necessary to apply these specific criteria purposively in light of the integrity of the legal system, assessing relevant public policies and (where appropriate) any disproportionality in denying the claim. This provides a much more flexible tool than the blunt technique of implied prohibition.

iii. How Should the New Criminal Offences in the Immigration Act 2016 be Analysed from the Perspective of Implied Statutory Prohibition?

Okedina was an unusual case in that it was concerned with a situation of employer criminality. In his concurring judgment, Davies LJ stated that 'the key to this case lies in the fact that s. 15 and s. 21 of the 2006 Act are directed at the employer. They are not, in my opinion, directed at the employee'.[85] Does it follow that the new regime of criminality in the Immigration Act 2016, with criminal offences for employers and workers, is a situation of implied statutory prohibition? Such a conclusion would be unwarranted, and the focus on a 'key' to any implied statutory prohibition represents a misplaced formalism. The offences of illegal working and illegal employing do not specify the express prohibition of employment contracts. They were introduced as part of a broad set of measures concerned 'to introduce tougher labour market regulation to tackle illegal working and exploitation'.[86] On the face of section 34, this looks like a much stronger case of implied statutory prohibition. The offence criminalises the specific activity of working where the individual is disqualified from working by reason of their immigration status. Does it not follow, by necessary and clear implication, that contracts for that illegal work are impliedly prohibited?

This conclusion should be rejected. The statutory purposes of the Immigration Act 2016 are undoubtedly pluralistic and complex. It represents a turn towards authoritarian public policy in using the criminal law to deter and punish breaches of the immigration regime by criminalising the daily activities of irregular migrants. It is also designed to prevent employers from exploiting the availability of cheap labour. In so doing it prevents the undercutting of law-abiding employers and the deprivation of employment opportunities from local workers. Even taking into account this complex (and, to some extent, contradictory) set of legislative purposes, these offences represent a new strategy of

[85] *Okedina* (n 21) [65].

[86] Conservative Party Manifesto 2015, 31; cited in ACL Davies, 'The Immigration Act 2016' (2016) 45 *Industrial Law Journal* 431.

worker-protective criminalisation, designed to deter working arrangements that facilitate the serious labour market exploitation of vulnerable workers.

The legality principle can assist us here. The court should adopt a construction of the penal statute that impairs the worker's fundamental social rights as minimally as possible. This would direct the courts to prioritise worker-protective purposes in construing the statutory purposes of the legislation. Since the offences in the Immigration Act 2016 are intended to be worker-protective by discouraging employment practices that facilitate abuse and exploitation, it would not further the purpose of the prohibition to deny the enforcement of fundamental social rights. The activation of the illegality doctrine to deny the enforcement of social rights would compound their vulnerability to abuse, not reduce it. This would be to subvert the legislative purpose of the Immigration Act 2016 offences, viewed in the wider context of supporting labour market enforcement. The penal purposes of the legislation are in any event served by the possibility of criminal liability for the various offences set out in the legislation, which provide for a range of significant criminal penalties. It is disproportionate to add to those penalties by also denying the contractual rights available to the vulnerable migrant worker.

B. Unpaid Wages and *Quantum Meruit*

Where the contract of employment is prohibited by statute, or its enforcement is otherwise barred by illegality, the question remains whether the employee can seek a restitutionary remedy for a *quantum meruit* where the employer is unjustly enriched. This will occur in situations where the employer has enjoyed the benefit of the employee's services without having paid for those services. Historically, the common law adopted a strict approach to *quantum meruit* in these circumstances. The interaction between illegality and *quantum meruit* appeared to raise the spectre of what Peter Birks has described as 'self-stultification' in the legal system.[87] The core of the contract of employment is the wage-work bargain. Where the employee is working in circumstances of illegality, and does not receive the wages due to them, would a *quantum meruit* not, in effect, be an enforcement of the wage-work bargain under different legal terminology? It might appear to be so, and in this way, the law on unjust enrichment provides a 'safety net' for participants in illegal activity where their contractual rights are forfeited.[88] It would also appear to be a situation where the law takes with one hand (through the illegality of the contract) and gives back

[87] P Birks, 'Recovering Value Transferred under an Illegal Contract' (2000) 1 *Theoretical Inquiries in Law* 155.

[88] ibid 162.

with another (in unjust enrichment).These arguments should not be regarded as decisive, and they can be addressed. However, the legal difficulty should be acknowledged.

Patel marked a clear liberalisation of the law on unjust enrichment for employees whose contractual claims are otherwise barred for illegality. The strongest signals may be found in Lord Toulson's judgment, in which he expressed the view that it was 'perhaps unfortunate that this court did not have the opportunity of considering a claim by Miss Hounga for a quantum meruit'.[89] This was supported by two authorities, both of which were affirmed as correct by Lord Toulson, and both of which were regarded as relevant to the *quantum meruit* point in *Hounga*.

The first decision was *Mohamed v Alaga and Co*.[90] The claimant alleged that he had entered into a contract with the defendant solicitors to introduce clients to the firm to pursue asylum claims. The plaintiff would then provide translation and interpretation services to the firm. The alleged contract provided that the claimant would receive a half share of the legal aid fees provided to the firm, on the basis of the introductions and the provision of professional translation services in the preparation of legal cases. The Court of Appeal concluded that the fee-sharing agreement was prohibited by the regulatory rules introduced under the Solicitors Act 1974. Those rules were introduced to protect the public interest in legal services provision, for example by avoiding the exploitation of vulnerable legal claimants for profit and avoiding conflicts of interest in the provision of legal advice. On that basis, the plaintiff could not sue for breach of contract. The Court of Appeal nevertheless allowed the plaintiff's *quantum meruit* claim to proceed, as a reasonable reward for the professional services that had been received by the solicitor. Lord Bingham CJ took the view that this sum could be regarded as distinct from the consideration payable under the illegal contract.[91] Furthermore, Lord Bingham CJ regarded it as relevant that the parties were not equal in blameworthiness. The solicitor could reasonably be assumed to have known of the rules prohibiting fee-sharing agreements, whereas the plaintiff did not.[92]

The second decision was the New York decision of *Nizamuddowlah* in which, as we have already seen, the claimant's *quantum meruit* claim was granted by the court. Taken together, *Alaga* and *Nizamuddowlah* were both used by Lord Toulson to support his positive view of a *quantum meruit* claim in cases similar to *Hounga*.

It is also significant that, despite the deep differences between Lord Toulson and Lord Sumption on the correct legal approach to illegality, Lord Sumption

[89] *Patel* (n 18) [119]
[90] *Mohamed v Alaga and Co* [2000] 1 WLR 1815.
[91] ibid, 1825.
[92] ibid.

expressed an identical view of the proper disposition of the *quantum meruit* point in *Hounga*. Thus, he observed that

> there was no claim under the employment contract itself, which was illegal, but it may well be that a claim for a *quantum meruit* for services performed would have succeeded on the same ground. There is New York authority for such a result: see *Nizamuddowlah v Bengal Cabaret Inc.*[93]

After *Patel*, the correct approach would be the application of Lord Toulson's trio of considerations. The first consideration is to examine the underlying purpose of the prohibition that has been transgressed. As has already been noted, in cases like *Hounga*, this is most likely to be the new offence in section 24B of the new offence of 'illegal working', inserted into the Immigration Act 1971 by the Immigration Act 2016. This provides under section 24B(5) that:

> [I]f a person is convicted of an offence under subsection (1) in England and Wales, the prosecutor must consider whether to ask the court to commit the person to the Crown Court under section 70 of the Proceeds of Crime Act 2002 [POCA] (committal with view to confiscation order being considered).

In this way, the policy of the legislation appears to treat wages earned in the course of illegal employment as potential 'proceeds of crime' which may be recouped by the state under a confiscation order.[94] This attenuates the relevance of cases like *Alaga* and *Nizamuddowlah*, where this statutory context was absent. It also creates difficulties for the legality principle, because here the legislation is couched in 'express language' (although it should be noted that the statute requires the prosecutor to 'consider' proceedings under POCA; it does not mandate them). This engages the more general issues of consistency and integrity of the legal system in a direct way, because by allowing the employee to recover the law appears to be speaking in two voices, not one. It therefore falls to be considered whether this might be affected by the other considerations in Lord Toulson's 'trio'.

The second consideration is the identification of any countervailing public policies that would support upholding the *quantum meruit* claim. The narrowest ground would be the public policy in favour of protecting the victims of trafficking, as in *Hounga* itself. This might be enough to resurrect the *quantum meruit* claims of trafficked workers, which may, strictly speaking, lead to the outcome in *Hounga* favoured by Lord Toulson and Lord Sumption. This narrow formulation of the relevant public policy would do little to assist highly vulnerable claimants who have not been trafficked, such as the claimant in *Nizamuddowlah*. Yet *Nizamuddowlah* was regarded by the Court in *Patel* as adopting the correct approach to the *quantum meruit* award.

[93] *Patel* (n 18) [243].
[94] Home Office (n 34).

There are a range of other possibilities in identifying the relevant fundamental right. For example, Birks explained *Nizamuddowlah* as based on a policy discouraging the evil of 'grievous exploitation' that was 'approaching slavery'.[95] This has obvious affinities with the freedom from forced labour, and could limit the scope of protection to extreme cases of exploitation. It is therefore very close to the characterisation of the wrong in *Hounga* itself. More broadly, Elaine Dewhurst has argued that there is a fundamental human right to back pay for irregular migrants, supported by international human rights instruments of the United Nations and International Labour Organization.[96] This conceptualisation would protect the full back-pay due under the contract. The most general formulation of the relevant fundamental right would be the right to a minimum or living wage, protected under the National Minimum Wage Act 1998. By pegging the level of the *quantum meruit* to the relevant statutory minimum rather than the contractual wage, as in *Nizamuddowlah* itself, this would undermine the 'self-stultification' argument against *quantum meruit* awards. This is because the quantum is set by the relevant statutory standard rather than the contractually agreed wage. In this way, a *quantum meruit* would not have the practical effect of indirectly enforcing the contractual wage-work bargain.

The third consideration examines the proportionality of denying the claim. This invites a consideration of the seriousness of the illegality, its centrality to contractual performance, the relative culpability of the parties, and so forth. Enquiries into the degree of culpability may serve to undermine the predictability of Lord Toulson's trio in difficult cases. In *Alaga*, for example, the assumed innocence of the plaintiff, reflected in his lack of knowledge about the legal prohibition of fee-sharing agreements (and, by contrast, the culpability of the defendant solicitor who must have been aware of the relevant rules), was regarded as critical to the outcome. Yet in *Hounga*, and in contrast to *Alaga*, the claimant *was* aware of the illegality of her employment situation. As the litigation in *Hounga* itself revealed, different judges took different views of her culpability and complicity in the arrangements. In circumstances where the parties have been complicit in fraudulent arrangements, this is likely to be fatal to the *quantum meruit* claim.[97] This is especially relevant where the employee has been actively and knowingly complicit in revenue fraud. It would also be relevant to situations where irregular migrants are judged to have been culpably dishonest in procuring employment. It also seemed highly significant to the outcome in *Okedina* that the claimant was viewed as a 'deserving' victim, and one who was innocent of culpability.

[95] Birks (n 87) 174.

[96] Dewhurst (n 39) 216.

[97] See, eg, *Taylor v Bhail* [1996] CLC 377. In *Patel* (n 18) [180], Lord Neuberger invites a comparison between *Bhail* and *Alaga*, observing that 'there is real room for debate in any particular case whether he should be entitled to claim payment on a *quantum meruit* basis'.

Overall, after *Patel* it would seem that in the ordinary case of an illegal employment contract, a *quantum meruit* will be awarded. This outcome, it is submitted, reflects the relative strength of the second of Lord Toulson's trio of considerations. It is an outcome that would be supported by the legality principle, even if the legality principle must do some significant work given the explicit nature of the statutory language in section 24B (5) on wages as 'proceeds of crime'.

V. CONCLUSION

The specific focus on this chapter has been on the English law of illegality as it applies to the social rights of irregular migrant workers, and in particular the right to back-pay. Nevertheless, the underlying normative challenges recur across all legal systems. The chapter has suggested some ways in which the ostensibly private law doctrine of illegality might be 'constitutionalised' through the common law principle of legality. This principle holds that fundamental human rights should only be cut back by legislation where the statutory language is clear and unambiguous. Ultimately, the limit of this principle is reached when it runs up against parliamentary sovereignty and the doctrine of legislative supremacy. If Parliament were to explicitly extinguish the social rights of irregular migrant workers through clear and unambiguous statutory language, there would be little that the English common law could do. The struggle for rights would then be a purely political one, at least in domestic terms. While these normative challenges are universal, other legal systems with different constitutional arrangements are likely to respond to those challenges in different ways. Further comparative work on the diversity of approaches to the social rights of irregular migrants, and the linkages with more general constitutional norms, is certainly warranted. In English law, at least, purposive statutory construction now lies at the heart of the legal enquiry into the illegality doctrine, in both its statutory and common law guises.

The special position of irregular migrants outlined in this chapter also has two important consequences for some important theoretical controversies in English labour law. First, the specific democratic vulnerabilities of irregular migrant workers, and their effective exclusion from the democratic process, provide a rationale for viewing this group of workers differently to other workers under the illegality doctrine. Where workers do not experience this pattern of democratic exclusion and civic precarity, the courts might justifiably adopt a different approach to the enforcement of their employment rights in circumstances of illegality. In this way, there *is* something distinctive about criminality arising in the immigration sphere, and there is a principled way of recognising this through the illegality doctrine. As a group exposed to formal democratic exclusion from the public sphere of the polity, and vulnerable to majoritarian hostility and/or neglect, the court occupies a special constitutional position for these claimants when they are seeking enforcement of their most basic rights. The lack of democratic voice justifies the most anxious scrutiny of any legislative curtailment of their rights. Second, there is still a strong thread of scepticism about the legitimacy of the judicial role among some scholars of English labour law and thinkers on the political Left.[98] This perspective is deeply-rooted and founded upon a constellation of factors: a social democratic preference for legislation as an instrument of progressive social and economic change; the undemocratic position of an unelected judiciary, especially where it impedes the popular will as expressed through legislation; and, concerns about the conservative bias of the judiciary and the common law and its gravitational pull towards established hierarchies, private property, and social order. The criminalisation of illegal working indicates the limitations of this sceptical tradition where a marginalised and stigmatised minority group is subjected to the targeted deregulation of its fundamental social rights through the statutory criminal law. In these circumstances, the insulation of the judiciary from the pressures of democratic politics appears to be more virtue than vice, in standing up for the social rights of a vilified and marginalised minority group.

[98] R Ekins and G Gee (eds), *Judicial Power and the Left: Notes on a Sceptical Tradition* (Policy Exchange, 2017). In a largely sceptical set of essays, there is a contribution from the current author that strikes a rather less sceptical note.

10

Counteracting Labour Exploitation: The Italian Response to Undeclared Work by Migrants

WILLIAM CHIAROMONTE*

I. THE BOUNDARIES OF THE INVESTIGATION: UNDECLARED WORK BY MIGRANTS

This chapter is concerned with 'undeclared work', which may be defined as employment relationships established within the informal economy, whose existence is unknown – in whole or in part – to the public authorities responsible for social security and collecting taxes.[1] In the Italian context, undeclared work is often associated both with labour exploitation and with illicit workforce recruitment, and all three phenomena are widespread. These phenomena now mainly concern migrant workers – ie, workers from non-EU countries – and above all those who are undocumented. They are especially associated with seasonal work,[2] particularly in the agricultural and construction sectors.[3]

* A first version of this chapter was presented and discussed at the *WORK 2017 – Work and Labour in the Digital Future* conference, held on 16–18 August 2017 at the University of Turku, Finland. I would like to thank all the participants for their fruitful comments. I would also like to thank Bernard Ryan and Ferran Camas Roda for their valuable suggestions. The normal disclaimer applies.

[1] On undeclared work in Italy see A Bellavista, *Il lavoro sommerso* (Torino, Giappichelli, 2002); V Pinto (ed), *Le politiche pubbliche di contrasto al lavoro irregolare* (Bari, Cacucci, 2007); A Viscomi (ed), *Questioni su lavoro sommerso e politiche di sviluppo locale* (Soveria Mannelli, Rubettino, 2008); M Esposito, 'Lavoro sommerso', in *Enciclopedia del diritto. Annali*, vol 5 (Milano, Giuffrè, 2012); M Sala-Chiri, *Il lavoro sommerso e il diritto del lavoro* (Napoli, Jovene, 2014); V Ferrante (ed), *Economia 'informale' e politiche di trasparenza. Una sfida per il mercato del lavoro* (Milano, Vita e Pensiero, 2017), as well as the contributions published in the *Rivista giuridica del lavoro e della previdenza sociale*, issue 2/2012. On European policies against undeclared work see M Giaconi, 'Le politiche europee di contrasto al lavoro sommerso. Tra (molto) soft law e (poco) hard law' (2016) 30 *Lavoro e diritto* 439 and S Varva, 'Undeclared work *e Unione europea, ultimo atto: una "piattaforma europea" per contrastare il lavoro sommerso*' (2016) 30 *Lavoro e diritto* 461.

[2] W Chiaromonte, 'Fisiologia e patologia dell'impiego stagionale di lavoratori stranieri in agricoltura' in W Chiaromonte and MD Ferrara (eds), *Bisogni sociali e tecniche di tutela giuslavoristica. Questioni aperte e prospettive future* (Milano, Franco Angeli, 2018), 127.

[3] In 2020, in the agricultural sector, 35.6% of employees were foreign, and it is estimated that 24.2% of foreign workers are irregular: see www.censis.it/lavoro/lavoro-agricoltura-18000-

This chapter will analyse the legislative measures which address both undeclared work and the exploitation of migrant workers (whether legally employed or undocumented) in Italy. In particular, the chapter will focus on the Italian legislative provisions aimed at sanctioning:

- the employers of undocumented migrant workers, ie, workers without residence permits;
- those who recruit workers to be employed by third parties in conditions of exploitation, taking advantage of persons in a situation of need;
- those who makes use of, hire, or employ workers – including by means of illicit labour recruitment – and impose conditions of exploitation upon them, taking advantage of persons in a situation of need.

The rest of the chapter will start by reflecting on the context of undeclared work by migrants in Italy (section II). It will then examine the ways in which legislation concerning labour migration contributes to the irregular situation of many migrant workers (section III), before moving on to evaluate the sanctions aimed at tackling undeclared work and labour exploitation (section IV).

II. UNDECLARED WORK BY MIGRANTS: THE CONTEXT

Over the past 30 years, notwithstanding an economic performance which has not always been brilliant, Italy has been a particularly attractive destination for migrants coming from southern countries with a younger population. This pattern has remained stable and independent of the general employment trend.[4]

stagionali-meno-nel-2020-19-perse-2-milioni-di-giornate-lavorate-24 [last accessed 17 March 2022]. In general, see also W Chiaromonte, 'The Italian Regulation on Labour Migration and the Impact and Possible Impact of Three EU Directives on Labour Migration: Towards a Human Rights-Based Approach?' in R Blanpain, F Hendrickx and P Herzfeld Olsson (eds), *National Effects of the Implementation of EU Directives on Labour Migration from Third Countries* (Alphen aan den Rijn, Kluwer Law International, 2016) 117; V Papa, 'Regulating Temporariness in Italian Migration Law' in J Howe and R Owens (eds), *Temporary Labour Migration in the Global Era. The Regulatory Challenges* (Oxford and Portland, Oregon, Hart Publishing, 2016) 259; and M Mc Britton, 'Lavoro in agricoltura e immigrazione' in E Rigo (ed), *Leggi, migranti e caporali. Prospettive critiche e di ricerca sullo sfruttamento del lavoro in agricoltura* (Pisa, Pacini, 2015) 101.

[4] See the data provided by the *Nota trimestrale congiunta sulle tendenze dell'occupazione* edited by the Ministry of Labour, ISTAT (*Istituto Nazionale di Statistica*, National Institute of Statistics), INPS (*Istituto Nazionale della Previdenza Sociale*, National Institute of Social Security) and INAIL (*Istituto Nazionale per l'Assicurazione contro gli Infortuni sul Lavoro*, National Institute for Insurance against Accidents at Work), published on 22 March 2022: www.lavoro.gov.it/documenti-e-norme/studi-e-statistiche/Documents/Nota%20trimestrale%20sulle%20tendenze%20dell%27occupazione%20IV%20trimestre%202021/Nota-Trimestrale-Occupazione-IV-2021.pdf [last accessed 25 March 2022].

Indeed, we are facing a paradox: massive immigration, even without economic growth.[5] In 1990, 2.5 per cent of the population residing in Italy were foreigners; by 2021, this percentage had grown to 8.7 per cent. In 2021, foreigners lawfully residing in Italy and aged between 15 and 74 years represented about 10 per cent of the workforce.[6]

While the reasons for the growth in the employment of migrants are numerous and interconnected, two main causes may be identified. On the one hand, the general rise in the standard of living of Italian citizens has meant that the majority of them are in a position to refuse so-called 'DDD' – dirty, dangerous and demeaning – jobs. On the other hand, demographic ageing has led both to a sharp increase in the number of elderly persons and therefore a new demand for labour in care work, and to an acute lack of young workers, due to comparatively low birth rates.[7]

The outcome in practice is a labour market in which migrant work is typically complementary to that of Italian workers.[8] The availability of migrant workers to perform 'DDD' jobs has allowed Italians to focus on jobs with higher salaries, as well as those that are less strenuous and more prestigious.[9] There has, moreover, been a remarkable reduction in the relative unemployment rate of women, as the availability of migrants to perform domestic work has led to the possibility for Italian women – especially those with higher education – to take employment.[10]

Undeclared work, particularly by migrant workers, has become a structural element in the Italian labour market. That is shown by the data presented in the annual reports of the National Labour Inspectorate concerning inspection activity in relation to work and social legislation. In 2020, for example, inspections were conducted in 103,857 companies, 70 per cent of which were found to have

[5] A Viscomi, 'La disciplina delle migrazioni economiche tra protezione dei mercati e promozione dei diritti. Spunti per una discussione' in *Studi in memoria di Mario Giovanni Garofalo* (Bari, Cacucci, 2015) vol II. S Allievi and G Dalla Zuanna, *Tutto quello che non vi hanno mai detto sull'immigrazione* (Bari-Roma, Laterza, 2016) 13 point out that during the recent economic crisis, while the employment of Italian workers decreased, that of migrant workers remained nearly stable. The same idea has been put forward by M Ambrosini, 'Perché e come gli immigrati continuano a lavorare in Italia' (2018) 67 *Rivista giuridica del lavoro e della previdenza sociale* 569. For an updated demographic analysis, see Ministero del Lavoro e delle Politiche Sociali – Direzione generale dell'immigrazione e delle politiche di integrazione, *Dodicesimo rapporto annuale. Gli stranieri nel mercato del lavoro in Italia* (Roma, 2022).

[6] Ministero del Lavoro e delle Politiche Sociali – Direzione generale dell'immigrazione e delle politiche di integrazione (n 5). On the impact of the migration crisis on Italy and EU see M Savino (ed), *La crisi migratoria tra Italia e Unione europea. Diagnosi e prospettive* (Napoli, Editoriale Scientifica, 2017).

[7] Allievi and Dalla Zuanna (n 5) 9.

[8] E Reyneri, *Introduzione alla sociologia del mercato del lavoro* (Bologna, il Mulino, 2017), 251. See also G Fullin and E Reyneri, 'Low Unemployment and Bad Jobs for New Immigrants in Italy' (2011) 49 *International Migration* 118.

[9] See F Cingano and A Rosolia, 'Non sono concorrenti ma complementari' [2010] *Libertàcivili* 45.

[10] S Allievi and G Dalla Zuanna (n 5) 22–23.

undeclared work of some form.[11] The number of undeclared workers discovered during the inspections was 267,677, of whom 22,366 were in a completely undeclared state (ie, their existence was wholly unknown to the public authorities). This data – although referring not only to undeclared migrant workers, but also to undeclared Italian and EU workers – confirm that 'the presence of a significant underground economy means that Italy exerts a particular pull effect on those migrants more prone to accepting irregular conditions'.[12]

Undeclared work is often performed by a migrant residing illegally in Italy, for instance because they entered the country in an irregular way, or their position became irregular because a residence permit expired, or was revoked, suspended or annulled.[13] Nevertheless, undeclared work by migrant workers should neither be confused nor identified with undocumented work.[14] For instance, a foreign national may be regularly residing in the Italian territory, with a residence permit not for the purpose of employment (eg, for tourism or medical care), or they may be authorised to take a specific employment, but then may obtain another one.

It is also the case that a foreign national illegally residing in Italy – as we will see in section III below – can only work within the informal economy. At most, they can hope to benefit, one day, from one of the ex post amnesties that, periodically, the Italian Government has experimented with and presumably will keep enacting.[15] As an alternative, they can hope that the informal work could represent a sort of 'probationary period' which precedes legal employment in compliance with the *Testo Unico sull'Immigrazione* (Consolidated Law on Immigration, Legislative Decree 286/1998).

The extent of undeclared work by migrants depends on several factors, many of which are of an extra-legal nature. That said, a key role has been played

[11] Ispettorato Nazionale del Lavoro, *Rapporto annuale dell'attività di vigilanza in materia di lavoro e legislazione sociale – anno 2020*, available from www.ispettorato.gov.it/it-it/in-evidenza/Documents/Rapporto-annuale-2020.pdf [last accessed 17 March 2022]. Some 2,000 cases involving the gangmaster system were discovered, including cases of unlawful or abusive conduct, serious labour exploitation and actual slavery.

[12] E Reyneri, 'The Role of the Underground Economy in Irregular Migration to Italy: Cause or Effect?' (1998) 24 *Journal of Ethnic & Migration Studies* 313.

[13] M Mc Britton, 'Lavoro degli immigrati e lavoro sommerso: l'inadeguatezza della normativa' [2014] *Questione giustizia* 172, 173.

[14] M-B Dembour and T Kelly (eds), *Are Human Rights for Migrants? Critical Reflections on the Status of Irregular Migrants in Europe and the United States* (Oxford, Routledge, 2011); C Morehouse and M Blomfield, *Irregular Migration in Europe* (Brussels, Migration Policy Institute, 2011).

[15] Since 1986, eight amnesty measures have been adopted in Italy, the most recent in 2020 (Art 103, Law Decree 34/2020): see W Chiaromonte and M D'Onghia, 'Cronaca di una sanatoria in tempo di emergenza sanitaria: genesi, finalità e limiti' (2020) 3 *Diritto, immigrazione e cittadinanza* 1. Such a frequent use of amnesties is an indicator of the failure of migration policies: see S Carrera, 'Integration of Immigrants in EU Law and Policy: Challenges to Rule of Law, Exceptions to Inclusion' in L Azoulai and K de Vries (eds), *EU Migration Law: Legal Complexities and Political Rationales* (Oxford, Oxford University Press, 2014) 149.

by the way in which the Italian legal framework on the work of migrants is structured. The main source is the *Testo Unico sull'Immigrazione*, which has numerous flaws, to the point of being itself a generator of illegal conduct.[16] The main paradox of the *Testo Unico* consists in the fact that a regime aimed at restricting illegal migration and undeclared work results in a restriction on the scope of legal migration. In other words, the legal framework not only does not tackle undeclared work by migrants, but ends up encouraging it.[17]

III. THE REGULATION OF LABOUR MIGRATION AS A CAUSE OF UNDECLARED WORK

Historically, Italy has struggled to formulate effective national immigration policies, especially since migration for economic reasons to the country began to occur consistently – approximately, since the 1970s, when Italy stopped being an emigration country.[18] Since then, the pattern has been that policy-makers have adopted an emergency approach to the phenomenon, instead of considering immigration as a structural feature which is characteristic of most of the countries of the developed West. Because of this 'original sin', the various legislative provisions adopted over time have almost never been able either to regulate the phenomenon properly, or to establish a regular and organised inflow of migrant workers, consistent with labour market demand.[19] To the contrary, the result is a legal framework on inflows and residence for employment purposes which is particularly complex. The regulation is so rigid and intricate that, in practice,

[16] For more extensive criticism, see S Sciarra and W Chiaromonte, 'Migration Status in Labour and Social Security Law. Between Inclusion and Exclusion in Italy' in C Costello and M Freedland (eds), *Migrants at Work. Immigration and Vulnerability in Labour Law* (Oxford, Oxford University Press, 2014) 121, especially 124–27; W Chiaromonte, MD Ferrara and F Malzani, 'The Migration Governance Through Labour Law: The Italian Case' (2019) 2 *Rivista del diritto della sicurezza sociale* 367; W Chiaromonte and V Federico, 'The Labour Market Needs Them, But We Don't Want Them to Stay for Good: The Conundrum of Migrants, Refugees and Asylum Seekers' Integration in Italy' in V Federico and S Baglioni (eds), *Migrants, Refugees and Asylum Seekers' Integration in European Labour Markets. A Comparative Approach on Legal Barriers and Enablers* (Cham, Springer, 2021) 193.

[17] W Chiaromonte, 'L'(in)evitabile nesso fra regolazione del lavoro immigrato e diffusione del lavoro sommerso: spunti ricostruttivi' in G Canavesi (ed), *Dinamiche del diritto, migrazioni e uguaglianza relazionale* (Macerata, EUM, 2019) 249; M D'Onghia, 'Immigrazione irregolare e mercato del lavoro. Spunti per una discussione' (2019) 2 *Rivista trimestrale di diritto pubblico* 463; Mc Britton (n 13); MG Garofalo and M Mc Britton, 'Immigrazione e lavoro: note al T.U. 25 luglio 1998, n. 286' [2000] *Rivista giuridica del lavoro e della previdenza sociale* 484.

[18] On the history of Italian migration policy, see L Einaudi, *Le politiche dell'immigrazione in Italia dall'Unità a oggi* (Roma-Bari, Laterza, 2007); M Colucci, *Storia dell'immigrazione straniera in Italia. Dal 1945 ai nostri giorni* (Roma, Carocci, 2018).

[19] For an overview of the evolution of the national legislation on migration, in particular for employment purposes, see W Chiaromonte, *Lavoro e diritti sociali degli stranieri. Il governo delle migrazioni economiche in Italia e in Europa* (Torino, Giappichelli, 2013) 97; W Chiaromonte, MD Ferrara and M Ranieri (eds), *Migranti e lavoro* (Bologna, il Mulino, 2020).

it tends to prevent migrant workers from entering Italy in a legal way, except through periodic and frequent ex post amnesties. This is especially problematic in a labour market such as the Italian one, within which informal hiring procedures are common, both for foreign nationals and for Italians.

The lack of accessible legal inflow mechanisms has made it very difficult to form an employment relationship with a migrant. Consequently, undeclared work has increased, and the legal labour market has been upset in crucial sectors for the country, such as agriculture and construction. Moreover, this scenario has favoured organised crime, which benefits from these phenomena by controlling irregular inflows and residence in Italy.[20]

It is apparent that in the Italian labour market there is a structural need for migrant workers. The main sectors where there is a structural need for migrant workers are care work (which is largely undeclared[21]) and seasonal work in agriculture (discussed further below). The gap between, on the one hand, the legislative obstacles to access the labour market, both as subordinate and self-employed workers, and, on the other hand, the structural need for migrant workers, remains extremely wide.

These key points may be identified: that the number of migrant workers who regularly enter the country for employment purposes remains low, mainly because there are insufficient places; that the system is too complex; that the norms elaborated in order to match labour supply and demand are systematically violated; and consequently, that there are too few legal migrants, and too many irregular migrants.

A. The Planning of Migration Flows

One of the causes of the spread of undeclared work of migrants is the procedure used by the State to determine the maximum threshold of migrant workers that may enter Italy for employment. In other words, the first defects of the system can be identified in the planning of migration inflows.

The *Testo Unico* provides for an articulation of national migration policies in two stages. The first is a three-year programmatic document 'concerning the policy on immigration and on migrant workers in the territory of the state' (Article 3(1)–(3)). This is aimed at establishing programmes and actions on migration as a whole, in particular the general criteria to determine annual inflows, and actions aimed at the integration of migrants. The second stage is represented by the so called *decreto flussi* (Article 3(4)), which every year establishes the maximum number of migrants who may be accepted for employment

[20] L Palmisano, *Mafia caporale* (Roma, Fandango Libri, 2017).

[21] For a comprehensive evaluation, see M Ambrosini, *Immigrazione irregolare e welfare invisibile. Il lavoro di cura attraverso le frontiere* (Bologna, il Mulino, 2013).

purposes. In compliance with this threshold, only a limited number of entry visa and residence permits may be issued. This can be seen from Table 1, which summarises the entry quotas for 2007–2021.

Table 1 Entry quotas, 2007–2021

Year	Non-seasonal	Seasonal	Total
2007	170,000	80,000	250,000
2008	150,000	80,000	230,000
2009	Not allowed	80,000	80,000
2010	104,080	80,000	184,080
2011	Not allowed	60,000	60,000
2012	17,850	35,000	52,850
2013	17,850	30,000	47,850
2014	17,850	15,000	32,850
2015	17.850	13,000	30,850
2016	17,850	13,000	30,850
2017	13.850	17,000	30,850
2018	12,850	18,000	30,850
2019	12,850	18,000	30,850
2020	12,850	18,000	30,850
2021	27,700	42,000	69,700

Source: Decrees of the President of the Council of the Ministers, 2007–2021.

In theory, the core of labour migration policies ought therefore to be represented by the three-year policy document, as it should establish the criteria applicable to match inflows for employment purposes with actual labour market demand. However, the last policy document approved was for the three-year period 2004–2006. Consequently, government action of more recent years has not been grounded upon a coherent medium-term migration strategy. Part of the explanation is presumably that the planning of migration inflows presupposes a stable macroeconomic context, which has often been lacking.[22]

Accordingly, the *decreto flussi* has acquired a central role, as it represents the only available policy instrument. Its original goal of regulating inflows through an estimate of the number of new admissions of migrant workers for employment has however been nearly entirely undermined. Instead, it has become the tool by which the irregular position of immigrants residing in Italy

[22] 'Il governo ha rinunciato a "governare" la migrazione': M Livi Bacci, 'Cronache di due fallimenti. L'Europa, l'Italia e le politiche migratorie' [2011] *Il Mulino* 437.

is 'decriminalised' on an annal basis. Moreover – as can be seen from Table 1 – the *decreto flussi* has been adopted each year only for seasonal workers, so that in some years non-seasonal subordinate employment and self-employment have not been provided for at all. Moreover, when provision has been made for non-seasonal subordinate employment and self-employment, the *decreto flussi* has typically foreseen too few admissions, especially in recent years.[23] This situation significantly reduces the number of admissions for employment purposes that are allowed, as admissions exceeding the quotas set by the *decreto flussi* are not allowed, other than in exceptional cases.

A first glance at Table 1 might suggest that Italy is not in need of migrant workers. However, such an approach does not properly consider that, without the contribution of migrants, the Italian working-age population would drastically decrease, because of a sharp reduction in the birth rate and improved life expectancy. As Allievi and Dalla Zuanna argue,

> In the next twenty years, in order to maintain the working-age population constant (20–64), approximately 325,000 potential workers should enter the Italian territory yearly; this amount is close to the admissions of the last two decades. Otherwise, within twenty years, the number of potential workers will decrease from 36 to 28 million.[24]

It is therefore impossible to dispense with migrants, if only to cover this deficit in the workforce.

A further consideration is that it has been estimated that in 2016, 8.8 per cent of Italy's GDP was produced by migrants, who provided €17.7 billion of tax revenues.[25] Several studies show that the costs borne by the public administration for migrants residing in Italy are more than compensated by the tax revenues and social security contributions paid by such migrant workers.[26]

Because the policy does not take account of the structural demand for migrant workers, at least in certain sectors of the Italian labour market, it contributes to the level of undeclared work. Indeed, a strongly restrictive policy towards inflows by migrants appears to trigger a vicious circle, as low quotas favour the irregular employment of migrants, which in turn permits lower quotas.[27]

[23] For example, in 2020, a very low number of new admissions for non-seasonal employment purposes (12,850) was allowed: see the Decree of the President of the Council of Ministers of 7 July 2020.

[24] Allievi and Dalla Zuanna (n 5) 10–11.

[25] It is estimated at around €15 billion, that is 1.75% of the public expenditure: see Fondazione Leone Moressa, *Rapporto annuale sull'economia dell'immigrazione. L'impatto fiscale dell'immigrazione. Edizione 2016* (Bologna, il Mulino, 2016).

[26] E Di Pasquale, A Stuppini and C Tronchin, 'Non solo profughi: l'economia degli immigrati' (*La Voce*, 27 January 2017), www.lavoce.info/archives/44832/non-solo-profughi-leconomia-degli-immigrati/ [last accessed 17 March 2022].

[27] C de Martino, M Lozito and D Schiuma, 'Immigrazione, caporalato e lavoro in agricoltura' (2016) 30 *Lavoro e diritto* 315.

B. The Admission Procedure for Subordinate Employment: Contradictions and Dysfunctions

The system of inflows planning can therefore be considered one of the causal factors of the rise in undeclared work. A similar analysis may be developed in relation to the rules that allow the entry and residence of migrant workers to perform contracted work in the private sector.[28]

Law 189/2002 – the so-called *Bossi-Fini* law, after the two members of Parliament who promoted it – significantly modified the original text of the *Testo Unico*, and generally made the entry and residence of migrant workers conditional upon the conclusion of a regular employment contract. The intending migrant worker has the obligation to have a document that legitimises their residence in the state for employment purposes. They must also be authorised to work by the *Sportello unico per l'immigrazione*, which is the office within each *Prefettura* (the provincial office of the state Police) which manages the entire procedure. This second element, which involves a special procedure for the employment of a migrant worker, is very different to the regular placement mechanism adopted for the national workforce. It deserves to be assessed further, with regard to the elements that favour the spread of undeclared work.[29]

First, the presupposition of the whole procedure is that the first matching between labour supply and demand takes place when the potential worker is still in their country of origin.[30] The administrative procedure requires the employer to apply for the work permit while the migrant is still residing outside the EU. The migrant worker is expected to remain in their country of origin until the entry procedure has been concluded. This duty stems from the fact that a job application by a foreign national already on the Italian territory is not allowed under Italian law, unless the migrant worker is already regularly residing in Italy for other reasons. However, this scenario conflicts with the recruitment procedure required by the law, based upon individual nomination ('*chiamata nominativa*'), which requires the employer to know the migrant worker at an early stage, notwithstanding that the latter is abroad. This system, which is rigid and intricate, does not facilitate the employment of migrants, and hampers

[28] This chapter does not deal with the issues related to the self-employment of migrants, or those connected to access by migrants to employment in the public sector.

[29] For a fuller assessment of the whole procedure, and in particular of the normative elements that constitute a disincentive to the employment of migrants, see Chiaromonte (n 19) 163; M Mc Britton, *Migrazioni economiche e ordinamento italiano. Una prospettiva giuslavoristica* (Bari, Cacucci, 2017) 118; GA Recchia, 'L'accesso al lavoro dei migranti economici' in Chiaromonte, Ferrara and Ranieri (n 19) 93; F Martelloni, 'L'accesso al mercato del lavoro dello straniero' in F Curi, F Martelloni, A Sbraccia and E Valentini (eds), *Imigranti sui sentieri del diritto. Profili socio-criminologici, giuslavoristici, penali e processualpenalistici* (Torino, Giappichelli, 2021) 58.

[30] Articles 22 et seq of the *Testo Unico*.

any direct contact between labour demand and supply. It therefore encourages the violation of the rules and gives rise to irregular behaviour. In practice, it is common for the migrant worker, who has irregularly entered Italy – or who has regularly entered Italy but with a permit that does not allow work, such as a travel visa – to make contact with an employer, before going back to their country of origin, in order to re-enter Italy in compliance with the procedure set out in the *Testo Unico*.

A second problematic element is the impossibility to enter Italy in order to search for a job. This circumstance is a consequence of the abrogation – again under the *Bossi-Fini* Law – of the possibility to sponsor a worker to enter for the purposes of a job search. Previously, a sponsor who was able to guarantee salary and accommodation was entitled to obtain, within the quota limits, authorisation for a third-country national to access the labour market for one year with the objective of finding a job (after one year, a migrant worker who had not found work was obliged to leave Italy).[31] The elimination of the sponsorship route makes the link between residence and employment even stricter, because access to the territory now depends on the existence of an employment contract. A third country national is now dependent on a request by an employer for a work permit, which is issued by the *Sportello unico per l'immigrazione*, after which the third-country national enters Italy and signs the contract of employment. It is after the formal conclusion of the employment contract that the police issue a residence permit for work, valid for the time indicated in the entrance permit.[32] This approach pushes the migrant worker who is looking for employment towards irregular employment and, hence, in most of the cases towards the informal economy.

A third factor is the so-called test of economic necessity, present for a long time in the law, then removed in 1998–2002, before being re-introduced by the *Bossi-Fini* Law. This test entails prior verification by the employer of the lack of a worker, already present in the national territory, who is available for the job in question. Only in that case may a work permit be issued in favour of the migrant worker.[33] This verification must be 'properly documented', having been conducted by the employer at the competent *Centro per l'impiego* (public placement office). For the employer, the choice to hire a migrant worker is quite burdensome, as the bureaucratic procedure to verify the unavailability of resident workers is complex.[34] Therefore, the principle of preference for the employment of workers already present in the territory and, consequently, the black mark

[31] Article 23 of the original version of the *Testo Unico*.

[32] This will be a maximum of nine months for short-term work, one year for a fixed-term employment contract and two years for a standard employment contract, though the permit is renewable.

[33] Article 22(2) of the *Testo Unico*.

[34] The *Centro per l'impiego* and the *Sportello unico per l'immigrazione* are no longer responsible for verification, which only directly involves the employer themselves.

against new entries of immigrants in the national labour market, is confirmed. In this way, the protection of the national labour market from potential regular immigrants is legitimised, without, however, obstructing irregular immigration or the informal economy.

A final problematic aspect is the considerable burden imposed by the 'contract of residence for subordinate employment' ('*contratto di soggiorno per lavoro subordinato*') upon an employer who wishes to hire a migrant worker. This form of contract was introduced by the *Bossi-Fini* Law and is now the primary form of 'work permit' employment.[35] The legal framework requires that the application to employ the migrant, presented by the employer to the competent *Sportello unico per l'immigrazione*, must be accompanied by documents guaranteeing: (i) the availability of accommodation which fulfils the minimum legal requirements for publicly-owned housing, for the migrant worker, as from the date of the application (hence long before the actual employment); and (ii) the payment of the repatriation costs of the migrant worker upon the termination of the employment relationship.[36] These burdens upon the employer make the procedure more demanding, and represent a deterrent to the employment of migrant workers, because of the costs of establishing the employment relationship. Indeed, the employer's duties to guarantee accommodation and the repatriation costs mean that the migrant worker is in a worse market position than Italian or EU citizens. These burdens end up discouraging legal employment, and again create a breeding ground for undeclared work.

In conclusion, the special framework on migrants' access to the national labour market, introduced by the *Bossi-Fini* Law, has seen a worsening of the already intricate entry procedures for employment purposes.[37] That has mainly been the result of linking access to the territory to access to employment. The legislation was intended to discourage the regular employment of migrant workers, but ended up triggering the diffusion of informal work. This is the consequence in particular of the system of individual nomination of workers still residing abroad; the removal of the residence permit for job search; the reintroduction of the so-called economic necessity test; and, the introduction of the residence contract for subordinate employment, with its heavy burdens on the employer.

[35] Article 5 *bis* of the *Testo Unico*.

[36] On the uncertain legal status of the residence permit contract in ordinary labour law terms, see L Calafà, *Migrazione economica e contratto di lavoro degli stranieri* (Bologna, il Mulino, 2013), 120, who defines it as an 'impossible contract'. Similarly, Viscomi, describes it as 'fantastical normative chimera': Viscomi (n 5) 1034.

[37] It has been descried as involving a 'Byzantine procedure, which makes almost impossible the regular admission into the labour market' (M Mc Britton, 'Prestazione di fatto e lavoro immigrato' [2010] *Rivista giuridica del lavoro* 551), and a 'kafkian bureaucracy' (Viscomi (n 5) 1029).

IV. THE FIGHT AGAINST INFORMAL AND IRREGULAR WORK: PUNITIVE PROVISIONS

This section is concerned with measures to tackle informal and irregular work by migrant workers. It will cover penal sanctions upon an employer who employs irregular workers (sub-section A) and the criminal offences of illicit workforce recruitment and labour exploitation (sub-section B). All of these are crucial elements in the State's response to the irregular employment of migrants.

A. Sanctions for Employing Irregular Migrant Workers

Article 22(12) of the *Testo Unico* imposes criminal sanctions upon an employer who employs migrant workers without a residence permit, or with a permit which has expired, or which has been revoked or cancelled. The penalties consist of prison sentences of between one and six years, and a fine of €5,000 for each worker employed.

The system of penalties for employers who employ irregular migrant workers was strengthened by Legislative Decree no 109/2012.[38] That in turn implemented EU Directive 2009/52 on employer sanctions.[39] The above-mentioned penal sanctions were increased by between a third and a half in cases of 'serious labour exploitation', which is defined to arise when more than three workers are employed irregularly, when a minor not of working-age is employed, or when workers are exposed to serious danger, taking into account the tasks and the working conditions. At the time of a conviction, the judge may also apply an administrative sanction, which consists of the payment of the average costs of the repatriation of the migrant worker recruited in an irregular manner.

A second change in 2012 was that Article 22 of the *Testo Unico* was enhanced by new paragraphs 5 *bis* and 5 *ter*, which define circumstances in which the

[38] On Legislative Decree no 109/2012, see T Vettor, 'Lavoro e immigrazione irregolare nel Decreto Legislativo n. 109 del 2012' (2012) 3 *Diritto, immigrazione e cittadinanza* 38; L Masera, 'La nuova disciplina penale in tema di contrasto allo sfruttamento del lavoro degli stranieri irregolari: l'inizio di una diversa politica criminale in materia di immigrazione?' (2012) 3 *Diritto, immigrazione e cittadinanza* 15; M Paggi, 'La tutela degli immigrati irregolari vittime di grave sfruttamento in ambito lavorativo: un percorso ad ostacoli per l'effettivo recepimento della direttiva 52/2009' (2013) 4 *Diritto, immigrazione e cittadinanza* 87; and A Ciervo, 'Una pura formalità. Alcune osservazioni critiche a margine del recepimento della direttiva 2009/52/CE da parte del legislatore italiano' (2014) 3 *Questione giustizia* 145.

[39] Directive 2009/52 providing for minimum standards on sanctions and measures against employers of illegally staying third-country nationals [2009] OJ L168/24. On Directive 2009/52, see B Fridriksdóttir, *What Happened to Equality? The Construction of the Right to Equal Treatment of Third-Country Nationals in European Union Law on Labour Migration* (Enschede, Ipskamp Printing, 2016) 139 ff.

Sportello unico per l'immigrazione must reject an application for a work permit, even though the standard conditions in the legislation and the *decreto flussi* are respected. This sanction applies where the employer has been convicted in the previous five years of any of the following: smuggling migrants into Italy or from Italy to another state, recruiting persons for prostitution or for the exploitation of prostitution, or recruiting minors to be employed in unlawful activities.

Prior to 2012, Article 22(12) contained the only penalty for the employment of an undocumented migrant. It was however limited to imposing penal sanctions upon the employer who had committed the offence, and did not regulate the consequences for the employment contract which had been established in an illicit manner. According to case-law, the illegitimate character of the employment relationship does not entail the loss of either the right to remuneration, or the worker's social security and insurance cover.[40] This solution is based upon the applicability of the Article 2126 of the Civil Code, which recognises that a de facto employment relationship, even if in violation of the law, is productive of legal effects.

The 2012 reforms implementing the Directive led to the employer of an undocumented migrant worker being obliged to pay the same amounts in respect of remuneration, social insurance contributions and taxes, as well as ancillary elements, as would have been paid in the case of regular employment. Until proven otherwise by the worker or the employer, it is presumed that the employment relationship has lasted at least three months.[41]

In practice, however, it will not usually be possible for the worker to receive any sum due before they are expelled. For that reason – again in order to implement the Directive – provision is made for the issuing of a residence permit for humanitarian reasons in favour of a worker who reports the employer, and who cooperates in related criminal proceedings, provided these concern serious exploitation or the unlawful employment of a minor.[42] The creation of this type of residence permit is an important innovation within the Italian legal system. Prior to the adoption of Legislative Decree 109/2012, the possibility to obtain a residence permit for 'social protection purposes' was limited to the victims of criminal associations that systematically exploited prostitution or committed other very serious criminal activities. As a consequence of the implementation of the Directive, an undocumented migrant is no longer treated as a potential criminal who may commit the offence of 'illegal immigration'. Instead, it is

[40] See, inter alia, Corte di Cassazione, 1 September 1982, n. 4755; Corte di Cassazione, 13 October 1998, n. 10128; Corte di Cassazione, 26 March 2010, n. 7380.

[41] Legislative Decree 109/2012, Art 3.

[42] This residence permit is initially for six months, but may be extended for 12 months, or for the longer period needed for the penal proceedings to be concluded. It may be revoked in the case of conduct incompatible with the purposes of the residence permit, or if the conditions for its issue cease to be met.

accepted that they may be the victim of a crime, because of their weak social and economic position.[43]

There are at the same time a number of deficiencies in Italy's implementation. According to Article 5 of the Directive, further administrative sanctions against an employer should be effective, proportionate and dissuasive, and should increase with the number of workers irregularly employed. The transposition Decree does not however provide for such further measures in the Italian legal system. Nor does it provide for the specific measures required by Article 8 of the Directive in cases of subcontracting, to ensure joint liability between the main contractor and the subcontractor where the latter employs undocumented migrants. Lastly, the Legislative Decree does not provide for instruments – other than the humanitarian permit – to facilitate complaints by migrant workers who have been irregularly employed, as required by Article 13 of the Directive.

B. The Fight against Labour Exploitation: Article 603 *bis* of the Penal Code

Besides the frequent involvement of migrants who are in an irregular position, undeclared work is often characterised by illicit workforce recruitment and/or the exploitation of workers. The discussion here will cover criminal offences linked to labour exploitation, provided for in Article 603 *bis* of the Penal Code.

Labour exploitation after recruitment by a third party often arises within the gangmaster system (in Italian called '*caporalato*').[44] This phenomenon is widespread in the agricultural sector and more generally throughout the food supply chain.[45] It is based upon intermediation by a so-called *caporale* (gangmaster), who recruits the workforce for third parties, who will employ the workers in conditions of exploitation, taking advantage of their vulnerable situation. Moreover, the gangmaster often governs the workers' living conditions, in certain

[43] See Masera (n 38) 31. The criminal offence of illegal immigration (Art 10 *bis Testo unico*) was introduced by Law 94/2009. It provided for the punishment of a foreign national who entered or resided in the territory of the state in violation of the rules of immigration law with a fine of between €5,000 and €10,000. This is a less serious crime (a '*reato contravvenzionale*'), which is punished solely with a financial penalty, without custodial remedies, such as detention or police custody.

[44] D Garofalo, 'Il contrasto al fenomeno dello sfruttamento del lavoro (non solo in agricoltura)' (2018) 2 *Rivista del diritto della sicurezza sociale* 229. On the UK experience see B Ryan, 'The Evolving Legal Regime on Unauthorized Work by Migrants in Britain' (2006) 27 *Comparative Labor Law and Policy Journal* 27.

[45] A Bonanno and JSC Cavalcanti (eds), *Labor Relations in Globalized Food* (Bingland, Emerald, 2014); W Chiaromonte, ''Cercavamo braccia, sono arrivati uomini'. Il lavoro dei migranti in agricoltura fra sfruttamento e istanze di tutela' (2018) 158 *Giornale di diritto del lavoro e di relazioni industriali* 321; P Campanella (ed), *Vite sottocosto. Secondo rapporto presidio* (Roma, Aracne, 2018); V Pinto, 'Rapporti lavorativi e legalità in agricoltura. Analisi e proposte' (2019) 161 *Giornale di diritto del lavoro e di relazioni industriali* 7; C Faleri, *Il lavoro agricolo. Modelli e strumenti di regolazione* (Torino, Giappichelli, 2020); S Borelli et al, 'L'altro art. 18. Riflessioni giuslavoristiche sullo sfruttamento del lavoro' (2021) 2 *Lavoro e diritto* 187.

cases by segregating them into 'ghettos' which the gangmaster manages.[46] The gangmaster will retain a certain amount of the salary – already likely to be far lower than the minimum wage established by collective bargaining – to cover the costs of transportation to the workplace, board and lodging, etc. Gangmasters may also transport workers from one area to another, according to the seasonal needs: for instance, tomatoes in Campania and Puglia in summer, apples in Trentino in autumn, oranges and tangerines on the Gioia Tauro plain (Calabria) in winter.

The gangmaster system involves mainly – though not only – undocumented migrant workers, who are particularly vulnerable from an economic, social and legal point of view. Given that a complaint filed to the public authorities would lead to their expulsion – subject to the limited possibility of a residence permit for humanitarian reasons – they tend not to report the situation of exploitation to which they are subjected. Therefore, they often accept working and living in particularly humiliating and unhealthy conditions.

In order to tackle this phenomenon, in 2011 the crime of labour exploitation and illicit job recruitment was introduced into Italian law, as Article 603 *bis* of the Penal Code.[47] In its original version, the 2011 legislation focused on the intermediary (ie, the third party to the employment relationship). It criminalised the conduct of the gangmaster conducting an intermediation activity (ie, recruiting or organising a workforce) which: (i) is characterised by exploitation; (ii) involves violence, threats or intimidation; and (iii) takes advantage of the difficult situation or the state of need of the workers.

The law on exploitation was subsequently modified by Law 199/2016, which amended Article 603 *bis*, by introducing rules aimed at making the policy against the gangmaster system more effective. In particular, it criminalised workforce exploitation by the direct employer, independently of any gangmaster activity. This penal crime of labour exploitation is unique in Europe.

Two elements characterise the criminal offence of both the gangmaster and the employer: on the one hand, labour exploitation and, on the other, the exploitation of the workers' state of need. The simultaneous presence of these two elements is necessary for the behaviour to amount to a criminal offence.

For both types of criminal conduct, the same penal sanctions are applicable. Both the gangmaster and the employer are punished by imprisonment of between one and six years, together with a fine of €500 to €1,000 for each

[46] An example is provided by the town of Rignano Garganico, Foggia, Italy. On the phenomenon see Y Sagnet and L Palmisano, *Ghetto Italia. I braccianti stranieri tra caporalato e sfruttamento* (Roma, Fandango Libri, 2015); M Omizzolo, *Sotto padrone. Uomini, donne e caporali nell'agromafia italiana* (Milano, Feltrinelli, 2019); Osservatorio Placido Rizzotto – FLAI-CGIL, *Agromafie e caporalato. Settimo rapporto* (Roma, Ediesse, 2022). In relation to exploitation as a 'method of production' in agriculture, see E Rigo, 'Lo sfruttamento come modo di produzione' in Rigo (n 3) 5. In general, see also J Fudge and K Strauss, *Temporary Work, Agencies and Unfree Labour. Insecurity in the New World of Work* (Oxford, Routledge, 2013).

[47] Article 12 of Law 148/2011.

worker recruited. Moreover, provision is made for a penalty of imprisonment of between five and eight years, and a fine of €1,000 to €2,000 for each worker, if the recruitment takes place through violence or intimidation. If the behaviour amounts to a more serious crime – for instance, slavery or trafficking in persons, prohibited by Articles 600 and 601 of the Penal Code – then these behaviours are punished by imprisonment of between eight and 20 years.

The concept of exploitation is central to these criminal provisions. In this regard, Article 603 *bis* paragraph 2 identifies several 'legal indicators of exploitation', most of which relate to conduct which can be perpetrated only by the employer. These may be grouped into four thematic clusters:

- Repeated payment of salaries which clearly diverge from the collective agreements at national and local level concluded by the most representative trade unions at national level, or which are disproportionate relative to the quantity and quality of the work performed[48]
- Repeated violation of the laws on working time, weekly rest, mandatory leave and holidays
- Persistent violation of the laws on health and safety at work
- Subjecting the worker to working conditions, monitoring methods or accommodation which is degrading.[49]

Ultimately, it can be argued that labour exploitation exists in those cases in which the 'hard core' of employment law, whether based in legislation or collective agreements, is not respected. Moreover, according to Article 603 *bis* (3) of the Penal Code, serious labour exploitation – as defined in section IV, above – represents a specific aggravating factor which implies a harsher punishment of between a third and a half.

Article 2 of Law 199/2016 allows for mitigating circumstances for the crimes enshrined in Article 603 *bis* of the Penal Code, which leads to a possible reduction of punishment of between one-third and two-thirds. This provision benefits a person who reports what they know, and thereby avoids a worsening of the consequences of the criminal behaviour, or alternatively who provides the authorities with evidence to identify and arrest their accomplices, or to enable the proceeds of the criminal activity to be confiscated.

Three other norms related to economic liability, introduced by Law 199/2016, also merit discussion. First, Article 603 *bis* (2) of the Penal Code extends legal provisions for the confiscation of properties used or destined to commit a crime, or properties which represent its price, product or profit, to the crime of illicit workforce intermediation.

[48] The reference to local collective agreement was added by Law 199/2016. Having regard to the Italian industrial relations system, there are in practice few sectors without effective collective agreements, as defined.

[49] The version of Art 603 *bis* had required that the working conditions, etc, were 'highly degrading'.

Moreover, in order to guarantee the continuation of the company that has employed workers in violation of Article 603 *bis* of the Penal Code, so as to protect their jobs, Article 3 of Law 199/2016 provides for judicial control of the company at which the crime has been committed. This is provided for where the suspension of the business activity 'may have an adverse impact on the employment levels or jeopardize the economic value of the business complex'.

Finally, under Article 6 of Law 199/2016, this criminal offence is included among those crimes that entail the mandatory arrest of the suspect caught *in flagrante delicto*, and also lead to the criminal-administrative responsibility of a company if the crime has been committed for its benefit.

From a labour law perspective – and thinking in particular about the fight against undeclared work – a critical weakness of the laws relating to illegal hiring and exploitation is the absence of a mechanism to oblige the employer to continue to employ the workers concerned, by regularising their status if they are undocumented. That would mean granting the full restoration of salary and social security protection.

V. CONCLUDING REMARKS: THE CONTINUING RELEVANCE OF A LABOUR LAW PERSPECTIVE

Within the Italian legal order, the regulation of the admission of migrants for work, and punitive measures against informal work, involve two conflicting – even contradictory – sets of rules. On the one hand, we have administrative regulations which – for the reasons described in this chapter – favour undeclared work by migrants. On the other hand, we find criminal law provisions which seek to combat informal work by punishing the employer.

If we assume that the prevalence of undeclared work is a socially and economically undesirable phenomenon, then the regulation of work performed by migrants should be designed so as to effectively combat it. We have seen in this chapter that that is not the case, however. Instead, the legislation hampers the admission of migrant workers to seek employment, and limits the duration of legal stay in the country once a job has been lost.[50] This unavoidably creates the conditions for an increase in the number of undocumented migrants. Many employers are pushed to make use of irregular work by migrants – which will typically be undeclared – by the low quotas and the administrative difficulties and delays of the hiring procedure.[51] Indeed, the repeated, uncoordinated changes to

[50] Termination of employment does not automatically invalidate the residence permit, which continues to be effective until its expiry. The period may not be less than one year, except in the case of a residence permit issued for seasonal work. Workers who are dismissed, or who have resigned from their jobs, can obtain unemployment benefits, and can search for a new job in Italy, but only for the remaining period of validity of the permit.

[51] M Barbieri, 'L'intervento comunitario di contrasto al lavoro nero alla luce dell'esperienza italiana' (2010) III *Rivista italiana di diritto del lavoro* 99.

the *Testo Unico* over the past 25 years have caused a degree of uncertainty which may itself have contributed to the spread of irregular work by migrants.[52]

The underlying perspective taken in this chapter is that, in order to tackle undeclared work, part of the solution is for punitive sanctions to be strengthened. We can see a tendency for the criminal law to displace labour law in addressing exploitative employment. It is inconceivable, however, that the phenomenon can be governed exclusively through criminal sanctions. On the contrary, to rely upon the most repressive legal instrument – that is, the criminal law – amounts to betting on defeat: the more the penal sanction is raised, the less are the chances that the sanction will be applied.[53]

Instead, the policy mix should include a strengthening of inspection mechanisms, and of employer incentives. In relation to inspection activity, the creation in 2015 of a National Labour Inspectorate – a single Agency for labour inspections which coordinates and conducts the inspection on the national territory of labour conditions, social security contributions, mandatory insurance and social norms, as well as the inspection on health and safety at work – represents a step forward, even if the number of inspectors is still insufficient. As for employer incentives, a key role could be played by norms in the agricultural sector that make the possibility to benefit from EU support measures conditional upon the fulfilment of certain production standards.[54] The same is true of ethical certification for goods produced by companies which respect workers' rights, and of a range of information and instruments aimed at orienting the consumers towards products produced without labour exploitation.[55]

As Cathryn Costello has argued, a labour law approach would entail an insulation of labour rights from migration status, better collective and institutional protections for labour rights and better regulation of intermediaries.[56] All of

[52] Mc Britton (n 13) 179–80. For a historical overview, see Chiaromonte (n 19) 131.

[53] Mc Britton (n 13) 176.

[54] I Canfora, 'La filiera agroalimentare tra politiche europee e disciplina dei rapporti contrattuali: i riflessi sul lavoro in agricoltura' (2018) 158 *Giornale di diritto del lavoro e di relazioni industriali* 259.

[55] In relation to agricultural work, see de Martino, Lozito and Schiuma (n 27). A leading example of 'ethical certification' is the label *Equapulia*, the 'ethical sticker' issued by the Puglia Region to enterprises which can demonstrate that they have not made use of undeclared work in any of the agricultural production phases (harvesting, processing and distribution).

[56] C Costello, 'Migrants and Forced Labour: A Labour Law Response' in A Bogg, C Costello, ACL Davies and J Prassl (eds), *The Autonomy of Labour Law* (Oxford and Portland, Oregon, Hart Publishing, 2014) 220–25. In relation to 'insulation', see M Freedland and C Costello, 'Migrants at Work and the Division of Labour Law' in Costello and Freedland (n 16) especially 16 ff; M Bell, 'Irregular Migrants: Beyond the Limits of Solidarity?' in M Ross and Y Borgmann-Prebil (eds), *Promoting Solidarity in the European Union* (Oxford, Oxford University Press, 2010) 151 ff; and L Calafà, *Undocumented Work (by foreigners) and sanctions. The situation in Italy* (CSDLE Massimo D'Antona working paper no 321/2017) 22–23. In relation to 'institutional' solutions, see L Hayes, T Novitz and P Herzfeld Olsson, 'Migrant Workers and Collective Bargaining: Institutional Isomorphism and Legitimacy in a Resocialised Europe' in N Countouris and M Freedland (eds), *Resocialising Europe in a Time of Crisis* (Cambridge, Cambridge University Press, 2013) 46 and V Mantouvalou, 'Organizing against Abuse and Exclusion. The Associational Rights of Undocumented Workers' in Costello and Freedland (n 16) 381.

these are important in properly reconciling the fight against undeclared work with more effective protection against the exploitation of migrant workers.[57]

In contrast, an excessive emphasis on promotion of the criminal law dimension risks marginalising the labour law perspective. That approach risks causing gaps in the protection of labour law, whereas it is better to establish a synergy between the two branches of law in fighting undeclared work.[58] That would imply the adoption of new norms and sanctions – including for companies – and increasing the capacity of trade unions to enforce rights before the labour courts.[59] The creation of faster channels for judicial protection before labour courts, which nowadays suffers from delays due to the procedures needed to confirm the existence of an employment relationship, would be a further desirable development.[60]

[57] On the Italian perspective see M D'Onghia and C de Martino, *Gli strumenti giuslavoristici di contrasto allo sfruttamento del lavoro in agricoltura nella legge n. 199 del 2016: ancora timide risposte a un fenomeno molto più complesso* (CSDLE Massimo D'Antona working paper no 352/2018).

[58] C Costello, 'EU Migration and Asylum Law: A Labour Law Perspective' in A Bogg, C Costello and ACL Davies (eds), *Research Handbook on EU Labour Law* (Cheltenham, Edward Elgar, 2016) 331.

[59] E Pugliese, 'Braccianti, caporali e imprese' in Rigo (n 3) 135. See also E Galossi (ed), *(Im) migrazione e sindacato. Nuove sfide, universalità dei diritti e libera circolazione – VIII Rapporto* (Roma, Ediesse, 2017).

[60] Pugliese (n 59) 326.

Part III

Reconciliations

11

New Labour Laws in Old Member States: The Impact of EU Enlargements on National Labour Law Systems in Europe

REBECCA ZAHN*

I. INTRODUCTION

ON 1 MAY 2004, eight post-communist states in central and eastern Europe joined the European Union (EU).[1] They were followed by Bulgaria and Romania on 1 January 2007, and by Croatia on 1 July 2013. In the years since, these enlargements resulted in an increase in the free movement of workers from 'new' to 'old' Member States, which had a visible and ongoing impact on the labour markets of old Member States. This chapter questions whether increased migration following the enlargements has also had an impact on the labour law systems of four 'old' EU Member States: Austria, Germany, Ireland, and the United Kingdom.[2] These countries are interesting for a number of reasons, despite the UK's subsequent decision to exit the EU. In particular, they illustrate to what extent migration controls affect actual migration flows and, by extension, labour law systems.

* I would like to thank Bernard Ryan for comments on earlier drafts of this chapter which substantially improved the final version. With a small number of exceptions, figures and the state of the law were last updated in January 2020 before the start of the COVID-19 pandemic and before the UK formally left the EU on 31 January 2020. All errors or omissions remain my own.

[1] The following countries acceded in 2004: the Czech Republic, Estonia, Cyprus, Latvia, Lithuania, Hungary, Malta, Poland, Slovenia and Slovakia. For ease of reference, workers from the central and eastern European Member States that joined the EU since 2004 are referred to collectively as 'new Member States' even though it is recognised that at the time of publication these Member States and their citizens are no longer 'new'.

[2] The research upon which this chapter is based is expounded in more detail in R Zahn, *New Labour Laws in Old Member States* (Cambridge, Cambridge University Press, 2017).

The different transitional measures put in place in these Member States following the enlargements allow the countries to be grouped into two categories.[3] On the one hand, Austria and Germany placed heavy restrictions on workers from new Member States entering their labour markets, which were only lifted in 2011 (for the 2004 enlargement) and in 2014 (for the 2007 enlargement) and, in the case of Germany, in 2015 for Croatia. Austria's restrictions on Croatian workers were maintained until June 2020. In addition, Austria and Germany negotiated and implemented special arrangements for posted workers. Nonetheless, Austria and Germany experienced significant inflows of new Member State workers. Ireland and the UK immediately opened their labour markets following the 2004 enlargements, and both countries witnessed a substantial increase in the numbers of new Member State workers compared with pre-enlargement levels. Largely as a result, they would each impose transitional measures on Bulgaria and Romania when those states joined the EU, and the UK would extend those measures to Croatia until June 2018.

In order to assess the impact of post-enlargement migration flows on the Austrian, German, Irish and British labour law systems, this chapter proceeds as follows. Section II contextualises the enlargements and explains their significance. Section III examines whether the increase in migration post-enlargement led to any changes in the labour law systems in these four countries. It concludes that limited legislative changes can be directly traced to increased migration, post-enlargement. Although, labour markets have absorbed the new arrivals, new Member State workers' impact on their host country's societies should not be under-estimated. Post-enlargement migration, regardless of the existence of transitional measures, led to an intensification of competition in the labour market and placed a burden on health, education and infrastructure in local communities at a time when these were already struggling to adapt to an increasingly globalised world. At the same time, workers from the new Member States played – and continue to play – an important role in filling gaps in the labour markets of old Member States, predominantly in low-wage sectors.

Section IV then discusses the labour law reforms at EU level which have occurred since the enlargements. These have focused on the posting of workers, against the background of allegations of wage undercutting, as the numbers increased substantially across the EU as a whole following the enlargements. Austria and Germany, in particular, recorded a substantial increase in posted workers in certain sectors. Ireland and the UK were affected less. The main relevant regulatory framework governing posted work had been the Posted

[3] The transitional measures lasted for seven years in total; two years initially, followed by a three-year period, followed by a further two-year period in the case of serious disturbances in the labour market. The transitional measures did not apply to Cyprus and Malta. The legal basis for the restriction can be found in the Accession Treaties at [2003] OJ L236; at [2005] OJ L157; and at [2012] OJ L112.

Workers Directive (PWD), adopted in 1996.[4] The PWD, and its interpretation by the Court of Justice of the European Union (CJEU) in *Laval*, was the subject of a plethora of critical commentary calling for a revision of the Directive.[5] Subsequent legislative developments include the adoption of the Enforcement Directive[6] in 2014, the revised PWD in 2018[7] and the establishment of the European Labour Authority in 2019.[8] These reforms are welcome but it remains to be seen whether and to what extent they will be effective.

II. CONTEXTUALISING THE ENLARGEMENTS

The enlargements in 2004, 2007 and 2013 differed from previous ones for a number of reasons, which help to explain the subsequent increase in migration. First, income differentials between the new and old Member States were markedly larger than those of previous enlargement rounds. Second, the iron curtain and the subsequent maintenance of immigration restrictions on the accession states throughout the 1990s prevented large scale migration movements from the CEE states pre-enlargement.[9] These circumstances led to a climate of fear amongst workers and trade unions in old Member States, particularly Austria and Germany, that the new Member States' economic integration following enlargement would lead to large migration flows, which would result in an intensification of competition within the labour market such as had not occurred after previous enlargements.[10]

As a result, transitional measures which severely restricted the right to free movement of citizens from central and eastern European states were proposed in 2000 by Germany, with the support of the main trade union

[4] Directive 96/71/EC concerning the posting of workers in the framework of the provision of services, [1996] OJ L18/1.

[5] Case C-341/05 *Laval un Partneri* [2007] ECR I-11767. There is a vast amount of literature on the judgments. For different views, see M Freedland and J Prassl, *Viking, Laval and Beyond* (Oxford, Hart, 2004), M Rönnmar (ed), *EU Industrial Relations vs National Industrial Relations. Comparative and Interdisciplinary Perspectives* (Deventer, Kluwer, 2008), R Blanpain and AM Swiatkowski (eds), *The Laval and Viking Cases: freedom of services and establishment v industrial conflict in the European Economic Area and Russia* (Deventer, Kluwer, 2009), and articles by A Dashwood, T Novitz, M Rönnmar, S Deakin and S Sciarra in *Cambridge Yearbook of European Legal Studies* (2007–2008) 10. For non-academic critiques of the decision see the ETUC's response to the judgment available at www.etuc.org/en/document/etuc-response-ecj-judgements-viking-and-laval [last accessed 17 March 2022] and A Bücker and W Warneck (eds), *Viking – Laval – Rüffert: Consequences and policy perspectives* (Brussels, ETUI, 2010).

[6] Directive 2014/67/EU [2014] OJ L159.

[7] Directive 2018/957/EU [2018] OJ L73.

[8] Regulation 2019/1149 [2019] OJ L186/21.

[9] European Integration Consortium, *Labour Mobility within the EU in the context of enlargement and the functioning of the transitional arrangements* (Nuremberg, EIC, 2009) 2.

[10] See further D Vaughan-Whitehead, *EU Enlargement versus Social Europe?: The uncertain future of the European Social Model* (Cheltenham, Edward Elgar, 2003).

confederation (DGB).[11] At the time of the 2004 enlargement, Germany had a high rate of unemployment which particularly affected low-skilled and unqualified workers.[12] As it was expected that central and eastern European nationals would primarily engage in these types of work in Germany, the government foresaw increasing tension and falling wages in the labour market, due to increased competition.[13] Similar arguments were put forward in Austria, and it was estimated that the Austrian labour market would need up to 20 years to prepare for free movement of labour without restrictions.[14] Geographical proximity between Germany, Austria, and the central and eastern European states also led to predictions of a greater influx of workers to Germany and Austria than to countries which are geographically more distant. It was hoped that the time between enlargement (2004 and 2007) and the lifting of the transitional arrangements (2011 and 2014 respectively) would enable the new Member States to improve their economic and social conditions, to reduce the incentives to migrate, or to post workers.[15] The legal basis for the transitional arrangements can be found in the Accession Treaties which (with the exception of those between the EU Member States and Cyprus and Malta) allowed Member States to enact national measures which restricted the free movement of workers from 'new' to 'old' Member States (and vice-versa) for the first two years following accession. The Accession Treaties further allowed the extension of these national measures for an additional period of three years. After that, an EU Member State that applied national measures could continue to do so for a further two years if it notified the Commission of serious disturbances in its labour market. Altogether, the national measures restricting access to the labour market could not extend beyond an absolute maximum of seven years. Individuals moving as service providers were not affected by these provisions. Only Austria and Germany were permitted, under the Accession Treaties, to restrict the free movement of services involving the posting of workers for up to seven years post-accession (discussed below).

In practice, the transitional measures meant that most new Member State workers (from the 2004, 2007 and 2013 enlargements) required a work permit

[11] See DGB, *Die EU wird größer* (Berlin, DGB, 2004) and E Jileva, 'Visa and Free Movement of Labour: The Uneven Imposition of the EU *Acquis* on the Accession States' (2002) 28 *Journal of Ethnic and Migration Studies* 683.

[12] In 2004 there were approximately 4 million unemployed people in Germany: see Bundesagentur für Arbeit, *Arbeitsmarkt in Deutschland – Zeitreihen bis 2011*.

[13] Bundeszentrale für politische Bildung, 'Fünf Jahre Arbeitnehmerfreizügigkeit in Deutschland', 28 April 2016 www.bpb.de/politik/hintergrund-aktuell/226107/arbeitnehmerfreizuegigkeit [last accessed 17 March 2022].

[14] See E Walterskirchen and R Dietz, *Auswirkungen der EU-Osterweiterung auf den österreichischen Arbeitsmarkt. Studie im Auftrag der Bundesarbeitskammer* (Wien, Österreichisches Institut für Wirtschaftsforschung, 1998).

[15] DGB (n 11).

in order to take up a job in Austria or Germany during the full seven-year transition period (although Germany lifted its restrictions on Croatian workers on 30 June 2015). In Austria, citizens from the new Member States had to obtain a work permit (*Beschäftigungsbewilligung*), through their employer, from the public employment service (*Arbeitsmarktservice* – AMS) before being allowed to work.[16] The AMS was required to carry out an economic needs check similar to that applicable to non-EU citizens before it could grant a work permit.[17] In addition, the regional advisory board (*Regionalbeirat*), made up of representatives of the social partners and the employment service, had to authorise the employment of the new Member State worker concerned in order for a permit to be issued. Work permits were initially granted for one year; subsequent permits were issued for two years, followed by five years. The geographical remit of the permit also varied.[18]

In Germany, work permits (*Arbeitsgenehmigung-EU*) which were granted by the German Federal Employment Agency (*Bundesagentur für Arbeit*) were required for most jobs[19] with exceptions for certain specific categories, namely students working during their holidays, managers and academics.[20] The work permit was initially in the form of a temporary permit (*Arbeitserlaubnis*) and, after 12 months of uninterrupted access to the labour market, the worker received a permanent work permit (*Arbeitsberechtigung*)[21] which conferred a right of unhindered access to the labour market and which was not linked to the employer. New Member State workers could apply for the permit before or after entering the country. Once a work permit was granted, the worker could avail themselves of their rights as a worker under EU law. Germany also had a large proportion of new Member State workers who entered the country as seasonal workers. These workers and their employers had to apply for a work permit from the Federal Employment Agency under a bilateral agreement signed between Germany and their home Member State. Germany signed bilateral agreements with all new Member States.[22]

[16] See § 32(a) *Ausländerbeschäftigungsgesetz* (AuslBG). See also G Chaloupek and J Peyrl, 'EU Labour Migration: Government and Social Partner Policies in Austria' in B Galgóczi, J Leschke and A Watt (eds), *EU Labour Migration since Enlargement: Trends, Impacts and Policies* (Aldershot, Ashgate, 2009).

[17] See S Schumacher, J Peyrl and T Neugschwendtner, *Fremdenrecht*, 4th edn (Wien, ÖGB Verlag, 2012) 305–7 and §4b AuslBG. In carrying out an economic needs check, citizens from new Member States had to be given preference over third-country nationals.

[18] See § 14a and § 15 AuslBG. This system was abolished in 2014.

[19] § 284 Abs. 1 *Sozialgesetzbuch* (SGB) III Arbeitsgenehmigungsrecht-EU.

[20] § 9 *Arbeitsgenehmigungsverordnung* (ArGV).

[21] § 12a Abs. 1 and 4 ArGV.

[22] For more information on the scheme as well as an overview of the legal framework see BMAS, *Information zur Beschäftigung ausländischer Saisonarbeitnehmer in der Landwirtschaft*, available at www.vsse.de/vsse/offene_dokumente/FAQSaisonarbeitskraefte.pdf [last accessed 17 March 2022].

In addition, Austria and Germany negotiated a concession which allowed them to introduce transitional measures applicable to posted workers in service sectors where serious labour market disturbances were likely should free movement be granted. In Austria these included gardening/horticultural services, construction, home care, industrial cleaning and social work. Austrian employers wishing to post new Member State workers were required to apply for a 'posting permit' (*Entsendebewilligung*) before being permitted to do so. Such a permit was granted only after a labour market check confirmed that Austrian workers were unable to carry out the relevant work.[23] In Germany, posted workers from the new Member States working in construction and related branches, industrial cleaning and interior decoration could work in Germany only within the framework of a service contract procedure (*Werksvertragsverfahren*) which imposed quotas on permissible numbers of workers entering the country which were administered by the Federal Employment Agency. Posted workers from the new Member States thus still needed a work permit but the requirement for a visa was abolished.[24]

The Austrian and German positions contrasted sharply with those of Ireland and the UK, where workers from the central and eastern European states that joined the EU in 2004 were granted free access to the labour market from the date of accession, with only minor restrictions being imposed. Both countries had adopted a more open approach to immigration before the 2004 enlargement, driven by labour market shortages.

In Ireland, migration had risen before enlargement, during the period of the Celtic Tiger boom, as a result of a shortage of labour, coupled with a relatively unregulated, flexible labour market.[25] Ireland did not therefore avail itself of the transitional measures in order to restrict the free movement of labour in the context of the 2004 enlargement. However, following the UK's decision to introduce the Worker Registration Scheme (WRS) – discussed below – the Irish Government felt it necessary to place minor restrictions on new Member State workers' access to social and welfare benefits, so that Ireland would not be more attractive to job-seeking new Member State workers. A 'habitual residence condition' was thus introduced in 2004 in response to public concerns about 'welfare tourism'.[26] That restricted new Member State workers' access to welfare benefits for at least two years from their date of arrival in the British-Irish common travel area.[27] In order to fulfil the condition,

[23] § 18(3) AuslBG.

[24] See further www.arbeitsagentur.de/unternehmen/arbeitskraefte/werkvertragsverfahren [last accessed 17 March 2022].

[25] G Collins and G Boucher, 'Irish Neo-Liberalism at Work?' in G Boucher and G Collins (eds), *The New World of Work: Labour Markets in Contemporary Ireland* (Dublin, Liffey Press, 2005) 8.

[26] J Heyes and M Hyland, 'Supporting, Recruiting and Organising Migrant Workers in Ireland and the United Kingdom: A Review of Trade Union Practices' in Galgóczi, Leschke and Watt (n 16).

[27] The benefits were inter alia jobseekers' allowance, state pension (non-contributory), carers' allowance, disability allowance, and child benefit.

a person needed to show both a right to reside in Ireland and habitual residence there. The latter was assessed by reference to five factors: whether Ireland was their main centre of interest; the length and continuity of residence; the length and purpose of any absences; the pattern of employment; and, their future intention to remain in Ireland.[28] A different approach was then taken as regards labour market access by nationals of Bulgaria and Romania, which Ireland restricted immediately following the 2007 enlargement (again in line with the UK's position). Bulgarian and Romanian nationals were required to apply for a 12-month work permit before being able to start work in Ireland. The Irish Government initially announced in December 2011 that the system would remain in place until 2014.[29] However, the transitional measures were lifted with immediate effect in July 2012, when free access was granted in response to the low numbers of workers applying for work permits.[30] No restrictions were placed on Croatian nationals.

The UK had initially announced in December 2002 that it would not impose restrictions on new Member State workers.[31] The decision not to impose transitional measures was informed by predictions that 13,000–15,000 new Member State workers would come to the UK per annum.[32] As the enlargement approached, and other countries restricted access to their labour markets, a widespread fear developed that migrants would pose a threat to the benefits system and disrupt the labour market.[33] The UK Government thus announced a modification of its plans in February 2004, to require workers from the new central and eastern European states to register under a Worker Registration Scheme as permitted by the Accession Treaties.[34] The rationale was to enable monitoring, so that 'if, contrary to our expectations, the numbers cause particular problems in one sector of the economy or across the board, we will be able to act swiftly and to take the necessary measures to protect our labour market'.[35] The WRS required the worker to register within a month of joining

[28] Department of Employment Affairs and Social Protection, 'HRC – Guidelines for Deciding Officers on the determination of Habitual Residence' www.welfare.ie/en/Pages/Habitual-Residence-Condition--Guidelines-for-Deciding-Offic.aspx [last accessed 17 March 2022].

[29] M Freeman, 'Ireland to keep restrictions on Romanian and Bulgarian workers' *The Journal* 17 December 2011.

[30] A Beesley, 'Government ends restrictions on hiring Romanians and Bulgarians' *Irish Times* 21 July 2012. In 2011, 29 Bulgarians and 313 Romanians applied for work permits under the scheme. See Department of Jobs, Enterprise and Innovation, *Labour Market Statistics* 2011, available at www.djei.ie/labour/workpermits/statistics.htm [last accessed 17 March 2022].

[31] For a detailed overview of the debate in Ireland see N Doyle, G Hughes and E Wadensjö, *Freedom of Movement for Workers from Central and Eastern Europe: Experiences in Ireland and Sweden* (Stockholm, SIEPS, 2006). For an overview of the UK's position see B Ryan, 'The Accession (Immigration and Worker Authorisation) Regulations 2006' (2008) 37 *Industrial Law Journal* 75.

[32] Home Office memorandum of 24 February 2004, 'Consequences of EU Enlargement', published by the House of Commons Home Affairs Committee in 2003–04 *House of Commons Papers* 435.

[33] See, eg, S Smith, 'Immigration Hysteria: What they said about … Immigration and the EU – Tabloids threaten "Flood" of Gypsies', *Guardian*, 21 January 2004.

[34] See s 7 of the Accession (Immigration and Worker Registration) Regulations 2004 SI 2004/1219.

[35] Home Office (n 32).

a new employer.[36] Under the Accession Treaty, once the worker had been in continuous employment for 12 months they obtained full labour market access, and the duty to register ceased at that point. The WRS also had implications for access to social benefits: as that was limited to those legally resident in the UK, for most nationals of central and eastern European states, it would be dependent upon their being in employment and registered.[37] Later, in light of the large numbers of new arrivals post-2004, the government took a political decision to restrict access to their labour market for Bulgarian and Romanian nationals (until 2014), and then for Croatian nationals (until 2018), all of whom were required to apply for permission from the Home Office to start work (for the first 12 months). In line with the various Accession Agreements, none of these restrictions applied however to posted workers or self-employed persons.

III. THE EFFECTS OF ENLARGEMENT UPON EMPLOYMENT LAW

A. Austria

Between 2004 and 2020, the number of new Member State citizens resident in Austria increased from 261,864 to 487,337 making up approximately one-third of foreign-born residents.[38] The vast majority of foreign workers still originate from 'old' Member States, particularly Germany, and from third countries.[39] Overall, it is thought that new Member State workers integrated well into the Austrian labour market and there is only limited evidence that wages for low-skilled work stagnated during this period.[40] After 2007, there was also a steady rise in the number of posted workers sent from the new Member States to Austria.[41] While Austria did not experience problems with posted workers such as those witnessed in Germany (see below), there were instances of workers being paid less than the collectively agreed wage.[42]

The lifting of the transitional measures in 2011 created the necessary momentum for the adoption of the Anti-Wage and Social Dumping Act (*Lohn- und Sozialdumpingbekämpfungsgesetz* or LSD-BG) which regulates the payment of workers whose employment relationship is governed by private law, including

[36] For a detailed overview see Ryan (n 31).

[37] S Currie, *Migration, Work and Citizenship in the Enlarged European Union* (Aldershot, Ashgate, 2008).

[38] Information available from Statistik Austria, 'Bevölkerung nach Staatsangehörigkeit und Geburtsland', www.statistik.at/web_de/statistiken/menschen_und_gesellschaft/bevoelkerung/bevoelkerungsstruktur/bevoelkerung_nach_staatsangehoerigkeit_geburtsland/index.html [last accessed 17 March 2022].

[39] For an in-depth discussion and analysis of the figures see BMASK, *Arbeitsmarktöffnung 2011*, (Wien, Sozialpolitische Studienreihe, Band 12: 2012) ch 3.

[40] ibid.

[41] ibid, 333.

[42] ibid, section 5.3.

posted workers.[43] According to one trade unionist the law 'would not have been possible without [the fear of low-wage immigration], so we have been pressing for this law for years and we could only push it through because Austrian politics was fearful of immigration'.[44] The LSD-BG mandates an administrative penalty for remuneration of any worker below minimum – and usually collectively-agreed – levels. In the case of posted workers, remuneration is assessed by reference to comparable Austrian workers.[45] The LSD-BG imposes joint liability upon the employer and the main contractor in this regard.[46] It requires employers to keep documentary records in German of the wages actually paid to posted workers, at their place of work.[47] Employers are also obliged to register postings with a central coordinating body.[48]

Enforcement in Austria is carried out by a number of public bodies, depending on the location of the employer and the subject-matter.[49] The *Kompetenzzentrum LSDB*, a body created by the LSD-BG, is primarily responsible for posted work, save that in the construction industry this task falls to the Construction Workers' Holiday and Severance Pay Fund (*Bauarbeiter-Urlaubs- und Abfertigungskasse* or BUAK).[50] The *Kompetenzzentrum* and BUAK receive notices of violation of the LSD-BG from the financial police, and can commission workplace inspections. Financial penalties arise in the case of failure to register posted work, failure to hold the relevant documents, and failure to pay appropriate wages.[51] For example, penalties range from €1,000–€10,000 per worker in the case of failure to pay appropriate wages, depending on the level of underpayment. The financial penalties are higher for repeat offenders and where more than three workers are concerned. The LSD-BG also makes provision for the enforcement of penalty notices abroad, although the actual enforcement of these notices may be difficult.[52]

The LSD-BG is considered to have been effective in ensuring that posted workers receive those rights to which they are entitled. Between 2011 and 2018 (latest figures available at time of writing), BUAK had served notices for underpayment of wages on 1,069 employers. Of these, at least two-thirds of notices

[43] § 1 *Lohn- und Sozialdumpingbekämpfungsgesetz* (LSD-BG) BGBI I Nr. 2011/24 amended in 2016 BGBI I 2016/44. This section outlines the amended law which came into effect on 1 January 2017. There has been a subsequent amendment in relation to applicable penalties which entered into force on 1 September 2021: BGBl. I Nr. 174/2021. This amendment is not discussed here.

[44] Author's interview, Proge, 2 July 2013. The interviews were carried out between 2008 and 2013 as part of a multi-year research project on the effects of the 2004 and 2007 EU enlargements on the Austrian, German, Irish, Swedish and British labour law systems. The research was in part funded by a British Academy Small Research Grant and the results were published in Zahn (n 1).

[45] *Lohn- und Sozialdumpingbekämpfungsgesetz*, § 3(3).

[46] ibid, §10.

[47] ibid, § 22.

[48] ibid, §19.

[49] ibid, § 11.

[50] ibid, §§ 13 and 15.

[51] ibid, §§ 26–9.

[52] See Part 3 of the Act and M Lindmayr, *Das neue Lohn- und Sozialdumpingbekämpfungsgesetz: Die neue Rechtslage ab 1.1.2017* (LexisNexis, 2016) 1.

were brought against companies posting workers from Slovakia, Slovenia and Hungary.[53] The success of the LSD-BG has been credited to the wide publication of the law amongst Austrian and foreign employers, the high penalties for breach of the law, and regular checks, particularly by BUAK, to ensure compliance.[54]

The specifics of the Austrian labour law system also merit mention in this context. Collective agreements, which are legally binding and have the same force as a statute, regulate a large part of the employment relationship, in particular in respect of wages.[55] Approximately 98 per cent of Austrian workers are covered by a collective agreement.[56] The main reason for the high coverage is the *Arbeitsverfassungsgesetz*, which provides that collective agreements extend to all members of the social partners.[57] Not only trade union members but also employers – and by extension all of their workers – who belong to the Economic Chambers (*Wirtschaftskammer Österreich* or WKÖ) are covered.[58] As membership in the WKÖ occurs *ex lege* as soon as an employer receives their licence to operate a business, the vast majority of employers are members of the WKÖ, and are thus covered by collective agreements.[59] When coupled with the joint liability provision of the LSD-BG, this system plays a vital role in ensuring that posted workers receive the same wages as comparable Austrian workers.

B. Germany

Despite the restrictions on access to its labour market, Germany remained an attractive destination for new Member State workers after 2004. The number of new Member State workers (including EU8, EU2 and Croatian nationals) increased from 438,828 in 2004 to 1.62 million in 2019.[60] Polish and Romanian workers, whose numbers rose particularly following the lifting of the transitional measures in 2011 and 2014, made up the largest groups. Taken as a whole, the increase in migration was described as 'manageable and

[53] A Riesenfelder, L Danzer, H Reichert and P Wetzel, *Endbericht. Entsendungen und Überlassungen nach Österreich, Lohndumping. Eine Studie mit Fokus auf dem Baubereich* (L&R Sozialforschung, 2019).

[54] ibid.

[55] *Arbeitsverfassungsgesetz*, §§ 2 and 11.

[56] R Mosler, 'Entwicklungstendenzen im Kollektivvertragsrecht' (2012) 3 *Das Recht der Arbeit* 283, 284.

[57] *Arbeitsverfassungsgesetz*, § 12.

[58] The WKÖ mainly represents small- and medium-sized enterprises.

[59] *Arbeitsverfassungsgesetz*, § 8.

[60] Bundesagentur für Arbeit, *Auswirkungen der Migration auf den deutschen Arbeitsmarkt Deutschland* (August 2019) statistik.arbeitsagentur.de/Statischer-Content/Statistische-Analysen/Statistische-Sonderberichte/Generische-Publikationen/Auswirkungen-der-Migration-auf-den-Arbeitsmarkt.pdf [last accessed 17 March 2022].

controllable'.[61] The vast majority of new Member State workers worked as skilled professionals, thereby filling labour market shortages.[62] The generally positive political response to EU migration (as opposed to non-EU migration which has received a more mixed response[63]) in Germany must be seen in the light of changing German demographics. As a result of a continual low birth rate and ageing population, Germany depends heavily on immigration of skilled labour.[64]

However, allegations of wage undercutting resulting in the loss of local jobs repeatedly emerged in certain sectors where posted work was prevalent, such as the meat industry and construction.[65] There was evidence that service providers from the new Member States often paid posted workers' wages well below the rates paid to Germans.[66] Workers who challenged their employer were often sent back to their country of origin only to be replaced by other workers.[67] Another issue which arose concerned social insurance contributions, which could be paid in the sending country and created the potential for non-payment because of a lack of cross-border enforcement.[68]

The 1996 Posted Workers Act (*Arbeitnehmer-Entsendegesetz* or AEntG) had introduced the concept of joint liability, applicable to the German signatory of a service contract and a foreign subcontractor.[69] However, the extensive use of sub-contracting through German and foreign letterbox companies, and the cross-border nature of posted work, made enforcement of liability difficult despite the existence of joint liability.[70] For example, the Food, Beverages and Catering Union (*Gewerkschaft Nahrung-Genuss-Gaststätten*, or NGG) reported that, in the meat sector, workers were posted for years to the same employer, but that their contract changed every six months to another letterbox company, which went bankrupt when the tax authorities start to check, or when workers demanded to be paid unpaid wages or holiday time.[71]

[61] Interior Minister, Thomas de Maizière, quoted in F Gathmann, 'Die aufgeblasene Armutseinwanderung', *Der Spiegel*, 26 March 2014.

[62] 'Deutschland profitiert von Zuwanderung aus Osteuropa', IZA Press, 30 December 2013.

[63] Particularly since the 2015 'refugee crisis' when Germany adopted an open-door policy which resulted in 890,000 refugees arriving in one year. This has led to intense and ongoing political debates in Germany. See further O Kösemen, *Willkommenskultur in Deutschland* (Policy Brief Migration, Bertelsmann Stiftung, 12.2017) and Deutscher Bundestag, *Auswirkungen von Migration auf die deutsche Volkswirtschaft*, WD 5-3000-011/19, 27 February 2019.

[64] Bertelsmann Stiftung, *Zuwanderung und Digitalisierung*, 2019.

[65] For an overview of the debates see H Fechner, 'Posting of workers before German courts' in Z Rasnača and M Bernaciak, *Posting of workers before national courts* (Brussels, ETUI, 2020).

[66] L Czommer and G Worthmann, *Von der Baustelle auf den Schlachthof: Zur Übertragbarkeit des Arbeitnehmer-Entsendegesetzes auf die Deutsche Fleischbranche*, IAT-Report 2005/3 (Gelsenkirchen, Institut Arbeit und Technik, 2005).

[67] ibid.

[68] ibid.

[69] *Arbeitnehmer-Entsendegesetz* (AEntG), § 14.

[70] K McGauran, *The Impact of Letterbox-Type Practices on Labour Rights and Public Revenue* (Brussels, ETUC, 2016).

[71] ibid 22.

The AEntG defines specific sectors in which a generally binding collective agreement for the sector applies to posted workers. From 1997 onwards, within the framework of the AEntG, sectoral minimum wages had been negotiated by the social partners in the construction industry and declared universally applicable by the Federal Ministry of Labour and Social Affairs. After 2010, as a result of post-enlargement migration, the AEntG's scope was successively widened, to extend negotiated minimum wages in a number of sectors, including the meat industry, waste management, cleaning, forestry, and care work. However, such sectoral minimum wages depended on the social partners being able to negotiate a collective agreement in the first place. In sectors where this was either not possible or which were not included in the AEntG, posted workers could be paid the minimum wage of their country of origin.

The payment of low wages to posted workers, and the increase in post-enlargement migration through posted work, therefore intensified an ongoing political debate as to the benefits and disadvantages of a minimum wage.[72] Between 1996 and 2013, low wage employment in Germany grew from 19.6 per cent to 24.3 per cent of workers.[73] At the same time, collective agreement coverage declined: in 2015, only 51 per cent of West German and 37 per cent of East German workers were covered by a collective agreement, down from 70 per cent and 56 per cent respectively in 1996.[74] The German trade union confederation (DGB) therefore launched a nationwide campaign for the government to introduce a statutory minimum wage in 2007 as a result of the increase in low wage employment and in light of the eventual lifting of the transitional measures in 2011.[75]

The campaign for a statutory minimum wage sought to place an obligation on the government to intervene in the labour market by setting a wage applicable across *all* sectors. Despite employer opposition, the introduction of a statutory minimum wage enjoyed broad public support, and the relevant law was adopted in April 2014, before coming into effect on 1 January 2015.[76] There are now two parallel minimum wage systems. The statutory rate acts as a minimum threshold applicable across the board. Higher sectoral minimum wages can be negotiated by the social partners. The statutory minimum wage is set by an independent commission (*Mindestlohnkommission*) made up of employer and trade union representatives. Enforcement is carried out by the relevant statutory authorities (*Finanzkontrolle Schwarzarbeit*), and the main penalties for non- or under-payment are fines and possible exclusion from public contracts.

[72] See A Buntenbach, 'Missbrauch von Werkverträgen' (Berlin, DGB, 29 July 2013).

[73] SK Futh, *Strategische Kommunikation von Gewerkschaften* (Wiesbaden, Springer, 2018) 254.

[74] ibid 255.

[75] See DGB, *DieMindestlohnkampagne im Rückblick* available at www.dgb.de/schwerpunkt/mindestlohn/kampagne [last accessed 17 March 2022].

[76] *Mindestlohngesetz* vom 11. August 2014 BGBI. I S. 1348.

The *Mindestlohnkommission* also runs a telephone hotline where workers can report breaches. An evaluation by the Ministry for Labour concluded in 2020 that the statutory minimum wage has had a positive effect on the low wage sector overall.[77] In-work poverty has decreased while wages in the low-wage sector have increased. However, there is continued evidence that enforcement of payment of the minimum wage remains problematic, particularly in the service/catering industry, home care and construction.[78] This can be traced back to the limited resources allocated to the relevant enforcement authorities, the lack of workplace representation in these sectors through either works councils or trade unions, and the lack of knowledge amongst workers in the low-paid sector about their rights and how to enforce them.

The experience of post-enlargement EU migration is heavily sector dependent. While Germany is reliant on immigration and the migration of skilled labour in particular is welcomed, its prevalence in the growing low-wage sector where workplace representation is weak or absent, has led to tensions in the labour market. Legislative reforms have had some success in tackling under-payment of wages and exploitation of workers but systemic enforcement problems remain.

C. Ireland

Ireland experienced a large influx of workers immediately following the 2004 enlargement. By 2007, new Member State workers made up nearly 3 per cent of the Irish population.[79] Between 2004 and 2007, a total of 422,958 Personal Public Service (PPS) numbers were issued to new Member State workers.[80] This was an unprecedented inflow of migrants looking for work in an economy whose labour force in 2004 was only 1.9 million.[81] The economic crisis which began in 2008 had a marked impact on migration flows to Ireland, however. Unemployment rose from 6.4 per cent in 2008 to 14.7 per cent in 2012.[82] Amongst new Member State workers, unemployment increased from 5.5 per cent in 2007 to almost 20 per cent by 2010.[83] New immigration also dropped sharply after 2007. Whereas in 2007, some 98,298 PPS numbers were issued to new Member State

[77] BMAS, *Gesamtbericht zur Evaluation des allgemeinen gesetzlichen Mindestlohns nach § 23 Mindestlohngesetz*, (Forschungsbericht 558, 2020).

[78] ibid.

[79] G Hughes, *Free Movement in the EU: The Case of Ireland* (Berlin, Friedrich-Ebert-Stiftung, May 2011) 13.

[80] Based on Central Statistics Office data. See *Table FNA02: Employment Activity of Foreign Nationals by Broad Nationality Group, Year of Entry and Year*, at statbank.cso.ie/px/pxeirestat/statire/SelectVarVal/Define.asp?Maintable=FNA02&PLanguage=0 [last accessed 17 March 2022].

[81] Hughes (n 79).

[82] Central Statistics Office, *Seasonally Adjusted Standardised Unemployment Rates (SUR)*, 2008–2012.

[83] Hughes (n 79) 15.

workers, the corresponding figures were 50,300 in 2008 and 18,448 in 2009.[84] Between 2010 and 2019, the rate remained relatively steady, with an average of 12,000–14,000 new PPS numbers issued to EU8 workers each year.[85] At the same time, the number of PPS numbers issued to Romanian, Bulgarian and Croatian workers steadily increased, from 2,914 in 2010 to 16,340 in 2017 and a slight fall to 15,901 in 2019.[86] There is limited reliable data on the number of posted workers in Ireland, but the overall numbers of posted workers have generally been small.[87]

It was generally thought that Ireland benefitted significantly from migration from the new Member States and the political debate around the effects of EU8 migration was positive in Ireland.[88] Reference was made repeatedly to Ireland's history of a country of emigration. For example, during the Second Stage of the Employment Permits Bill 2005, it was suggested that:

> The Government's progressive strategy was demonstrated by its brave decision to allow workers from the new EU member states to live and work in Ireland. This decision has benefited not only our economy but also our society in terms of the diversity one sees in every town in the country. [...] It is wonderful, therefore, that the Minister and the Government are giving an opportunity to people from abroad to come to Ireland and secure employment. We are reciprocating what was done for us in Britain and elsewhere.[89]

Despite such positive rhetoric, concerns around social integration of new Member State workers remained. As Hughes points out, the social partners 'expressed concerns about the strain which [EU migration] had placed on infrastructural, educational and other resources and about the speed at which the foreign-born population increased from around three per cent to 10 per cent in the ten year period 1996–2006'.[90] In addition, even though workers who came to Ireland from the new Member States were predominantly young, and often highly educated, they were willing to 'downgrade' and to work for low wages in low-skilled jobs.[91] Some data indicated that new Member State workers in

[84] Department of Social Protection, *Annual Allocations: PPS Numbers* available at www.gov.ie/en/collection/a78027-statistics-on-personal-public-service-pps-numbers-issued/#2020 [last accessed 17 March 2022].

[85] ibid.

[86] ibid.

[87] See further M Doherty, 'Posting of workers before Irish courts' in Rasnača and Bernaciak (n 65).

[88] Hughes (n 79).

[89] Seanad Éireann Debate, vol 183, No 50, Employment Permits Bill 2005: Second Stage, 24 May 2006.

[90] Hughes (n 79) 25. See also ICTU, *Observations and Recommendations on the Application of Transitional Measures on the Accession of Bulgaria and Romania to the EU on 1st January 2007* (Dublin, ICTU, 2006); and Dáil Éireann Debate, vol 625, 11 October 2006, Priority Questions – EU Enlargement for Fine Gael's position.

[91] See A Barrett, S McGuinness and M O'Brien, 'The Immigrant Earnings Disadvantage across the Earnings and Skills Distribution: The Case of Immigrants from the EU's New Member States' (2012) 50 *British Journal of Industrial Relations* 457.

certain, labour-intensive sectors earned less than comparable native employees, or were paid less than collectively-agreed rates of pay.[92] There was, however, no evidence of a major displacement of Irish workers by new Member State workers.[93] In large part, this seems due to the reforms promised following the Gama and Irish Ferries disputes which occurred shortly before (Gama) and immediately after (Irish Ferries) the enlargements.

The first phase of the Irish Ferries dispute began in December 2004, when it reflagged one of its vessels – which operated between Ireland and France – to the Bahamas, and then sought to replace 150 Irish-based workers with agency staff, who were to be paid substantially less than the Irish minimum wage.[94] Although that initial dispute was settled in early 2005 following industrial action, in September 2005 the company announced the replacement of a further 543 Irish-based workers on its British-Irish routes, by central and eastern European agency workers who would be posted to work. To facilitate this change, three further ships were to be flagged in Cyprus, in order to circumvent applicable Irish labour law and, in particular, minimum wage legislation. In response, SIPTU, the trade union concerned, requested the Labour Court to recommend that the terms and conditions of employment of those Irish-based workers who wished to stay with the firm would remain at current levels, and that the collective agreement be maintained until it could be voluntarily renegotiated. The Labour Court acceded to both requests.[95] A deal between SIPTU and Irish Ferries would be reached in mid-December 2005 which allowed the outsourcing to proceed, but on the basis that the Irish minimum wage would be enforced.

The Gama case did not involve EU nationals but it raised similar concerns to the Irish Ferries dispute in that posted workers were being paid less than the mandated minimum. It was also linked with the Irish Ferries dispute in subsequent campaigns and so merits mention. The case began in 2000 and involved the posting by a Turkish company of 600 Turkish workers to work on a number of public infrastructure projects for its wholly owned Irish subsidiary (Gama Ireland).[96] In 2005, it came to light that Gama was paying workers below both the registered employment agreement which set wage rates in the construction industry, and the national minimum wage. Following an investigation by the

[92] ibid

[93] FÁS, *The Irish Labour Market Review 2006* (Dublin, FÁS, 2006) 7.

[94] For a detailed overview of the facts see T Krings, 'Irish Ferries, Labour Migration and the Spectre of Displacement' in M Corcoran and P Share (eds), *Belongings: Shaping Identity in Modern Ireland* (Dublin, Institute of Public Administration, 2008).

[95] *Irish Ferries v Seaman's Union of Ireland* CD/05/1016 Recommendation No 18390 11th Nov. 2005.

[96] See further A Afonso, 'The Domestic Regulation of Transnational Labour Markets: EU Enlargement and the Politics of Labour Migration in Switzerland and Ireland' in L Bruszt and R Holzhacker (eds), *The Transnationalization of Economies, States and Civil Societies: New Challenges for Governance in Europe* (London, Springer, 2009).

Labour Inspectorate and the relevant trade unions, it became clear that work records had been destroyed and workers' money was being paid into a complex web of international bank accounts. The dispute was initially resolved through the Labour Relations Commission in August 2005, when Gama agreed to abide by the relevant registered employment agreement. However, a separate action was brought on behalf of 491 Turkish workers in the Irish courts claiming inter alia unpaid overtime, punitive damages and accumulated interest, for a total amount of €40.3 million.[97] The Court of Appeal upheld two High Court decisions permitting the Irish courts to hear the claims. However, after the case was brought, the majority of workers left Ireland and Gama Ireland ceased to operate, highlighting the difficulty of sanctioning a non-compliant employer based in a foreign jurisdiction.

In response to the Irish Ferries and Gama cases, in December 2005, the Irish Congress of Trade Unions organised a national day of protest under the heading 'Equal Rights for all Workers'.[98] It also delayed its agreement to participate in new social partnership negotiations (planned for 2006) until it received guarantees from the government and employers that employment laws and their enforcement would be strengthened, in order to prevent a recurrence of such cases.[99] The outcome of the social partnership negotiations was the ten-year agreement – *Towards 2016* – concluded in June 2006, which set out a number of measures designed to improve the protection of workers' rights in Ireland.[100] These measures included the establishment of a statutory office dedicated to employment rights compliance, a substantial increase in the number of labour inspectors, and higher penalties for non-compliance with employment law. A National Employment Rights Authority (NERA) was set up on an interim basis in 2007 as an agency of the Department of Jobs, Enterprise and Innovation, to provide impartial information on employment rights legislation to employers and employees and to monitor enforcement of employment rights through labour inspections. The Employment Law Compliance Bill 2008 was to have given a statutory footing to NERA and to enact the other measures agreed in *Towards 2016*, but the pressures of the economic crisis meant that the Bill was allowed to lapse in 2011. At the same time, as Doherty pointed out, 'one consequence of austerity [was] a reduction in resourcing of all State agencies, compromising their ability to adequately carry out their functions'.[101]

[97] See *Abama & ors v Gama Construction (Ireland) Ltd & anor* [2015] IECA 179 (31 July 2015) and 'Court upholds right of Gama workers to take cases in Ireland' *Irish Times*, 31 July 2015.

[98] Hughes (n 79) 23.

[99] ibid.

[100] www.welfare.ie/en/downloads/Towards201626June06.pdf [last accessed 17 March 2022]. As a result of the economic crisis, *Towards 2016* was modified by a Transitional Agreement in 2008–2009: www.ictu.ie/download/pdf/t16_review_and_transitional_agreement_oct_08.pdf [last accessed 17 March 2022].

[101] M Doherty, 'New Morning? Irish Labour Law Post-Austerity' (2016) 39(1) *Dublin University Law Journal* 29.

The Workplace Relations Act 2015 then introduced a range of reforms to the enforcement of employment standards.[102] It established the Workplace Relations Commission (WRC), which subsumes the existing employment tribunals, including a labour inspectorate to replace NERA, so ensuring that one single body dealt with all employment claims at first instance.[103] The focus of the Act is on early resolution of disputes as close to the workplace as possible. The WRC has a statutory duty to ensure high standards of compliance with employment legislation.[104] Inspectors appointed under the Act have extensive powers to enter workplaces, to inspect records, and to issue compliance notices and fixed payment notices where an employer has breached its obligations.[105] Failure to comply with a compliance notice is a criminal offence.[106] Overall, the reforms of the Act have been welcomed, as it makes the system of rights enforcement easier to navigate for all workers. However, the emphasis on the resolution of individual rights-based disputes leaves room for doubt as to the extent to which its mechanisms will be effective for migrant workers, given the lack of support for individual workers at workplace level, through trade unions or otherwise.

Irish employment legislation applies in principle in its entirety to all workers, including posted workers. That principle included registered employment agreements (REAs) in those sectors where they had been agreed, such as the construction industry. However, in 2013 the Supreme Court declared the system of universally-applicable REAs unconstitutional, on the grounds that it was an impermissible exercise of legislative power to bind employers who were not party to an REA. Although the Industrial Relations (Amendment) Act 2015 reintroduced the REA system, REAs now only bind the workers and employer(s) that are parties to the agreement. Ireland thus lacks a mechanism to declare collective agreements universally applicable, and posted workers are entitled to the national minimum wage, but cannot enforce higher rates of pay contained in collective agreements, if their employer is not party to the agreement. The 2015 Act permitted this problem to be alleviated in some sectors through Sectoral Employment Orders (SEOs). Applications to adopt an SEO may be made by a trade union alone, by an employer organisation alone, or jointly by both, provided the union or employer organisation is 'substantially representative' of the workers or employer 'of the particular class, type or group in the economic sector' concerned'.[107] An SEO does not involve bargaining between employers and unions, but rather the unilateral imposition of

[102] For an overview and discussion of the reforms see M Bolger, 'The Workplace Relations Bill: World-class or Legally Flawed?' (2015) 12(1) *Irish Employment Law Journal* 21; A Kerr, 'The Workplace Relations Reform Project' (2016) 7(1) *European Labour Law Journal* 126.

[103] Workplace Relations Act 2015, s 41.

[104] ibid, s 11.

[105] ibid, ss 28 and 36.

[106] ibid, s 7

[107] Industrial Relations (Amendment) Act 2015, s 14(2).

standards in relation to pay, sick pay and pensions by Ministerial Order, after a recommendation from the Labour Court.[108] It is a pre-condition to examination of a recommendation by the Labour Court that it is satisfied that it is 'normal and desirable' or 'expedient' to have the SEO proposed, and that a recommendation would promote 'harmonious relations' in the sector.[109] An employer in a sector where an SEO operates may apply for an exemption for a maximum period of 24 months, but only on the basis that the employer's business is 'experiencing severe financial difficulties'.[110] The first SEO was adopted in October 2017 in the construction sector (it was updated in 2019 and 2021), and was followed by Orders for mechanical engineering in 2018 and electrical contracting in 2019.[111]

Overall, new Member State workers integrated well into the Irish labour market due, in large part, to its flexibility, a growing economy, and a shortage of low-skilled labour at the time of the 2004 enlargement. Although enforcement problems of labour rights remain, the rapid increase in migration did not lead to negative reactions from Irish-based workers (unlike in the UK – see below). In part, this is due to a wave of legislative reforms triggered by three concurrent events: the arrival of large numbers of new Member State workers after 2004, the Irish Ferries dispute, and the Gama case. Taken together, these three events provided the necessary momentum for substantial employment law reforms. As David Begg, the General Secretary of Congress, explains:

> We had to make a working assumption that, if not addressed, it was only a matter of time before we had another Irish Ferries situation, albeit on land. Without a robust legal and enforcement architecture to deal with it our evaluation was that such a dispute would release very damaging social and racial tensions.[112]

The measures which were negotiated in 2006 were described by Congress's General Secretary in the following terms:

> I have no hesitation in saying that these measures in their totality, and in the context of the legislation necessary to implement them, represents the single biggest leap forward in social policy initiated in this country. Other important social policy changes were inspired by the EU but this is the biggest thing we have ever done of our own volition.[113]

[108] ibid, ss 16 and 17.
[109] ibid, s 15.
[110] ibid, s 21.
[111] Sectoral Employment Order (Construction Sector) 2017 (SI 2017/455) and Sectoral Employment Order (Construction Sector) 2021 SI 598/2021 which amends SI 234/2019; Sectoral Employment Order (Mechanical Engineering Building Services Contracting Sector) 2018 (SI 2018/59) and Sectoral Employment Order (Electrical Contracting Sector) 2019 (SI 2019/251). All of these cover pay rates, sick pay and pensions.
[112] D Begg, 'Managing the Labour Market: Implications of EU Expansion and Ireland's Experience', Address to conference on Race and Immigration in the New Ireland, University of Notre Dame, 14–17 October 2007.
[113] D Begg, 'Immigration, Integration and Cultural Identity' (2007) 2 *Translocations* 181, 185.

Although not all of the measures were implemented due to the onset of the economic crisis, there have nonetheless been a number of reforms in recent years which, in their entirety, mean that Irish labour law has changed significantly due, in part, to post-enlargement migration.

D. United Kingdom

At the time of the 2004 enlargements, employers in the UK labour market – as in Ireland's – were often struggling to find workers to fill posts, typically for low-skilled or physically strenuous work, in key areas of employment such as agriculture, construction, food-processing and hospitality. After the opening of the labour market, by 2007, nationals of new Member States made up about 1 per cent of the population in the UK.[114] Between 2004 and 2008, 1.24 million National Insurance Numbers were allocated to new Member State workers in the UK, and a total of 926,000 applications were approved under the Worker Registration Scheme.[115] By May 2016, it was estimated that 2.1 million EU citizens were working in the UK.[116] The global financial crisis, and its disproportionate impact on southern European states, also led to an increase in migration to the UK from the old Member States. The number of EU citizens migrating to the UK fell after the 2016 referendum on EU membership, but as of December 2019 there were still an estimated 2.31 million EU citizens working in the UK.[117] Data on posted workers in the UK is limited but overall the numbers seem to be low.[118] The majority work in construction, education and industry.

As in the case of Ireland, the UK's flexible labour market made it an ideal host country for workers from the new Member States who were often willing to work for low wages in low-skilled jobs.[119] There was no evidence that the presence of new Member State workers led to a lowering of employment terms and conditions. Yet this did not prevent a significant perceived negative impact of post-enlargement migration in the UK which conflated posted work (where numbers are comparatively low in the UK) and free movement of workers.

[114] European Integration Consortium (n 9) 23.

[115] Migration Advisory Committee, *Review of the UK's transitional measures for nationals of member states that acceded to the European Union in 2004*, April 2009, 17.

[116] Office for National Statistics, *Migration Statistics Quarterly Report: May 2016.*

[117] Office for National Statistics, *UK and non-UK people in the labour market: February 2020.*

[118] European Commission, *Country factsheet: posted workers in the UK 2016* (2018) available at ec.europa.eu/social/main.jsp?pager.offset=25&advSearchKey=posted+workers+&mode=advancedSubmit&catId=1307&doc_submit=&policyArea=0&policyAreaSub=0&country=0&year=0 [last accessed 17 March 2022].

[119] See M Sumption and W Somerville, *The UK's New Europeans: Progress and Challenges Five Years after Accession* (Equality and Human Rights Commission Policy Report, together with the Migration Policy Institute, January 2010) 5.

The best known example is the Lindsey oil refinery dispute.[120] In December 2008, part of the work on the construction of a new unit at the plant was subcontracted to an Italian company (IREM), which posted its own permanent workforce of foreign nationals to the UK to carry it out. The decision not to use any local labour resulted in a series of wildcat strikes at the Lindsey Oil Refinery and across the country in 2009. Particular concern was raised in the dispute that it had been awarded the contract because they were able to supply labour at rates that under-cut the British firms who had agreed to an industry standard contained in a collective agreement.

The PWD in force at the time gave Member States two options to use collective agreements as a method of implementation of the requirements of the Directive. The first option required collective agreements to be declared universally applicable, ie, binding on all undertakings in the geographical area and in the profession or industry concerned. The second option allowed Member States to base themselves on either: (i) collective agreements which are generally applicable to all similar undertakings in the geographical area and in the profession or industry concerned; or (ii) collective agreements which have been concluded by the most representative employers and labour organisations at national level and which are applied throughout the national territory. The UK does not rely upon either possibility, as it has no legal mechanism which allows collective agreements to be declared universally applicable. IREM was, therefore, by law, not obliged to pay the level set in the relevant collective agreement for the industry.[121] Although there was no evidence that IREM had breached the industry's standard terms and conditions, the dispute at the time generated a large amount of political and public support. There was a widespread feeling, as evidenced by many of the placards bearing Gordon Brown's pledge of 'British Jobs for British Workers', that British workers should be accorded preference over foreign nationals, in this case EU workers, in the allocation of employment contracts. The underlying issues surrounding the PWD were not well understood in the public debate and were obscured by broader concerns around immigration (particularly, but not limited to, EU migration). Following the election of the Conservative-Liberal Democrat government in 2010, from 2014 changes were made to all EU migrants' entitlement to out-of-work benefits, and to the habitual residence test which proves entitlement to benefits.[122]

[120] See further ACAS, *Report of an Inquiry into the Circumstances Surrounding the Lindsey Oil Refinery Dispute*, 16 February 2009, www.acas.org.uk/CHttpHandler.ashx?id=1019&p=0 [last accessed 17 March 2022]; and R Zahn, '"British Jobs for British workers": The problem of collective agreements in the UK' [2010] *Juridical Review* 181.

[121] See further C Barnard, '"British Jobs for British Workers": The Lindsey Oil Refinery Dispute and the Future of Local Labour Clauses in an Integrated EU Market' (2009) 38(3) *Industrial Law Journal* 245, 256–57.

[122] See the Immigration (European Economic Area) (Amendment) (No 2) Regulations 2013 (SI 2013/3032), the Jobseeker's Allowance (Habitual Residence) Amendment Regulations 2013 (SI 2013/3196), and the Housing Benefit (Habitual Residence) Amendment Regulations 2014 (SI 2014/539).

Concerns around EU immigration would continue to come to the fore strongly in the run-up to the 'Brexit' referendum held in June 2016 and ending the free movement of workers became a priority in the negotiations on the UK's withdrawal from the EU and the UK-EU future relationship.[123]

The 'employment rights enforcement landscape in Britain is fragmented, uneven and incomplete'[124] with the Employment Tribunal (a form of labour court) remaining the dominant avenue. In addition, enforcement of workers' terms and conditions is done through a number of organisations which adopt different 'philosophies of enforcement':[125] His Majesty's Revenue and Customs (HMRC) and the Low Pay Commission (the minimum wage); the Health and Safety Executive (HSE) (health and safety); the Employment Agency Standards Inspectorate (EASI) (the rights of agency workers); and the Gangmasters Licensing Authority (GLA).[126] The GLA was created to enforce the licensing requirement upon labour market intermediaries (agencies and gangmasters) in the farming, food processing and shellfish gathering sectors which was imposed by the Gangmasters (Licensing) Act 2004. The 2004 Act was introduced following the death of Chinese cockle pickers at Morecambe Bay and heavy campaigning by trade unions who saw the GLA as a way to integrate new Member State workers into the labour market.[127] It is an offence to operate as a gangmaster without such a licence. Since 2012, the GLA has focused on cases where criminal activity has been alleged and on 'the most severe extremes of worker exploitation'.[128] As Barnard and Ludlow point out, that meant that 'individuals suffering from lower level denial of employment rights do not get the support they need'.[129]

The Immigration Act 2016 then introduced changes to the GLA, including renaming it as the Gangmasters and Labour Abuse Authority (GLAA), and widening its remit to cover what are termed 'labour market offences' under the Employment Agencies Act 1973, the National Minimum Wage Act 1998, the

[123] See further M Goodwin and C Milazzo, 'Taking Back Control? Investigating the Role of Immigration in the 2016 Vote for Brexit' (2017) 19(3) *British Journal of Politics and International Relations* 450.

[124] L Dickens, 'Another "A" for the GLA in enforcing labour rights and preventing exploitation' in L Dickens and G Meardi (eds), *Labour market exploitation: Emerging empirical evidence* (Warwick Papers in Industrial Relations No 108, 2017) 5.

[125] ibid.

[126] For a broader discussion of the powers of the different agencies and their role in relation to the enforcement of migrant workers' rights, see C Barnard, A Ludlow and S Fraser Butlin, 'Beyond Employment Tribunals: Enforcement of Employment Rights by EU-8 Migrant Workers' (2018) 47 *Industrial Law Journal* 226.

[127] See further B Ryan, 'The Evolving Legal Regime on Unauthorized Work by Migrants in Britain' (2005) 27 *Comparative Labor Law and Policy Journal* 27 and Author's Interview, National Development Manager for Migrant Workers, UNISON Headquarters, London, 20/10/2008.

[128] See the written ministerial statement of Department for Environment, Food and Rural Affairs minister Lord Holbeach, House of Lords 24 May 2012, col WS95 and Department for Environment, Food and Rural Affairs, *Report of the Triennial Review of the Gangmasters Licensing Authority* (April 2014).

[129] Barnard, Ludlow and Fraser Butlin (n 126) 28.

Gangmasters (Licensing) Act 2004 Act and the Modern Slavery Act 2015.[130] The GLAA's newly-created Labour Abuse Prevention Officers have the power to arrest suspects, to enter and search premises where they have a reasonable belief that labour market offences are being committed, and to seize evidence.[131] The changes concerning labour market offences apply to all sectors of the labour market. The 2016 Act also gave the Secretary of State the power to extend GLAA licensing to cover sectors other than farming, food processing and shellfish gathering, though that power has not been used at the time of writing.[132] These reforms implemented the 2015 Conservative Party manifesto commitment to 'introduce tougher labour market regulation to tackle illegal working and exploitation'.[133]

As in Ireland, new Member State workers, including posted workers (whose numbers are small), generally integrated well into the labour market. However, the perceived uncontrollable nature and negative impact of post-enlargement migration has continued to dominate policy debates on the regulation of immigration in the labour market even as labour market shortages persist in many sectors of the economy. Enforcement of labour rights also remains an issue. The large increase in EU migration after 2004 gave the necessary momentum for the introduction of the GLA but other employment law reforms were limited. In addition, the budget cuts introduced in 2010 following the economic and financial crises had a significant impact on the resources and work of the Health and Safety Executive, the Low Pay Commission and the GLAA. Although more money was made available after 2016, the resources are still relatively modest in comparison to the agencies' remit.

IV. EUROPEAN LABOUR LAW REFORM

The period since the end of the twentieth century and up until 2020 has largely been one of legislative stagnation in the social policy sphere at the EU level. Increased migration after 2004 brought to the surface underlying tensions between economic policy and social integration. The main debates over post-enlargement labour law reform have centred on a revision of the PWD, prompted by the decision of the CJEU in *Laval*. In an initial response, in March 2012 the European Commission published two legislative proposals. One proposal – known as 'Monti II' – was for a Regulation to regulate the right of workers to take collective action in the context of the freedom of establishment and the freedom to provide services.[134] That proposal was eventually withdrawn after objections

[130] Immigration Act 2016, ss 3 and 10. The 2016 Act also introduced a number of other changes including a Labour Market Enforcement Agency which are discussed in detail in ACL Davies, 'The Immigration Act 2016' (2016) 45(3) *Industrial Law Journal* 431.

[131] Immigration Act 2016, s 12.

[132] Gangmasters (Licensing) Act 2004, s 3(5), as amended by Immigration Act 2016, Sch 3, para 17.

[133] *Conservative Party Manifesto 2015*, 31.

[134] COM (2012) 130 final, 21 March 2012.

by national parliaments and others.[135] The second proposal was for a Directive concerning the enforcement of the Posted Workers Directive, and that was adopted with minor amendments in May 2014.[136] The Enforcement Directive aimed inter alia to raise the awareness of posted workers and companies of their rights and obligations as regards the terms and conditions of employment; to improve cooperation between national authorities in charge of posting; to clarify the definition of posting increasing legal certainty for posted workers and service providers; and, to define Member States' responsibilities to verify compliance with the rules laid down in the PWD. The Enforcement Directive also introduced joint liability for subcontractors in the construction industry. However, the Directive did not address inequality of treatment between posted and local workers, and failed to introduce an EU-wide monitoring system to reduce problems of differential treatment across Member States, or the non-payment of social security contributions in either the home or host Member State.[137]

In a second phase, on 8 March 2016, as part of a 'mobility package', the European Commission proposed a Directive amending the PWD, to complement the Enforcement Directive. The revised Directive was adopted on 28 June 2018.[138] The revised PWD replaces the reference to 'minimum rates of pay' in Article 3(1) of the PWD with the term 'remuneration', and imposes an obligation on Member States to publish information on the constituent elements of remuneration. This means that employers have to apply the rules of the host country in relation to pay/remuneration, as laid down by law or by universally applicable collective agreements, and not just the minimum rates of pay. This amendment builds on the case law of the CJEU in *Sähköalojen ammattiliitto ry*[139] by entitling posted workers to some of the same advantages such as bonuses, or pay increases according to seniority as local workers. In addition, rules set by universally-applicable collective agreements will become mandatory in all sectors, whereas previously they were only so in the construction sector. The amendments extend the equal treatment principle to posted temporary agency workers, with respect to remuneration and working conditions. The duration of posting will be limited to twelve months with a possible six-month extension. After this time, the posting can continue but host Member States shall apply all national terms and conditions of employment to the posted worker

[135] For an overview of the difficulties encountered by the Regulation see The Adoptive Parents, 'The Life of a Death Foretold: The Proposal for a Monti II Regulation' in M Freedland and J Prassl (eds), *Viking, Laval and Beyond* (Oxford, Hart Publishing, 2016).

[136] COM (2012) 131 final, 21 March 2012 and Directive 2014/67 [2014] OJ L159. For an analysis of the Enforcement Directive, see J Cremers, 'Economic Freedoms and Labour Standards in the European Union' (2016) 22(2) *Transfer* 149.

[137] See D Schiek, *EU Social and Labour Rights and EU Internal Market Law: Study for the EMPL Committee* (European Parliament, 2015) 62 and R Zahn, 'Revision of the Posted Workers' Directive: a Europeanisation perspective' [2017] *Cambridge Yearbook of European Legal Studies* 187.

[138] Directive 2018/957 amending Directive 96/71/EC concerning the posting of workers in the framework of the provision of services [2018] OJ L173/16.

[139] *Sähköalojen ammattiliitto ry v Elektrobudowa*, C-396/13, EU:C:2015:86.

(rather than just the mandatory list contained in Article 3(1)) as set down in law or collective agreement.[140] Road transport workers are excluded from the revised PWD; they are subject to a 'lex specialis' on the mobility sector adopted in 2020.[141] The revised PWD does not make provision for shared liability which is particularly unfortunate in light of the problems that have arisen with subcontracting chains in all four countries discussed in this chapter.

The Directive is a step in the right direction in that it recognises a problem with the status quo. The introduction of the equal treatment principle, in particular, is to be welcomed. In addition, the use of the term 'remuneration' allows for the inclusion of a variety of different elements as part of a pay package. The inclusion of a limit on posting periods is also to be welcomed. However, the Directive falls short in three areas. First, it disregards the full range of wage-setting mechanisms in the Member States. As such, the proposed Directive does little to tackle inequality in those countries which make limited or no use of universally applicable or generally applicable collective agreements, but rely instead on other forms of agreement.

Second, although the European Commission recognised the unreliability of existing data on posted work, the proposed Directive fails to establish a more reliable system for the collection of data.[142] The difficulty at present is that the collection of data depends on the host state's requirements. In Ireland, for example, the lack of a requirement to register a posting makes identification of posted workers, and determining their length of time in the country, difficult. Although Article 5 mandates Member States to provide effective, proportionate and dissuasive penalties against undertakings that fail to comply with the Directive, it does not establish a uniform system for the collection of reliable data. It therefore remains to be seen whether the PWD's revised provisions will be effective.

The revised Directive also does not address cross-border enforcement. Regulation 2019/1149[143] establishes a European Labour Authority (ELA) which was launched in October 2019. The European Labour Authority's remit is to assist the Member States and the Commission in their effective application and enforcement of EU law related to labour mobility across the EU and the coordination of social security systems. A number of cases involving posted workers were referred to the ELA for investigation as soon as it commenced work.[144] Although the ELA cannot enforce decisions, it provides a welcome forum

[140] Article 3(1a) although there are limited exceptions contained in Arts 3(1a)(a)-(b).

[141] See Directive 2020/1057/EU. The application of the PWD to the road transport sector was at issue in Case C-815/18 *Federatie Nederlandse Vakbeweging v Van den Bosch Transporten BV and Others*, judgment of 1 December 2020.

[142] See European Commission, *Impact Assessment accompanying the document Proposal for a Directive of the European Parliament and the Council amending Directive 96/71/EC concerning the posting of workers in the framework of the provision of services* SWD (2016) 52 final.

[143] Regulation 2019/1149 of 20 June 2019 establishing a European Labour Authority OJ L186/21.

[144] www.etuc.org/en/pressrelease/unions-refer-first-exploitation-cases-new-european-labour-authority-investigation [last accessed 17 March 2022].

for national authorities to cooperate and exchange information on issues of concern around labour mobility, in particular posted workers.

Finally, Brexit adds an extra layer of complexity to the enforcement of posted workers' rights. The PWD no longer applies to postings between the UK and the EU from 1 January 2021, including to postings that commenced before the UK's exit. EU workers posted to the UK must henceforth navigate a complex set of immigration and social security rules, with potential criminal penalties for non-compliance. See further Novitz, ch 13 in this volume. There are transitional rules for workers posted to the EU for a period of up to 15 years contained in the EU-UK Trade and Cooperation Agreement.[145] Cross-border enforcement is likely to be difficult and dependent on national agency co-operation.

V. CONCLUSION

The EU's eastern enlargement – unprecedented in terms of its size, historical significance and political and economic consequences – led to a large rise in the number of workers availing of their rights under EU free movement law to move from one Member State to another. Most new Member State workers travelled to Austria, Germany, Ireland and the UK despite the existence of transitional measures in the former two countries. New Member State workers integrated well into the host labour markets, but the rapid increase in migration placed a burden on local infrastructure, particularly in the UK and Ireland which did not expect large numbers of new arrivals.

There were employment law reforms in all four countries in the period after enlargement, although the links to post-enlargement migration are not always clear and often formed part of broader immigration debates. The increase in post-enlargement migration served as a trigger for the adoption of measures to regulate low-wage sectors and low-skilled employment. The reform that was most directly linked to fears of wage undercutting by EU workers was in Austria, where the comprehensive LSD-BG, adopted in 2011, appears to have had its intended effect of preventing payment of wages below collectively agreed-rates. In Germany, from 2010 onwards, the widening of the scope of the Posted Workers Act (the AEntG) was a result of increased migration. At the same time, the introduction of a statutory minimum wage in 2014–2015 was not as a direct consequence of the EU enlargement, although fears over low-wage migrant labour contributed to the success of the campaign. In Ireland, the presence of migrant workers, including posted workers, contributed to the creation of the National Employment Relations Agency (2007) and then the Workplace Relations Commission (2015) to strengthen the enforcement of employment rights, and to establishment by the Industrial Relations (Amendment) Act 2015

[145] See further ec.europa.eu/commission/presscorner/detail/en/qanda_20_2532 [last accessed 17 March 2022].

of sectoral minimum rules. In the UK, the GLA was seen as a way to integrate new Member State workers into the labour market.

At EU level, reforms concentrated on dealing with the consequences of an increase in posted work following the enlargements whose negative effects (although well-publicised) are largely concentrated in certain sectors and limited to particular countries. The revision of the PWD coupled with the adoption of the Enforcement Directive and the establishment of the European Labour Authority addressed many of the problems flagged up in relation to posted workers, and the reforms are therefore to be welcomed. Yet concerns remain over effective cross-border enforcement, shared liability, and the collection of reliable, comparable data. Brexit adds to these concerns in relation to postings between the UK and the EU.

Overall, the Austrian, German, Irish and British labour law systems were able to accommodate large numbers of new Member State workers, the majority of whom work in low-skilled, labour-intensive sectors. There is limited causality between the EU enlargements and labour law reforms although the increase in migration (or the fear thereof) was used in all four countries to introduce legislation to better regulate low-wage employment. Yet, although labour markets have absorbed the new arrivals, new Member State workers' impact on their host country's societies should not be under-estimated. Long-term, social integration has not been straightforward. Post-enlargement migration has led to an intensification of competition in the labour market and placed a burden on health, education and infrastructure in local communities at a time when these were already struggling to adapt to an increasingly globalised world; effects that 'the law' – particularly at EU level – has not been able to deal with adequately and which, in many countries, have polarised debates on immigration.

12

Revisiting the Ethics of Temporary Labour Migration Programmes: The Role of Exit in Migrant Work Relations

MIMI ZOU

I. INTRODUCTION

IN RECENT DECADES, temporary labour migration programmes (TLMPs) have expanded in a number of advanced industrialised countries. 'Well targeted' and 'carefully designed'[1] TLMPs have been touted in international, supranational, and national policy arenas as a 'triple-win' instrument for industrialised host countries, lower-income home states, and migrants and their families.[2] Advocates of such schemes argue that, if properly designed, they would enable the 'more humane treatment' of migrant workers, compared to past guest worker programmes.[3] Yet, critics maintain that these 'labour import' regimes have highly exploitative elements built into them, where migrants are denied an array of social, economic, political and civil rights in law and in practice.[4] Numerous scholars have highlighted the precarious nature of these workers' migration status that creates the conditions for exploitative work relations.[5]

[1] Global Commission on International Migration (GCIM), *Migration in an Interconnected World: New Directions for Action* (Geneva, GCIM, 2005) 16.

[2] M Ruhs, 'The potential of temporary migration programmes in future international migration policy' (2006) 145 *International Labour Review* 7; G Hugo, 'Best Practice in Temporary Labour Migration for Development: A Perspective from Asia and the Pacific' (2009) 47 *International Migration* 23.

[3] M Ruhs, *The Price of Rights: Regulating International Labor Migration* (Princeton, Princeton University Press 2013) 9.

[4] S Castles, 'Guestworkers in Europe: A Resurrection?' (2006) 40 *International Migration Review* 741; D Nakache and P Kinoshita, 'The Canadian Temporary Foreign Worker Program: Do Short-Term Economic Needs Prevail over Human Rights Concerns?' (2010) 5 *IRPP Study* 1; C Dauvergne and S Marsden, 'The Ideology of Temporary Labour Migration in the Post-Global Era' (2014) 18 *Citizenship Studies* 224.

[5] J Fudge, 'Precarious Migrant Status and Precarious Employment: The Paradox of International Rights for Migrant Workers' (2012) 34 *Comparative Labor Law and Policy Journal* 101; B Anderson,

For liberal democratic societies, restricting a range of rights in relation to a subset of residents who are granted official admission into their territory poses certain ethical conundrums. Various accounts of 'exploitation' have been put forward in this context. For example, Walzer claims that the exploitation of guest workers is rooted in the denial of equal membership rights and access to citizenship for this group. For Walzer, the political subordination of this 'exploited or oppressed class' institutionalises and locks them into a position where they are dominated by 'a band of citizen-tyrants'.[6] Meanwhile, Attas conceptualises exploitation under TLMPs as the unfair advantage taken from the vulnerable position of migrants who are denied equal economic rights as citizens. Due to the restrictions placed on their labour rights (such as the right to free choice of employment), Attas points out that guest workers are forced to accept wages lower than the equilibrium price for their labour in a competitive marketplace.[7]

For the purposes of this chapter, I adopt a working definition of exploitation that expands on general understandings of 'exploitation' as taking unfair advantage of another person[8] and the use of a vulnerability of the exploited person for the exploiter's ends.[9] In the case of some migrants under TLMPs, the unfair advantage arises from a key condition of their vulnerability: their precarious migration status and the rights restrictions associated with such status. Employers may use this vulnerability to impose wages and working conditions that are inferior to what these migrants could command if they were resident workers with permanent residence or citizenship status, or, worse, to subject these migrants to extreme domination and precariousness. (This I have described elsewhere as 'hyper-dependence' and 'hyper-precarity'.[10])

The major aim of this chapter is to develop a substantive normative foundation for remedying the most ethically problematic institutional features of contemporary TLMPs in liberal democratic host states. It focuses on one of the most criticised features: the restrictions attached to these migrants' status that effectively 'tie' them to a personal work contract specific to a

'Migration, Immigration Controls and the Fashioning of Precarious Workers' (2010) 24 *Work, Employment and Society* 300; M Freedland and C Costello 'Migrants at Work and the Division of Labour Law' in C Costello and M Freedland (eds) *Migrants at Work: Immigration and Vulnerability in Labour Law* (Oxford, Oxford University Press, 2014); M Zou, 'The Legal Construction of Hyper-dependence and Hyper-Precarity in Migrant Work Relations' (2015) 31 *International Journal of Comparative Labour Law and Industrial Relations* 141.

6 M Walzer, *Spheres of Justice: a Defense of Pluralism and Equality* (New York, Basic Books, 1983) 52, 54, 59.

7 D Attas, 'The Case of Guest Workers: Exploitation, Citizenship and Economic Rights' (2000) 6 *Res Publica* 73, 88.

8 A Wertheimer, *Exploitation* (Princeton, Princeton University Press, 1996).

9 A Wood, 'Exploitation' (1995) 12 *Social Philosophy and Policy* 136.

10 Zou (n 5).

particular employer, occupation, sector and/or workplace. A key ethical (and legal) concern is how such 'ties' may potentially lead to forms of unfree labour such as servitude or forced labour.[11] The main idea proposed is that an ethically tenable TLMP should have in place the necessary conditions that maximise the viability of exit for migrants, as regards leaving any employment relationship at any time during their stay in the host state. Creating these conditions for exit in the regulatory design of such schemes is crucial if the host state wants to impose certain restrictions on migrants' rights but minimise the risk of the TLMP enabling the most severe forms of labour exploitation which offend basic moral principles and laws found in liberal democratic states.

The chapter is structured as follows. Section II starts with a critique of two common justifications for restricting migrants' rights under TLMPs in liberal states: the consent theory and the number versus rights trade-off. Section III analyses several proposals that accept the legitimacy of rights restrictions under TLMPs while attempting to articulate which 'core rights' should be protected and which 'non-core' rights could be restricted. In my view, these proposals lack a strong normative basis for distinguishing 'core' rights from 'non-core' rights. Section IV, drawing on Hirschman's 'Exit, Voice, and Loyalty' thesis,[12] highlights the important role of exit in migrants' work relations and argues that it should be the normative basis for identifying the 'core' rights that should be granted to migrants under TLMPs.

While recognising that there are different yet overlapping categories of migrants who perform paid work in the host state on a temporary basis (such as students and working holidaymakers), the scope of this chapter is limited to schemes that formally admit migrants for the specific purpose of undertaking paid work in the host state for a fixed period. There exists a wide range of TLMPs in advanced industrialised countries. Some schemes are designed to enforce the temporary labour migrants' repatriation or return to their home countries at the end of their stay. There are also TLMPs that include conditional pathways for migrants to apply for more secure legal status after a certain period of employer sponsorship in the host state.[13] In this regard, I refer to TLMPs in this chapter as any labour migration regimes that do not create an automatic and independent right or entitlement of the migrant worker to permanent residence in the host state.

[11] J Fudge and K Strauss, 'Migrants, Unfree Labour, and the Legal Construction of Domestic Servitude: Migrant Domestic Workers in the United Kingdom' in P Kotiswaran (ed), *Rethinking Trafficking through Migration Policy* (Cambridge, Cambridge University Press 2017) 524–55; Zou (n 5).

[12] A Hirschman, *Exit, Voice, and Loyalty* (Cambridge, MA, Harvard University Press 1970) 93.

[13] See, eg, Australia's Temporary Work (Skilled) Visa (subclass 457) Scheme (which was 'replaced' by/renamed the 'Temporary Skill Shortage Visa (subsection 482)' on 18 March 2017) and Canada's Live-In Caregiver Program.

II. COMMON JUSTIFICATIONS FOR RESTRICTING TEMPORARY LABOUR MIGRANTS' RIGHTS

This section examines two prevalent types of argument that seek to justify or defend the various restrictions on migrants' rights under TLMPs. The first category of arguments is based on the idea that migrants have consented to work under these schemes. The second type of justification arises from a proposed trade-off between the openness of a host state's admission policy (the numbers of migrants admitted) and the rights granted to the migrants admitted.[14]

A. Consent and Choice

Some advocates of TLMPs draw attention to the 'consent' of migrants who have 'voluntarily' contracted to work in the host state and have waived certain rights for a period of time in exchange for such an opportunity.[15] Such arguments have an underlying presumption, however, that migrants are indeed 'willing participants' entering into contractual arrangements under TLMPs with full information of what to expect. In reality, this may not be the case for some migrants who lack requisite knowledge of, or have been misinformed by sponsors and intermediaries about, their employment and residence arrangements and conditions in the host state.

Mayer argues that exploitative guest worker schemes may be acceptable under some conditions: 'the unfairness may be tolerated if the exploitation is modest, not severe, and if the most likely non-exploitative alternative worsens the plight of disadvantaged'.[16] Mayer maintains that 'we judge their exploitability by whether they will have enough if they do not migrate, and we judge exploitable workers to be exploited if they gain less than one with enough at home would likely accept'.[17] In other words, if migrants' wages and working conditions are equivalent to a living wage in their home countries, then (based on Mayer's reasoning) the scheme should not be deemed as exploitative. In liberal democratic societies, it is however extremely difficult to justify that the reference point of normatively acceptable labour standards should be those of migrants' countries of origin.

The types of contractual relations under these schemes can differ vastly between groups of migrants under different TLMPs. Mayer asserts that it would be difficult to view skilled temporary migrants, who are sponsored by a specific

[14] Ruhs (n 3) 167–72; H Chang, 'Guest workers and Justice in a Second-Best World' (2008) 34 *University of Dayton Law Review* 3.

[15] R Mayer, 'Guestworkers and exploitation' (2005) 67 *Review of Politics* 311.

[16] ibid.

[17] ibid 322.

employer, as exploited: 'If the pay is good and the workers have alternatives, it does not seem unfair to ask them to yield their (alleged) right to freedom of occupation in exchange for admission.'[18] I would suggest however that a distinction needs to be made between highly paid executives and highly skilled specialists on the one hand and semi-skilled migrants who are paid considerably less on the other hand. Depending on the conditions of entry, both groups of migrants may be admitted under the same 'skilled' TLMP. As I have argued elsewhere, the admission criteria of TLMPs can directly and indirectly shape the occupations and sectors that migrants are recruited into, as well as other characteristics such as migrants' countries of origin, age, gender, and family status.[19] These factors can have an important bearing on different migrants' bargaining power and propensity to exploitation.

In another account of TLMPs that is based on the notion of 'consent', Ottonelli and Torresi argue that migrants under these schemes have voluntarily 'chosen temporary migration as a worthwhile, albeit sometimes painful, part of their life-plans'.[20] These migrants' intention is not to remain and settle in the host state in the long term. Accordingly, Ottonelli and Torresi maintain that temporary migrants engage with the resident labour market and host society in order to serve their life plans upon returning home. Therefore, temporary migrants tend to work longer hours, take on insecure jobs, tolerate inferior wages and conditions, accept standards of housing, public education, and health care far below those that the host state sets for its own citizens. Their strategies also involve maximising earnings and savings and pursuing a 'life of austerity' during their short stay in the host state. In addition, they generally show little political participation and social engagement with the host society and invest little time in 'making themselves at home in the new country'.[21]

Ottonelli and Torresi refer to the notion of 'temporary migration projects', which entail persons migrating to a host state for a certain period of time and acquiring the expertise and money required to advance long-term goals upon returning to the home state.[22] They claim that 'the effectiveness and meaning of civil, social and political rights are grounded in a web of economic and social preconditions that are simply lacking in the case of temporary migrants'.[23] These 'preconditions' are based on the particular orientation of the migrant's life plans that involves returning to their country of origin.

[18] ibid 317.

[19] M Zou, 'Employer Demand for 'Skilled' Migrant Workers: Regulating Admission under the United Kingdom's Tier 2 (General) Visa' in J Howe and R Owens (eds), *Temporary Labour Migration in the Global Era: The Regulatory Changes* (Oxford, Hart, 2016) 113–30; M Zou, 'Immigration Law as Labour Market Regulation: Temporary Migration Status and Migrant Work Relations' [2015] *Mondi Migranti* 43.

[20] V Ottonelli and T Torresi, 'Inclusivist Egalitarian Liberalism and Temporary Migration: A Dilemma' (2012) 20 *Journal of Political Philosophy* 202.

[21] ibid 209–10.

[22] ibid 202.

[23] ibid 213.

I would contend that Ottonelli and Torresi's thesis regarding 'temporary migration projects' does not fully address the predicament of migrants with 'temporary' legal status who have life-plans and life-courses that involve seeking permanent residency in the host state. Moreover, according to Piore, as migrants 'develop a more permanent attachment, their time horizon expands: instability of employment is no longer a matter of indifference'.[24] Migrants who acquire a more permanent presence in the host state may start to display expectations akin to those of the resident workforce. Yet their legal statuses may create a cohort of long-term but 'temporary' residents without an unconditional right to remain in the host state. Indeed, a TLMP may allow for consecutive renewals of migrants' work permits but without ever granting them permanent residence status. Despite the host state's expectation that temporary migrant workers will return home once their labour is expended, Castles and Miller point out the 'inexorable pressures for settlement and community formation' that come with time.[25]

I would further argue that, for some migrants, TLMPs may engender or induce significant dependence on a particular sponsor/employer where the migrant has the goal of acquiring more secure legal status in the host state. As mentioned earlier, the regulatory design of some TLMPs provides a conditional pathway or 'stepping stone' for a migrant to obtain permanent residence.[26] This 'stepping stone' is often contingent on an employer's continued employment and sponsorship of the migrant, which can exacerbate the latter's dependence on the former. As I have examined in the context of Australia's 'skilled' TLMP (formerly known as the '457 Visa'), temporary migrants with aspirations for permanent residency are less willing than those without such aspirations to 'antagonise' their sponsoring employer.[27] An Independent Review of the scheme found that some visa holders, particularly those in less-skilled and lower-paid occupations, 'may be more concerned with gaining permanent residency in Australia than ensuring that they receive appropriate wages and conditions in the short term'.[28]

B. Numbers versus Rights

A separate, and influential, justification for the expansion of TLMPs that has been advanced emphasises the opportunities they give to migrants to access

[24] M Piore, *Birds of Passage: Migrant Labor and Industrial Societies* (Cambridge, Cambridge University Press, 1979) 64.

[25] S Castles and M Miller, *The Age of Migration: International Population Movements in the Modern World* (Basingstoke, Palgrave Macmillan, 2003).

[26] Wertheimer (n 8).

[27] Zou (n 19).

[28] B Deegan, *Visa Subclass 457 Integrity Review Final Report* (Australian Government Department of Immigration and Citizenship, 2008) 33.

employment in high-income host states.[29] Those opportunities are better than those these workers enjoy in their home countries, and benefit migrants' families and those who stay behind through remittances. Proponents of TLMPs view such labour migration regimes as an alternative to the 'politically unfeasible' option of permanent migration, which is unlikely to be accepted by residents of the host state, and as an alternative to zero migration.[30]

Underpinning these arguments is a 'numbers versus rights' trade-off, which has become quite influential in global migration policy debates over the past decade. Ruhs, a leading proponent of this trade-off, has argued that the rights a host state grants to migrants are based on policymakers' appraisal of the 'costs' and 'benefits' that 'critically depend on their impacts on the existing population in the host country'.[31] He compared 104 labour migration programmes in 46 host states based on the 'openness' of the host state's admission regime and the level of rights protection afforded to migrants in that state.[32] From this quantitative analysis, Ruhs found that higher-skilled migration programmes tend to be more open and to grant more rights than those admitting lower-skilled migrants. His explanation was that host states generally expect greater gains from higher-skilled than lower-skilled migrants; while the granting of rights often comes at a 'price' – especially social rights such as access to social security and social housing. Ruhs concluded that host states restrict the rights of lower-skilled migrants in order to maximise their net benefits, while confer rights to higher-skilled migrants in order to 'attract talent'.[33] Overall, Ruhs found a certain correlation between the openness of labour migration regimes and the restrictions on the rights granted to the migrants admitted. The most commonly restricted right found in the migration regimes of the countries in Ruhs' study is the right to free choice of employer.

Ruhs' work raised a relatively unexamined and thought-provoking issue regarding the interests of future migrants. His claim was that rights-based rationales often fail to consider the economic welfare benefits for migrants, mainly the interests of future migrants in seeking access to the labour markets of high-income countries. As he put it, the 'price' of granting more rights or insisting on equal rights (as citizens) for existing migrants in the host state is likely to be the adoption of more restrictive admission policies towards future migrants.

[29] Ruhs (n 3); H Chang, 'The Immigration Paradox: Poverty, Distributive Justice, and Liberal Egalitarism' (2003) 52 *De Paul Law Review* 759.

[30] Chang (n 29); D Bell, 'Justice for Migrant Workers? Foreign Domestic Workers in Hong Kong and Singapore' in Sor-hoon Tan (ed), *Challenging Citizenship: Group Membership and Cultural Identity in a Global Age* (Farnham, Ashgate, 2005).

[31] Ruhs (n 3) 13.

[32] ibid; M Ruhs, *Openness, Skills and Rights: An empirical analysis of labour immigration programmes in 46 high- and middle-income countries* (Centre on Migration, Policy and Society, 2011).

[33] Ruhs (n 3).

However, we may query whether it is truly possible to objectively measure and assess the actual (as opposed to perceived) impacts of granting migrants certain rights, particularly the purported effect on the number of future migrants admitted. Indeed, there have been empirical challenges to the 'numbers versus rights' postulation. Most notably, using international and regional databases and indices of migrants' rights, Cummins and Rodriguez did not find obvious support for a negative correlation between the stock of migrants in OECD countries and the inclusiveness of rights accorded to them.[34] Ruhs has responded by highlighting the methodological problems with the select cross-national indices and measures used by Cummins and Rodriguez.[35] From this debate, it can be seen that attempts to theorise the types of trade-offs made in labour migration policies require, as Ruhs acknowledged, more 'systematic empirical research … that investigates alternative explanations'.[36]

Moreover, Ruhs' inquiry largely focused on migrants' rights 'on paper' and stopped short of examining whether the rights prescribed in laws and regulations were exercised or denied in practice. In particular, his work paid little attention to the role of temporary migration statuses themselves in undermining the enforcement of migrants' labour rights in the host states in practice. Other scholars have highlighted the substantial difficulties of enforcing employment rights protection for migrants under TLMPs. For example, in their analysis of the European Union's Seasonal Workers Directive, Fudge and Herzfeld Olsson point out the challenge for seasonal migrant workers to 'claim obligations to which they would have been entitled had the work authorisation not been withdrawn on account of the employer's violation'.[37]

The 'number versus rights' trade-off has nevertheless been influential in respect of the case for expanding TLMPs in high-income countries. Such a case entails the argument that larger numbers of labour migrants (and their families and communities) from low-income sending states would benefit if some rights could be legitimately curtailed under TLMPs. These restrictions on migrants' rights can limit the perceived costs for the host state and as such, allow greater openness toward admitting future migrant workers. The next section examines various proposals for 'making temporary labour migration programs work', which focuses on which and how rights under TLMPs may be legitimately restricted.[38]

[34] M Cummins and F Rodriguez, *Is There a Numbers versus Rights Trade-off in Immigration Policy? What the Data Say* (UNDP 2009).

[35] M Ruhs, 'Numbers versus Rights in Low- Skilled Labour Immigration Policy? A Comment on Cummins and Rodríguez' (2010) 11 *Journal of Human Development and Capabilities* 305. See also M Cummins and F Rodríguez, 'A Rejoinder to Ruhs' (2010) 11 *Journal of Human Development and Capabilities* 311.

[36] M Ruhs, 'Migrant Rights, Immigration Policy and Human Development' (2010) 11 *Journal of Human Development and Capabilities* 259, 276.

[37] J Fudge and P Herzfeld Olsson, 'The EU Seasonal Workers Directive: When Immigration Control Meets Labour Rights' (2014) 16 *European Journal of Migration and Law* 439, 459.

[38] Ruhs (n 3) 178.

III. EXISTING PROPOSALS FOR RIGHTS RESTRICTIONS

There has been growing interest in the idea of redesigning contemporary TLMPs so as to promote such schemes as a 'triple-win' for host states, sending states, and migrants and their families. Numerous proposals have included the granting of a set of 'core' rights for migrants under TLMPs while restricting a wider range of rights in exchange for migrants' access to the host state's labour markets. For example, Pevnick argues that these migrants should have the right to work for different employers and the protection of their basic employment rights. In regard to rights that can be excluded or restricted, he asserts that there would be '(a) no promise of future access to citizenship; (b) no access to membership services (such as social security); and (c) no access for their families'.[39]

Similarly, Ruhs argues for the combination of 'realistic, feasible' aspects of immigration policymaking with idealistic considerations.[40] Migrants' basic civil and political rights must not be restricted (except for the right to vote in elections). Other rights can be restricted if there is evidence that those rights create net costs for host states. On this basis, he argues that there is a strong case for restricting the right to free choice of employment, the right to access means-tested public welfare benefits, the right to family reunion, and the right to permanent residence.

In my view, the case for granting a set of 'core' rights to migrants under TLMPs, while restricting other rights, requires a substantive normative foundation for identifying and justifying exactly what those rights are to be. Distinguishing between core and non-core rights granted to migrants would need to go beyond arguments based on the 'price' of rights. Such arguments have little appeal to those who underline the intrinsic values of human rights and moral equality in liberal democratic states. For example, Castles has raised the question of whether it is normatively acceptable to trade off workers' rights for economic gains.[41] As Taran puts it, rights should not be 'commodified as negotiable bundles that may be traded, sold or renounced in exchange for the economic benefits deriving from access to foreign labour markets'.[42]

Recognising that liberal democracies are morally constrained in distinguishing between citizens and non-citizens in the allocation of legal rights, Carens has provided a more substantive normative account that identifies the circumstances in which liberal democratic states may legitimately admit migrants for

[39] R Pevnick, *Immigration and the Constraints of Justice* (Cambridge, Cambridge University Press, 2011) 178.

[40] Ruhs (n 3) 164.

[41] Castles (n 4) 749.

[42] P Taran, 'The Need for a Rights-based Approach to Migration in the Age of Globalisation' in R Cholewinski, P de Guchteneire and A Pecoud (eds), *Migration and Human Rights: The United Nations Convention on Migrant Workers' Rights* (Cambridge, Cambridge University Press, 2009) 158.

employment on a temporary basis and impose certain rights restrictions. He accepts that a small handful of restrictions on social rights can be justified on the basis of the temporariness of migrants' stay in the host state, with their claims to membership rights strengthening over time. For Carens, the admission of temporary migrant workers with explicit restrictions on their right to stay in the host state is morally permissible, provided that these workers are actually present only for a short time. For migrant workers admitted on a temporary visa 'who have no other moral claim to residence than their presence in the state', it would be reasonable to expect that they leave the host state after a year or two when their visa expires.[43]

For Carens, 'it is not acceptable to keep people in a temporary status which is constantly renewed, so that they actually stay for a long time but remain in a vulnerable and restricted situation'.[44] In my view, Carens' proposition is useful for addressing the predicament of the cohort of 'temporary' long-term residents with precarious legal statuses. Some migrants partaking in TLMPs may have life-plans and life-courses that ultimately involve acquiring permanent residency and/or citizenship in the host state. These migrants' claims to full membership strengthens with the duration of their stay in the host state, which provides a normative basis for extending to them a full range of social, economic, political, and civil rights.

Temporary migration projects entail a high degree of vulnerability for those involved, who are exposed to the risk of losses arising from failed migration projects (due to a lack of necessary resources and/or difficulties of returning home), and from acquiring a lesser and marginal status in the host society.[45] Instead of extending membership rights to migrants, Ottonelli and Torresi propose the need for accessible exit options to mitigate the risks of failed temporary migration projects, including measures to enable migrants to change jobs; to allow them to return to their home country whenever they wish; to permit them to divert part of their income taxes and social security payments to some form of social guarantee for usage in their home states; to grant the portability of pension and social security payments from the host state to migrants' home state; to create special funds for migrants' voluntary repatriation; and, to enable migrants to frequently visit and interact with their home state.[46]

Ottonelli and Torresi allude to the prospect of personal failures or successes of temporary migration projects that 'can be induced by institutional factors', and observe that 'in the case of immigrants, as in the case of nationals, liberal states set up the relevant conditions for success by enacting the appropriate

[43] J Carens, 'Live-in Domestics, Seasonal Workers, and Others Hard to Locate on the Map of Democracy' (2008) 16 *Journal of Political Philosophy* 419, 422.

[44] J Carens, 'Who Belongs? Immigration, Democarcy, and Citizenship' in O Schmidtke and S Ozcurumez (eds), *Of States, Rights, and Social Closure* (Basingstoke, Palgrave Macmillan, 2007).

[45] Ottonelli and Torresi (n 20) 210–11.

[46] ibid 220.

social policies'.[47] However, a weakness of their argument is that they do not venture further into how these 'institutional factors … that are under the control of the liberal state'[48] structure migrants' vulnerability to the risks of failure in their projects. I would argue that such institutional factors as the restrictions of various rights under TLMPs, can have a significant bearing on the contours of migrants' choices and goals in their migration projects.

Ottonelli and Torresi argue that the availability of exit options concerns 'actual options to change one's immigrant status',[49] but again, stop short of elaborating on what these options actually entail and the institutional factors (such as immigration laws) that construct such status. As I have argued, the regulatory design of labour migration schemes can constitute and shape the precariousness of these migrants' legal status and the constraints on their options to change such status.[50] As stated earlier, migrants may appear to have the 'option' of applying for permanent residence through a TLMP, but are subject to the condition of continued employer sponsorship that could exacerbate their dependence and vulnerability to exploitative work relations. Nevertheless, Ottonelli and Torresi's general insights on the need to provide 'exit' options for migrants in their migration projects are promising. The next section builds on their arguments by focusing on how exit should be embedded in the institutional design of TLMPs, and how exit relates to voice in this context.

IV. MOVING FORWARD: THE ROLE OF EXIT

Having reviewed two common justifications for restricting migrants' rights under TLMPs as well as several notable proposals of where rights restrictions may be deemed ethically acceptable, the chapter now turns to the task of developing a normative approach for identifying the 'core' rights that a redesigned TLMP ought to protect. The basic idea that I put forward is that any ethically viable TLMP in a liberal democratic society should not deprive migrants of the possibility to exit an employment relationship at any stage of their migration project in the host state. Recourse to exit mechanisms not only enables migrants to leave highly exploitative labour relations, but also enhances their freedom to plan for the future – including the life plans and life courses emerging from their migration projects. This normative approach can help policymakers identify and reform some of the most ethically problematic rights restrictions under contemporary TLMPs.

Hirschman's seminal work on 'exit', 'voice', and 'loyalty' has been widely applied to diverse contexts to analyse how members of an organisation respond

[47] ibid 212.
[48] ibid.
[49] V Ottonelli and T Torresi, 'When is Migration Voluntary?' (2013) 47 *International Migration Review* 783, 801.
[50] Zou (n 5).

to a deteriorating or dissatisfying situation in respect of the organisation. There are essentially two types of responses: (1) exit, by ceasing to participate in or withdrawing from the organisation; and (2) voice, by articulating the grievance and complaint in order to effect change in the situation.[51] Drawing on insights from Hirschman's treatise and applications of his ideas by other scholars, I argue that exit is more important than voice in dealing with 'an objectionable state of affairs'[52] in migrants' work relations under TLMPs. Migrants may be unable to voice discontent against their sponsor/employer where exit is not a viable possibility. I have previously advanced a thesis regarding the need for exit and voice in migrants' work relations.[53] The argument here further develops the exit element of this earlier thesis and proposes ways in which contemporary TLMPs may be redesigned to maximise the viability of exit options in migrants' work relations.

According to Hirschman, the initial high costs of entry and stiff penalties and sanctions for exit can diminish and repress the salience of both exit and voice. Hirschman identifies these entry fees and exit penalties as devices for organisations to generate or reinforce the loyalty of consumers or employees. In other words, loyalty disrupts the functioning of exit and voice by causing consumers or employees to stay with an organisation.[54] Applying this idea to the context of migrant workers admitted under a TLMP, it may be argued that entry costs for such a migrant (and possibly their families and communities) can include the large amounts of time, money, resources, and energy invested to embark on the migration project. These costs include finding a job and sponsor (potentially through an intermediary) and acquiring the requisite visas and work permits. At the same time, migrants may be presented with hefty penalties for exit. If a migrant under a TLMP leaves their employment with a specific sponsor/employer, they could promptly lose their legal authorisation to remain in the host state and face the risk of removal. Other sanctions for exit may arise from the need to repay large sums of debt often owed to intermediaries or even the shame and humiliation of returning home early.

Freeman and Medoff borrow insights from Hirschman to posit a trade-off in situations where dissatisfied workers can respond through quitting their job to seek better working conditions elsewhere or resorting to 'voice' mechanisms such as trade unionism and collective bargaining.[55] Based on this proposition, a lack of 'voice' can increase the likelihood for 'exit' and vice versa, as exemplified in Freeman's association of unionism with lower quit rates.[56] However, the

[51] Hirschman (n 12).

[52] ibid 30.

[53] M Zou, 'Towards Exit and Voice: Redesigning Temporary Migrant Workers Programmes' (2017) 31 *Lavoro e Diritto* 91.

[54] Hirschman (n 12) 93.

[55] R Freeman and J Medoff, *What Do Unions Do?* (New York, Basic Books, 1984).

[56] R Freeman, 'The Exit-Voice Tradeoff in the Labor Market: Unionism, Job Tenure, Quits, and Separations' (1980) 94 *Quarterly Journal of Economics* 643.

existence of such a trade-off has been contested. As Taylor points out, a lesser-known aspect of Hirschman's thesis is the idea that:

> voice is most effective when it carries a threat (implicitly or explicitly) to impose a cost on the power, and exit is one of the main things that makes such threats credible, especially when it is properly resourced; potential exit can empower voice by diminishing its threshold for efficacy and thereby encouraging it.[57]

Adopting a neo-republican theoretical framework, Taylor's reading of Hirschman posits that voice within relationships is most effective as a means of limiting arbitrary power when it is backed by a credible threat of exit. His broader thesis is that the state's efforts should be targeted at empowering people to get out of relationships of potential domination and exploitation. For Taylor, efforts to directly empower voice run the risk of increasing direct domination by public or quasi-public agents. In the labour domain, he provides three examples of the state's efforts to empower labour's voice for countering the arbitrary power of employers and managers: workplace regulations or labour laws, state-directed employee participation mechanisms (such as work councils), and the 'privatisation' of power to trade unions. Taylor argues that such efforts will entail regulatory agents possessing discretionary powers to monitor, assess, and redress employer abuse that silences labour's voice. He is suspicious about the potential abuse of such powers, which pose the threat of increasing overall domination by countering one source of power with another.[58] Taylor ultimately advocates the state's resourcing of exit and encouraging of competition as indirect empowerment of voice.

In line with Taylor's approach, I would argue that exit is more important than voice in protecting migrant workers against domination and exploitation by less scrupulous employers. However, my argument is premised on different grounds to Taylor's. I take issue with Taylor's questionable assumption that collective action, such as trade unionisation, entails domination. His arguments also place too much faith in competition and markets to resource exit.[59] In contrast, I would argue that voice is rendered meaningless without exit, or the threat of exit, for migrants with precarious migration statuses under TLMPs.

In my view, voice-based means to effect change in temporary migrants' work relations (such as unionisation and collective bargaining, workplace grievance mechanisms, legal proceedings, protections for whistle-blowers, etc) and beyond their work relations (such as participation in political processes) cannot exist where exit is not possible due to their precarious migration status. I would

[57] R Taylor, *Exit Left: Markets and Mobility in Republican Thought* (Oxford, Oxford University Press, 2017) 5.

[58] ibid 23–24.

[59] See W Roberts, 'Book Review: *Exit Left: Markets and Mobility in Republican Thought*, by Robert S. Taylor' (2018) 46 *Political Theory* 147.

argue that the tethering of migrants' legal status to an employer sponsorship under TLMPs can be seen as mandating the 'loyalty' of a group of extremely immobile workers through substantial entry fees and prohibitive exit penalties. In these circumstances, migrants may become unable or unwilling to use voice mechanisms against their sponsor/employer if doing so would entail the risk of losing their legal authorisation to work and reside in the host country. The existence of viable exit options, rather than voice, may be seen as a precondition for the effective enforcement of rights granted to migrants under TLMPs. Where a migrant's legal status is tied to a mandated employer sponsorship, fears of reprisal for bringing any claims against their employers can render any formal rights meaningless.

Having highlighted the salient role of exit (vis-à-vis voice) in migrant work relations, we may now consider what an ethically viable TLMP that expands the contours for exit would look like. To start with, such a scheme should have as few as possible restrictions attached to migrants' status that could leave them beholden to a specific employer and employment relationship. Migrants must be able to quit their job and change employers without adverse consequences for their legal status in the host state. Ruhs argues that the portability of work permits/visas between different employers could be acceptably limited for a short initial period (such as six months), as otherwise it would 'substantially reduce the propensity of local employers to recruit migrant workers because the latter would be free to leave the employer who recruited them before at least part of that employer's recruitment costs have been recovered'.[60] Carens proposes that three months would be the maximum period for limiting migrants' freedom to change employers, so that any 'recruitment costs' may be recouped. Even with this restriction, there ought to be an escape clause if the employer engages in abusive behaviour during this period.[61]

Here, I would go further than the qualified conditions proposed by Ruhs and Carens. Without the freedom to exit an employment relationship at any time, a migrant worker can be vulnerable to forms of unfree labour that would not be legally or ethically acceptable even for a 'short initial period'. While Carens proposes an escape clause, he does not make it clear how this would actually operate in practice. Such a clause seems to be aimed at responding to highly exploitative labour situations when they occur, rather than preventing the very source of migrants' vulnerabilities that stem from immigration restrictions in the first place. A reasonable response to the practical need for employers to recuperate their recruitment costs would be to reduce visa application and administration costs for employers and migrant workers – something which could also reduce any debt incurred by migrants.

I would argue that a migrant's legal authorisation to work and reside in the host state must be detached from an employment contract with a specific

[60] Ruhs (n 3) 175.
[61] Carens (n 43) 433.

sponsor. Migrants under TLMPs could be issued with a transferrable work permit that is not tied to a mandated employer sponsorship but enables them to change employers and to search for alternative employment throughout the duration of the permit. Migrants' choice of employment could potentially be limited to a defined list of demonstrated shortage occupations and sectors in the host state's labour market. Their work permits would allow them to choose between and switch into any of the occupations on this list during their stay in the host state. Such a proposal, in addition to promoting exit in migrants' work relations, would address labour market considerations of 'shortages' that underpin many TLMPs.

Expanding the contours for exit also require the provision of some safeguards in terms of social protections for migrants under TLMPs. Without such safeguards, the risks of destitution in the host state – exacerbated by the need to repay debts incurred in their migration projects – may severely constrain migrants' ability to leave an extremely exploitative employment relationship. As mentioned earlier, restriction of migrants' access to a range of social protections is often defended on the basis of maximising the 'fiscal net contribution of migrants' and minimising the 'cost' to the host state in extending public services and welfare benefits to migrants.[62] As against that, however, I would argue that the principle of inclusion in liberal democratic states requires the minimum provision of 'universal' social benefits in host states, such as public health services and education, to migrants and their family members under TLMPs.

In determining what other social benefits should be extended to migrants under TLMPs, I would support Carens' reasoning regarding migrants' claims to different types of social protections, which depend on the nature and purpose of such protections. Based on principles of reciprocity, Carens maintains that temporary migrants should be entitled to the same rights or to reimbursement for contributions to social protection programmes that are tied to their workforce participation. Where migrant workers and their families are prevented from receiving such benefits under applicable national laws, the International Convention on Migrant Workers' Rights urges states to reimburse the 'amount of contributions made by them with respect to that benefit on the basis of the treatment granted to nationals who are in similar circumstances'.[63]

In this regard, I would suggest that one feasible proposal could be that a proportion of income taxes and social security payments collected by the state from migrant workers (and any accompanying family members) go into a special fund set up to finance their access to social benefits during their stay in the host state. To enable migrants to exercise exit options in respect of their employment

[62] Ruhs (n 3) 47.

[63] International Convention on the Protection of the Rights of all Migrant Workers and Members of their Families, Art 27(2).

relationships, and their broader migration projects in the host state, bilateral agreements between host and home states to secure the portability of such funds would be vital to protect migrants and their families against the risks of destitution during their residence in the host state and upon their return home.

V. CONCLUSION

This chapter has reviewed influential positions and proposals in recent scholarship on the ethics of restricting migrants' rights under contemporary TLMPs. Considering the strong push-pull factors driving global labour migration to high-income countries, the use of TLMPs is unlikely to cease in the near future. Rather than advocating for the immediate elimination of TLMPs in favour of zero-migration or permanent settlement policies, I have focused on developing a normative basis for redesigning the institutional architecture of such schemes. Recognising that migrants are unlikely to be granted a full range of rights under TLMPs, the proposed approach seeks to identify the core rights that should be protected at a minimum. Enabling migrants to exit from any employment relationship at any stage of their migration projects is essential to liberal democratic states' espoused commitments to moral principles, especially the elimination of forms of unfree labour. It is hoped that this chapter can direct the attention of policymakers to the normative legitimacy and practical feasibility of addressing particularly exploitative work relations for some migrants under TLMPs, without relying upon the contested numbers versus rights trade-off.

13

Rationales for Regulation of Temporary Movement of Natural Persons: Options for a Post-Brexit Model

TONIA NOVITZ

I. AN INTRODUCTION TO THE LAW AND ISSUES

TEMPORARY MOVEMENT OF natural persons has become an increasing feature of trade in services.[1] This is regulated within the European Union through Article 56 of the Treaty on European Union (TEU) and the Posting of Workers Directive,[2] as well as internationally under Mode 4 of the World Trade Organisation (WTO) General Agreement on Trade in Services (GATS)[3] and preferential trade agreements.[4] In this scenario, services are traded between countries, involving the temporary movement of natural persons across borders from a 'home state' to a so-called 'host state'. Such persons may be temporarily deployed to work by their own employer abroad, or they may be part of an inter-corporate transfer connecting to another related enterprise, or they may be dispatched as an agency worker.[5] They may even be notionally self-employed as a service provider hired by a third party.[6]

[1] For a review of the expansion of these forms of temporary migration, see J Howe and R Owens, 'Temporary Labour Migration in the Global Era: The Regulatory Challenges' in J Howe and R Owens (eds), *Temporary Labour Migration in the Global Era: The Regulatory Challenges* (Oxford and Portland, Oregon, Hart, 2016) 12.

[2] Directive 96/71 concerning the posting of workers in the framework of the provision of services [1997] OJ L18/1.

[3] General Agreement on Trade in Services, Annex IB to the World Trade Organisation Agreement, available at: www.wto.org/english/docs_e/legal_e/26-gats.pdf [last accessed 16 March 2022].

[4] See, eg. the EU-Singapore Free Trade Agreement, which under Appendix 8 includes a 'Schedule of Specific Commitments in Conformity with Articles 8.14 (Key Personnel and Graduate Trainees) and 8.15 (Business Services Sellers)'.

[5] Directive 96/71, Art 1(3).

[6] GATS, Art 1(b) and Annex on Movement of Natural Persons Supplying Services Under the Agreement, Art 1. False self-employment can potentially be addressed, and employment law provisions applied, under the laws of the home or host state.

Under both the Posting of Workers Directive and GATS, it is stated that the temporarily 'posted' worker will not gain access to the labour market of the host state.[7] The differences between the Posting of Workers Directive and GATS should though be highlighted. The EU posting of workers regime applies to all EU Member States, regardless of their enthusiasm for this regulatory regime or otherwise. By way of contrast, under GATS, contracting parties have the option to make specific undertakings to be bound under Mode 4 in relation to particular 'sectors', which are then registered in their 'schedule of commitments'.[8] Further, EU posted workers lie outside the immigration rules which would otherwise apply to temporarily present non-nationals – even when these posted workers do not independently possess free movement rights, because they are not EU nationals or are nationals of recent accession countries covered by a transitional arrangement.[9] By contrast, under GATS, states are permitted to apply 'measures to regulate the entry of natural persons into, or their temporary stay in, its territory' – provided that 'such measures are not applied in such a manner as to nullify or impair the benefits accruing to any Member under the terms of a specific commitment'.[10]

As I have argued elsewhere, the treatment of labour as a 'service' to be traded can become divorced from recognition of the type of work provided and the products that work produces.[11] Services are conventionally understood as 'immaterial labour' – that is, labour not linked to an identifiable product or commodity.[12] Typical examples concern care work or health services.[13] Services can also be provided in the form of 'analytical labour', connected to knowledge-based jobs, such as data entry and word-processing, which can be high or low-skilled.[14] Significantly, however, services can also arise from the decentralisation of

[7] Case C-113/89 *Rush Portuguesa v Office national d'immigration*, 27 March 1990, [1990] ECR I-1417, para 15; Annex on Movement of Natural Persons Supplying Services Under the Agreement, Art 1.

[8] The EU Schedule of Commitments (2006) which lists Mode 4 commitments is available at: trade.ec.europa.eu/doclib/docs/2012/november/tradoc_150087.pdf [last accessed 16 March 2022].

[9] See the facts of *Rush Portuguesa* (n 7); also *Intra-EU Mobility of Third-country Nationals* (European Migration Network Study 2013), 28, citing inter alia Case C-43/93 *Van der Elst*, 9 August 1994 and Case C-445/03 *Commission v Luxembourg*, 21 October 2004.

[10] Annex on Movement of Natural Persons Supplying Services Under the Agreement, Art 4.

[11] See T Novitz, 'Evolutionary Trajectories for Transnational Labour Law: Trade in Goods to Trade in Services?' [2014] *Current Legal Problems* 239 and T Novitz, 'Supply Chains and Temporary Migrant Labour: The Relevance of Trade and Sustainability Frameworks?' in D Ashiagbor (ed), *Re-Imagining Labour Law for Development: Informal Work in the Global North and South* (Oxford, Hart/Bloomsbury, 2019).

[12] This typology is extrapolated from the categorisation offered by M Hardt and A Negri, *Empire* (Cambridge, Mass., Harvard University Press, 2000) 290–93.

[13] J Kelsey, *Serving Whose Interests? The Political Economy of Trade in Services Agreements* (London, Routledge 2008) 119.

[14] Hardt and Negri (n 12) 291–2.

production through networks,[15] 'labour for institutionalised production',[16] which are also termed 'human supply chains'.[17] This type of service-provision is more concerned with subcontracting than with the absence of a specific product. For example, a worker may be placed in a different country to provide a 'service' as a cook, a designer, or a lawyer, and there may be a product at the end of the day, such as an item of food, an architectural plan, or a legal contract. Yet, we talk about catering services, design services, and legal services, as if there were no end product in sight. In the same way, agencies can be regarded as providing the 'service' of supplying people to do a job in another state which involves production of a manufactured item.[18] This form of trade in services, recognised under both EU law and GATS, allows additional profit to be made by the supplier of the labour (usually the recruitment and placement agency) before the workers begin to make the products in question.

This form of temporary migration in the context of trade in services has been problematic, because of the ways in which the workers concerned can be housed, paid and treated.[19] Significant concerns have also arisen regarding health and safety – for example in relation to construction workers,[20] and care workers[21] within supply chains sent through agencies. There have been negative impacts on access to work for local workers in host states.[22] There is also a troubling potential for a loss of skilled labour in the home state, often described as a 'brain drain', which can be more prevalent in relation to movement from low income states to high income states.[23] The need for some form of regulation is clear, but its scope remains contested, with significant reform of the Posting of Workers Directive only having been achieved in 2018.[24]

[15] ibid 293–4.

[16] Kelsey (n 13) 12.

[17] J Gordon, 'Regulating the Human Supply Chain' (2017) 102 *Iowa Law Review* 445.

[18] Novitz (n 11) 244.

[19] See G Bosch and C Weinkopf, 'Transnational Labour Markets and National Wage Setting Systems in the EU' (2013) 44(1) *Industrial Relations Journal* 2; N Lillie and M Sippola, 'National Unions and Transnational Workers: The Case of Olkiluoto 3, Finland' (2011) 25 *Work, Employment and Society* 292, 302–3; and I Wagner, 'The Political Economy of Borders in a "Borderless" European Labour Market' (2015) 53 *JCMS* 1370.

[20] Discussed in the European Parliament at: www.europarl.europa.eu/sides/getDoc.do?pubRef=-//EP//TEXT+OQ+O-2011-000168+0+DOC+XML+V0//EN [last accessed 16 March 2022].

[21] A Stewart, *Gender, Law and Justice in Global Markets* (Cambridge, Cambridge University Press, 2011).

[22] These concerns have been documented in J Cremers, *In Search of Cheap Labour in Europe: Working and Living Conditions of Posted Workers* (Brussels, CLR Studies: European Institute for Construction Labour Research, 2011). See also the European Commission Impact Assessment on the proposal to amend the Posting of Workers Directive, SWD (2016) 52 (8 March 2016) 13 and 36.

[23] PA Martin, *GATS, Migration and Labour Standards* DP/165/2006 (ILO, 2006) www.ilo.org/inst/publication/discussion-papers/WCMS_193612/lang--en/index.htm, 11–13 [last accessed 16 March 2022]; and C Kanchanachitra et al, 'Human Resources for Health in Southeast Asia: Shortages, distributional challenges and international trade in health services' (2011) 377 *The Lancet* 769.

[24] On 21 June 2018 the Council adopted the new revised Posting of Workers Directive, see www.consilium.europa.eu/en/press/press-releases/2018/06/21/posting-of-workers-council-adopts-the-directive/ [last accessed 16 March 2022].

The treatment of temporary movement of natural persons is a particular issue in the context of Britain's exit from the EU, as the United Kingdom (UK) is no longer bound by the original Posting of Workers Directive,[25] the related Enforcement Directive,[26] or the newly agreed Amended Posting of Workers Directive.[27] Instead, the UK is faced with new policy choices regarding the treatment of temporary migration as an aspect of trade in services.

In March 2018, the Confederation of British Industry proposed that the UK negotiate swiftly with the EU 'a reciprocal agreement on intra-company transfers and posting of workers'.[28] However, in the White Paper on 'The Future Relationship Between the United Kingdom and the European Union' published in July 2018, the UK Government offered a more limited commitment:

> Given the depth of the relationship and close ties between the peoples of the UK and the EU, the UK will make a sovereign choice in a defined number of areas to seek reciprocal mobility arrangements with the EU, building on current WTO GATS commitments. The UK has already proposed that this should be achieved in an appropriate framework for mobility, in line with arrangements that the UK might want to offer to other close trading partners in the future, where they support new and deep trade deals.[29]

UK legislation on its face offers natural persons temporarily working in the UK potentially the same entitlements as resident workers, provided the categories of eligibility (namely 'worker' or 'employee') are satisfied, that conflicts of law rules are satisfied and that they are not engaged in illegal working.[30] However, the Posting of Workers Directive and the freedom to provide services under Article 56 of the Treaty on the Functioning of the European Union (TFEU) have notoriously restricted (at least in practice) access to industrial action in the UK regarding the terms and conditions of posted workers, exemplified by the notorious East Lindsey unofficial industrial action and sympathy strikes in which placards were paraded seeking 'British jobs for British workers'.[31] This raises

[25] See (n 2).

[26] Directive 2014/67 on the enforcement of the Posting of Workers Directive [2014] OJ L159/11.

[27] Directive 2018/957 amending the Posting of Workers Directive [2018] OJ L173/16.

[28] CBI, *5 Steps to Protect Services Post-Brexit*, 8 March 2018, available as of 9 November 2018 at www.cbi.org.uk/index.cfm/_api/render/file/?method=inline&fileID=FA2619F6-B44A-437E-9942AB4F6727C2E2 [last accessed 16 March 2022]. Since removed from the public CBI website but the reference to its plans can be found at: www.icas.com/technical-resources/five-steps-to-protect-services-after-brexit and https://www.cbi.org.uk/policy-focus/brexit-and-eu-negotiations/articles/cbi-calls-government-to-take-five-steps-to-protect-services-post-brexit/ [last accessed 16 March 2022].

[29] *The Future Relationship Between the United Kingdom and the European Union* Cm 9593 July 2018, 32–33.

[30] See the Immigration Act 2016, s 34 inserting s 24A of the Immigration Act 1971; J Fudge, 'Illegal Working, Migrants and Labour Exploitation in the UK' (2018) 38(3) *Oxford Journal of Legal Studies* 557.

[31] Regarding the East Lindsey Oil Refinery Dispute, see C Barnard, '"British Jobs for British Workers": The Lindsey Oil Refinery Dispute and the Future of Local Labour Clauses in an Integrated

questions regarding the rationales which could govern future UK regulatory choices.

That is not to say that policy choices after Brexit would be unconstrained. As was clear from the White Paper, the UK will still wish to continue membership of the WTO. Indeed, the government submitted a revised tariff schedule under GATT in July 2018,[32] with a schedule of commitments under GATS following in December 2018. The latter replicates external EU services schedule commitments with the removal of what would be 'inappropriate' references to EU terms and EU law.[33] In January 2021, the UK issued a statement regarding its WTO commitments, which included its assertion that 'the period for objections to the certification of that schedule and list of Article II GATS (MFN) exemptions expired on 17 January 2019'.[34] The terms of GATS also determine the validity of any preferential trade agreement entered into by the UK, with the EU or a third country, which sought to substantially liberalise trade in services with 'substantial sectoral coverage' under Article V of GATS, or which included a 'labour integration agreement' under Article V bis of GATS. The UK does not therefore, within the WTO, have complete freedom to determine its future trade in services arrangements with other states regarding temporary movement of natural persons, but will have to do so in accordance with the GATS schedule of commitments and, if any state is to be given preferential treatment in excess of these commitments, must abide by the requirements established in Article V and Vbis of GATS. Moreover, the UK will also be bound by the terms of the preferential trade agreements that it enters into, a case in point being the EU-UK Trade and Cooperation Agreement (TCA),[35] which requires certain enforcement of labour standards and protection of International Labour Organization (ILO) and European Social Charter

EU Market' (2009) 38(3) *Industrial Law Journal* 245. On subsequent developments, see L Hayes, T Novitz and H Reed, 'Applying the Laval Quartet in a UK Context: Chilling, Ripple and Disruptive Effects on Industrial Relations' in A Bucker and W Warneck (eds), *Reconciling Fundamental Social Rights and Economic Freedoms after Viking, Laval and Ruffert* (Baden–Baden, Nomos Publishers, 2011); and T Novitz and P Syrpis, 'The UK Report' in M Freedland and J Prassl (eds), *Viking and Laval and Beyond* (Oxford, Hart Publishing, 2014).

[32] This schedule was submitted on 24 July 2018. See www.wto.org/english/news_e/news18_e/mark_24jul18_e.htm [last accessed 16 March 2022].

[33] Available at: assets.publishing.service.gov.uk/government/uploads/system/uploads/attachment_data/file/762808/SCW380_-_UK_GATS_Schedule-FINAL_03_12_2018.pdf [last accessed 16 March 2022].

[34] For more detail, see 'End of the UK-EU Transition Period Communication from the United Kingdom' 31 December 2020, WT/GC/226, 4 January 2021 available at: assets.publishing.service.gov.uk/government/uploads/system/uploads/attachment_data/file/949410/201231_General_Council_Statement_FINAL.pdf [last accessed 16 March 2022].

[35] Trade and Cooperation Agreement (TCA) between the European Union and the European Atomic Energy Community, of the one part, and the United Kingdom of Great Britain and Northern Ireland, of the other part [2021] OJ L149/10, version approved by European Parliament (following provisional application of the TCA from 1 January 2021).

standards so as to avoid certain regulatory action and even trade sanctions.[36] The UK cannot simply 'take back control'.

This chapter seeks to re-consider UK regulation of posted work, given that the UK is no longer bound by the requirements regarding the freedom to provide services under Article 56 TFEU or the Posting of Workers Directive (as amended). In their 2017 report on 'Human Rights and Business', the UK Parliamentary Joint Committee on Human Rights indicated that it would expect the types of human rights clauses in EU bilateral and multilateral preferential trade agreements to be replicated (and even improved upon) in UK external relations relating to trade.[37] These have tended to include reference to international instruments considered key to 'sustainable and good governance', such as the four fundamental ILO principles, reflected in the eight 'core' ILO Conventions.[38] The EU has also gradually been extending the remit of its legitimate concerns and enhancing enforcement of labour rights in this context.[39] For example, Chapter 23.3 of the Comprehensive Economic Trade Agreement (CETA) between the EU and Canada goes beyond acknowledgement of core or fundamental ILO standards, also recognising such issues as health and safety standards and 'non-discrimination in respect of working conditions, including for migrant workers'. How the latter protection is to be linked with Chapter 10 on 'Temporary Entry and Stay of Natural Persons For Business Purposes' is though unclear.[40] In the same way, it is unclear what constraints the UK would place on protection of those engaged in temporary

[36] Set out in the 'Trade and Sustainable Development' chapter found in 'Part Two – Heading 1 – Title XI: Level playing field for open and fair competition and sustainable development', discussed for example by KD Ewing, 'The EU-UK Trade and Cooperation Agreement: Implications for ILO Standards and the European Social Charter in the United Kingdom' (2021) 32(2) *King's Law Journal* 306.

[37] 'Human Rights and Business 2017: Promoting responsibility and ensuring accountability' HL Paper 153, HC 443 available at: publications.parliament.uk/pa/jt201617/jts [last accessed 16 March 2022] and assets.publishing.service.gov.uk/government/uploads/system/uploads/attachment_data/file/762808/SCW380_-_UK_GATS_Schedule-FINAL_03_12_2018.pdf elect/jtrights/443/44302.htm [last accessed 16 March 2022].

[38] See, eg, the 'special incentive arrangement for sustainable development and good governance chapter' ('GSP+'), which was initially set out in Council Regulation 732/2008 and is maintained in the current incarnation of the GSP under Council Regulation 978/2012. The fundamental ILO principles to which the EU refers are: freedom of association and the effective recognition of the right to collective bargaining (linked to the 'fundamental' ILO Conventions Nos 87 and 98), elimination of all forms of forced and compulsory labour (ILO Conventions Nos 29 and 105), effective abolition of child labour (ILO Conventions Nos 138 and 182) and elimination of discrimination in respect of employment and occupation (ILO Conventions Nos 100 and 111).

[39] For discussion see T Novitz, 'Sustainable Labour Conditionality in EU Free Trade Agreements? Implications of the EU-Korea Expert Panel Report' (2022) 47(1) *European Law Review* 3; and the EU Trade and Sustainable Development (TSD) Review consultation which closed in November 2021 available at: policy.trade.ec.europa.eu/consultations/open-public-consultation-trade-and-sustainable-development-tsd-review_da [last accessed 16 March 2022].

[40] See ec.europa.eu/trade/policy/in-focus/ceta/ceta-chapter-by-chapter/ [last accessed 16 March 2022].

migrant labour or, as it is known more technically, trade in services. We are seeing the first indications of a distinctive UK approach in the free trade agreements (FTAs) which are being concluded with Australia[41] and New Zealand (NZ),[42] although at the time of writing neither FTA is yet in force.

It is suggested that the regulatory rationales available can be divided into at least four discernible categories. The first regulatory rationale is, as the Parliamentary Joint Committee properly identified, the protection of 'human rights', which should apply to EU 'posted workers' and now those 'natural persons' supplying temporary services abroad as human beings. As we shall see, this regulatory rationale is potentially problematic by virtue of disputes over the scope of human rights, such that it may be seen as too minimalistic (if focused on narrow civil and political rights or only 'core' international labour rights) or too extensive (if determined with reference to the broader recognition of socio-economic rights internationally). In this sense, it may need to be supplemented by other regulatory rationales, to assist in determination of its scope and application.

A second regulatory possibility is to make provision for minimum labour standards imposed by the host state, in order to establish the basic terms of 'fair competition'. In this respect, Article 3(1) of the Posting of Workers Directive offers a model, by requiring a state to extend basic standards relating to such matters as working time, holidays, a minimum wage, and health and safety to posted workers. This justification for regulation, which can also be linked to concerns over 'social dumping' and unfair competitive advantage in trade,[43] will be considered in further detail below.

A third option is to consider those persons temporarily working in the UK as entitled to 'equality of treatment' in the labour market of the UK as a host state and to insist on reciprocal obligations in FTAs concluded by the UK. This last option may be preferable not only because it is simpler, but because it is fairer. This potential approach is evident in the 2018 amendment to the Posting of Workers Directive although not before a 12-month period has expired,[44] and

[41] Hereafter 'UK-Australia FTA'. Text signed on 16 December 2021 and available at: www.gov.uk/government/collections/free-trade-agreement-between-the-united-kingdom-of-great-britain-and-northern-ireland-and-australia [last accessed 16 March 2022].

[42] Hereafter 'UK-NZ FTA'. Text signed on 22 February 2022 and available at: www.gov.uk/government/collections/free-trade-agreement-between-the-united-kingdom-of-great-britain-and-northern-ireland-and-new-zealand [last accessed 16 March 2022].

[43] Drawn in part from the discussion in T Novitz, 'Collective Bargaining and Social Dumping in Posting and Procurement: What Might Come from Recent Court of Justice Case Law and the Proposed Reform of the Posted Workers Directive?' in A Sanchez-Graells (ed) *Smart Public Procurement and Labour Standards: Pushing the Discussion after RegioPost* (Oxford and Portland, Oregon, Hart, 2018) 215–41.

[44] Amended Posting of Workers Directive 2018, Art 1(2)(b) creating Posting of Workers Directive, Art 3(1a). This is consistent with the limitations for 'inter-corporate transferees' under, for example, the EU-Singapore Trade Agreement, Art 8.13, with thanks to Mijke Howerzijl for pointing out this connection to me.

there are precedents for an 'equal treatment' principle in response to migrant workers more generally. The scope for equal access to legislative protections will be considered in comparison to contractual terms and conditions such as pay. The chapter also considers the material consequences of equal access to 'human rights' such as freedom of association.

Finally, there is potentially a broader social sustainability rationale – namely, that the levels of wage and other forms of inequality that follow from treating temporarily 'posted' workers so very differently have profound short- and long-term social costs, which ultimately need to be tackled. Justification of regulation on 'sustainability' grounds is complicated by contestation of the concept and its application, although the adoption by the United Nations (UN) General Assembly of 17 Sustainable Development Goals (SDGs) in 2015 may assist in remedying such complications.[45] While the EU has taken a turn towards describing its own trade regulation in sustainability terms when setting labour standards,[46] the UK seems less interested in doing so in recent FTAs. It is suggested here that sustainability may yet be useful as a supplement to the human rights, competition based and equality rationales for regulation.

II. THE HUMAN RIGHTS RATIONALE

All workers temporarily 'posted' or otherwise possess human rights as human beings. Under international law, for example, 'all human beings' and 'all persons' can claim protections under the International Covenant on Civil and Political Rights 1966. Additionally, 'everyone' has entitlements under the International Covenant on Economic, Social and Cultural Rights (ICESCR), adopted the same year, in particular the right to just and favourable conditions of work in Article 7 (including 'safe and healthy working conditions') and the right to form and join a trade union under Article 8.[47] The notion that 'everyone' has such entitlements is also reflected in the wording of the European Convention on Human Rights, in relation to the right to a fair trial under Article 6, the right to privacy under Article 8, freedom of expression under Article 10, and the right to assembly and association under Article 11. These provisions of the ECHR are relevant to the access of posted workers to respectively: enforcement of their rights under employment and human rights legislation, achievement of decent

[45] Resolution adopted by the UN General Assembly on 25 September 2015 – Transforming our world: the 2030 Agenda for Sustainable Development A/Res/70/1 available at sustainabledevelopment.un.org/post2015/transformingourworld/publication [last accessed 16 March 2022].

[46] T Novitz, 'Labour Standards and Trade: Need we choose between "Human Rights" and "Sustainable Development"?' in H Gött (ed) *Labour Standards in International Economic Law* (Berlin, Springer, 2018).

[47] On the complementarity of labour and social rights and their potential application to migrants, see B Ryan and V Mantouvalou, 'The Labour and Social Rights of Migrants in International Law' in R Rubio Marin (ed), *Human Rights and Immigration* (Oxford, Oxford University Press, 2014).

housing conditions which allow for privacy, as well as scope for voice at work including collective bargaining and a right to strike.[48] Evidence of acceptance of the significance of these 'Convention rights' can be found in their domestic effect in the UK by virtue of the Human Rights Act 1998, at least for the time being.[49] There is also the supplementary protection from discrimination in respect of the exercise of these human rights under Article 14 of the Convention. A broader span of workers' rights is further recognised under the European Social Charter, which the UK has also ratified.[50] However, the coverage of these rights is though limited by the Appendix to the ESC, which states that (apart from protection for refugees), 'the persons covered by Articles 1 to 17 include foreigners only insofar as they are nationals of other Contracting Parties lawfully resident or working regularly within the territory of the Contracting Party concerned'. Third country nationals cannot readily claim these entitlements.

At the outset, a principled objection can be made to a human rights-based regulatory rationale. To protect a bare 'human right' may be not to protect very much at all, since when migrants are reduced to mere human beings, we are only looking at subsistence, rather than the greater well-being we aspire to in a workplace (or a country).[51] The Arendtian paradox is that being barely human is insufficient for the meaningful exercise of rights. Much depends on whether we conceive of only basic civil and political rights being available to temporarily 'posted' workers, or the broader span of socio-economic entitlements recognised under international law. If specific socio-economic rights are to be included, it will be significant whether these are limited merely to the 'core' labour rights under the International Labour Organisation Declaration on Fundamental Principles and Rights at Work 1998 (as is the case in, for example, the EU Generalised Scheme of Preferences (GSP) and now UK GSP, both of which offer incentives for compliance with the fundamental ILO Conventions which map onto these rights),[52] or whether they extend to a wider set of claims

[48] For further elaboration, see L Hayes and T Novitz, 'Workers without Footprints: The Legal Fiction of Migrant Workers as Posted Workers' in B Ryan (ed) *Labour Migration in Hard Times: Reforming Labour Market Regulation?* (Liverpool, Institute of Employment Rights, 2013) 99–118.

[49] In election manifestos in 2010 and 2015 the Conservative Party (currently in government) indicated a determination to 'scrap' the Human Rights Act and to replace this legislation with a British Bill of Rights which would seemingly become much more limited in its scope and effects: see S Greer and R Slowe, 'The Conservatives' Proposals for a British Bill of Rights: Mired in Muddle Misconception and Misrepresentation?' (2015) 4 *European Human Rights Law Review* 372.

[50] See for further elaboration, Ryan and Mantouvalou (n 47). It should however be noted that the UK has not ratified the more extensive European Social Charter or the Collective Complaints Protocol, which would enable complaints to be made to the European Committee of Social Rights, see for relevant background information www.coe.int/en/web/turin-european-social-charter [last accessed 16 March 2022]. The UK's commitment to instantiation of social rights is less evident than in relation to civil and political rights.

[51] See H Arendt, *The Origins of Totalitarianism* (New York, Harcourt Brace, 1951), 297–302.

[52] See ILO Declaration on Fundamental Principles and Rights at Work 1998 amended by ILC.110/Resolution 1, 10 June 2022 to include a safe and healthy working environment. See also Annex 8 to EU Regulation 978/2012 applying a scheme of generalised tariff preferences [2012] OJ L303/1;

including socio-economic entitlements set out in the European Social Charter (as seems to be envisaged in the TCA).[53] An even broader set of labour objectives promoting employment, social protection and social dialogue were added in the 2008 ILO Declaration on Social Justice for a Fair Globalization as part of a 'Decent Work Agenda' and may not qualify straightforwardly as human rights, although their relevance is clear from the social sustainability arguments discussed later in this chapter.[54]

In the UK-Australia and the UK-NZ FTAs, there are signs that the UK is willing to agree to a more extensive bundle of 'human rights' in relation to labour standards than had been contemplated previously. Chapter 21 of the UK-Australia FTA and Chapter 23 of the UK-NZ FTA recognise not only the 'labour rights' set out in the 1998 ILO Declaration but also affirm obligations 'with respect to minimum wages, hours of work, and occupational safety and health'.[55] This is an interesting development reflecting the terms of the 'Universal Labour Guarantee' endorsed by the ILO Global Commission on the Future of Work and the 2019 ILO Centenary Declaration.[56] It indicates that this ILO prompt to expand the sphere of core labour standards to encompass further socio-economic entitlements has been effective in the context of trade. Moreover, both instruments explicitly impose obligations regarding 'modern slavery' and non-discrimination and 'gender equality'.[57] The UK-NZ FTA goes even further to more broadly recognise 'the importance of decent work' and obligations to promote the ILO Decent Work Agenda.[58] The difficulty is that there is no express connection made in either FTA between the obligations set out in the chapter addressing labour rights and the chapter relating to what is termed 'temporary entry of business persons', which would include the types of movement contemplated under GATS Mode 4.[59]

Given that the UK is now willing to consider a broader span of labour standards as encompassed in a 'labour rights' rationale, there may be scope to design more extensive protection of temporary migrant workers in the context of trade in services. Indeed, being aware of their vulnerability, there might need

and the UK Generalised Scheme of Preferences as of 1 January 2021 available at: www.gov.uk/government/publications/trading-with-developing-nations [last accessed 16 March 2022].

[53] See the obligations regarding enforcement arising under Art 388 of the TCA (n 35), discussed by Ewing (n 36).

[54] ILO Declaration on Social Justice for a Fair Globalization 2008, Article IA. Available at: www.ilo.org/wcmsp5/groups/public/---dgreports/---cabinet/documents/genericdocument/wcms_371208.pdf [last accessed 16 March 2022].

[55] UK-Australia FTA, Art 21.4; UK-NZ FTA, Art 23.5.

[56] T Novitz, 'Past and Future Work at the International Labour Organization: Labour as a Fictitious Commodity, Countermovement and Sustainability' (2020) 17(1) *International Organizations Law Review* 10, 33–35.

[57] UK-Australia FTA, Arts 21.7 and 21.8; UK-NZ FTA, Arts 23.8 and 23.9.

[58] UK-NZ FTA, Art 23.7.

[59] UK-Australia FTA, ch 11; and UK-NZ FTA, ch 13 and Annex 13A.

to be additional protection for such workers and access to enforcement of their rights.[60] Within the UK, this could be achieved in the form of labour inspection, which could be operationalised through existing mechanisms such as the Anti-Slavery Commission[61] and the Gangmasters and Labour Abuse Authority,[62] while enhancing the powers and resources of the Health and Safety Executive inspectors.[63] Ensuring access to justice through employment tribunals and the ordinary courts will also be crucial.[64] The proposed introduction by the UK of a Single Enforcement Body could also chime with such commitments, although this seems to be delayed.[65]

An additional issue is the scope and weight of human rights protection when balanced against other legal entitlements. Historically, under EU law, human rights-based protections of posted workers were not given priority. Instead, a more market-based rationale gained precedence. Human rights claims of workers were mentioned in *Laval*, insofar as the Court of Justice recognised a right to strike.[66] The Court appreciated that 'the right to take collective action for the protection of the workers of the host State against possible social dumping may constitute an overriding reason of public interest', limiting the application of freedom to provide services under Article 56 TFEU.[67] However, social dumping was not considered to be at issue in the *Laval* case. Accordingly, the right to strike under Article 28 of the EU Charter of Fundamental Rights did not fall to be weighed against the employer's exercise of the entitlement to free movement of services. Instead, the Court considered it unacceptable that union collective action rendered 'it impossible or excessively difficult in practice' for a service provider 'to determine the obligations with which it is required to comply as regards minimum pay'.[68] The 2018 amendments to the Posting of Workers Directive (such as Article 1a) would seem to have addressed this issue.

[60] See rather different obligations arising regarding enforcement under the TCA (n 35), Art 388; also UK-Australia FTA, Art 21.6 and UK-NZ FTA, Art 23.13.

[61] Under the Modern Slavery Act 2015, see www.antislaverycommissioner.co.uk/ [last accessed 16 March 2022].

[62] See www.gla.gov.uk/.

[63] See www.hse.gov.uk/.

[64] This is now more likely following the Supreme Court judgment in *R on the Application of UNISON v the Lord Chancellor* [2017] UKSC 51; discussed by A Bogg, 'The Common Law Constitution at Work: *R (on the application of UNISON) v Lord Chancellor*' (2018) 81 *Modern Law Review* 509; and M Ford, 'Employment Tribunal Fees and the Rule of Law: *R (Unison) v Lord Chancellor in the Supreme Court*' (2018) 47(1) *Industrial Law Journal* 1.

[65] UK Department for Business, Energy and Industrial Strategy, *Establishing a New Single Enforcement Body for Employment Rights: Government response* (June 2021) available at assets.publishing.service.gov.uk/government/uploads/system/uploads/attachment_data/file/991751/single-enforcement-body-consultation-govt-response.pdf [last accessed 16 March 2022].

[66] Case C-341/05 *Laval un Partneri v Svenska Byggnadsarbetareförbundet (Laval)* [2007] ECR I-11767, para 91.

[67] ibid, para 103.

[68] ibid, para 110. *Cf* Case C-438/05 *International Transport Workers' Federation (ITF) and Finnish Seamen's Union (FSU) v Viking Line* [2007] ECR I-10779, para 77.

The question is whether comparable concerns could arise in the context of FTAs concluded by the UK.

A difficulty with FTAs is the formal distinction commonly found between the different chapters contained therein, which as is evident in the UK-Australia and UK-NZ texts can relate to apparently discrete matters such as 'investment', Mode 4 services (that is, movement of natural persons) and labour rights, without explaining the connections between them.[69] The UK might have to innovate in this respect, so as to ensure that human rights protections (including labour rights) are consistently embedded in key provisions and effective mechanisms for their implementation, as contemplated by the Joint Parliamentary Committee on Human Rights.[70] There are new signs of synergies being acknowledged in the text of the recently concluded FTAs with Australia and NZ; for example, the former does contemplate potential use of the general dispute settlement mechanism for enforcement of the labour chapter,[71] but a more extensive Interpretive Joint Statement (of the kind appended later to CETA)[72] would helpfully elaborate on the connections.

III. A FAIR COMPETITION OR SOCIAL DUMPING RATIONALE

A second basis for regulation of temporary movement of natural persons is that the potential to exploit and underpay those engaged in such work can create 'unfair competition' between resident and temporary migrant workers, as well as between home and other external service providers. This may seem illogical, given that these workers are assumed not to gain or to seek access to the employment market of the host state.[73] Nevertheless, as noted above, empirical evidence suggests that this form of migration can have palpable effects on the domestic job market. In some cases in the EU, the standard rate of pay for a job may be undercut by 50 per cent, thereby affecting thereby the usual terms of employment.[74] One option is to set the terms of fair competition by requiring

[69] B Sjafjell et al, 'Securing the Future of European Business: SMART Reform Proposals' (2020) University of Oslo Faculty of Law Research Paper No. 2020-11 available at: papers.ssrn.com/sol3/papers.cfm?abstract_id=3595048 [last checked 16 March 2022], 48–49.

[70] See UK Parliamentary Joint Committee on Human Rights, *Human Rights and Business 2017*.

[71] UK-Australia FTA, Art 21.16, although the labour consultations set out in Ch 21 (Labour) have to be exhausted prior to recourse to dispute settlement under Ch 30 (Dispute Settlement).

[72] See Joint Interpretative Instrument on the Comprehensive Economic and Trade Agreement (CETA) between Canada and the European Union and its Member States [2017] OJ L11/3 available at: eur-lex.europa.eu/legal-content/EN/TXT/?uri=CELEX%3A22017X0114%2801%29 [last accessed 16 March 2022] which addressed the use of 'letter box companies' which can feature in EU posting; regarding which see T Novitz and R Andrijasevic, 'Reform of the Posting of Workers Regime – An Assessment of the Practical Impact on Unfree Labour Relations' (2020) 58(5) *Journal of Common Market Studies* 1325, 1331.

[73] A principle restated in the UK-Australia FTA, Art 11.2.2; and UK-NZ FTA, Art 13.3.2.

[74] See European Commission Impact Assessment, 13 and 36.

compliance with certain basic labour standards, as illustrated by Article 3 of the Posting of Workers Directive. There is also potential for recourse to the general notion of 'social dumping', as recognised in the *Laval* case, although the content of this term and its application are more contested.[75] It will be demonstrated that, to date, the fair competition rationale has had little effect on the actual implementation of FTAs and should possibly be viewed with caution. It is more common for the terms of entry in schedule commitments under GATS Mode 4 and FTAs to be limited to more 'highly skilled workers' defined in terms of, for example, a tertiary level degree and work experience;[76] although the difficulties of circumscribing immigration in such terms has been widely acknowledged.[77]

The difficulty of discerning what preventing 'social dumping', and fair competition, should entail has been highlighted in a study by Magdalena Bernaciak.[78] While social dumping is often understood merely in terms of the effects of trade in goods made in other states where labour standards are lower, it can be understood more generally as corporate exploitation of differential labour standards for profit.[79] For example, social dumping may arise, in the context of posted work or Mode 4 services, where the temporary worker can be paid considerably less than – or is treated very differently in terms of working time to – a worker usually resident in the host state performing the same job.

As Bernaciak observes, 'an inflow of migrant workers from low-wage countries does not automatically imply social dumping …'.[80] She notes that migrants may be deployed through agency work, to perform work needed by employers where there is a temporary boom in demand for goods and services. In that case, the migrant and the economy of the host state benefit. Social dumping arises 'when foreign or local companies employ their workers at conditions inferior to those laid down in the host country's employment regulations or collective agreements'. This may be because the employment laws of the posted workers or Mode 4 worker's home state are considered to be applicable, or because such workers are not in law or practice covered by local collective agreements. In that scenario, Bernaciak observes that 'firms, and in the short-term their workers' profit, while those adhering to the existing

[75] *Laval* (n 66), paras 103–10.

[76] See, eg, UK-NZ FTA, Annex 13.

[77] See A Boucher, 'Measuring Migrant Worker Rights Violations in Practice: The example of Temporary Skilled Visas in Australia' (2019) 61(2) *Journal of Industrial Relations* 277; and E Kofman, 'Towards a Gendered Evaluation of (Highly) Skilled Immigration Policies in Europe' (2014) 52(3) *International Migration* 116.

[78] M Bernaciak, *Social Dumping? Political Catchphrase or Threat to Labour Standards* (Brussels, ETUI, 2012) WP 2012/06.

[79] E Bengtsson, 'Social Dumping Cases in the Swedish Labour Court in the Wake of Laval, 2004–2010' (2016) 37(1) *Economic and Industrial Democracy* 23, 24. See also D Vaughan-Whitehead, *EU Enlargement versus Social Europe? The Uncertain Future of the European Social Model* (Cheltenham, Edward Elgar, 2003) 325.

[80] Bernaciak (n 78) 26.

conditions lose out. Moreover, '[i]n the long run … dumping practices do not only lead to the erosion of employment protection systems in the host states, but might also hinder the gradual improvement of wages and working conditions in the poorer sending countries'.[81] Dumping can then be identified by its corrosive effects on the effective regulation of terms and conditions of work – whether through law or collective bargaining – within both the home and host states.

Bernaciak seems to assume that what amounts to unacceptably low labour standards, and thereby social dumping, will depend on the application of legislative norms already established in the host state, and the terms of relevant collective agreements. This offers a national-based touchstone for the UK to consider. Alternatively, we could view social dumping in terms of what is considered unacceptable in human rights terms. For example, reference could be made to internationally agreed standards concerning prohibitions on child labour or forced labour, and requiring fair terms and conditions of employment (under the ILO Decent Work Agenda and the European Social Charter). Any violation of basic freedom of association principles, such as the right to engage in collective bargaining or industrial action, would also constitute social dumping and unfair competition. In this way, a fair competition and human rights rationale for regulation could be combined.

The question then is whether the UK could seek to utilise FTAs to establish the terms of fair competition, for example with reference to freedom of association. If the UK is to do so, the government may wish to learn some obvious lessons from the outcome of the dispute between the US and Guatemala regarding the Central American Free Trade Agreement (known as CAFTA).[82] CAFTA contains a standard provision that the parties undertake to comply with their own labour laws, but this is only enforceable to the extent that any non-compliance takes place 'in a manner affecting trade'.[83] The dispute centred not on Mode 4 trade in services, or the position of migrant workers, but rather Guatemala's treatment of freedom of association which had involved a series of human rights violations, ranging from prohibitions on trade union organisations to detention and killing of trade unionists. This was alleged to be a violation of labour conditions which had occurred in a manner affecting trade; Guatemala maintained that trade had not been affected.

The panel acknowledged that the very purpose of CAFTA was 'to promote conditions of fair competition in the free trade area'.[84] The US then argued

[81] ibid.

[82] See *In the Matter of Guatemala: Issues Relating to the Obligations Under Article 16.2.1(a) of the CAFTA-DR: Final Report of the Panel* (14 June 2017). On the history of the case, see ILO, *Labour Provisions in Trade Agreements* (ILO, Geneva, 2016) 45–47.

[83] For use of this phrase in other US trade agreements, see Art 17.2(2) of the US-Colombia Trade Agreement, and Art 19.4 of the unratified Trans-Pacific Partnership Agreement (2016).

[84] *Guatemala* Final Report (n 82) para 120.

that the term 'affecting trade' should be given a broad scope 'so as to include measures that might adversely affect conditions of competition between domestic and imported products on the internal market'. Guatemala argued however that the US needed to actually demonstrate 'a change in prices of or trade flows in particular goods or services'.[85] While rejecting such a specific requirement, the panel nevertheless found that the US had 'not met its burden to prove that one or more exporter or exporters obtained a competitive advantage from failures to effectively enforce labor laws against the shipping companies, and thus that the failures were in a manner affecting trade'.[86] Indeed, '[a] complainant must demonstrate that labor cost effects reasonably expected in light of the record evidence are sufficient to confer some competitive advantage'.[87] In particular, the panel were not convinced that 'a failure to effectively enforce labor laws protecting the right to organize or the right to bargain collectively necessarily affects conditions of competition'.[88] This was not quantifiable. What the panel findings indicate is that it may be near impossible to demonstrate empirically in a simple concrete (and legalistic) fashion that non-compliance with labour law affected prices and thereby the terms of trade (and fair competition) between the states. For the UK, then, in renegotiating the terms of FTAs with the EU and third countries, much may depend in practice on the wording of provisions in the labour (and services) chapters to such FTAs and, as stressed above, their potential enforceability.

In the EU-Korea FTA dispute, the EU based its complaint regarding breach of freedom of association on a provision which did not rely on any effect on trade.[89] The panel of experts responsible for assessing the merits of the complaint rejected any contention that an effect on trade was implicitly required, referring to the Vienna Convention on the Law of Treaties to guide their interpretation of the FTA.[90] Moreover, even if there was a requirement to find an effect on trade, the expert panel considered that this might be regarded as present, given the FTA's recognition of 'dynamic interactions between economic, social and environmental objectives as interdependent and mutually reinforcing components of sustainable development',[91] which was lacking in the Guatemala case.[92]

[85] ibid, para 165.
[86] ibid, para 455.
[87] ibid, para 488.
[88] ibid, para 485.
[89] See Art 13.4.3 in Ch 3 (Trade and Sustainable Development) of the Free Trade Agreement between the European Union and its Member States, of the one part, and the Republic of Korea of the other part (hereafter 'EU-Korea FTA') [2011] OJ L127/6, eur-lex.europa.eu/legal-content/EN/TXT/PDF/?uri=CELEX:22011A0514(01) [accessed 16 March 2022].
[90] Report of the Panel of Experts (2020) Proceeding constituted under Art 13.15 of the EU-Korea FTA, 25 January 2021, Panel: Dr J Murray (Chairperson), Professor L Boisson de Chazournes and Professor J Lee; available at: trade.ec.europa.eu/doclib/docs/2021/january/tradoc_159358.pdf [accessed 16 March 2022].
[91] ibid, para 74.
[92] ibid, paras 93–94.

We will return to this issue in the context of sustainable development as a regulatory objective later in this chapter. In the meantime, it is sufficient to note that the UK does not seem to be interested in connecting sustainable development and labour standards in the same way as the EU has done, such that this principle cannot be applied straightforwardly to the UK-Australia or UK-NZ FTAs. However, these FTAs do, like the EU-Korea FTA, seem to contemplate certain overarching obligations to respect core labour standards, such as freedom of association, without linking these explicitly to trade effects.[93]

IV. EQUAL TREATMENT

An equal treatment rationale would be simpler than an assessment of the human rights of those workers temporarily moved for the purpose of trade in services, or of the impact of violation of labour standards on fair competition. This is the dominant norm regarding treatment of migrant workers under international human rights law. As Judy Fudge has observed, ILO Convention No 97 makes provision for equality in terms of access to legal protections,[94] whereas, Convention No 143 is concerned with guarantees of equal treatment by employers.[95] So, Article 12(g) of Convention No 143 states that each party will 'guarantee equality of treatment, with regard to working conditions, for all migrant workers who perform the same activity whatever might be the particular conditions of their employment'. The UK has ratified Convention No 97 but not Convention No 143.

The potential difficulty, however, as Fudge observes, lies in the exceptions made in these ILO instruments regarding temporary migrants. Article 11 of Convention No 97 excludes members of the liberal professions and artists who are given permission to enter for an undefined short period. Article 11 of Convention No 143 contains the more far-reaching exclusion of

> employees of organisations or undertakings operating within the territory of a country who have been admitted temporarily to that country at the request of their employer to undertake specific duties or assignments, for a limited and defined period of time, and who are required to leave that country on the completion of their duties or assignments.

[93] See UK-Australia FTA, Art 21.4 (*cf* Art 21.6 which does address failure to effectively enforce labour laws 'through a sustained or recurring course of action or inaction in a manner affecting trade or investment') and UK-NZ FTA, Art 23.5 (*cf* Art 23.6.4 which provides that: 'Neither Party shall, through a sustained or recurring course of action or inaction, fail to effectively enforce its labour laws to encourage trade or investment' such that effect on trade or investment will be irrelevant, and it will be the use of non-enforcement as a means of encouragement of trade and investment that matters).

[94] Article 6(1)(a) of ILO Convention No 97 guarantees equality 'in so far as such matters are regulated by law or regulations, or are subject to the control of administrative authorities'.

[95] J Fudge, 'Precarious Migrant Status and Precarious Employment: The Paradox of International Rights for Migrant Workers' (2012–13) 34 *Comparative Labor Law and Policy Journal* 95.

This statement seems to exclude temporary migrant work from the more general equality principle which is usually to be applied.

A comparison may be made with the UN International Convention on the Protection of the Rights of all Migrant Workers and their Families 1990 (ICRMW), which extends a series of guarantees to all migrant workers, whether documented or undocumented. Under Article 18, all migrant workers are entitled to equal access to justice. Under Article 25(1), migrant workers benefit from a general guarantee of equality of treatment by employers as regards remuneration and other terms and conditions. It is made clear in Article 25(2) that these entitlements cannot be contracted out of and in Article 25(3) that they are not affected by irregular status. It would therefore be most peculiar were they not to apply also to temporary migrant workers. There are however certain entitlements to equality set out in Part IV, which only apply to documented (that is, not irregular) workers, such as equality of access to such aspects of community life as education, vocational services, housing and health care, as well as equal protection against dismissal (Article 54) and equality of treatment in the exercise of authorised remunerated activity (Article 55). Limited rights to join, participate in the activities of trade unions and seek trade union assistance apply under Article 26 to all migrant workers, regardless of whether their status is regular; a more wide-ranging entitlement to form a trade union is provided in Article 40 for regular migrants under Part IV.[96]

There remains scope for exceptions regarding claims by temporary migrants who come within the definition of a 'seasonal' or 'project-tied' worker. Article 2(2)(b) defines a 'seasonal worker' as 'a migrant worker whose work by its character is dependent on seasonal conditions and is performed only during part of the year'. Such a worker is only entitled to those rights in Part IV 'that can be applied to them by reason of their presence and work in the territory of the State of employment and that are compatible with their status in that State as seasonal workers'. It is unclear whether they are entitled to claim the right to form a trade union if it will only be operative for a short part of the year; a government might argue that to do so is inconvenient and incompatible with their short stay in the country; whereas the better response is that such an entitlement should arise given its widespread recognition as a human right under Article 22 of the International Covenant on Civil and Political Rights 1966. But, if the latter is such a powerful argument, why is the right to form trade unions omitted from application to all migrant workers under Article 26? To the extent that temporary seasonal work features in trade in services, the principle of equality for such workers is arguably undermined. Art 2(2)(f) provides that 'the term "project-tied worker" refers to a migrant worker admitted to a

[96] *Cf* B Ryan, 'In Defence of the Migrant Workers Convention: Standard-setting for Contemporary Migration' in SS Juss (ed), *The Ashgate Research Companion to Migration Law, Theory and Policy* (London and New York, Routledge, 2013) 499.

State of employment for a defined period to work solely on a specific project being carried out in that State by his or her employer'. Under Article 61, 'project tied' workers retain access to justice under Article 18, but many of the equal treatment rights in Part IV will not apply to them, including expressly Articles 54 and 55, so the ICRMW provides only limited protection of the equal treatment principle and, even then, has yet to be ratified by the UK.

There would seem to be potential overlap between a 'project-tied' worker and the temporary movement of natural persons under Mode 4 of GATS.[97] It is, however, worth bearing in mind that the ICRMW was concluded before the adoption of GATS at the international level (or even the Posting of Workers Directive at the European level). The drafters of that international human rights instrument cannot be expected to have contemplated the concrete problems experienced by those engaged in temporary migration in the context of trade in services. Given the evidence of exploitation which has since come to light, the desirability of any apparent departure from equality principles should be regarded as questionable. Rather, it is arguable that the basic principle of equal treatment that underlies the ILO Conventions and the ICRMW should prevail.[98]

One difficulty with a straightforward equal treatment approach is the longstanding political opposition to its adoption. Wage equality is particularly controversial. The problem has its roots in the differences between the standard pay available for certain sorts of work in different countries.[99] Imposition of the same local rate of pay on an incoming service provider might mean that posted workers lose their chance of competing for jobs which would make a substantial difference to their income,[100] and could deprive that service provider of what is perceived to be their 'comparative advantage'.[101] This is the concern raised by Bernaciak in an EU context regarding the scope of social dumping.[102] Given that many states now rely heavily on remittances from migrants temporarily resident elsewhere, there are also costs for these

[97] S Engblom, N Kountouris and A Odin Ekman, 'Temporary Labour Migration and the Trade in Services: European and Global Perspectives in an Age of Economic Integration' in Howe and Owens (n 1) 74–75.

[98] Although it should be noted that the application by the EU of equal treatment is also notoriously inconsistent in the context of migrant work. See B Ryan, 'The European Union and Labour Migration: Regulating Admission or Treatment' in A Baldiccini et al (eds), *Whose Freedom, Security and Justice?* (Oxford, Hart, 2007) 510.

[99] For discussion of this issue in the context of EU trade in services at the time of the *Laval* litigation, see G Majone 'Legitimacy and Effectiveness: A Response to Professor Michael Dougan's Review Article on Dilemmas of European Integration (2007) 32 *European Law Review* 70, 74.

[100] For example, Gordon (n 17) 461 observes that Bulgarian workers migrating to the Netherlands can earn roughly six times what they would at home, while for those moving from Vietnam to Korea temporarily it is at least eleven to one.

[101] See the WTO Singapore Declaration 1996, which says that: 'We reject the use of labour standards for protectionist purposes, and agree that the comparative advantage of countries, particularly low-wage developing countries, must in no way be put into question.'

[102] See also Bernaciak (n 78) 26.

countries.[103] For that reason, certain academic commentators endorsed the *Laval* judgment, precisely because it prevented national unions using industrial action to impose going wage rates on a building contractor employing posted workers.[104] Concern with preservation of comparative advantage would also seem to have obstructed the EU from regulation of pay under the 'Social Policy' title in the TFEU previously,[105] and has blocked the ILO from actively enhancing wage rates in the context of trade.[106] Express reference to 'protectionist' trade purposes and 'comparative advantage' is made in the 'Labour' chapters of both the UK-Australia and UK-NZ FTAs.[107] Arguably, host states also aid and abet the lack of regulation of migrant wages, because unequal wages can enable cheaper procurement of certain services and even forms of foreign direct investment, as the export processing zones (EPZs) demonstrate.[108]

It may, however, be possible to overcome this objection with recourse to a human rights approach. It has been observed that a feature of the minimal 'core labour standards' in the 1998 ILO Declaration is that they do not tend to impose simple quantifiable costs on employers or developing states, but instead offer significant procedural entitlements.[109] By the same token, an equal treatment approach can dovetail with a procedural human rights approach in terms of access to law, for example, under Article 18 of the ICRMW. This is, however, potentially too sparse a construction of the human rights approach, as explained above, since the experiences of temporary migrant workers indicate that their physical and material well-being can be placed in jeopardy.

What can be granted as a matter of equal treatment to migrant workers is access to at least the minimum statutory standards regarding wages, hours and holidays, of which a service provider can be informed prior to making the

[103] Again, Gordon (n 17) 475 notes the World Bank report that 'worldwide migrant remittance flows to developing countries reached an all-time high of $441 billion in 2015' making up, eg, 18% of GDP in El Salvador and 29.8% in Nepal.

[104] See, eg, R Blanpain in the special issue, 'The Laval and Viking Cases: Freedom of Services and Establishment v Industrial Conflict in the European Economic Area and Russia', *Bulletin of Comparative Labour Relations* (2009) who (at xxii) considered that '[t]he European Court took the right decision' in *Laval*.

[105] TFEU, Art 153(5). Cf adoption of the EU Adequate Minimum Wage Directive in 2022.

[106] For a powerful challenge to ILO reticence in this regard see A Chan, 'Racing to the Bottom: International Trade without a Social Clause (2003) 24(6) *Third World Quarterly* 1011, 1024. ILO Convention No 131 on Minimum Wage Fixing Convention 1970 has only had 54 ratifications and makes no reference to migrant labour or trade.

[107] UK-Australia FTA, Art 21.3; and UK-NZ FTA, Art 23.3.2 and 23.6.1.

[108] See for a useful overview, K Jayanthakumaran, 'Benefit–Cost Appraisals of Export Processing Zones: A survey of the literature' (2003) 21(1) *Development Policy Review* 51, and more specific discussion of the regulatory role of the state in R Andrijasevic and T Novitz, 'Supply Chains and Unfree Labour: Regulatory failure in the case of Samsung Electronics in Slovakia' (2020) 6 *Journal of Human Trafficking* 195.

[109] C McCrudden and A Davies, 'A Perspective on Trade and Labour Rights' (2000) *Journal of International Economic Law* 43, 51.

decision to set up business in the country. In this way the predictability stressed by the CJEU in *Laval*[110] can be achieved. Going beyond this however, equal access to the going rate of pay for a job for temporarily migrant (or posted) workers could be achieved through the 'process' right to freedom of association and effective recognition of the right to collective bargaining (with reference to Article 2 of the 1998 ILO Declaration) to the extent that they wish to engage in this type of bargaining.[111] Recent studies by Bernaciak and Zahn indicate some interest from unions in cooperation across new and old EU Member States regarding collective bargaining for posted work.[112] This bare minimum entitlement to a 'core' labour standards sets up the potential for material equality through coverage by a collective agreement, with access to industrial action to improve pay terms and conditions (under Articles 7 and 8 of the ICESCR and Articles 2, 5 and 6 of the European Social Charter). In this context, the UK need not be bound by the niceties of a requirement that the collective agreement in question be of statutory effect, universal or general application, especially given the current lack of such mechanisms in UK legislation.[113]

The difficulty is that there is, as yet, no sign in FTAs of explicit recognition of a right to freedom of association and collective bargaining coverage for natural persons temporarily resident in another country. In part, this comes from the artificial divide between labour and services chapters in such instruments, discussed above. The UK has the opportunity to be innovative and forward thinking on this, and it may be that its policy-based approach will continue to evolve as is evident in the UK-Australia and UK-NZ FTAs. Notably, both the UK-Australia FTA and the UK-NZ FTA make commitments regarding 'Non-Discrimination and Gender Equality in the Workplace'.[114] The UK-Australia FTA goes further by creating the scope to 'cooperate' 'on the promotion and protection of equality and elimination of discrimination in respect of employment and occupation for migrant workers'.[115]

V. SUSTAINABILITY

A final potential justification for regulation of temporary labour migration linked to service provision is the idea of 'sustainability'. This broad idea has

[110] See *Laval* (n 66) para 110.

[111] For recognition of the significance of collective bargaining in establishing fair wages, see Commission Proposal for a Directive of the European Parliament and of the Council on adequate minimum wages in the European Union COM(2020) 682 final, 28 October 2020.

[112] M Bernaciak, 'Polish Trade Unions and Social Dumping Debates: Between a Rock and a Hard Place' (2016) 22(4) *Transfer* 505, 512–13; R Zahn, *New Labour Laws in Old Member States: Trade Union Responses to European Enlargement*. (Cambridge, Cambridge University Press, 2017) chs 5 and 11.

[113] See discussion in T Novitz, 'Collective Bargaining, Equality and Migration: The Journey to and from Brexit' (2017) 46(1) *Industrial Law Journal* 109, 126.

[114] UK-Australia FTA, Art 21.8 and UK-NZ FTA, Art 23.8.

[115] UK-Australia FTA, Art 21.12.6.

been garnering international recognition and has particular pertinence for labour standards.

The notion of environmental sustainability emerged from the Stockholm Conference on the Human Environment in 1972, and the consequent 'Stockholm Declaration of Principles'. Some 15 years later, the Brundtland Report indicated that 'sustainable development' arose where a policy 'meets the needs of the present without compromising the ability of future generations to meet their own needs', in other words recognising inter-generational sustainability.[116] In addition to inter-generational sustainability, we can understand intra-generational sustainability as the need to make just distributions within present generations, for example of the costs of environmental protections. The issue of time, endurance and longevity is significant, and is now seen not just to protect environmental standards, but to have 'economic' and 'social' dimensions too. The 'social pillar' of sustainability was more powerfully acknowledged in the 1986 UN Declaration on Right to Development, Article 1 of which stresses the idea of 'economic, social, cultural and political development' as 'an inalienable' human right.

Sustainable development gives an additional reason for promotion of equal treatment, as being, in the long term, desirable for the promotion of social harmony and well-being in any country. For all to have access to minimum statutory labour standards limits opportunities for exploitation, such as the 'social dumping' Bernaciak identifies; moreover, access to human rights such as freedom of association, including collective bargaining and the right to strike, can ensure all workers meaningful voice and scope to improve terms and conditions.[117] In this way, labour standards, as a key facet of a sustainability 'social pillar' can reduce intra-generational social and economic tensions, while the prevention of poverty (especially for the children of those working, whether migrants or otherwise) promotes intergenerational well-being. Doing so avoids the kinds of protests and animosity fuelled by Posting of Workers Directive rules in the UK, for example in the East Lindsey dispute.[118] Indeed, the idea of sustainability can also enable a less minimal interpretation of 'human rights' as a rationale for regulation and assist in explaining how breach of labour standards can have an impact on trade.[119]

There are indications that sustainable development may play various 'interpretive functions' in legal proceedings, leading to consideration of balancing. Thus far, this has been recognised in the context of international environmental law proceedings, but could have implications for investment arbitration

[116] World Commission on Environment and Development (WECD) Our Common Future, The Brundtland Report (1987), 51.
[117] Bernaciak (n 78).
[118] Barnard (n 31).
[119] EU-Korea FTA expert panel report (n 90) paras 93–94.

disputes regarding labour standards too.[120] There is also scope to use sustainability as a foundation for policy-making. For example, the EU has done so in recent years by appending a 'trade and sustainable development' chapter to key trade agreements (such as CETA discussed above, at Chapter 22 which is linked to Chapter 23 on 'trade and labour'). The benefits of this EU approach are contested, however; others view a human rights based approach as preferable.[121] My view is less negative,[122] but there is certainly scope for the UK to improve on past EU practice. For example, one step would be to remedy the uncertainty surrounding the application of the provisions in a sustainable development FTA chapter to other chapters concerning such matters as investment or temporary presence of natural persons. Moreover, in this policy context, given past contestation over the meaning of sustainability and its application to workers,[123] the UK could look to the UN approved Sustainable Development Goals (SDGs) for guidance.

The SDGs indicate an awareness of the need to protect migrant workers (under SDGs 8 and 10) and to change the architecture of international trade (for example under SDG 17), but they do not provide straightforward specific policy prescriptions which might be of assistance for the UK when considering regulation of temporary migrant workers in a trade in services context.[124] Rather, it is necessary to extrapolate, from the main body of the UNGA Resolution on the 2030 Agenda and the specific SDGs, principles which could guide UK responses. For example, the 2030 Agenda does 'recognize the positive contribution of migrants for inclusive growth and sustainable development' and that 'international migration is a multidimensional reality of major relevance for the development of countries of origin, transit and destination, which requires coherent and comprehensive responses'.[125] In this way, the potential economic benefits of trade in services involving migrant work, identified by Bernaciak, are also recognised.[126] Nevertheless, the acceptance of migrant workers as a facet of

[120] V Barral, 'Sustainable Development in International Law: Nature and Operation of an Evolutive Legal Norm' (2012) 23(2) *European Journal of International Law* 377.

[121] L Van den Putte and J Orbie 'EU Bilateral Trade Agreements and the Surprising Rise of Labour Provisions' (2015) 31(3) *International Journal of Comparative Labour Law and Industrial Relations* 263; and L Bartels, *Human Rights and Sustainable Development Obligations in EU Free Trade Agreements* in Legal Studies Research paper Series, University of Cambridge Faculty of Law, Paper No 24/2012, www.academia.edu/1902855/Human_rights_and_sustainable_development_obligations_in_EU_free_trade_agreements [last accessed 16 March 2022].

[122] Novitz (n 46).

[123] T Novitz, 'The Paradigm of Sustainability in a European Social Context: Collective Participation in Protection of Future Interests?' (2015) 31(3) *International Journal of Comparative Labour Law and Industrial Relations* 243.

[124] Resolution adopted by the UN General Assembly (UNGA) on 25 September 2015 – Transforming our world: the 2030 Agenda for Sustainable Development A/Res/70/1 available at sustainabledevelopment.un.org/post2015/transformingourworld/publication [last accessed 16 March 2022] (the 2030 Resolution).

[125] ibid, para 29.

[126] Bernaciak (n 78) 26.

trade requires a regulatory response from the UK, preferably one coordinated with the EU and other third country actors. This international cooperation is termed 'global partnership' under SDG 17 and involves under target 17.14 'policy coherence for sustainable development'. This can be achieved with reference to minimal WTO (GATS) rules (as is acknowledged under SDG target 17.10), but there is also scope to improve on these through FTAs. The 2030 Agenda also makes a commitment to 'cooperate internationally to ensure safe, orderly and regular migration involving full respect for human rights and the humane treatment of migrants regardless of migration status'.[127] This indicates the ongoing significance of human rights as a regulatory rationale. The text does not require 'equal treatment', perhaps taking account of the limited ratification of the ICRMW with its extensive provisions to this effect,[128] but rather 'humane treatment'. However, the 2030 Agenda does not distinguish between 'project-tied workers' or 'posted workers' or temporary migrants and others. All migrant workers seem to come within its embrace.

SDG 8 is aimed at promoting 'sustained, inclusive and sustainable economic growth, full and productive employment and decent work for all'. The reference to 'decent work' is aligned with the 'Decent Work Agenda' promoted by the ILO, and encompasses not only fundamental principles and rights at work (as narrowly defined in the 1998 ILO Declaration), but also broader objectives promoting employment, social protection and social dialogue (set out in the 2008 Declaration). This suggests that, while a human rights approach could be helpful, we may need to also consider the significance of other concrete labour standards which make a difference to workers, migrant or otherwise. This leads us back to an inclusive human rights approach which would entail reference to the ICESCR and the full gamut of labour rights in the European Social Charter.

SDG 8.8 also sets out the aim to provide 'safe and secure working environments for all workers, including migrant workers, in particular women migrants, and those in precarious employment'. Temporary migrant workers will often fall in this precarious category, given what we know about industrial accidents in the construction industry in the context of posted work[129] and the vulnerability of female care workers.[130] Notably 8.8.1 adds a further 'indicator', namely 'an increase in national compliance of labour rights (freedom of association and collective bargaining) based on ILO textual sources and national legislation, by sex and migrant status'. This suggests that the UK can and should be promoting migrant worker engagement in collective bargaining, including

[127] The 2030 Agenda Resolution (n 124) para 29.

[128] Having only 52 state parties, for which see indicators.ohchr.org/ [last accessed 16 March 2022].

[129] N Rogelja and K Toplak (eds), *Occupational Safety and Health of Posted Workers: Conference Proceedings* (Lubljana, ZRC Publishing House, 2017).

[130] Stewart (n 21); and L Hayes, *A Labour of Care: Gender and Class at Work* (London, Palgrave, 2017).

temporary workers. Further, freedom of association is arguably implicit in the commitment in SDG 16.7 to: 'Ensure responsive, inclusive, participatory and representative decision-making at all levels.' A UN Special Rapporteur report has also said that 'freedom of association' must be understood as encompassed the broader protection of 'fundamental freedoms' in SDG target 16.10.[131]

Moreover, SDG 8.7 suggests that enforcement of labour standards should not only be a matter for migrant workers, but also the state, which should take 'immediate and effective measures to eradicate forced labour, end modern slavery and human trafficking and secure the prohibition and elimination of the worst forms of child labour'. This suggests an urgent need for the UK to improve its labour inspection practices, as observed above. Moreover, the significance of the capacity for temporary migrants to send remittances home (under SDG 10c) is duly recognised and would need to be actively protected by the UK.

Finally, SDG 17.10 seeks 'a universal, rules-based, open, non-discriminatory and equitable multilateral trading system under the World Trade Organization', which must be understood to relate both to trade and services, including Mode 4 provision. This entails, under SDG 17.17, the obligation to 'encourage and promote effective public, public-private and civil society partnerships, building on the experience and resourcing strategies of partnerships'. The UK then, even in the context of Brexit cannot regard itself as entirely free to redesign its own regulatory strategies in place of what was once 'posted work'. Instead, this will have to be crafted at the national and transnational level in dialogue with other international institutions (whether the WTO or EU), states and civil society actors. In this context the issues of fair competition (and equal treatment) between service providers in the context of trade, but also between migrant and other workers, will have to be addressed, with all the difficulties that this entails. Once again, the normative touchstone of human rights protection, already acknowledged as vital by the SDGs and the UN Resolution, may offer some assistance within this process. It is curious that, at least for the time being, the UK seems to have steered away from linking labour rights and protections for migrant workers to sustainable development. 'Sustainable development' is mentioned repeatedly in the 'Environment' chapters of the Australian and NZ FTAs,[132] but not in those chapters relating to 'Temporary Entry of Business Persons' or 'Labour'.

[131] Report of the Special Rapporteur on the rights to freedom of peaceful assembly and association, 7 August 2018, A/73/279, para 6. This is also the view taken by the trade union movement globally, regarding which see *A trade union take on the SDGs* (2019) available at: www.ituc-csi.org/IMG/pdf/tudcn_sdgs_global_report_2018_en.pdf [last accessed 16 March 2022].

[132] UK-Australia FTA, Ch 22 (Environment) and UK-NZ FTA, Ch 22 (Environment). The latter also makes express reference to the UNGA 2030 Agenda. See further UK-NZ FTA, Ch 27 (Trade and development) which makes commitments regarding 'sustainable economic growth' without reference to the 2030 Agenda or SDG 8.

VI. A CONCLUSION

This chapter has sought to examine various rationales for regulation of temporary migrant work connected to trade in services, understood previously as 'posted work' in an EU context. These have been addressed in the peculiar situation of the UK, which is no longer subject to the Posting of Workers Directive regime following Brexit, and which has important regulatory choices to make. Those choices are not unconstrained, since what has been understood in the UK to be 'posted work' is akin to 'temporary movement of natural persons supplying services', already potentially regulated under GATS Mode 4. Further, GATS provisions will determine the legitimacy of FTAs that the UK concludes, whether with the EU or third countries.

Nevertheless, this effort to engage with regulatory rationales may be helpful in the elaboration of possibilities for UK conduct in relation to temporary migrant workers sent to the UK by their employer, as part of intercorporate transfers or as agency workers. This analysis may also be of interest to EU scholars analysing the merits of the 2018 Amended Posting of Workers Directive.

The rationales that I have outlined in this chapter span human rights protections, fair competition, equal treatment and sustainability. In my view, the first of these remains the most significant as a guide for UK conduct. There is an argument for taking an expansive view of human rights protections, which includes not only civil and political rights recognised internationally, but also socio-economic rights of more direct relevance to workers. Further, from an ILO perspective, the rights set out in the 1998 Declaration on Fundamental Principles and Rights at Work, are at a bare minimum deserving of respect, strongly suggesting that the UK needs to step up protection (and inspection) regarding forced labour (which may be of particular relevance to temporary migrant workers). Additionally, freedom of association as a 'process right' may offer such workers greater agency and voice. There is a strong case now to extend the reach of labour standards to encompass the ILO 'Decent Work Agenda', as well as wages, hours and health and safety as contemplated by the ILO Centenary Declaration.

Issues of what constitutes 'fair competition' between service providers, and indeed between migrant workers and local host state workers, will also be relevant to the UK's policy choices. This chapter has investigated the model offered by the EU posting regime, amended in 2018. Broader reference to the idea of 'social dumping' could be helpful to the UK, and can be understood not only in relation to nationally determined terms and conditions (whether through legislation or collective agreement), but also with reference to broader international human rights including freedom of association. It would be helpful to recognise the significance of trade union representation and action as constitutive of fair competition, despite the approach taken in the *Guatemala* case.[133] Arguably, the statement of the expert panel in EU-Korea offers an alternative way forward, which links to a sustainable development approach.[134]

A policy based on 'equal treatment' has the advantage of simplicity as well as ethical merit, as reflected in the key provisions of ILO Conventions and the ICRMW. The exceptions in these instruments regarding temporary migrant workers and in particular (as detailed in the ICRMW) project-tied workers are partial and problematic. They predate the expansion of trade in services that we have witnessed within the EU and globally and the evidence found of vulnerability and exploitation of such workers. There remain some political obstructions to a full equal treatment approach, according to which each migrant worker could claim parity of treatment with every comparable home state worker. However, it is suggested here that a hybrid approach, enabling parity of treatment regarding legislative minimum entitlements and equal access to freedom of association (including collective bargaining and the right to strike) might offer a solution.

In a 'sustainability' context, we are reminded of the importance of intergenerational and intragenerational environmental, economic and social justice. A durable approach which prevents crisis in the labour market, but which also fosters social cohesion, will be vital for the UK in renegotiating the parameters of trade in services involving natural persons. The EU has long placed 'sustainable development chapters' in its FTAs, but this is a model that has yet to be perfected. In this context, the UK could use the 2015 SDGs as a reference point. These arguably reinforce the significance and utility of a human rights approach. They also require engagement with competition arguments and equal treatment issues, when engaging with other international institutions, states and civil society. In this sense, the regulatory rationales discussed here, while conceptually discrete, will all merit attention.

The first steps are now being taken by the UK towards devising a strategy and, as has been highlighted in this chapter, all of these regulatory rationales can be detected in the texts provisionally agreed. It will be interesting to see how UK policy now develops within the parameters of international trade law on services alongside the UN frameworks of human rights and sustainability.

[133] See *Guatemala* Final Report (n 82).

[134] See the EU-Korea FTA expert panel report (n 90).

14

Migration in Employment Law Scholarship in Britain: Going Beyond Methodological Nationalism

BERNARD RYAN

I. INTRODUCTION

THE SHARE OF the foreign-born among employed workers in the United Kingdom has grown substantially in recent decades. Whereas in 1997 the Labour Force Survey showed 1.9 million foreign-born workers, comprising 7.3 per cent of those employed, by 2021 those figures had increased to 6.1 million and 18.8 per cent.[1] Over the same period, the UK has had a flexible employment law regime, with limited reach of, and a lack of support for, collective bargaining, permissiveness toward precarious employment contracts, a lack of licensing for labour market intermediaries, and a fragmented approach to the enforcement of labour standards. That flexible approach to labour standards appears connected to the evidence of migrant workers facing poor conditions, especially in low-wage occupations.[2] It has probably also enabled higher levels of labour migration to become embedded in the economy.

Against that background, this chapter considers the treatment of migration-related questions within employment law scholarship in the UK. For this purpose, 'migration-related' questions include labour migration policy and the effects of migration or migration policy upon employment law. The 'scholarship' to be considered is literature on employment law in academic publications, including by legal practitioners.[3] As used here, the notion of labour migration

[1] Data from Office for National Statistics, *Employment by Country of Birth and Nationality* (dataset EMP06, released on 17 August 2021). Further detail concerning labour migration trends in the UK is provided in ch 1 of this volume.

[2] See for example Migration Advisory Committee, *Migrants in Low-skilled Work* (July 2014) 167–79.

[3] The publications of the Institute of Employment Rights are included, as its authors and audience are a mixture of trade unionists, legal practitioners and academics.

has no time horizon: it ranges from actual or potential short-term stay for employment purposes (often termed 'labour mobility'), through to migrant workers who remain in employment in another state for most or all of their working lives.

The chapter will start by outlining the concept of 'methodological nationalism', which has provided the basis for a generalised critique of academic scholarship which takes the state for granted (section II). In this chapter, the alternative is taken to be what is termed 'cosmopolitan realism', which involves recognition *both* of transnational influences upon political and social life, *and* of the continuing importance of states. Applying the related ideas of methodological nationalism and cosmopolitan realism, the chapter will explore the extent to which migration-related questions have been covered by employment law scholarship (section III). It will show that, while migration-related questions were only occasionally addressed in previous decades, since the late 2000s – and especially after the EU enlargements of 2004 and 2007 – it has become far more common to do so. The notions of methodological nationalism and cosmopolitan realism are then used to explore how migration, and related policy choices, are approached within employment law literature, in two broad areas: restrictions on access to employment (section IV), and the equal application of employment standards (section V). It will be argued that there remains a tension within employment law scholarship between methodologically nationalist tendencies, oriented to the agenda of the state, or the interests of resident workers, and cosmopolitan realist approaches, which recognise the presence of migrant workers and give due weight to their interests. It should be noted at the outset that the purpose of this chapter is exclusively methodological: it explores the extent to which, and the ways in which, writers on employment law approach migration-related questions. Observations to the effect that certain scholarship is consistent with forms of methodological nationalism are not intended to imply political nationalism on the part of the writers concerned.

II. METHODOLOGICAL NATIONALISM, EMPLOYMENT LAW AND MIGRATION

The concept of 'methodological nationalism' initially emerged in the 1970s and 1980s to critique the orientation within sociology to the study of social systems within nation-states.[4] In Wimmer and Glick Schiller's leading account, methodological nationalism is evident across the social sciences, and has three

[4] D Chernilo, 'Methodological Nationalism and the Domestic Analogy: Classical Resources for their Critique' (2011) 23 *Cambridge Review of International Affairs* 87, 88–89. Chernilo credits Herminio Martins with coining the phrase in 'Time and Theory in Sociology' in J Rex (ed), *Approaches to Sociology* (London, Routledge and Kegan Paul, 1974).

inter-related elements.[5] The first is 'ignoring or disregarding the fundamental importance of nationalism for modern societies'.[6] The second is what they term the 'naturalisation of the nation-state', which means that 'nationally bounded societies are taken to be the naturally given entities to study' and that, 'national discourses, agendas, loyalties and histories' are taken for granted.[7] The third, which they term the 'territorialization of social science imaginary', occurs when scholarship 'confines the study of social processes to the political and geographic boundaries of a particular nation-state'.[8] This is also known as the 'container' model of analysis: 'the web of social life was spun within the container of the national society, and everything extending over its borders was cut off analytically'.[9] The criticism of such an approach is that it leaves 'no room for transnational and global processes that connect … national territories'.[10]

The critique of methodological nationalism came to be deployed from the early 1990s as part of theorisation of the implications of neoliberal globalisation – ie, the growing internationalisation of economic activity, politics, culture and social life.[11] Literature on transnationalism called for methodological openness to 'transnational' social phenomena which involve 'sustained linkages and ongoing exchanges among non-state actors across national borders', including the social networks which enable migration.[12] Similar ideas featured within the cosmopolitan sociology developed by Ulrich Beck and others.[13] That approach started from the idea of a 'second age of modernity', in which the established arrangements of industrial society tend to dissolve.[14] In Beck's words

> A new kind of capitalism, a new kind of economy, a new kind of global order, a new kind of politics and law, a new kind of society and personal life are in the making which both separately and in context are clearly distinct from earlier phases.[15]

[5] A Wimmer and N Glick Schiller, 'Methodological Nationalism and Beyond: Nation-State Building, Migration and the Social Sciences' (2002) 2 *Global Networks* 301, and 'Methodological Nationalism, the Social Sciences and the Study of Migration: An Essay in Historical Epistemology' (2003) 37 *International Migration Review* 576. The summary here draws upon the interpretation of the three elements in A Sager, 'Methodological Nationalism, Migration and Political Theory' (2016) 64 *Global Networks* 42.

[6] Wimmer and Glick Schiller (2003) (n 5) 577–78.

[7] Wimmer and Glick Schiller (2002) (n 5) 304–07.

[8] Wimmer and Glick Schiller (2002) (n 5) 307; Wimmer and Glick Schiller (2003) (n 5) 578.

[9] Wimmer and Glick Schiller (2002) (n 5) 307.

[10] Wimmer and Glick Schiller (2003) (n 5) 578.

[11] Chernilo (n 4) 89–90.

[12] S Vertovec, *Transnationalism* (London, Routledge, 2009) 3 and 38–40.

[13] For Beck's usage of 'methodological nationalism', see U Beck, *What is Globalization?* (Oxford, Polity, 2000), and the discussion in D Chernilo, 'Social Theory's Methodological Nationalism' (2006) 9 *European Journal of Social Theory* 5.

[14] The links between the 'second age' theory and cosmopolitanism are explored in U Beck, 'The Cosmopolitan Perspective: Sociology of the Second Age of Modernity' (2000) 51 *British Journal of Sociology* 79. A fuller account of the 'second age' theory is in U Beck and C Lau 'Second Modernity as a Research Agenda: Theoretical and Empirical Explorations in the 'Meta-Change' of Modern Society' (2005) 56 *British Journal of Sociology* 525.

[15] Beck (n 14) 81.

These changes meant that nation-state-centred thinking had become unviable: 'the assumed congruence of state and society is broken down and suspended: economic and social ways of acting, working and living no longer take place within the container of the state'.[16]

An awareness of the limits to methodological nationalism does not imply treating the state as irrelevant, however. On any view, states continue to provide a primary framework for culture, society, economic activity and politics. This reality has been addressed within cosmopolitan sociology, which treats states as under pressure to become more cosmopolitan. That was encapsulated in the concept of a 'cosmopolitan nation' developed by Beck and Levy, who identified a role for 'national attachments [as] potential mediators between … individual and cosmopolitan horizons'.[17] States have contributed to greater cosmopolitanism through the establishment of international human rights and world trade regimes, and through the institutionalisation of international migration.[18] Beck and Levy argued for a 'cosmopolitan realism' of nation-states, which 'basically means the recognition of the legitimate interests of others and their inclusion in the calculation of one's own interests'.[19] Their expectation was that 'the more cosmopolitan the political structures and activities, the more successful [states] are in promoting national interests'.[20]

The related concepts of methodological nationalism and cosmopolitan realism will be relied upon in the analysis of UK employment law scholarship throughout this chapter. It is unsurprising that the three aspects of methodological nationalism identified by Wimmer and Glick Schiller above – unstated nationalism, naturalising the nation-state, and exclusion of transnational processes – have all been historically evident in employment law scholarship. After all, modern systems of employment law and industrial relations typically developed in industrialised countries with the consolidation of the nation-state in the second half of the nineteenth century and early twentieth century.[21] Similarly, as employment law emerged as an academic field around 1900 in Germany and elsewhere, it was oriented to employment contracts and collective bargaining of individual states, and emphasised the distinctiveness of national systems.[22] In the post-1945 era, when protective employment law and developed systems of industrial relations became elements of the universal welfare state, they were conceived in terms of a guarantee of 'industrial citizenship'

[16] ibid 87–88.

[17] U Beck and D Levy, 'Cosmopolitanized Nations: Re-imagining Collectivity in World Risk Society' (2013) 30 *Theory, Culture and Society* 3, 9.

[18] ibid 12–15.

[19] ibid 24.

[20] ibid.

[21] B Hepple, 'Introduction' in B Hepple (ed), *The Making of Labour Law in Europe: A Comparative Study of Nine Countries up to 1945* (London, Mansell, 1986) 15–22.

[22] Ibid 7–10.

or 'social citizenship', which implied a close link to a particular nation-state.[23] In that period, as employment law scholarship became more widely formalised as an academic subject, it retained its orientation to individual states.[24] That was reflected in Kahn-Freund's influential approach to comparative labour law, which was rooted in the idea of national 'traditions' concerning the relationship between employer and labour organisations, and the respective roles of the judiciary and governments within each state's constitution.[25] Famously, he expressed scepticism about legal transplants in employment law, especially in the area of collective labour law.[26]

In the era of neoliberal globalisation, the interpretation that employment law systems are separate and distinctive has typically remained the starting point for comparative analysis.[27] In the UK, one modification has concerned the significance within employment law of developments at the international level, covering the EU, the ILO and the ECHR.[28] Others have recognised the effects of neoliberal globalisation trends upon employment law systems in different countries, including the UK.[29]

A consideration of globalisation leads to the central question of this chapter: what would it mean for employment law scholarship to go beyond methodological nationalism, and to adopt a cosmopolitan realist position, in respect of migration? Two possible dimensions may be proposed. The first is simply recognition of migration-related questions – including access to employment by migrant workers, and equality of treatment for them in the labour market – as coming within the terrain of employment law. We shall see in section III that there is extensive evidence for such recognition in the case of the UK, especially in literature published since the late 2000s. The second involves

[23] C Zhang and N Lillie, 'Industrial Citizenship, Cosmopolitanism and European Integration' (2015) 18 *European Journal of Social Theory* 93.

[24] B Hepple and B Veneziani, 'Introduction' in B Hepple and B Veneziani (eds), *The Transformation of Labour Law in Europe: A Comparative Study of 15 Countries, 1945–2004* (Oxford, Hart, 2009).

[25] O Kahn-Freund, 'On the Uses and Misuses of Comparative Law' (1974) 37 *Modern Law Review* 1, 20.

[26] ibid 21.

[27] For example, M Pittard and S Butterworth, 'The Rich Panoply of Source of Labor Law: National, Regional and International' in M Finkin and G Mundlak (eds), *Comparative Labor Law* (Cheltenham, Edward Elgar, 2015).

[28] Leading examples are B Bercusson, 'The Conceptualization of European Labour Law' (1995) *24 Industrial Law Journal* 3 and B Bercusson, *European Labour Law*, 2nd edn (Cambridge, Cambridge University Press, 2009); K Ewing, 'Article 11 and the Right to Freedom of Associations' and J Hendy, 'Article 11 and the Right to Strike', both in K Ewing (ed) *Human Rights at Work* (London, Institute of Employment Rights, 2000); B Hepple, *Labour Laws and Global Trade* (Oxford, Hart, 2005) ch 2; and, T Novitz, *International and European Protection of the Right to Strike* (Oxford, Oxford University Press, 2003).

[29] B Bercusson and C Estlund (eds), *Regulating Labour in the Wake of Globalisation: New Challenges, New Institutions* (Oxford, Hart, 2008) ch 1; R Dukes and W Streeck, 'From Industrial Citizenship to Private Ordering? Contract, Status, and the Question of Consent' *MPIfG Discussion Paper* No 20/13 (Max Planck Institute for the Study of Societies, Cologne, 2020).

not being limited by the interests of resident workers. It is well-known that the interests of migrant workers are often defined by continuing connections in their place of origin, even if they have settled in the destination country.[30] Their interests may therefore diverge from those of resident workers engaged, actually or potentially, in the same work, but who do not face the same pressures as regards their earnings. Employment law scholarship may be classed as cosmopolitan realist when it openly recognises these potentially divergent interests and treats them as legitimate.

Finally, how are these elements to be elaborated concretely in the analysis of employment law?[31] This aim should be to find a model which avoids exclusive orientation to resident workers on the one hand (methodological nationalism), while not simply permitting migrant workers to accept inferior conditions to resident workers on the other (economic liberalism). One possibility in that regard may be termed the 'reconciliation' of the situation and interests of resident and migrant workers, so that they are in an equal position, both in theory and practice. This corresponds to what Freedland and Costello have described as 're-integrative responses' within employment law, 'to … impacts coming from labour migration and migration law'.[32] Such 're-integration' may not always be possible however, because the situations and interests of resident and migrant workers diverge, or because of policy constraints. In that case, cosmopolitan realism implies what Freedland and Costello have termed 'the appropriate balancing of [migrants'] interests with those of the local workforce'.[33] We shall see in section IV on access to employment, and in section V on the equal application of standards, that cosmopolitan realism – based on reconciliation and balancing – is an emergent tendency, though not a universal one, in the practice of employment law scholarship.

III. EMPLOYMENT LAW SCHOLARSHIP ON MIGRATION

In the introduction to their edited collection *Migrants at Work* (2014), Freedland and Costello observed that 'labour lawyers have tended to regard migration

[30] This insight is at the heart of Piore's theory of labour migration: M Piore, *Birds of Passage: Migrant Labor and Industrial Societies* (Cambridge, Cambridge University Press, 1979) chs 3–4. It also fits with what has been termed the 'new economics of migration', focused on decisions by families in places of origin rather than individual action: D Massey et al, *Worlds in Motion: Understanding International Migration at the End of the Millennium* (Oxford, Oxford University Press, 1998) 21–28 and 277–81.

[31] On the difficulty of addressing 'the relative situations of local workers and migrant workers', see ACL Davies, 'Identifying "Exploitative Compromises": The Role of Labour Law in Resolving Disputes Between Workers' (2012) 65 *Current Legal Problems* 269, 276.

[32] M Freedland and C Costello, 'Migrants at Work and the Division of Labour Law' in C Costello and M Freedland (eds) *Migrants at Work* (Oxford, Oxford University Press, 2014) 11.

[33] ibid 1.

law, generally speaking, as outside their purview'.[34] For our purposes that observation may be understood as their recognition of a form of methodological nationalism in employment law scholarship, that of excluding migration law and policy, and migration phenomena, from the assumed subject-matter. The discussion in this section will show that, while that characterisation had some truth in the post-war era of migration, the more recent period of neoliberal globalisation has seen more frequent engagement with migration-related questions.[35]

A. Post-War Period

The post-war decades in the UK saw an increase in labour migration, particularly from Commonwealth territories and states in the Caribbean, South Asia and East Africa. That prompted a reaction, both socially and in the political sphere, aimed at non-white migration, with restrictions upon immigration by Commonwealth nationals introduced by the Conservative Government in 1962, and reinforced by the Labour Government between 1965 and 1970.[36] The significance of these developments was recognised by leading employment law scholars of the time. Writing in 1967, Kahn-Freund classed the UK's new immigration controls as an example of legislation promoting 'status', and as a deviation from the historic tendency 'in the direction of promoting and not of restricting access to the labour market and that mobility of labour'.[37] Similarly, Hepple's study of race discrimination in employment, published in 1968 and 1970 included an outline of immigration law and policy concerning employment.[38] In contrast, the first two editions of Wedderburn's classic work *The Worker and the Law* (1965, 1971), contained a discussion of racial discrimination in employment, but did not go on to address immigration law and policy.[39]

Through the 1970s and 1980s, governments sought to limit immigration, and debate over it, leading Layton-Henry to describe the UK as the 'would-be zero-immigration country'.[40] Instead the policy focus was upon the integration

[34] ibid 1. They added that: 'migration lawyers have somewhat similarly tended to neglect labour law'.

[35] On these two periods of international labour migration, see ch 1 in this volume.

[36] P Foot, *Immigration and Race in British Politics* (Harmondsworth, Penguin, 1965) and Z Layton-Henry, *The Politics of Immigration* (Oxford, Blackwell, 1992) ch 4.

[37] O Kahn-Freund, 'A Note on Status and Contract in British Labour Law' (1967) 30 *Modern Law Review* 635, 639, and the discussion in C Costello, 'Migrants and Forced Labour: A Labour Law Response' in A Bogg, C Costello, ACL Davies and J Prassl (eds), *The Autonomy of Labour Law* (Oxford, Hart, 2015) 190.

[38] B Hepple, *Race, Jobs and the Law*, 2nd edn (Harmondsworth, Penguin, 1970).

[39] KW Wedderburn, *The Worker and the Law* (Harmondsworth, Penguin, 1965) 330–31; KW Wedderburn, *The Worker and the Law*, 2nd edn (Harmondsworth, Penguin, 1971) 84.

[40] Z Layton-Henry 'Britain: The Would-Be Zero Immigration Country', in W Cornelius, P Martin and J Hollifield (eds) *Controlling Immigration: A Global Perspective* (Stanford, Stanford University Press, 1994).

of ethnic monitories, including measures against racial discrimination.[41] The political orientation of the time was reflected within employment law scholarship in the 1980s, which treated measures against race discrimination within a general account of employment equality law, but contained either no or limited discussion of immigration law and policy. For example, the collection *Labour Law in Britain* edited by Lewis addressed race discrimination within a chapter entitled 'women and minorities', but did not include any treatment of immigration policy.[42] The third edition of Wedderburn's *The Worker and the Law* added a chapter on 'social discrimination at work', which covered legislation on race discrimination, but had only a short section on 'foreign workers', with a paragraph on permission to work for Commonwealth and alien nationals, and another on the free movement of workers.[43] The textbook by Benedictus and Bercusson contained a general chapter on discrimination, equality and the law, while covering controls on aliens, but not the rights of Commonwealth or EU workers, in a separate part of the work.[44] The exception was Davies and Freedland's textbook, which divided its treatment of anti-discrimination law between chapters on 'constituting' the employment relationship, and its 'content' and – consistently with that approach – covered the free movement of workers and the employment of non-EU nationals in the first of those chapters.[45]

The general lack of interest in migration-related questions was also seen in the *Industrial Law Journal*, the UK's main academic review of employment law. It contained only two contributions on labour migration policy between its foundation in 1972 and 1990: a summary by Duysens of the work permit system, and an article on free movement rights in the public sector by Morris, Fredman and Hayes.[46] Nor was the question of race discrimination prominent in the journal: only one full-length article by Lustgarten in that period addressed the Race Relations Act in detail, within a discussion of problems of proof which also covered sex discrimination claims.[47]

[41] Layton-Henry (n 36) ch 3; A Favell, *Philosophies of Integration: Immigration and the Idea of Citizenship in France and Britain*, 2nd edn (Basingstoke, Palgrave, 2001) ch 3.

[42] M Redmond, 'Women and Minorities' in R Lewis (ed), *Labour Law in Britain* (Oxford, Blackwell, 1986).

[43] KW Wedderburn, *The Worker and the Law,* 3rd edn (Harmondsworth, Penguin, 1986) ch 6 and 448–49, respectively.

[44] R Benedictus and B Bercusson, *Labour Law: Cases and Materials* (London, Sweet and Maxwell, 1987) chs 6 and 33, respectively.

[45] P Davies and M Freedland, *Labour Law: Text and Materials*, 2nd edn (London, Weidenfeld and Nicolson, 1984) chs 1 and 3, and 13–24, respectively. There was no equivalent discussion in the first edition of the work, published in 1979.

[46] D Duysens, 'Work Permits – Department of Employment Control of the Labour Market' (1977) 6 *Industrial Law Journal* 85; G Morris, S Fredman and J Hayes, 'Free Movement and the Public Sector' (1990) 19 *Industrial Law Journal* 20.

[47] L Lustgarten, 'Problems of Proof in Employment Discrimination Cases' (1977) 6 *Industrial Law Journal* 22.

B. The 1990s and After

As migration increased in extent and significance in the period of neoliberal globalisation from the early 1990s, discussions of labour migration by employment law scholars gradually became more commonplace. The inclusion of measures against race discrimination within employment equality law had by now become normalised, something which was reflected in the leading textbooks in the field.[48] For that reason, the focus here will be on the treatment of migration and migration policy by employment law scholars, as distinct from race-based discrimination.

The treatment by employment law textbooks of migration-related questions has seen divergent views as to the scope of the field. The first six editions of Deakin and Morris (published 1995–2012), included a passage on 'access to the labour market' within a section on recruitment, which covered both EU and non-EU nationals.[49] From its second edition onwards, it added a discussion of employer checks of the right to work under immigration law, which had been introduced in 1996.[50] ACL Davies' *Employment Law* also provided comprehensive coverage of labour migration policy within a chapter entitled 'migration', in addition to discussions of employer checks and the principle of illegality (ie, the position in employment law of workers without a right to work).[51] Among other leading textbooks, a more piecemeal approach has been taken. In their textbook, Collins, Ewing and McColgan address posted work, the exploitation of migrant workers, and the principle of illegality, but not immigration policy or right to work checks.[52] The most recent editions of Selwyn and Smith and Wood cover employer checks of immigration status, and the principle of illegality, while works by Bowers and Cabrelli cover only the latter.[53] Moreover, the most recent edition of Deakin and Morris (2021) – the first since the EU free movement of workers ceased to apply to the UK – saw a change of tack. It removed the previous coverage of immigration policy and of right to work checks, on the basis that 'access to the national labour market … lie[s] outside

[48] In addition to examples given from the 1980s, see I Smith and J Wood, *Industrial Law,* 5th edn (Butterworths, London, 1993) ch 5; S Deakin and G Morris, *Labour Law* (Oxford, Hart, 1995) ch 6.

[49] Deakin and Morris (n 48) 132–34, and 6th edn (Oxford, Hart, 2012) of the same work, 139–41.

[50] S Deakin and G Morris, *Labour Law*, 2nd edn (Oxford, Hart, 1998) 141–43, and 6th edn (Oxford, Hart, 2012) 141–42. Employer checks had been introduced by the Asylum and Immigration Act 1996.

[51] ACL Davies, *Employment Law* (Boston, Pearson, 2015) ch 3.

[52] H Collins, K Ewing and A McColgan, *Labour Law,* 2nd edn (Cambridge, Cambridge University Press, 2019) 63–76 and 162–63.

[53] A Emir, *Selwyn's Law of Employment*, 21st edn (Oxford, Oxford University Press, 2020) 62–63; I Smith, A Baker and O Warnock, *Smith and Wood's Employment Law*, 14th edn (Oxford, Oxford University Press, 2019) 88–89 and 103–04; J Bowers, *A Practical Approach to Employment Law,* 9th edn (Oxford, Oxford University Press, 2017) 220; and D Cabrelli, *Employment Law in Context*, 4th edn (Oxford, Oxford University Press, 2020) 100–01.

the scope of this book'.[54] Accordingly, it too addresses immigration law and policy only in the context of the principle of illegality.[55]

A more definitive shift to coverage of migration-related questions can be seen in the *Industrial Law Journal*, from around 2008. Between 1991 and 2007, the journal contained only three notes concerning migration questions: one by the present author on the introduction of right to work checks; a second by Davies covering a series of CJEU rulings about posted workers between 1997 and 2002; and a third by Forshaw and Pilgerstorfer on the principle of illegality.[56] Greater coverage of migration-related questions was triggered by labour market changes and related policy debate after the accession of central and eastern European states to the EU in 2004 ('EU 8') and 2007 ('EU 2'). Accordingly, much of this work had an EU law dimension. In 2008, there were notes by the present author summarising the labour market arrangements for Bulgarian and Romanian nationals, and by Davies which included the CJEU's *Laval* judgment on posted workers.[57] In the following year, Barnard published pieces on the CJEU judgment in *Commission v Luxembourg* concerning posted workers, and the 'British jobs for British workers' protests of that year.[58] Barnard also published a further analysis of national and international developments relating to posted workers.[59] Papers by Barnard, Ludlow and Fraser Butlin analysed the comparatively low rate of applications to employment tribunals and the Employment Appeal Tribunal by EU8 workers.[60]

[54] Z Adams, C Barnard, S Deakin and S Fraser Butlin, *Deakin and Morris' Labour* Law, 7th edn (Oxford, Hart, 2021) 105.

[55] ibid 122.

[56] B Ryan, 'Employer Enforcement of Immigration Law after Section Eight of the Asylum and Immigration Act 1996' (1997) 26 *Industrial Law Journal* 136; P Davies, 'The Posted Workers Directive and the EC Treaty' (2002) 31 *Industrial Law Journal* 298; S Forshaw and M Pilgerstorfer, 'Illegally Formed Contracts of Employment and Equal Treatment at Work' (2005) 34 *Industrial Law Journal* 158.

[57] B Ryan, 'The Accession (Immigration and Worker Authorisation) Regulations 2006 (2008) 37 *Industrial Law Journal* 75; ACL Davies, 'One Step Forward, Two Steps Back? The *Viking* and *Laval* Cases in the ECJ' (2008) 37 *Industrial Law Journal* 126. *Laval* was Case C-341/05 [2007] ECR I-11767: see discussion in ch 1 of this volume.

[58] C Barnard 'The UK and Posted Workers: The Effect of *Commission v Luxembourg* on the territorial application of British Labour Law' (2009) 38 *Industrial Law Journal* 122, C Barnard, '"British jobs for British workers": The Lindsey Oil Refinery Dispute and the Future of Local Labour Clauses in an Integrated EU Market' (2009) 38 *Industrial Law Journal* 245.
Commission v Luxembourg was Case C-319/06 [2008] ECR I-04323. In that period, a Swedish academic published on the domestic effects of the *Laval* litigation: M Rönnmar, '*Laval* Returns to Sweden: The Final Judgment of the Swedish Labour Court and Swedish Legislative Reforms' (2010) 39 *Industrial Law Journal* 280.

[59] C Barnard, 'More Posting' (2014) 43 *Industrial Law Journal* 194, which covered the *STX* litigation before the EFTA Court and the Norwegian Supreme Court, and a complaint about the implications of the *Laval* ruling made by the Swedish Trade Union Confederation to the European Committee on Social Rights.

[60] C Barnard and A Ludlow, 'Enforcement of Employment Rights by EU-8 Migrant Workers in Employment Tribunals' (2016) 45 *Industrial Law Journal* 1; C Barnard, A Ludlow and S Fraser Butlin, 'Beyond Employment Tribunals: Enforcement of Employment Rights by EU-8 Migrant Workers' (2018) 47 *Industrial Law Journal* 226.

The years since the mid-2010s have also seen a series of contributions on other migration-related topics in the *Industrial Law Journal* by UK-based scholars.[61] Many of those have concerned the legal regime concerning work in breach of immigration law. Bogg and Green analysed the law on illegality after the Supreme Court judgment in the migration case of *Hounga*, which Bogg later followed with a note on the similar case of *Okedina*.[62] Davies wrote about the Immigration Act 2016, which inter alia included reforms to the criminal law sanctions for breach of immigration law.[63] Bales analysed the law relating to immigration enforcement raids at workplaces.[64] Others have concerned the place of migrant workers in the labour market. Novitz highlighted the problematic lack of statutory support for sectoral collective bargaining in the UK in the context of labour migration.[65] Dias-Abey focused on the links between a flexible employment law regime which encourages segmentation in the labour market, and the channelling of migrant workers into less desirable employment.[66]

A growing interest in migration-related questions by UK employment law scholars has also been reflected in articles appearing in other legal journals. Prior to the mid-2000s, such literature remained rare: examples included an article by Davies on posted workers in the *Common Market Law Review*, and by the present author on work without immigration permission in the *Comparative Labor Law and Policy Journal*.[67] The period from the late 2000s onwards would though see a marked increase in literature of this type. First, the *Laval* ruling in 2007 was followed by articles which wholly or partly addressed the legal regime relating to posted workers, including by Barnard and Deakin in the *Cambridge Yearbook of European Legal Studies* and by Kilpatrick in the *European Law Review*.[68] Zahn wrote both about the 'British jobs' protests

[61] Two further articles were published by academics based in Ireland and Australia, respectively: C Murphy, 'Tackling Vulnerability to Labour Exploitation through Regulation: The Case of Migrant Fishermen in Ireland' (2017) *Industrial Law Journal* 417; and, J Howe, 'A Legally Constructed Underclass of Workers? The Deportability and Limited Work Rights of International Students in Australia and the United Kingdom' (2019) 48 *Industrial Law Journal* 416.

[62] A Bogg and S Green, 'Rights are Not Just for the Virtuous: What *Hounga* Means for the Illegality Defence in the Discrimination Torts' (2015) 44 *Industrial Law Journal* 101; A Bogg, '*Okedina v Chikale* and Contract Illegality: New Dawn or False Dawn?' (2020) 49 *Industrial Law Journal* 258. The judgments in question were *Hounga v Allen* [2014] UKSC 47 and *Okedina v Chikale* [2019] EWCA Civ 1393.

[63] ACL Davies, 'The Immigration Act 2016' (2016) 45 *Industrial Law Journal* 431.

[64] K Bales, 'Immigration Raids, Employer Collusion and the Immigration Act 2016' (2017) 46 *Industrial Law Journal* 279.

[65] T Novitz, 'Collective Bargaining, Equality and Migration: The Journey to and from Brexit' (2017) 46 *Industrial Law Journal* 109.

[66] M Dias-Abey, 'Determining the Impact of Migration on Labour Markets; The Mediating Role of Legal Institutions' (2021) 50 *Industrial Law Journal* 532.

[67] P Davies, 'Posted workers: Single Market or Protection of National Labour Law Systems?' (1997) 34 *Common Market Law Review* 571; B Ryan, 'The Evolving Legal Regime on Unauthorized Work by Migrants in Britain' (2005) 27 *Comparative Labor Law and Policy Journal* 27.

[68] C Barnard, '*Viking* and *Laval*: An Introduction' (2008) 10 *Cambridge Yearbook of European Legal Studies* 463; S Deakin, 'Regulatory Competition after *Laval*' (2008) 10 *Cambridge Yearbook of European Legal Studies* 581; C Kilpatrick, 'Laval's Regulatory Conundrum: Collective Standard-setting and the Court's New Approach to Posted Workers' (2009) 34 *European Law Review* 844.

of 2009 in the *Juridical Review* and later about the revision of the Posted Workers Directive in the *Cambridge Yearbook of European Legal Studies*.[69] Aspects of the legal regime relating to work without immigration permission were explored in articles by Bogg and Novitz in the *Law Quarterly Review* and by Fudge in the *Oxford Journal of Legal Studies*.[70] Articles by Mantouvalou and Pavlou addressed the situation of migrant domestic workers, who were taken to be at particular risk of exploitation and forced labour.[71]

Finally, increased coverage of migration-related questions has been evident in books and other longer-form works from the mid-2000s. The Institute of Employment Rights was something of a pioneer, publishing a report and a collection on migrant labour and the law edited by the present author, and a collection on posted workers edited by Ewing and Hendy.[72] Freedland and Costello's collection, *Migrants at Work* included contributions inter alia by Barnard, Bogg and Novitz, Dewhurst and Mantouvalou among UK-based legal scholars.[73] The first monographs in the field have appeared: Zahn's study of the impact of EU enlargement upon the labour laws of selected states, and Pavlou's comparative study of the legal status of migrant domestic workers in Europe.[74] Other edited collections featured contributions on migration-related questions by UK scholars. Prominent examples include a chapter on the reform of the Posted Workers Directive co-authored by Countouris in a collection entitled *Viking, Laval and Beyond*; chapters by Costello on forced labour, modern slavery and related questions in edited collections on *The Autonomy of Labour Law*, *Temporary Labour Migration in the Global Era* and *Criminality at Work*; and a chapter by Aliverti on the enforcement of immigration law at work in *Criminality at Work*.[75]

[69] R Zahn, '"British Jobs for British workers": The Problem of Collective Agreements in the UK (2010) *Juridical Review* 181; R Zahn, 'Revision of the Posted Workers Directive: A Europeanisation Perspective' (2017) 19 *Cambridge Yearbook of European Legal Studies* 187.

[70] A Bogg and T Novitz, 'Race Discrimination and the Doctrine of Illegality' (2013) 129 *Law Quarterly Review* 12; J Fudge, 'Illegal Working, Migrants and Labour Exploitation in the UK' (2018) 38 *Oxford Journal of Legal Studies* 557.

[71] V Mantouvalou, 'Human Rights for Precarious Workers: The Legislative Precariousness of Domestic Labour' (2012) 34 *Comparative Labor Law and Policy Journal* 133; V Mantouvalou, '"Am I Free Now?" Overseas Domestic Workers in Slavery' (2015) 42 *Journal of Law and Society* 329; V Pavlou, 'Where to Look for Change? A Critique of the use of Modern Slavery and Trafficking Frameworks in the Fight Against Migrant Domestic Workers' Vulnerability' (2018) 20 *European Journal of Migration and Law* 83.

[72] B Ryan (ed), *Labour Migration and Employment Rights* (London, Institute of Employment Rights, 2005); B Ryan (ed), *Labour Migration in Hard Times: Reforming Labour Market Regulation?* (Liverpool, Institute of Employment Rights, 2013); K Ewing and J Hendy (eds), *The New Spectre Haunting Europe: The ECJ, Trade Union Rights and the British Government* (Liverpool, Institute of Employment Rights, 2009).

[73] Costello and Freedland (n 32).

[74] R Zahn, *New Labour Laws in Old Member States: Trade Union Responses to European Enlargement* (Cambridge, Cambridge University Press, 2017); V Pavlou, *Migrant Domestic Workers in Europe: Law and the Construction of Vulnerability* (Oxford, Hart, 2021).

[75] N Countouris and S Engblom, 'Civilizing the European Posted Workers Directive' in M Freedland and J Prassl (eds), *Viking, Laval and Beyond* (Oxford, Hart, 2016); C Costello,

It can be seen therefore that employment law scholarship has moved beyond an earlier methodologically nationalist tendency to omit migration-related questions from consideration. The theme which is explored in the next two sections concerns the divergent approaches which scholars have taken in addressing such questions. That topic is examined separately in respect of access to the labour market (section IV) and the equal application of labour standards (section V).

IV. ACCESS TO THE LABOUR MARKET

This section considers the treatment within employment law scholarship of two types of restriction on access to the labour market – state labour migration policy, and discrimination by labour market actors (ie, employers or trade unions). These are considered together, as each implies a preference for resident workers, through the exclusion of migrant workers either from employment, or from more desirable jobs.

A. Labour Migration Policy

For employment law scholarship to go beyond methodological nationalism in respect of labour migration policy, it appears necessary to avoid being limited by a state's own agenda. In deciding about labour migration, policy makers typically face significant competing pressures.[76] On the one hand, there are reasons for openness to labour migration, as employers have an interest in enhanced labour supply, while the state has a fiscal incentive to increase the population in employment. On the other hand, governments and political parties frequently face demands from within the resident population to restrict immigration as a whole, or labour migration specifically. Meanwhile, actual and potential labour migrants mostly lack representation within the domestic political system. The policy mixture which emerges from these contradictory pressures frequently involves restrictions and conditions on migrant workers'

'Migrants and Forced Labour: A Labour Law Response' in A Bogg, C Costello, ACL Davies and J Prassl (eds), *The Autonomy of Labour Law* (Oxford, Hart, 2015); V Mantouvalou, 'Temporary Labour Migration and Modern Slavery' in J Howe and R Owens (eds), *Temporary Labour Migration in the Global Era* (Oxford, Hart, 2016); C Costello, 'Victim or Perpetrator? The Criminalization of Migration and the Idea of "Harm" in the Labour Market Context' and A Aliverti, 'Doing the Dirty Job: Labour at the Intersections of Criminal Law and Immigration Controls', both in A Bogg, J Collins, M Freedland, and J Herring (eds), *Criminality at Work* (Oxford, Oxford University Press, 2020).

[76] G Menz, *The Political Economy of Managed Migration* (Oxford, Oxford University Press, 2009); C Wright, 'Employer Organizations and Labour Immigration Policy in Australia and the United Kingdom: The Power of Political Salience and Social Institutional Legacies' (2017) 55 *British Journal of Industrial Relations* 347.

freedom of action and equality of treatment, which are hard to rationalise in normative terms. Particularly for that reason, the evaluation and critique of labour migration regimes appears a legitimate and desirable task within employment law scholarship.

Viewed in that light, one form of methodological nationalism within employment law scholarship involves taking a neutral or descriptive approach to state labour migration policy. An older example is provided by Hepple's work on racial discrimination in 1968–1970, which outlined immigration policy, but did not offer any evaluation of it, despite its association with such discrimination.[77] The present author also took a neutral approach in papers on employer checks of status, and on their implications for workers who are both lawfully employed and undocumented.[78] Davies's discussion of immigration policy in her textbook and in the article on the Immigration Act 2016 is similarly cautious in style.[79] A neutral approach has a certain logic if the primary aim is to introduce immigration law material into discussion within the employment law field. Nevertheless, in Glick Schiller and Wimmer's terminology, it can be seen as 'naturalising' the state, by ostensibly accepting the state agenda, without evaluation or critique.

Other commentators on employment law have been willing to scrutinise state policy on labour migration, though with very different perspectives. A more critical school of thought has objected to aspects of labour migration policy for being *too open*, because it favours business interests in access to a flexible labour supply. A general example is the position taken in the Collins, Ewing and McColgan textbook, which speaks of 'globalisation having contributed to the emergence of new forms of exploitation, as developed countries import workers to do work that cannot be exported'.[80] A more specific example is the objections by Hayes and Novitz to the supply of labour through service provision under EU law and other international trade regimes.[81] Another is Zou's criticism of the employer-led character of the UK's skilled migration system.[82] These critical positions in the literature arguably exhibit a type of methodological nationalism, however, in that they implicitly give primacy to the interests and positions of resident workers in reaching their conclusions.

An alternative school of thought is more willing to approve of state policy which enables the employment of foreign nationals. In the late 2000s, Paul

[77] Hepple (n 38) 23–24, 51–52 and 56–57.

[78] B Ryan 'The Evolving Legal Regime on Unauthorized Work by Migrants in Britain' (2005) 27 *Comparative Labor Law and Policy Journal* 27 and 'Employer Checks of Immigration Status and Employment Law' in Costello and Freedland (n 32).

[79] Davies (n 51) and Davies (n 63).

[80] Collins, Ewing and McColgan (n 52) 67.

[81] L Hayes and T Novitz, 'Workers without Footprints: The Legal Fiction of Posted Workers' in Ryan (2013) (n 72). See further Novitz, ch 13 in this volume concerning the regulation of temporary mobility post-Brexit.

[82] M Zou, 'Employer Demand for "Skilled" Migrant Workers: Regulating Admission Under the United Kingdom's Tier 2 (General) Visa' in Howe and Owens (n 75). See too Zou's discussion of temporary labour migration schemes in ch 12 in this volume.

Davies and Freedland justified the relatively open labour migration policy of the time on the basis that it favoured economic growth and addressed labour supply shortages.[83] Others have favoured greater openness in specific aspects of labour migration policy. Examples include Costello's argument for the regularisation of migrants without status as an alternative to criminalisation, and Mantouvalou's criticism of the limiting of migrant domestic workers' permission to stay to six months.[84] While this scholarship avoids the methodological nationalism of naturalising the state, or orientation to the resident population, its cosmopolitan realism is somewhat circumscribed, in that it is focused either on economic benefits to the UK, or upon a more humane policy towards the specific category of migrants lacking status.

B. Discrimination

Access to the labour market by migrant workers who possess a legal right to work may be affected by the actions and policies of labour market actors, leading to the denial of employment to migrant workers, or to segmented employment patterns.[85] The question here is how employment law scholarship has responded to discrimination on nationality or related racial grounds against migrant workers. The case of the UK in the 1960s and 1970s shows the challenges for scholars which can arise. In that period, racial discrimination by employers against non-white Commonwealth migrants was widespread, including through denial of employment, and concentration in lower-skilled work.[86] These practices were often supported by white British workers, which in turn led trade unions not to oppose discrimination in workplaces, and to be unwilling to actively support industrial action taken by Caribbean and South Asian workers.[87] The TUC too avoided engagement with the issue of race discrimination until the mid-1970s.[88]

[83] P Davies and M Freedland, *Towards a Flexible Labour Market; Labour Legislation and Regulation since the 1990s* (Oxford, Oxford University Press, 2007) 216–23. The quoted sentence is at 217.

[84] C Costello, 'Victim or Perpetrator? The Criminalization of Migration and the Idea of "Harm" in the Labour Market Context' in Bogg, Collins, Freedland, and Herring (n 75); V Mantouvalou, 'Human Rights for Precarious Workers: The Legislative Precariousness of Domestic Labour' (2012) 34 *Comparative Labor Law and Policy Journal* 133; Mantouvalou (n 71); and Mantouvalou in Howe and Owens (n 75).

[85] On migration and labour market segmentation, Piore (n 30) ch 2.

[86] WW Daniel, *Racial Discrimination in England* (Harmondsworth, Penguin, 1968) chs 3–8; D Smith, *Racial Disadvantage in Employment* (London, PEP, 1974).

[87] B Radin, 'Coloured Workers and British Trade Unions' (1966) 8 *Race* 157; J Wrench, 'Unequal Comrades: Trade Unions, Equal Opportunities and Racism' in R Jenkins and J Solomos (eds), *Racism and Equal Opportunity Policies in the 1980s* (Cambridge, Cambridge University Press, 1987).

[88] R Miles and A Phizacklea, *The TUC, Black Workers and New Commonwealth immigration, 1954–1973* (S.S.R.C. Research Unit on Ethnic Relations, University of Bristol, 1977); R Miles and

The initial response of leading employment law scholars to these developments was limited. For example, the first edition of Wedderburn's classic work *The Worker and the Law* (1965) did not consider racial discrimination by employers at all. Instead, it recognised that workers might support racial discrimination, and treated trade unionism as the antidote:

> In recent decades local groups have ... raised xenophobic or racial objections to the intake of workers, e.g., against Italian miners or coloured workers on buses; but these rare outbursts have so far been contained and overcome by resolute pressure from union leaders and members and by the strong tradition in the British labour movement opposed to any such racial, religious or even political discrimination.[89]

In the context of the 1960s, this passage was rather blasé in respect of discrimination on racial grounds.[90] The second edition of the work (1971) contained no equivalent, with Wedderburn instead discussing the Race Relations Act 1968, while recognising that it had been enacted after extensive evidence of race discrimination in employment.[91]

A second example from the same period is Hepple's reluctance to critique the limitations to the provisions of the 1968 Act concerning racial discrimination in employment. First, he endorsed the 1968 Act arrangements for race discrimination complaints to be referred to voluntary industry bodies, on the basis that that had more likelihood of reducing discrimination than did individual legal remedies.[92] That position was not however shared by liberal advocates of anti-discrimination legislation, and mandatory complaints to industry arrangements were removed by the Race Relations Act 1976.[93] Second, Hepple accepted the omission of nationality from the prohibited grounds of employment discrimination in the 1968 Act, on the basis that discrimination between British subjects and aliens was 'an accepted principle of legislation and industrial practice'.[94] 'Nationality' did though become a prohibited ground of discrimination, including in respect of employment, under the Race Relations Act 1976.[95] Finally, Hepple was unwilling to criticise the permission given in the 1968 Act for racial

A Phizacklea, 'The TUC and Black Workers 1974–1976' (1978) 16 *British Journal of Industrial Relations* 195.

[89] Wedderburn (1965) (n 39) 330–31.

[90] See the works by Foot and Layton-Henry, cited above (n 36).

[91] Wedderburn (1971) (n 39) 84. This referred inter alia to research by Political and Economic Planning (Daniel, n 86).

[92] These provisions were in Race Relations Act 1968, s 16 and Sch 2. See the discussion in Hepple (n 38) 185–95 and 252–53.

[93] See H Street, G Howe and G Bindman, *Report on Anti-Discrimination Legislation* (London, PEP, 1967) 73 and Home Office, *Racial Discrimination* (Cmnd. 6234, September 1975) para 88. Between 1968 and 1974, discrimination was found in only 10 complaints out of 536 disposed of by industry arrangements: Select Committee on Race Relations and Immigration, *Employment* (House of Commons Papers 312-I, 25 July 1974) para 33.

[94] Hepple (n 38) 49–54.

[95] For the background, see Race Relations Board, *Report for 1971–72* (HC 296, 20 June 1972) para 88 and Home Office (n 93) para 58. See now Equality Act 2010, s 9(1)(b).

discrimination, where the employer's objective was to achieve 'a reasonable balance of persons of different racial groups', arguing that it had led many employers to drop racial quotas.[96] In the event, after widespread criticism that this exception enabled racial discrimination, especially against first-generation migrants, it was removed by the Race Relations Act 1976.[97]

A reluctance among employment law scholars to criticise discrimination against migrants was also arguably evident in the responses to industrial action and protests in 2009 concerning posted and foreign workers in construction projects in the energy sector.[98] Most commentary on those developments focused on the deficiencies of the legal regime concerning the extension to posted workers of the terms and conditions of collective agreements.[99] On the ground, however, participants had advocated 'British jobs for British workers', which amounted to a call for nationality-based discrimination in access to employment.[100] It was though unusual for employment law scholars to focus on that aspect of the protests.[101] In the terminology of this chapter, that difference of approach was between the methodological nationalism of prioritising resident workers and the cosmopolitan realism of accepting the legitimacy of the supply of labour by migrant workers.

V. EQUAL APPLICATION OF LABOUR STANDARDS

As indicated in section II, a 'cosmopolitan realist' approach within employment law scholarship implies giving due weight to the interests of each of resident and migrant workers. As regards statutory and collective labour standards, scholarship would aim for reconciliation of those interests through equal application of standards, or – if that cannot be achieved – a 'balancing' of interests. The key question is often whether scholarship takes the situation of resident workers as its sole or primary reference point, or whether it also recognises and gives weight to the potentially distinct situation of many foreign workers, The approach taken will have consequences for how the equal application of legal and contractual labour standards is conceptualised, and how it is to be achieved. The general

[96] Race Relations Act 1968, s 8(2) and Hepple (n 38) 118–20.

[97] Race Relations Board (n 95) para 87 and Home Office (n 93) para 62.

[98] For an outline of these events, B Ryan 'Transnationalism and Labour Law: The "British Jobs" Protests of 2009' in MA Moreau (ed), *Before and After the Economic Crisis: What Implications for the 'European Social Model'?* (Cheltenham, Edward Elgar, 2011).

[99] See the literature on the terms and conditions of posted workers in section V, below.

[100] 'Dawn of a New Age of Unrest: Strikes at 19 sites over 'British jobs for British workers'' *Times*, 31 January 2009.

[101] Examples are Barnard (n 58) and Ryan (n 98). In comparison, scholars of industrial relations were more willing to identify a preference for local labour within these disputes: see G Meardi, 'Union Immobility? Trade Unions and the Freedoms of Movement in the Enlarged EU' (2012) 52 *British Journal of Industrial Relations* 99, 112–14 and G Gall, 'The Engineering Construction Strikes in Britain, 2009' (2012) 36 *Capital and Class* 411.

point may be illustrated by an examination of three questions concerning the equal application of labour standards seen in recent literature: the standards applicable to posted workers, the position of workers without a right to work, and the enforcement of labour standards.

A. Posted Workers

A key migration-related topic addressed by employment law scholars in the UK in recent times concerned the (pre-Brexit) EU legal regime relating to posted workers, ie, employees sent by a service provider from one Member State to another. Up to the early 2000s, scholars had taken a broadly descriptive approach to the topic, as the CJEU began to map out the options for Member States under the EU treaties, and the 1996 Posted Workers Directive provided for the application of host state employment law and collective agreements to incoming workers.[102] A more extensive literature followed the CJEU judgments in *Laval*, *Rüffert* and *Commission v Luxembourg* in 2007–2008.[103] In broad terms, these cases treated the Posted Workers Directive as a ceiling rather than a floor for the application of host state employment law. In addition, in *Laval*, the CJEU held that the TFEU precluded trade unions from industrial action aimed at extending collective agreements to posted workers, where the aims of the action went beyond the scope of the Posted Workers Directive, and the outcome was uncertain.[104] UK-based scholars were among the leading voices arguing that these judgments unduly favoured the free movement of services over national labour laws and trade union rights.[105]

The terms and conditions applicable to posted workers acquired greater significance in the UK with the 'British jobs' protests of 2009 (above), as the initial dispute at East Lindsey had involved complaints of undercutting by posted workers.[106] Those events led to widespread commentary on the deficiencies of the legal regime concerning the extension of terms and conditions in collective agreements to posted workers. That commentary concerned both the limitations of post-*Laval* EU law, and those of British law, which did not

[102] P Davies (n 67) and Davies (n 56).

[103] *Laval* (n 57); *Rüffert* Case C-346/06 [2008] ECR I-1989 and *Commission v Luxembourg* (n 58).

[104] *Laval* (n 57) paras 86–111.

[105] For overviews, M Freedland and J Prassl, '*Viking*, *Laval* and Beyond: An Introduction' in M Freedland and J Prassl (eds), *Viking, Laval and Beyond* (Oxford, Hart, 2016) and C Barnard, 'The Calm after the Storm: Time to Reflect on EU (Labour) Law Scholarship Following the Decisions in *Viking* and *Laval*' in A Bogg, C Costello and ACL Davies (eds), *Research Handbook in EU Labour Law* (Cheltenham, Edward Elgar, 2016). These also considered the CJEU ruling in *Viking Line* Case C-438/05 [2007] ECR I-10779, which concerned industrial action and businesses' freedom of establishment.

[106] ACAS, Report of an Inquiry into the Circumstances Surrounding the Lindsey Oil Refinery Dispute (16 February 2009).

(and does not) provide a mechanism for the extension of collective agreements to non-parties.[107]

Within the post-2007 literature concerning posted workers, an important difference of perspective among UK scholars concerned the question of whose interests the posted workers regime was to protect. The dominant school of thought focused on the implications of the CJEU rulings for the position of resident workers and of the trade unions representing them. Within that approach, the central issues were the potential for unfair competition ('social dumping'), and the restricted capacity of trade unions to take industrial action to respond to it.[108] Typical solutions were to roll back EU single market laws, for example through a Social Protocol to the TFEU, or recourse to ILO and ECHR standards.[109] A variant of this school of thought identified the weakness of EU law concerning posted workers as a contributory cause of the xenophobia in the UK that manifested in 2009, and of the evolution of public opinion which led to Brexit.[110]

An alternative approach sought to recognise the interests both of resident workers and of foreign service providers and their workers, to avoid discrimination or protectionism. The Posted Workers Directive had earlier been interpreted in this way by Paul Davies, when he highlighted the separateness of posted workers' interests, relative to home state workers, and rejected as 'erroneous' the view that competition by lower-paid posted workers that undercut higher-paid ones was inherently 'unfair'.[111] That anti-protectionism was developed by Kilpatrick in response to *Laval*, when she argued that 'It is not inappropriate ... for EU law to require those making collective bargains to demonstrate that adequate account has been taken in their agreements of the rights and needs of posted workers and posting undertakings.'[112] The same theme was reflected in ACL Davies's account of conflicts of interest among workers, in which she interpreted the Posted Workers Directive as 'an attempt to strike a balance between 'host' states' interests in protecting their own workers and maintaining certain

[107] C Kilpatrick, *British Jobs for British Workers? UK Industrial Action and Free Movement of Services in EU Law* (LSE Legal Studies Working Paper 16/2009) (EU law); Zahn (2010) (n 69) (British law); K Ewing and J Hendy, 'The ECJ Decisions and Trade Union Freedom: Lessons from the United Kingdom' in Ewing and Hendy (n 72) (both).

[108] T Novitz, 'A Human Rights Analysis of the *Viking* and *Laval* Judgments (2008) 10 *Cambridge Yearbook of European Legal Studies* 541 and P Syrpis and T Novitz, 'Economic and Social Rights in Conflict: Political and Judicial Approaches to their Reconciliation' (2008) 33 *European Law Review* 411.

[109] K Ewing and J Hendy, 'Conclusion' in Ewing and Hendy (n 72).

[110] T Novitz and P Syrpis, 'The United Kingdom' in Freedland and Prassl (n 105); N Contouris and S Engblom, 'Civilizing the Posted Workers Directive' in Freedland and Prassl (n 105); and Novitz (n 65) 112.

[111] P Davies (n 67) 574–75 and 598.

[112] Kilpatrick (n 68) 864, which includes a discussion of Davies (n 67) at 863.

minimum standards in their labour markets, and 'home' states' interests in enabling their firms to compete for business around the EU'.[113]

A conceptual framework oriented primarily to resident workers and their trade unions may be classed as methodologically nationalist in that it focuses on the interests of those already securely established within the labour market. In contrast, recognition of the separate interests of service-providers and posted workers is in line with cosmopolitan realism, in that claims from outside the state are also being recognised. In practice, the compulsory extension of a host state's legal standards and collective agreements to posted workers, whether by legislation or industrial action, appears defensible on either approach. That said, two differences in the implications of the two approaches may be suggested. One concerns whether the standards to be extended are already effective domestically within a given sector: that appears unimportant if the goal is the protection of resident workers from 'external' competition, but critical from a cosmopolitan realist perspective, where discrimination against external competitors is considered objectionable. A second concerns the potential role of private actors such as trade unions in extending labour standards: should they be free to choose which employers and workers to target? Again, this is of less concern if the underlying goal is the protection of the resident workforce, whereas, from a cosmopolitan realist perspective, discrimination against foreign service providers and their workers casts doubts upon the legitimacy of industrial action.[114]

B. Migrant Workers Without a Right to Work

A second topic concerning the equal application of labour standards addressed by UK scholars concerns the position in employment law of workers who are present or working in breach of immigration law. In English law, such claims have historically been excluded by private law rules concerning illegality, which cover both tort-based claims (including claims of discrimination) and contract-based claims (including claims for wages and relating to dismissal).[115]

[113] ACL Davies (n 31) 278.

[114] The 'cosmopolitan realist' position suggested here is broadly that followed in EU law after the 2018 revision of the Posted Workers Directive by Directive 2018/957 [2018] OJ L173. That now requires the extension to posted workers of all statutory and collectively agreed standards on core subjects, and not only minimum standards. It also applies in all sectors, and not only in construction. The extension of collective agreements is conditional on general applicability, however, while the freedom to engage in industrial action probably continues to be constrained by the material scope of the Directive and by requirements of certainty. For a discussion of the Commission's proposals on which Directive 2018/957 was based, see Zahn (2017) (n 69).

[115] *Hall v Woolston Hall* [2001] ICR 99 (CA). The common law position in Northern Ireland and Wales may be assumed to be the same as that in England. The author is unaware of any discussion of case law relating to Scottish law on the point.

Three distinct approaches to the illegality principle in employment law claims may be identified in the literature: neutral acceptance, modification of the defence to protect vulnerable workers, and rejection of the defence on principle.

A note by Forshaw and Pilgerstorfer in the *Industrial Law Journal* provides a good example of neutral acceptance.[116] That followed the Court of Appeal judgment in *Vakante* (2004), which reaffirmed the orthodox position that a discrimination law action was barred if there was an 'inextricable link' between an individual's illegal act and the claim, and applied that test to preclude a claim of race discrimination by a migrant worker who had deceived their employer as to their right to work.[117] In their discussion, Forshaw and Pilgerstorfer offered only marginal criticism, arguing that the 'inextricable link' test had been too broadly interpreted, so that discrimination should be actionable where it was separate from the original illegality.[118] But they accepted the logic of excluding claims for wages in the context of remedies for unlawful discrimination, arguing that that could amount to unjust enrichment.[119] By accepting the policy underlying the law, their approach may be considered an example of methodological nationalism.

A second position, which has been elaborated especially by Bogg, focuses on mitigating the effects of the illegality defence in the case of workers who may be thought 'vulnerable'. In 2013, he wrote of the 'special vulnerabilities that some migrant workers experience', as 'social, cultural and linguistic barriers can lead to alienation and disorientation, and a lack of familiarity with and confidence in asserting one's legal rights and remedies', and concluded that it was indefensible that 'the most vulnerable migrant workers [were] denied protection'.[120] A similar understanding emerged in his commentary on the Supreme Court ruling in *Patel v Mirza*, where Lord Toulson proposed that the illegality defence in contract law should be subject to a proportionality assessment, with 'potentially relevant factors includ[ing] the seriousness of the conduct, its centrality to the contract, whether it was intentional and whether there was marked disparity in the parties' respective culpability'.[121] Bogg argued for that approach to be applied in the present context: committing the criminal offence of working without immigration permission should not lead to a worker's contract being classed as illegal, as the offence was 'designed to deter working arrangements that facilitate the serious labour market exploitation of

[116] Forshaw and Pilgerstorfer (n 56).

[117] *Vakante v Addey and Stanhope School* [2004] EWCA Civ 1065.

[118] Forshaw and Pilgerstorfer (n 56) 169–76. For similar observations about the inextricable link test, A Bogg and T Novitz, 'Race Discrimination and the Doctrine of Illegality' (2013) 129 *Law Quarterly Review* 12, and Bogg and Green (n 62) 116–19.

[119] Forshaw and Pilgerstorfer (n 56) 177.

[120] A Bogg, 'The Immoral Trap: Migrant Workers and the Doctrine of Illegality' in Ryan (2013) (n 72) 119–20.

[121] *Patel v Mirza* [2016] UKSC 42, para 107.

vulnerable workers'.[122] It may be argued however that it is only those migrant workers who are exploited through being taken advantage of by their employers who are likely to be protected by a *Patel v Mirza*-style proportionality assessment.[123] Such an assessment is unlikely to benefit other migrant workers in an irregular situation, if they may be thought to have responsibility for their actions, and therefore 'culpability'. For that reason, the cosmopolitanism of such an approach is incomplete, in that it does not imply a complete reconciliation between resident and migrant workers' interests by fully equalising their legal situation.

A third approach rejects the illegality defence as inconsistent with the labour market position of migrant workers as a category. An example can be seen in the present author's critique of the post-*Vakante* legal position, that it favoured immigration law enforcement over guarantees of labour standards, and was therefore an element of the 'low road' strategy of 'penalizing unauthorized work in the hope of thereby deterring it'.[124] A more elaborate version is found in Dewhurst's comparative research identifying three legal models concerning employment law claims by those lacking a right to work.[125] One model is found in the UK, Australia and Ireland, where employment law offers little or no protection.[126] A second model, described as 'protection with consequences', taken by the ILO, EU law, and by many states, makes employment law rights available, but leaves the worker exposed to immigration law penalties and removal.[127] The final model, described as the 'full protection approach', protects workers from the immigration status-related consequences of taking employment law claims – eg, by denying the employer information about their immigration status, and by penalising retaliatory action based upon lack of status, and is the model followed in the US, and by the UN Migrant Workers Committee.[128] The significance of Dewhurst's analysis is that it aims to ensure that *all* migrant workers have the protection of employment law, and does not depend upon vulnerability and exploitation by employers. It may be considered 'cosmopolitan realist' in that it achieves a full reconciliation between resident and migrant workers through an equal legal position.

[122] A Bogg, 'Illegality in Labour Law after *Patel v Mirza*: Retrenchment and Restraint' in S Green and A Bogg (eds), *Illegality after Patel v Mirza* (Oxford, Hart, 2018) 272–273 and Bogg (n 62) 277. See further Bogg's discussion of the *Patel v Mirza* approach in ch 9 in this volume.

[123] This observation draws upon the present author's discussion of concepts of exploitation in ch 1 of this volume.

[124] Ryan (n 78) 158.

[125] E Dewhurst, 'The Right of Irregular Immigrants to Back Pay: The Spectrum of Protection in International, Regional and Legal Systems' in Costello and Freedland (n 32) and 'Models of Protection of the Right of Irregular Immigrants to Back Pay: The Impact of the Interconnection between Immigration Law and Labor Law' (2014) 35 *Comparative Labor Law and Policy Journal* 217.

[126] Dewhurst in Costello and Freedland (n 125) 232 and Dewhurst (2014) (n 125) 222–24.

[127] Dewhurst in Costello and Freedland (n 125) 224–25 and Dewhurst (2014) (n 125) 228–32.

[128] Dewhurst in Costello and Freedland (n 125) 224, 235–36 and Dewhurst (2014) (n 125) 235–39.

C. Enforcement

A third strand of employment law scholarship concerned with equal application has focused on the enforcement of labour standards in the context of migration. In this area, there have been significant policy developments over the period. The Gangmasters Licensing Authority (GLA) was established under legislation adopted in 2004, to license and supervise labour market intermediaries in agriculture and food processing, against the background of poor labour conditions concerning migrants in those sectors.[129] The Immigration Act 2016 introduced a range of employment law enforcement measures expressly set in a migration policy context. These included the re-naming of the GLA as the Gangmasters and Labour Abuse Authority (the GLAA); the creation of a power – as yet unused – to extend the GLAA's licensing scheme to other sectors than those provided for in 2004; the extension of the GLAA's remit to enforcement of legislation on employment agencies and the national minimum wage in all sectors; and, the creation of the role of Director of Labour Market Enforcement to oversee and coordinate the activities of the GLAA, the Employment Agency Standards Inspectorate and national minimum wage enforcement by Her Majesty's Revenue Commissioners. The criminal offence of requiring another person to perform forced labour, introduced by the Modern Slavery Act 2015, is a further innovation of relevance, in that it often concerns employment by migrants with very poor labour conditions.[130]

One type of employment law commentary on these developments has been descriptive of the linkages between migration developments and changes in labour market enforcement structures and policies. For example, the present author discussed the legislation establishing the GLA in 2004, including the prior policy debates and the impact of the Morecambe Bay tragedy of February that year.[131] A second and more critical strand has focused on the inadequacy of these developments for the employment law system. Costello criticised the focus upon criminal and human rights law in addressing forced labour, to the apparent exclusion of solutions aimed at upholding labour standards.[132] ACL Davies meanwhile has noted the limitations to the provisions concerning labour market enforcement in the Immigration Act 2016 as a means of upholding labour standards in general.[133] From the perspective of this chapter, *all* of this work appears to lack a discussion of the challenges posed for enforcement by migrant workers' specific situation.

In contrast, a series of empirically oriented papers by Barnard and collaborators focused directly on the position of migrant workers from the eight

[129] Gangmasters (Licensing) Act 2004.
[130] Modern Slavery Act 2015, ss 1, 3 and 5.
[131] Ryan (n 78) 50–57.
[132] Costello (n 37).
[133] Davies (n 63) 440–42.

central and eastern European states which joined the EU in 2004. Two of those documented the comparatively low rate of applications to employment tribunals and the Employment Appeal Tribunal by such workers.[134] A third drew upon interview material to explain the far lower rates of recourse to employment tribunals by these migrant workers.[135] The authors' analysis was that that was due to a combination of 'practical and legal impediments to bringing claims', such as precarious employment relationships, a lack of knowledge of tribunals, and a lack of advice in their native language. They also observed the relevance of individuals' migration plans, with those who intended to stay and maximise their income for a short or medium period (up to five years) unwilling to spend time on legal action. The analysis supported their conclusions that enforcement should be less individualised, with a single enforcement agency, supported by an employment ombudsman. This series of papers illustrates the potential for employment law scholarship to open out to transnational elements, by recognising that the actual social position of migrants may differ from that of resident workers.

VI. CONCLUSION: VARIATIONS WITHIN EMPLOYMENT LAW SCHOLARSHIP ON LABOUR MIGRATION

The review in this chapter of UK-based employment law scholars' work relating to labour migration, applying the lens of methodological nationalism – including cosmopolitan realism – may be summarised as follows. First, since the mid-2000s, there has been much more extensive engagement with questions concerning migration than previously. Second, there is significant divergence between work which takes a neutral, descriptive approach in respect of changes in employment law, and that which is evaluative or critical. Third, a distinction is to be made between an approach oriented to the situation of migrant workers deemed vulnerable, and migrant workers at large. Fourth, there are crucial differences of approach as to which workers' interests are taken as the reference point, with some authors focusing primarily on the position of resident workers, while others look for a reconciliation or balancing of interests. Finally, examples of direct engagement with the distinct situation of migrant workers remain rare. Each of these points may be elaborated in turn.

As to the first, this chapter has shown the breadth and depth of current engagement with aspects of labour migration within employment law

[134] C Barnard, 'Enforcement of Employment Rights by Migrant Workers in the UK: The Case of EU-8 Nationals' in Costello and Freedland (n 32) and C Barnard and A Ludlow, 'Enforcement of Employment Rights by EU-8 Migrant Workers in Employment Tribunals' (2016) 45 *Industrial Law Journal* 1.

[135] C Barnard, A Ludlow and S Fraser Butlin, 'Beyond Employment Tribunals: Enforcement of Employment Rights by EU-8 Migrant Workers' (2018) 47 *Industrial Law Journal* 226.

scholarship, covering both access to the labour market and the equal application of labour standards. Until the mid-2000s, a form of methodological nationalism could be seen in the reticence of writers on employment law in the face of such questions. That historic tendency can still be seen in the treatment of access to the labour market by leading textbooks: only some address employer checks of the right to work, with the fuller treatment of labour migration policy in ACL Davies's textbook an exception. In contrast, since the late 2000s, employment law scholars have extensively discussed a range of migration-related topics in the *Industrial Law Journal* and other publications. The topics covered include employer checks, temporary labour migration schemes and discrimination in respect of access to the labour market, the position of posted workers, claims by irregular workers, and the enforcement of labour standards. This engagement must be considered an essential first step in 'going beyond' methodological nationalism.

Second, a methodological nationalism lens calls attention to tendencies to neutrality and descriptiveness in addressing the implications of migration for employment law. In this chapter, we have seen examples of this tendency – including by the present author – in respect of labour migration policy, employer checks, the principle of illegality, and changes to enforcement regimes. Such an approach can be defended on the basis that exposition has value in itself, in respect of the challenges posed by labour migration and immigration law and policy for employment law, and in respect of political and judicial law and policy-makers' attempts to respond to those challenges. The danger however is one of acquiescence in the terms of the national debate, and of the range of interests and policy agendas expressed within it. It is far from clear that scholarship should be confined in this way, not least given that the voice of migrant workers is already weak in law- and policy-making.

Third, the review in this chapter has shown an orientation in some scholarly work to the position of especially vulnerable migrant workers. The main topics where that has been seen here are admission policy in respect of domestic workers and the principle of illegality in employment law. That is in contrast to work which is primarily concerned with labour migration at large, where migration and nationality are the key variables. Awareness of tendencies to methodological nationalism can help illuminate the downside of an exclusive focus on vulnerable workers. To the extent that such scholarship either accepts the legal regime applicable to other migrant workers, or appears to do so by implication, it is open to the same objection as to 'neutral' scholarship – that it acquiesces in the terms of the state-level political debate relating to labour migration.

Fourth, reflection on methodological nationalism calls attention to important differences of approach as to which workers' situation is prioritised. One school of thought treats the central question for regulatory design as whether resident workers are protected. In a previous period, that was evident in the limits to support for interventionist legislation to protect Commonwealth workers against discrimination, and more recently has been seen in opposition to the posting of workers. The other school of thought – which it is argued here is in line with cosmopolitan realism – argues for reconciliation or balancing of the interests of resident and migrant workers. An approach emphasising reconciliation or balancing will be inherently more favourable to rights relating to access to the labour market by migrant workers.

Finally, consideration of methodological nationalism leads to the question whether employment law scholarship has succeeded in capturing the often distinct situation of migrant workers. This review shows that this engagement is rare, with the empirically-oriented work on enforcement of Barnard and her collaborators offering the only clear counter-examples. Even scholarship which addresses vulnerability, or which aims at a balancing of interests, typically makes assumptions about migrant workers' situations and interests, which may not always be true, either generally, or in particular cases. For example, if the absence of worker agreement is central to conceptions of vulnerability, do we know which conditions migrant workers *expect* in their employment? Do we know whether and in which circumstances migrant workers welcome the equal application of labour standards?[136] Labour migrants' perspectives on these questions are important – even if they are not determinative of public policy – and not including them risks an orientation to the interests and perspectives of resident workers by default. Even if direct empirical evidence may be hard to acquire, that should not preclude reflection on these questions, taking into account what is understood about labour migration.

In conclusion, it bears repeating that the purpose of this chapter has been a methodological one. The identification of tendencies to methodological nationalism in employment law scholarship is revealing about the orthodoxies in the field, not the political outlook of the scholars concerned. We may speculate that the explanations for such orthodoxies lie in scholars' understandable orientation to one or more of the following: defence of the labour market position of resident workers in the context of neoliberal globalisation; support for trade unions and other organisations who represent resident workers; and a standpoint that resident and migrant workers' interests are essentially similar. It is hoped that this chapter will promote further evolution in a cosmopolitan realist direction, through scholarship which gives due recognition to the often divergent interests of resident and migrant workers.

[136] For recent examples within labour sociology, see the discussion of hand-car washes in Leicester in I Clark and T Colling, 'New Insights into Informal Migrant Employment: Hand Car Washes in a Mid-sized English City (2019) 40 *Economic and Industrial Democracy* 755, and of the Leicester garment sector in N Hammer and R Plugor, 'Disconnecting Labour? The Labour Process in the UK Fast Fashion Value Chain' (2019) 33 *Work, Employment and Society* 913, 924.

Index

www.ingramcontent.com/pod-product-compliance
Ingram Content Group UK Ltd.
Pitfield, Milton Keynes, MK11 3LW, UK
UKHW020235290926
15470UKWH00002B/550

9 781509 919147